TOWER SNIPER

THE TERROR OF AMERICA'S FIRST ACTIVE SHOOTER ON CAMPUS

Monte Akers,
Nathan Akers,
Dr. Roger Friedman, Ph.D.

TOWER SNIPER

THE TERROR OF AMERICA'S FIRST ACTIVE SHOOTER ON CAMPUS

Monte Akers,
Nathan Akers,
Dr. Roger Friedman, Ph.D.

Published by John M. Hardy Publishing, Inc.,
Houston Texas

TOWER SNIPER: The Terror of America's
First Active Shooter on Campus

Lora Gray
Text and Cover Design

Sarah Le Pichon
Editing

Cover photo of UT Tower, circa 1980
Larry D. Moore CC BY-SA 3.0.

First Printed Edition 2016

2 4 6 8 10 9 7 5 3 1

ISBN: 978-0- 9903714-3- 4 Hardback
ISBN: 978-0- 9903714-2- 7 Trade Paper

John M. Hardy Publishing Co.
Houston, Texas
www.johnhardypublishing.com

Printed in Canada

*This book is dedicated to the many people who
were injured physically, emotionally, and otherwise,
by the events of August 1, 1966, and to those who
courageously stepped forward to protect, save, and serve
those who were placed in peril that day.*

TABLE OF CONTENTS

ACKNOWLEDGMENTS

The authors are grateful for the help of dozens of people who assisted us with this book, in particular the numerous people who were willing to be interviewed about their experiences on August 1, 1966 and thereafter. In some cases they had told their stories repeatedly over five decades, and yet were willing to put up with one more set of researchers. In other cases we were the first to whom they had told their stories, which was particularly gratifying. Their names appear throughout the book and are specifically listed in the primary sources in the bibliography.

The staff at the Austin History Center was very helpful, particularly Susan Rittereiser, Mike Miller, Molly Hults, Grace McEvoy and Nicole Davis. Rachael Penman, of the Crime Museum in Washington, D. C. was very gracious to provide us with the numbers written on the piece of tape on the butt of Whitman's rifle, and we never could have figured out the meaning of those numbers without the expertise of Kyle Wineman.

Dr. Friedman extends his appreciation to Dr. Rosa Eberly and Dr. Mary Ellen O'Toole, as well as the other persons he interviewed listed in the bibliography. He also thanks Monika McCoy and Alfred McAlister for their patience and guidance, and Sara Taber for her editorial support.

To Francis J. Schuck, the former roommate and friend of Charles Whitman, we express our sincere appreciation for the insight he provided.

Of particular importance in regard to the "why did he do it" question was Dr. Mitchell Berger, who was extremely cooperative, as was Thomas Marshall, Executive Director of the American Association of Neurological Surgeons, who put us in touch with him.

The generosity of Monika McCoy in providing information and photographs cannot be underestimated, and Susan Dirks, of the Texas Archive of the Moving Image was extremely professional and cooperative with our efforts to include stills from the films of August 1, 1966 in the Archive's possession. We also want to thank those we interviewed who provided photos of themselves circa 1966. We particularly appreciate the skill of Adam Allen in preparing the map, and for Adam's father-in-law's efforts to put us in touch with Ron Oliviera. We also appreciate Nell Carroll's granting of permission to publish photos from the *Austin American Statesman*. Particularly helpful was the aid we obtained from Jannah Tompson and her friend, David Hayden, in gathering, formatting, and upgrading the resolution of photos included in the book.

The book could not have concluded in a positive way without the enthusiastic contribution of Erica Saenz, of the University of Texas. As of this writing, June 1, 2016, it remains to be seen if the university is able to accomplish what she described as being planned a year previously, and which is discussed in Chapter 14. However, any disappointments in that regard should not be considered to have been for lack of Ms. Saenz's efforts. Finally, of course it could not have become possible at all without its merit being recognized by Edysol D. Price of John W. Hardy Publishing, or without the superior technical skills of Lora Gray in laying out and putting the book in form for publication, and the editing skills of Sarah Le Pichon.

To everyone mentioned above, and to our wives, Patty Akers, Alexis Akers, and Roz Beroza, we extend a sincere thank you for your patience over the last several months. We could not have done it without your support.

FOREWORD

The Sanctuary of Time

Today, if you drive down Pecos, a hilly, meandering residential street in North Austin, you'll probably pass right by the neighborhood park across the road from the earth-hugging, red-brick rambler where my first best friend, Paul Sonntag, and his family, lived in 1957. If you get to 35th Street, you've gone too far. Turn around and come back slowly. Watch closely and you will spot the park entrance marked by a small wooden placard hanging between two cedar posts that are sunk deep in the dry Texas dirt. The marker stands on the edge of a grove of old Live Oak trees that have shaded the rolling hills in this part of Austin for a hundred years. REED PARK is chiseled in the sign's weathered wood and underneath in neat cursive you can make out the words, "City of Austin – 1954."

In a city that even then was known for its expansive and lush public parks, Reed Park was an unheralded, pint-sized community space. It had a smallish, fenced in swimming pool in the back. But what really drew me, my friend Paul and other neighborhood kids most weekends from 1957 to 1961—with a centripetal force that I can still feel soaring through my body, was the grass and dirt meadow in the front part of the park. Paul and I were nine years old when we met in 4th grade at Casis Elementary, our local public school. I remember him seeming kind of small for his age, skinnier and shorter than me, with light brown hair he combed to the side, just so. He was incredibly fast and could easily outrun me and most other kids we played ball with at Reed Park. He could catch anything that came near him; a loopy, spiraling football or a long hard throw from the outfield bouncing in the dirt. I was built more like a tall, wide-shouldered quarterback, and wore my dark brown hair in a proud crew-cut. I was the better hitter and had the stronger throwing arm of the two of us. But in blue jeans, white-t shirts and gym shoes, we were a perfect team. That meadow in the front of Reed Park was the sports stadium of our dreams. Springtime was baseball season at Reed Park, and fall and winter belonged to football.

Every kid I knew loved the University of Texas Longhorn football team in the late fifties and early sixties. On Saturday nights during football season, we watched to see if the Library Tower on campus was lit up in orange or white, the school colors. If it was orange, it meant we'd won, and if it was white, the Longhorns had lost. Our mutual love for the Longhorns and our dreams of becoming big-time athletes drew Paul and me together in the 4th grade. We had similar desires to play football or baseball at the drop of a hat and with boundless, childhood passion. But there was more than that. My family had just moved from Houston in 1957 so my Dad could finish a doctorate in Education at U.T., and I was looking for a new friend in Austin. Paul and I both liked school and we were good, serious students. He was eager to show me his Civil War soldier collection and I was eager to learn. And though I couldn't put it into words as a nine-year-old, I think we were both introverts, more comfortable spending time around our families or with just one good friend, rather than hanging out with a whole gang of kids.

Paul idolized the Longhorns' little half back, James Saxton; we'd both read the newspaper story that said Saxton was "as quick as a minnow." I wanted to be Mike Cotten, the tall Texas quarterback with an amazing arm. On TV in the fall of 1959, Paul and I had seen Cotten pump fake a long throw and then flip a perfect spiral, *underhanded*, for 25 yards to Saxton who ran for a touchdown. It was the coolest play we'd ever seen and for the week following that game we secretly practiced the play in Paul's backyard. The next weekend, when we had enough guys together to play a game at Reed Park, I faked a long one and then flipped Paul the same perfect underhanded pass. He caught it mid-stride and took off like he was chasing down jack rabbits and scored. The other team's only defense was to scream in unison, "Eeleeegal play," but we knew better.

In the spring of 1960, I would run around the outfield, dive all-out to catch sinking line drives, scramble to my feet and fire the ball back to Paul at home plate. We always pretended it was the bottom of the ninth and we had to stop a rally by the Los Angeles Dodgers, a team we both hated. I hated them because they'd beaten my family's beloved Chicago White Sox in the 1959 World Series, and Paul hated them just because he was my best friend. Our ball games stopped only when it got too dark to see the ball coming at you. We walked across the street, then to Paul's house, and his mother served us bologna sandwiches on white Wonder Bread that she'd pre-made and kept in her freezer.

The only time Paul ever got mad at me was when, in his room after one of those dinners, I said I thought it was weird to freeze sandwiches like that. He said I was being disrespectful toward his mother. He got a stern look on his face when he thought I was out of line. Unlike me, Paul didn't cuss and would never argue with his parents. He said, "I learned that it was important to respect my parents in Bible School," and he thought it was part of being a good Methodist. Paul was the first non-Jewish kid I'd ever had as a friend, and I was the first Jewish kid Paul had ever played with so much. We were kindred spirits though and had become curious about our differences. Fifteen minutes later that evening, as we worked in silence setting up a new Civil War scene with his tin soldiers, I apologized for saying his mother's sandwiches were weird.

In June of 1962, Paul and I finished 8th grade together at O. Henry Junior High. We were both thirteen years old. As fate would have it, my family moved further into north Austin and I started high school across town in the fall at A. N. McCallum. Paul continued on to his local high school, Stephen F. Austin. I had my Bar Mitzvah that fall and we invited Paul and his family, and he showed up so spit and polished I barely recognized him. The loss of common ground, the geographical distance and our desperate need to get anchored in big and competing public high schools seemed to loosen the bond we had. Entering adolescence meant we were leaving the sanctuary of time that nourished our boyhood friendship and the simple super-hero sports life we had created at Reed Park. We were nervously brave and serious, full of ourselves, thrilled to be going to high school, and totally unaware of the horror that lay four years ahead.

The 307-foot granite Tower stood tall in the center of the University of Texas at Austin campus. Its observation deck commanded a panoramic view that included the great mall crisscrossing the campus grounds as well as the busy streets and shops that form its border. All of Austin saw the Texas Tower as the University's most distinguishing landmark and a symbol of academic excellence, personal opportunity, and Lone Star pride.

On Monday noon, August the 1st, 1966, the summer Paul and I finished high school, Charles Whitman, a muscular, crew-cut 26-year-old engineering student and Marine, brought a footlocker full of rifles, pistols and 700 rounds of ammunition up to the Tower's Observation Deck. He'd stabbed his wife and mother to death the night before and for 90 minutes he rained terror down on the world. He shot and killed 14 people on campus and wounded 32.

The ninth person Charles Whitman killed that day, shooting from a distance of about 1200 feet from the Tower's Observation Deck, was Paul Sonntag. One shot, directly into Paul's mouth with a hollow-point bullet that exploded on impact and destroyed the back of his head. Claudia Rutt, who was walking with Paul, turned to help him when he fell forward onto the ground. She was the tenth victim. Shot in the chest, near her heart. The news reports said "she died instantly," just like Paul. Two Austin cops, Houston McCoy and Ramiro

Martinez, finally snuck up on Whitman on the observation deck and gunned him down from sixty feet away with a 12 gauge shotgun at 1:24 p.m.

I was working that summer as the wrangler at my family's children's camp in the hill country about 200 miles west of Austin. My mother sent a counselor out to get me on a horseback ride I was leading that Monday morning. The message was that someone was shooting from the Tower in Austin and she thought that Paul Sonntag, a friend of mine, had been hurt. I drove the dusty red ranch pickup into Austin that evening. What was often a leisurely two hour drive on Highway 290 seemed endless and full of dread. The closer I got to Austin, the more overwhelmed I felt.

I listened to frantic news bulletins on the radio from the Emergency Room at Brackenridge Hospital and learned that Paul Sonntag was dead, along with his fiancée, Claudia Rutt. I had heard they were dating, but wasn't sure that fiancée thing was right. I knew Claudia too. She was part of the small group of Jewish kids my age in Austin. We'd been in the same class in religious school for ten years at Temple Beth Israel. The reporter said that Paul had just graduated from high school, worked as a lifeguard at Reed Park Pool that summer, and had come downtown to pick up his final paycheck from the Parks and Recreation Office that was a block off of the U.T. campus. Claudia, also a recent graduate of Austin High School, had gone along for the ride.

I decided to go to Claudia's home first because I thought it would be easier emotionally. I knew her home would be packed with relatives, Temple friends, and lots of food. That was Jewish tradition—grieve together, say a Kaddish, cry, tell stories, laugh a little, then eat a lot. I was drained when I pulled into her neighborhood and found a parking spot about 8:00 p.m. The front door was propped open and I entered the crowded first floor with lots of familiar sad faces. A few parents and kids turned to silently welcome me with a nod and then I saw my good friend from high school standing in the corner of the dining room, holding a massive roast beef sandwich, looking gloomy and alone.

I was glad to see Mark and I made my way through the crowd to him. I told him I'd just gotten into town from camp and had heard everything on the radio. He said he'd been at work at his family's downtown clothing store that morning. He heard all the sirens, turned on the TV in the store office and couldn't believe his eyes. He said that Claudia was wearing Paul's senior ring on a chain around her neck when she died. Mark told me that he wasn't sure about the fiancée thing either. He had heard that Paul was going to be buried in what he was wearing when he was shot: a surfer shirt, blue jean cut-offs and flip-flops. That image burned itself into my mind. I suddenly pictured my friend, face–up and eyes closed, stretched out on his back with his arms to his sides in a coffin—wearing a bloody surfer shirt and his cut-offs. It made it seem that Paul was really dead. If Paul could be killed and buried just like that, the same thing could happen to me. I was speechless. The room went silent. I stared at the floor. I felt ancient tectonic plates shifting deep in the earth right under my feet. I felt thrown off balance, like I might faint or collapse on the floor right there in the dining room.

Then rage flooded through my body. I'd never felt any of it before. I mumbled that I was set to leave for Northwestern University in a few weeks, but who the fuck really cared anymore? The world had changed around me forever in a fucking blink of an eye. My old buddy had gotten the back of his head blown off by a crazy student Marine. Everyone thought that guy was normal until he showed he was not. And Claudia was killed just because she wanted to hang out with Paul. It made no sense. "That could've been you or me, Mark, buying a book at the Co-op or getting some Mexican food on the Drag," I said. Underneath my 18-year-old rage was a terrifying, sorrowful awareness that I tried to ignore, that life was totally fragile, dangerous and could be snuffed out at any minute. As a kid, I'd been taught that the world was a safe and stable place, but that was a cruel fairy tale.

I picked up the phone in the back of the crowded den and dialed Paul's home number from memory. A silver metallic wall clock read 9:25 p.m. The phone rang maybe five times and Paul's Dad finally answered with an irritated voice, "Hello, Hello….who is this?" When he heard it was me, his tone softened and he said that they would love for me to stop by. I said "Well, it's pretty late, Mr. Sonntag, I can come by in the morning just as well." He quickly responded, "No, Roger, tomorrow is going to be crazy with everyone coming in and the funeral and all. We haven't seen you in a long time. We'd really like you to come over tonight. Don't wait until the morning."

I hadn't been to Paul's house since the days I'd ridden by bike there to play ball at Reed Park. When I pulled up it looked empty and dark save for the porch light—just one car in the driveway. As I rang the doorbell it occurred to me that only Paul's parents were home—my God, what was I going to say? Where the hell were all their relatives and Church friends? I had naively expect-ed the same kind of tearful, crowded gathering as there had been at Claudia's. I wondered if Methodists just did their grieving alone. At least that night, Paul's family did.

His parents looked terrible. Their faces were drawn, eyes red from crying. His Dad wore a wrinkled old robe that hung sadly from his skinny shoulders. His

Mom was trying to be perky and wore a pair of jeans and a baggy Longhorn sweatshirt. She gave me a soft tentative hug and said they'd sent George and Barney, Paul's younger brothers, over to their grandparents' house for the week. They led me down the long narrow hall to Paul's room. When we got there, his mom switched on the overhead light, and his Dad and I sat down on the neatly made bed. She collapsed into a bean bag chair that wasn't there when Paul and I were kids. They asked me about camp that summer and where I was going to college, and how my mom and dad were. The chit chat was too normal. Finally there was silence. Looking at no one, I said as calmly as I could, "I'm really sorry about what happened." I began to tear up and Mr. Sonntag openly cried.

Mrs. Sonntag broke the enveloping sadness. She blew her nose softly into a piece of Kleenex and said with a funny smile, "Now Roger... I want to know the truth about those baloney sandwiches. Paul told me you loved them, but I know how boys eat and you never finished a one!" Then we all started laughing. I told them about Paul and me secretly practicing that underhand pass play in their backyard, and we laughed and cried again. The tears were sweeter now, not so bitter. I felt safer crying, not afraid. It was the strangest, saddest night of my 18 year old life. I had the uncanny feeling that his parents were confusing me with Paul. The Sonntags invited me to spend the night but I declined. I was deadened, empty and amazingly hungry again. I drove back home that night, wondering what happens now to my friendship with Paul? What happens inside of you when a 10 year old soulmate is killed and you can't ever share another conversation, or joke or ballgame with him, ever? Death was so unreal to me. Part of me thought, I'll call Paul in the morning and this horrible day will be over; the nightmare will end when the light of day arrives. No one had ever told me a best friend could be killed walking around on the Drag with his girlfriend on a Monday afternoon. I was learning terrible knowledge about life.

After I left that night I stayed in touch with the Sonntags through occasional letters, but I didn't see them again for 15 years. In the spring of 1981, I was in Austin with Roz, my wife-to-be, visiting from Maryland where we were living together at the time. I was thirty-three years old and Roz was thirty-one. I was finishing up a doctoral program in developmental psychology and Roz had started working as a clinical social worker for Montgomery County. I'd found myself thinking a lot about Paul those days—mostly in the spring or early summer when I played pickup baseball and wished I could be 10 years old again at Reed Park running plays with him. I missed Paul terribly, but it was hard to admit that to myself, because it made me too sad and reminded me of just how tenuous life was, including my own and Roz's. How could I marry someone who might be taken from me in an instant? I think staying in touch with the Sonntags over time was a way to keep Paul alive for myself and for them, to avoid, even after 15 years, the unnerving lesson that his violent death had forced upon me. There is a sudden finality in life that is unbearable to think about; I have no control over when I or a loved one will have to face that truth.

I knew that I wanted the Sonntags to meet Roz. After leaving a message that we were coming by on their answering machine, we drove over to their house. I rang the doorbell and Mrs. Sonntag happily welcomed us into the living room as though no time had passed. She called out for Jim to come see who'd dropped in. He gave us both big bear hugs. I introduced Roz to them and they eagerly asked all about our lives. I said I'd like to hear about George and Barney, and Mr. Sonntag cautiously responded that one of them was just fine but the other wasn't doing so well. could tell answering my question was hard on him. Half an hour later, as we were leaving, I said "I was nervous about coming by because I thought it might bring up sad memories of Paul for you." Mrs. Sonntag laughed, "No, honey, it's just the other way around. We love knowing that someone else out there remembers Paul. It means so much to us. It means his life made a difference. You two were such good friends. And by the way, you all please call us Beverly and Jim now. Just makes sense, doesn't it?"

We returned in 1986, after my mother died, because I wanted Beverly and Jim to meet our two year-old first child, Amanda. In a fantasy I was not conscious of at the time, I think I was hoping the Sonntags would feel that Paul was still around because I was still around, and more than that, a new generation was coming into the world, and maybe my daughter could be their granddaughter as well. Maybe we all actually could live forever. The visit started off joyfully with hugs all around. Then I asked about the large tent I noticed in the back yard, and Jim softly said it was where one of the boys came to stay in bad weather because he was homeless right now.

Beverly invited us to see her collection of dolls gathered from yard sales that she and Jim frequented over the years. We followed her down the hallway but held up abruptly as we entered Paul's old bedroom: it was empty of furniture except for large metal book shelves that lined the walls and were wedged full of hundreds of dolls—fashion dolls, Shirley Temples, Cowgirls, Raggedy Anns, and Granny dolls. Some were made of porcelain, others of plastic, and all were staring out into space with empty eyes and tiny smiles. Beverly seemed in a reverie but it was kind of eerie. She sweetly offered Amanda a little Shirley Temple and my daughter accepted the doll with a worried grin. Roz glanced at me, concerned about the hint of fear she saw in Amanda's eyes. We thanked Beverly for the generous gift and then I took Amanda's hand and turned to leave the room. When we came back to the living room, Jim didn't notice us. He was sitting in his tattered easy chair, staring hypnotically into the cold, empty fireplace.

In 1994, I got a note from Beverly in barely legible cursive saying Jim had died at the age of 68, and she was moving into assisted living. I wrote her back several times, called and left messages, but never heard from her again. In 1998, Beverly died at 71 and was buried next to Jim and Paul in the Austin Memorial Park Cemetery.

Since Paul's death, I have learned through almost 50 years of life experience and more than three decades of clinical practice in psychology, that trauma is not just an event that takes place sometime in the past; it is also the imprint left by that experience on a person's mind, brain and body.[1] Trauma refers not only to the blow that is delivered, but to the enduring injury that lingers long after the precipitating assault is over. Our memory, perception and entire nervous system repeat to us what we haven't yet come to terms with, what still haunts us.

I'd noticed for many years, that at moments of deep personal loss throughout my life, my thoughts always turned back to Paul Sonntag, and how much I'd missed him since boyhood. In August of 2013, after long family debate, we'd closed the children's camp in Texas that my parents had founded in 1952. So approaching the next summer, 2014, the first one with the camp shuttered, I was grieving over the loss of the camp community and missing the excitement of opening day. Instead of being in Texas on June 6th, as I had been as the camp director for ten years, I found myself in my office in Maryland, with a pressing need to talk with anyone who would understand about Paul and camp. With great irony, I went searching online for his name and came up with "Find a Grave Memorial Website." I decided to leave a message there about Paul, for someone, anyone out there in that empty vastness of the Internet. As I typed the words below a deep sadness settled over my shoulders and moved into my chest, and almost out of nowhere, I felt tears flowing down my face.

As summer approaches, I'm thinking about Paul again. So many years ago, in the 1960s, we were such good friends in Austin—endless hours of pickup football or baseball in the park off Pecos Drive, lots of private talks back in his house, eating his mom's sandwiches that she had defrosted for us! My home away from home. I miss all of that time in my life, and I miss Paul as well—an early best friend.

-Roger Entered: June 6, 2014.

It is staggering how the impact of traumatic events endures in our lives. It hovers over us, and gradually like dust, settles imperceptibly into our bodies, minds, hearts, our relationships and our communities. I saw it with Paul's parents, how the random and public murder of their first born son at the age of 18 broke their spirits, brought them closer together in their pain, and isolated them as well from their community.

Writers and historians who want to know where a story starts, like therapists who need to identify a precipitating cause to help a client, are naturally interested in beginnings and facts about proximate causes. These details provide the archive for an accurate narrative of the event itself and the motives and actions of the perpetrator. It is necessary, with reasoned and up-to-date clinical insight, to discuss how it is possible for a person, like Charles Whitman, to look conventionally "normal," but because of his psychopathy and Antisocial Personality Disorder, still engage in well-thought-out, terrifying and murderous behavior. But these reflections on the perpetrator do not tell the story of the victims, survivors, the first responders, or the witnesses—everyone who experienced terrible knowledge about life that day, including my friend Paul's family and myself. It is how we in Austin reacted then and through the years since, that is giving the event its gripping traumatic quality. It is the psychological and social damage caused, the healing or lack of it, and the narrative or lack of an adequately complex narrative for the individuals and community involved, that really defines, gives shape, and provides the story of the public human disaster that took place on the Texas campus in 1966 .[2]

Trauma is a social and individual concept. It has both centripetal and centrifugal effects on every person and every relationship that it touches; it can draw people together but also drives people apart. In the immediate aftermath of the shootings, individuals who'd experienced the trauma very personally became painfully isolated from each other because neither the University of Texas, the City of Austin, nor any group of concerned citizens provided public leadership, a process to mourn and remember, or emotional support to the victims' families, survivors or the campus community. There was no effort to bring the wounded city together, to publically and formally memorialize and honor the dead, or celebrate the bravery of first responders, police, and medical staff. Remarkably, it was not until 2007, forty-one years after the shootings, that the University placed a small plaque on a stone near the base of the Tower, "remembering with profound sorrow the tragedy of August 1, 1966." A University press release at the time of the plaque's unveiling concluded that, "A detailed plan for a more extensively landscaped Tower Garden, including memorial elements, has been developed but private fund-raising efforts have been unsuccessful to date." In important psychological, social and institutional ways, the shootings changed and isolated everyone involved and continue to affect us all. "Everywhere You Go, It's There," is the title of an essay about the shootings that refers to the ever present Tower that looms over the campus and the memory of the sniper shootings that the iconic Tower constantly evokes; that phrase perfectly captures the feeling one has while walking across the University of Texas at Austin campus today.[3]

On January 27, 2015, I received an email from someone named Monte Akers, who said he was an attorney and author in Austin, and that he'd seen the message I'd left in June of 2014 at Paul Sonntag's "Find a Grave Memorial Site." He said that he and his son were under contract to write a book about the U.T. Sniper shootings in which Paul was killed. He wondered if I was interested in talking to them about Paul and if so, he'd love to hear from me. I was thrilled to receive their email. Someone out there had actually responded to the note I'd left on the Memorial Site eight months before. During those months I'd thought a lot about Paul and had already finished a draft of a memoir about my relationship with him entitled "The Sanctuary of Time." I sent the Akerses the memoir and jumped at the chance to meet them in person. I booked a flight and two weeks later I was in Austin driving my rental car to Monte and Nathan's office on the north side of town. After spending a full day with them, I felt like I'd found two kindred spirits. We talked endlessly in their office about the book and the many important issues that the Texas shootings raised about public violence in our culture, the lingering impact of trauma on individuals and communities, gun control, insanity and delusional disorders, and of course, Paul Sonntag and his family, and how each of us felt drawn to explore the topic of the Texas shootings. We visited the UT Campus and saw the small plaque on a rock near the Tower which was placed there in 2007 and is the only memorial to the victims of the tragedy. They showed me the pock marks from the sniper's bullets that still remain in the aging concrete of a bench and sidewalk that sit beside an old live oak on the campus mall, in full view of the Texas Tower. We drove across Austin to see Reed Park where Paul and I grew up over fifty years ago. At the end of the visit, instead of having satisfied our curiosities, the three of us were even more engaged by what the U.T. Tower shootings had meant and done, so much so that Monte and Nathan invited me to contribute to the book.

Tower Sniper: The Terror of America's First Active Shooter on Campus is an important book that will help mark the fiftieth anniversary of the Tower shooting in the summer of 2016 with seriousness and human concern. More than that, it honors the memories of the victims not only by providing a complex and nuanced historical narrative, but also by describing the enduring social and psychological effects of this massive trauma. At best, it may also serve as a vehicle for continuing personal and communal healing for all of us who were touched by the events of that tragic day.

The Texas Tower shooting was a public human disaster of intense and resounding proportions. Its traumatic fifty year legacy lingers over Austin and the University community, as well as for me and the Sonntags, and hundreds of other victim's families, friends, first responders and witnesses who were on campus that day.

We didn't realize back then that this attack would become the first of an enduring series of similar tragedies in supposedly safe colleges, public schools, office buildings and shopping centers all over the country. To this day, these disasters confound our understanding of violence prevention and gun control, mental health diagnosis and treatment, the lasting power of trauma, the need for individual and communal healing, and the preciousness of life itself. This book re-opens a public dialogue about all of these contemporary concerns, and in so doing, sheds light and offers direction for fresh, salient and lasting solutions.

Roger Friedman, PhD
Silver Spring, Maryland, March, 2015

---

1. Bessel van der Kolk, The Body Keeps the Score: Brain, Mind, and Body in the Healing of Trauma (New York: Viking Penguin, 2014).

2. Kai Erikson, A New Species of Trouble: Explorations in Disaster, Trauma and Community (New York: W. W. Norton, 1994).

3. Rosa A. Eberly, "Everywhere You Go, It's There: Forgetting and Remembering the University of Texas Tower Shootings," Chapter 3, in Framing Public Memory, Kendall R. Phillips (ed.), (Tuscaloosa: University of Alabama Press, 2004).

THOUGHTS TO START THE DAY.
READ AND THINK ABOUT, EVERY DAY:

STOP procrastinating (Grasp the nettle)
CONTROL your anger (Don't let it prove you a fool)
SMILE (Its contagious)
DON'T be belligerent
STOP cursing, improve your vocabulary
APPROACH a pot of gold with exceptional caution
(look it over - twice)
PAY that compliment
LISTEN more than you speak, THINK before you speak
CONTROL your passion; DON'T LET IT lead YOU - - Don't
let desire make you regret your present actions later
(Remember the lad and the man)
If you want to be better than average, YOU HAVE TO
WORK MUCH HARDER THAN THE AVERAGE
NEVER FORGET: when the going gets rough,
the ROUGH get going!!!!!

PROLOGUE

The perpetrator should never be glorified, but neither should he or she be demonized, to avoid glorification by rebellious countercultures.

-Antonio Petri, M.D.[1]

The writing of this book was my son's idea. We had a minor connection to the U.T. Tower shootings in that Saralynn Lankford, the first cousin of Nathan's mother/my wife, was present for the duration of the event and had friends killed and wounded, but neither he nor I had intently considered its meaning, not at the beginning. We knew only that it was a large story in the history of a place we adore. Once engaged, however, it seeped into our every thought crack as no other historical analysis has done.

The popularity of the story after fifty years, which has endured longer than we anticipated, should not be about the man who caused it all. That man's question marks have been erased and his ferret mind strangled. Over fifty years he has become embalmed with research words, statistic quotes and careful evasions. Even his indecisions are footnoted, and yet his whole life serves only as a warning to others. If this story could be told without mentioning his name, as many of the living he would prefer, then that would be the nature of its telling. Yet such a story would swim like a shark in a lightless sea, something we cannot entice to the surface.

The story of Charles Whitman, the 17 people he murdered, the 31 he injured with bullets and the hundreds or more he wounded emotionally should not need to be enticed to the surface at all. It should be ancient history. It isn't a Jack the Ripper tale that will never be solved. It isn't a presidential assassination about which conspiracy theories orbit. No American

The ironic words of a note that Charles Whitman made for himself, which was found after the tregedy in August of 1966.

1

celebrities died as a result, no world events were altered, no office-holders were turned out in scandal. Indeed, when we started this book we expected it to just be history, another telling of an oft-told tale, made timely principally because of American fascination with anniversaries divisible by ten.

Instead we found an undercurrent of unhealed wounds because of a societal failure in 1966 to know how to respond to the event, exacerbated by a quickness to seize on a false explanation for why it occurred, made particularly unsettling by the prolific propagation of similar events that Whitman's crimes seem to have inspired. Long before we had completed the manuscript, we had discovered information and reached conclusions we had neither hoped nor dreamed of acquiring, and our effort also ceased to be ours alone.

During the course of our research we talked to some 25 people who were there or were directly affected, and while searching for witnesses and participants, as described by Dr. Friedman in his *Foreword*, I visited the "Find-a-Grave" Internet site for each of the victims and made what has turned out to be an important connection. His resulting contribution to this book provides a perspective—as one touched personally by the incident and as a person educated and trained to recognize and analyze its effect—that few others could offer. His description of the effect of trauma on those involved with the shootings, and the extent to which the community failed the victims in 1966, due to a lack of understanding of what to do, adds a rich layer of information and value to this book that its father and son authors could not hope to contribute on their own.

So saying, come now to Austin, Texas at mid-morning on a summer Monday. The University of Texas Tower stands proud, a symbol of peace and majestic learning. It is still possible that the date will be unremarkable, will not become a wounded day that leaves an arterial stain across a purple sky. The collective lifeblood of its citizens has not begun to flow upward from broken bodies. There is no wraparound sound of distant dogs barking or sirens approaching. Nothing about the Tower darkens the mind, as though misgiving is built into its stones. Not yet.

- Monte Akers, June 30, 2015

---

1. "School Shootings as a Culturally Enforced Way of Expressing Suicidal Hostile Intentions," *Journal of American Academy of Psychiatry Law*" 36:4, 544-550 (December, 2008).

CHAPTER ONE
July 31, 1966

I don't really understand myself these days. I am supposed to be an average, reasonable and intelligent young man. However, lately (I can't recall when it started) I have been a victim of many unusual and irrational thoughts.

- Charles Whitman, July 31, 1966

On July 31, 1966, the cords tethering Charles Whitman to reality finally came undone. Whitman knew they had been unraveling, and he snipped the last few himself. He may have believed they held him down and that he would soar to greater heights without them. He did not.

The cords had secured him rather than restrained him, and without them he crashed rather than flew. In so doing, he crushed the dreams of a multitude. His victims were not people who found a cause to die for. There was nothing significant, like freedom or the future, to justify their sacrifice. People fifty years later are not alive at their expense. Their deaths were a waste.

Nothing about the known actions and activities of Charles Whitman immediately prior to July 31, 1966 portend the horror he decided to unleash. Certainly, by March, he had said things that would make armchair judges wise to his intentions through the wizardry of hindsight, but nobody who was there, including Whitman, knew what was coming before the preceding Saturday, July 30. In fact, his actions in the days preceding that weekend suggest that the things on his mind were normal and totally inconsistent with what followed.

On July 22, he visited the U.T. Tower, but only to show it off. Charles's younger brother, Johnnie Mike, and a friend named Jim Poland were in Austin as part of a summer excursion, including a visit to Charles' and Johnnie Mike's mother, Margaret, as well as Charles

Charles Whitman in 1963

and his wife, Kathy, so Whitman took them up to see the breath-taking view. Later that same day, he went to the Travis County Blood Bank and donated a pint.

On Saturday, July 23, Charles and Kathy drove to Devine, Texas, which is 25 miles southwest of downtown San Antonio, to return a deer rifle to a friend, Brock Huffman. The three had gone deer hunting the previous December and Huffman left the rifle, a high-powered Remington with a scope that be-longed to Huffman's father-in-law, with the Whitmans. They had other reasons for traveling in that direction. Huffman's wife, Sherron, gave birth that day to their son, Bart, in San Antonio, and it is probable the couple also stopped in San Antonio to shop for furniture. They did not see Huffman, but left the rifle and a congratulatory note about the baby at his law office in Devine, which was open that Saturday.[1]

Brock Huffman, a friend of Whitman's at U.T. A law student when he knew Whitman, Huffman went deer hunting with him in December 1965 and left a high-powered, scoped rifle belonging to Huffman's father-in-law at Whitman's home. A minor mystery is why Whitman chose to go out of his way to return the rifle on July 23, 1966, one week before he might have used it in his killing spree.

On Sunday, July 24, the three young men, Kathy, and Margaret had breakfast at the home of a friend of Margaret's from Wyatt's Cafeteria, where she worked, named Goldie Harris, and then the four young people drove to San Antonio to see the Alamo so Kathy and Charles could shop some more, or perhaps so that Charles could purchase and arrange for the shipment of furniture they had found the previous day. They took cameras and recorded several scenes, including the last photo of Kathy and Charles together, standing and smiling beside an Alamo plaza arch, and another of Charles sitting on the Alamo Cenotaph. A week later Charles would pen a polite note, after murdering his mother and wife, requesting that the film be developed.

The next day, the 25th, Charles attended classes at U.T. and went to work at his part-time job as a research assistant for a traffic study on campus. On Thursday, the 28th, he remembered to remind a classmate named

Tom Brightman to return some lecture notes Whitman had loaned him, explaining that he needed to study them for upcoming exams. Later that same day, he went to the Zales Jewelry store in Austin to make his first payment, $13.29, on a senior class ring he had ordered previously, and on which he owed a balance of $80.10.[2]

Why would a man with plans to commit murder and be killed in a few days focus on exams he won't take, furniture he won't use, or obtaining a ring he won't be around to wear? In particular, why would a man who is planning to take multiple rifles to the top of a tower to shoot people abandon a high-powered, scoped rifle so useful for that purpose?[3]

Friday, July 29, was the last day of his part time job at the University. Students who saw him said he acted normal and was in good spirits. He was dressed nicely in a blue shirt and khaki trousers, and that morning at 11:30 he visited a Gulf Mart convenience store and asked the store clerk if they stocked distilled water in plastic jugs. The clerk told him the store did not.

It is conceivable Whitman was already planning his shooting spree, stocking up for thirsty work at a high elevation, but he could just as well have needed the water for a steam iron, a humidifier, or any number of purposes. He had no reason to spend money on distilled water for drinking purposes when he could get all he wanted at home from the kitchen tap, and if he was making plans to kill and be killed by then, it isn't likely he was concerned about the health benefits of distilled water. The probable explanation is that distilled water was the only type sold by the jug in 1966, and he and co-workers needed it to drink while working outside at their traffic control research assistant jobs, which Whitman wrapped up that afternoon.

On Saturday the 30th, Whitman played racquetball with a friend in the morning, and then supposedly spent a relaxing day at home. He may have attended a training session in karate, in which he held a brown belt, because he was wearing his karategi that afternoon when he took a nap on the living room couch with their dog Schocie curled at his feet. Kathy thought it was cute and snapped a picture of it. It would be the last photo taken of Whitman in life.

There is another account about what he did that day, however, that portrays Whitman in a different light, and which places him near the base of the U.T. Tower on Friday the 29th, as well as the next day, quite possibly stepping off distances and scanning the area for lines of sight from the

Tower's observation deck. It is an interesting account, but not one that can be told in this book. Suffice it to say that a woman who was one of his closest friends—"Betty" for present purposes—came forward years later and told another close friend of Whitman's about the incident, and that the latter close friend intends to write his own book. It is his account to tell and its truth or otherwise provides more fodder for speculation than it does answers.

If Betty's recollection is accurate, it means the incident that tipped Whitman over the edge and caused him to finally decide to climb the Tower occurred the morning of Friday the 29th, rather than Saturday, July 30, 1966, which is how his uncle remembered it. In the great scheme of a man's life, even Whitman's, it should not have been a game-changer, certainly not one of the magnitude with which it manifested itself. It would have been bad news for any young college student strug-gling with finances, but it was only a stick in the bundle of sticks that are the elements of life. Nevertheless, when it was heard by Whitman there occurred in his consciousness the instant when music shatters glass.

We can never know positively that the incident occurred. Those who do are dead, and Whitman may simply have made an impulsive decision to commit mass murder that day or the next, or he may have carefully planned his moves for months and successfully camouflaged his intent from the world. However, there is evidence that the incident occurred and that it had a totally irrational effect on Whitman. The incident is Whitman's learning that his father had announced he would no longer provide financial support to either Charles or his mother.

Coming as it did, when it did, combined with everything else, the elder Whitman's announcement scrapped Charles' tenuous grip on rationality. Despite having been trained from boyhood about the importance of making money and being self-reliant, despite having a paper route from age 12, earning enough to purchase a motorcycle, and despite consis-tently seeking employment in Austin, Whitman was never able to escape dependence on his father's largesse. However short on emotional support C.A. Whitman's parenting and marital skills proved to be, his willingness to spend money on his family cannot be disputed. Doing so was one of his primary means of control, and once Margaret and Charles were in Texas, it was his only means.[4]

Accepting the money, conversely, was a major reason Charles loathed himself and, in turn, his father. For years his father had been sending money, sometimes as much as $380 per month.[5] The fact that Charles was receiving money from his father was not something he let be known to his friends. Francis J. Schuck said he did not know anything about the money coming from C.A. Whitman until he heard about it after Whitman's death. With regard to Whitman's finances in general, he described them as always being "in disarray."[6]

C.A. Whitman's decision, and ability, to ravage Charles's financial security from afar meant C.A. proved himself the better man. It told Charles all too clearly that he was not only unable to compete with his father for a career, but that he couldn't even stop being dependent on him to pay each month's bills. It was the last straw, the last drop in the teacup before it overflowed. He was worn out worrying about success and money and the future, that nervous worry that had been a hallmark of his existence since childhood, and that had been particularly intense

Johnnie Mike Whitman, left, and his friend, Jim Poland, taken during their visit to Austin during the third week of July, 1966. This was one of the photos from the two Kodak Instamatic cameras Whitman left behind in the Whitman bedroom, with a written request from Charles that the photos be developed.

during the previous six months. He had made quick, irrational, impulsive decisions of a huge magnitude before. Now he made another. It was time to end it all and to do so in a huge way.

The exact means and timing by which C.A. Whitman communicated his decision to Margaret and Charles is not clear. Charles did not allude to it directly in his final letters, although a reference to his father's "fight to keep her below her usual standard of living" may be an indirect reference. In any event, Margaret's brother, Walter, stated during the FBI's investigation in August that their father had in fact made this decision, and that he believed it was the cause of Whitman's breakdown.[7] C.A. had been calling Charles on an almost daily basis since March to try to convince him to intervene and persuade Margaret to return to Florida. Although one account concluded that the last such call occurred on June 18, 1966,[8] this is inconsistent with what C.A. and other family members said after August 1. C.A. probably did not deliver the news personally to Charles or Margaret, but to Walter, who lived close to C.A. in Florida, knowing it would be conveyed quickly and directly to Margaret, after which mother conveyed the news to son by telephone sometime on Saturday.

Sunday morning at approximately 11 a.m., after dropping Kathy off at the Southwestern Bell office for the first of her two shifts that day, Whitman launched his mission. First he went to a 7-11 convenience store on Barton Springs Road, not far from his house, and purchased $6.65 worth of Spam and other canned food. Next he went to an Academy Surplus store and bought a pair of binoculars for $18.98 and a bowie knife for $5.44. The canned goods were not routine household purchases, and the knife and binoculars would play major roles in his plans. He had other knives, one of which was inscribed with his name, but he may not have wanted to use a blade he treasured for such odious tasks.

He maintained a façade around his family, of course, and at 1 p.m. he returned to Kathy's office, picked her up, and took her to a movie. No record remains of which movie they saw, but it was probably *The Russians are Coming; The Russians are Coming,* a farcical comedy starring Jonathan Winters, Carl Reiner, and Eva Marie Saint, at the State Theatre. Of the eight theaters in the city, it was the only movie convenient by location and time of showing for their schedule. Located on Congress Avenue, a short drive from the Southwestern Bell office, the State began the movie at 1:10 p.m. and it had a running time of 126 minutes, which put them out in time to make their next appointment. It is tempting to believe that the last movie Charles Whitman saw was the first show of the double feature at the Austin Theatre, *How to Murder Your Wife*, starring Jack Lemmon and Virna Lisi, but the doors to the Austin Theatre did not open until 1:45 and the movie's running time of 118 minutes effectively rules it out.[9]

Their appointment after the movie was at Wyatt's Cafeteria, where they had a late lunch with Whitman's mother, Margaret, timed so they arrived when her afternoon break began at 3:30. Next, the couple dropped in on friends, Fran and John Morgan, arriving about 4:10. The Morgans said later that Whitman seemed uncharacteristically subdued and quiet.[10] They departed about 5:45 and Charles drove Kathy back to the Southwestern Bell office for her second shift of the day, which began at 6 p.m. Charles then went home to 906 Jewel Street and soon after arriving he retrieved a small typewriter he and Kathy owned, placed it on the coffee table in the living room,[11] and sat down on the couch to begin typing.

Sunday, July 31, 1966 6:45 P.M.

I don't quite understand what it is that compels me to type this letter. Perhaps it is to leave some vague reason for the actions I have recently performed. I don't really understand myself these days. I am supposed to be an average reasonable and intelligent young man. However, lately (I cannot recall when it started) I have been a victim of many unusual and irrational thoughts. These thoughts constantly recur, and it requires a tremendous mental effort to concentrate on useful and progressive tasks. In March when my parents made a physical break I noticed a great deal of stress. I consulted a Dr. Cochrum at the University Health Center and asked him to recommend someone that I could consult with about some psychiatric disorders I felt I had. I talked with a Doctor once for about two hoursand (sic) tried to convey to him my fears that I felt come overwhelming violent impulses. After one session I never saw the Doctor again, and since then I have been fighting my mental turmoil alone, and seemingly to no avail. After my death I wish that an autopsy would be performed on me to see if there is any visible physical disorder. I have had some tremendous headaches in the past and have consumed two large bottlesof (sic) Excedrin in the p ast (sic) three months.

It was after much thought that I decided to kill my wife, Kathy, tonight after

I pick her up from work at the telephone company. I love her dearly, and she has been as fine a wife to me as any man could ever hope to have. I cannot rationally pinpoint any specific reason for doing this. I don't know whether it is selfishness, or if I don't want to her to have to face the embarrassment my actions would surely cause her. At this time, though, the prominent reason in my mind is that I truly do not consider this world worth living in, and am prepared to die, and I do not want to leave her to suffer alone in it. I intend to kill her as painlessly as possible.

Similar reasons provoked me to take my mother's life also. I don't think the poor woman has ever enjoyed life as she is entitled to. She was a simple young woman who married a very possessive and domineering man. All my life as a boy until I ran away to join the Marine Corps...

There was a knock on the screen door. The front door was open and Whitman saw it was Larry and Elaine Fuess, another couple who were friends. Whitman removed the page he was typing and placed it in a black attaché case he used to carry school work, went to the door and greeted them. It was 7:05 p.m.

Whitman invited them in and mentioned he had been writing a letter to a friend in Washington he had not seen in years. They chatted for awhile. The Fuesses found Charles unusually calm and quite happy. He told stories, talked of his plans to buy land on Canyon Lake near San Antonio, as he'd done once before, and spoke very sentimentally of Kathy. Elaine remembered him speaking about her in a way she considered odd, saying later, "You don't just sit in front of your best friends and just moon over your wife. He was unusually tender."[12] Twice he started to say something that might have seemed considerably more unusual had he finished the sentence: "It's a shame that she should have to work all day and then come home to..."

It was one of the hottest days of the summer, the temperature hitting 101, and the Whitmans did not have air conditioning, so when a Blue Bonnet Ice Cream vender came down Jewel Street the three friends bought cones and chatted awhile longer outside in the cooling evening. The Fuesses left around 8:30 p.m.

An hour later, as Charles was preparing to leave to pick up Kathy when her second shift ended, the phone rang. It was Eva Bayne, Kathy's fellow school teacher at Lanier High School. She asked for Kathy, and

Charles, sounding happy and in good spirits, told her he was about to pick her up at work. When Eva said she would call back in the morning, Charles insisted that she call back that evening instead, saying the reason she should do so was because Kathy had to be back at work by 8 a.m., although her shift didn't actually begin until 8:30.

At 9:45, when Kathy exited the phone building with a co-worker, Kay Pearce, the Whitmans' black 1966 two-door Chevrolet Impala was waiting at the curb. Kathy told Kay she hoped they would not stop on the way home at the new Dunkin Donut shop on Congress because the donuts were bad for her figure, then walked to the Impala, opened the door, looked back, waved and said "bye" to Kay.

In the meantime, Margaret Whitman left her job as a cashier at Wyatt's cafeteria at 9:15 p.m., and accepted an invitation from Goldie Harris to come to Goldie's house. There, the two talked and ate ice cream for over an hour. After an abusive marriage of nearly 26 years with few close acquaintances, living almost like a prisoner within a world her husband had created, Margaret was enjoying making friends and living her own life in her new hometown. She was only 43 years old, and had every intention of enjoying that life for plenty of years to come.

Kathy and Charles were home shortly after 10 p.m, with no stop at Dunkin Donuts, and between 10:30 and 11:00 they had three phone conversations, all close together. Eva Bayne called again to invite Kathy to her party and they talked for 15-20 minutes. Eva said later that Kathy was in high spirits, and she believed she hung up the phone around 10:40 or 10:45.[13] Either shortly before or after that phone conversation, Kathy called her parents, Raymond and Florence Leissner, in Needville, and when the phone was not being used, Margaret Whitman called from Goldie Harris's home to check in with her son. Whitman asked his mother if he and Kathy could come over to her air conditioned apartment to study and "cool off before bed." Margaret said of course and, Ms. Harris reported, rushed home to meet them.

Kathy didn't accompany Whitman to his mother's place at the Penthouse Apartments. She went to bed instead, first removing her wedding band, a gold watch, and a women's dinner ring, and placing them together on the dresser in the front bedroom. She removed her clothes and got into bed nude, as she often slept during the scorching Austin summers. The windows and front door were left open, allowing any breeze to come in through the screened door and windows.

Charles left the house around midnight, and a few minutes later Margaret rode the elevator to the lobby of her apartment complex wearing pajamas, told the doorman her son was coming over to study, then greeted Charles and they rode the elevator to the fifth floor.

When they were inside apartment 505, Charles attacked her.

Largely because no autopsy was performed on Margaret's body, the exact circumstances of her killing are not known. Immediately after her body was found it was reported that she was shot in the back of the head, but that is highly unlikely, as noise from adjoining apartments was easily heard and nobody reported anything similar to a gunshot. The ease with which a loud noise could be heard by others is demonstrated by the fact that two men, Steven Foster and Scott Smith, walked down the hall at 12:15 a.m. to visit a friend in Apartment 511, while Whitman was in his

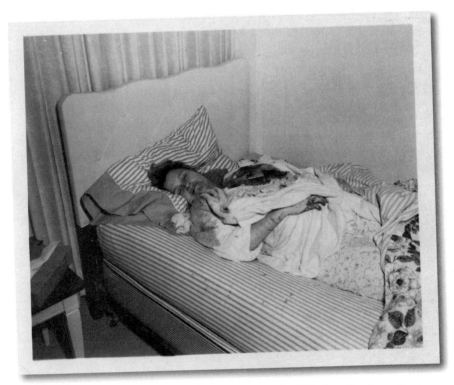

Margaret Whitman in death in her bed in apartment number 505 of the Penthouse Apartments on 12th Street in Austin. Whitman stabbed his mother, after hitting her in the back of the head with an iron bar shortly after midnight the morning of August 1, 1966.

mother's room, and heard what they thought was a child "crying and whimpering" in an apartment. They did not know which one, did not try to investigate, and only reported their experience after learning about the murder in Apartment 505.[14]

Another theory is that Whitman choked Margaret from behind with a length of rubber hose found in the black attaché case the doorman saw him carrying when he arrived, but that is also unlikely. She suffered a massive wound in the back of her head that was mistaken for a bullet wound, and a large bloodstain the size of a dinner plate was left on the carpet at the lower corner of the twin bed in which her body was found. Choking her to death, which can take four minutes to accomplish, would not have been consistent with Whitman's intent to end his mother's life painlessly. Choking her was also completely unnecessary considering she was struck in the back of the head with sufficient force to leave her bleeding copiously on the floor.

Although not suggested by anyone at the time or later, the object with which Whitman most likely killed his mother was an iron rod about 12 inches in length. It was found after Whitman's death among the possessions he took to the top of the Tower. It would have been the right size to conceal in the attaché case and of sufficient heft to strike down Margaret with one vicious blow. What likely happened is that Margaret led Charles into her apartment and he followed her into the bedroom while removing the iron rod from his case, then struck her with tremendous force while her back was turned.

The iron rod would account for another mystery related to Margaret's murder. The fingers of her left hand were broken, her wedding ring damaged—its diamond dislodged from its setting—and her hand bore the mark of a blow from a straight or straight-edged object. Some speculated that Margaret realized Charles's intentions, tried to stop him from entering the apartment and that her hand was caught and crushed in the door jam. This could explain the damage, injury, and wound, but it doesn't make sense. Margaret had no inkling her son intended to kill her, and rather than try to slam a door in his face, she probably would have stared in disbelief had he come at her with a weapon. Also, had she slammed a door and caught anyone's hand, it likely would have been Charles's rather than her own.

A more probable explanation is that Whitman, aware that the previous May his father had tried to forcibly take Margaret's wedding ring from her hand when she returned to Florida to retrieve personal belongings, and knowing that C.A. Whitman's top priorities in life were things of value, decided to deny him the ring he coveted. Charles knew that his father would inherit Margaret's possessions, considering their divorce was not final. He despised his father and it was in keeping with his personality and goals to intentionally smash the ring, post-mortem, with another blow from the iron rod, intending not to damage her fingers but to destroy the ring and send his father a message. In fact, the diamond from the ring was never found, meaning Whitman probably took it with him to make certain his father never recovered it.[15]

However she was assaulted, Whitman picked her body up from the floor, laid her in her bed, and then stabbed her in the chest with a hunting knife, probably the one he'd purchased earlier and which he'd secreted in the attaché case along with the iron rod and the rubber hose. He probably brought a pistol as well, as he was always prepared for contingencies. Whether she was still breathing when he stabbed her, or was not and the final wound was simply insurance, is not known, but Margaret Whitman was dead by 12:30 a.m.

Whitman arranged his mother's body on the striped sheets with matching striped pillow case so that she appeared to be sleeping. Then he placed a throw rug over the bloodstain on the floor and sat down to write another letter of explanation.

Monday, August 1, 1966 12:30 A.M.

To Whom It May Concern,

I have just taken my mother's life. I am very upset over having done it. However, I feel that if there is a heaven she is definitely there now. And if there is no life after, I have relieved her of her suffering here on earth. The intense hatred I feel for my father is beyond description. My mother gave that man the 25 best years of her life and because she finally took enough of his beatings, humiliation and degradation and tribulations that I am sure no one but she and he will ever know—to leave him. He has chose to treat her like a slut that you would bed down with, accept her favors and then throw a pittance in return.

I am truly sorry that this is the only way I could see to relieve her sufferings but I think it was best.

Let there be no doubt in your mind I loved that woman with all my heart.

If there exists a God let him understand my actions and judge me accordingly.

Charles J. Whitman

He re-read the letter, saw he had omitted the word "all" in the next to last sentence and inserted it with a caret. Charles Whitman was a meticulous man. He then placed the note on her chest and pulled the covers up to her chin. He may also have taken one of her pillowcases.

Before leaving, he wrote another note and taped it to the front door. It was meant for the building caretaker, and said "Roy, I don't have to be to work today and I was up late last night. I would like to get some rest. Please do not disturb me. Thank you. Mrs. Whitman."

Charles left the Penthouse Apartments about 1:30 a.m., but returned a short while later and told the doorman, a different one than the one who was on duty when he arrived, that he was Mrs. Whitman's son and needed to get into her apartment to get a prescription he'd promised to fill for her. He explained that his mother was sleeping and he didn't want to wake her by knocking. The doorman verified his identity in the apartment files, took him upstairs and let him in the door. He noticed but did not read the note on the door, and when Whitman did not return immediately, he went back down. Whitman followed a few moments later, exited the elevator and held up a pill bottle for the guard to see as he walked toward the door. It was likely his Dexedrine, which he expected to need during the upcoming day and which he'd forgotten, perhaps having removed it from the attaché as he was retrieving a weapon, perhaps in order to take a few pills in preparation for a busy night's work. He left for good at about 2 a.m.

Kathy was asleep when Charles returned home. It is unknown whether he spent time pondering, admiring his wife while she still lived, or acted quickly and without hesitation. He pulled back the bedding and stabbed her repeatedly in the chest.[16] She died instantly.

At 3 a.m., an hour after leaving the Penthouse Apartments, he retrieved the letter he began at 6:45, before the Fuesses arrived. Since then, having spent almost two hours visiting, picking up Kathy and driving her home, talking to her and participating in phone calls, going to his mother's apartment and murdering her, returning home and murdering his wife. Whitman took up writing again in mid-sentence, right where he left off, the only difference being that he was then writing by hand with a blue ballpoint pen instead of typing.

No one can say he was not organized and in an orderly frame of mind. He was even careful to annotate and explain the disconnection in the letter by writing "friends interrupted 8-1-66" and "Mon. 3:00 A. M. Both Dead" in the left margin of the letter. Then picking up his train of thought about what occurred before he joined the Marines, he wrote:

I was a witness to her being beat at least once a month. Then when she took enough my father wanted to fight to keep her below her usual standard of living.

I imagine it appears that I brutally kill (sic) both of my loved ones. I was only trying to do a quick thorough job.

If my life insurance policy is valid please see that all the worthless checks I wrote this weekend are made good. Please pay off all my debts. I am 25 years old and have never been financially independent. Donate the rest anonymously to a mental health foundation. Maybe research can prevent further tragedies of this type.

Charles J Whitman

Give our dog to my in-laws. Please tell them Kathy loved "Schocie" very much.

R.W. Leisner (sic)

Needville, Texas

If you can find in yourself to grant my last wish Cremate me after the autopsy.

Next he turned his attention to the rest of his family. Heading both of them "8-1-66, Monday, 3:00 a.m.," he wrote short letters to his brothers. To Johnnie Mike he penned:

Dear Johnnie: Kathy and I enjoyed your visit. I am terribly sorry to have let you down. Please try to do better than I have. It won't be hard. John, Mother loved you very much.

Your brother, Charles

The note to his other brother, Patrick, reflected that the middle son had sided with C.A. when it came to assigning blame for their parents' estrangement:

Pat: You are so wrong about Mom. Maybe someday you will understand why she left Daddy. Pat, Mom didn't have any desire to harm Daddy whatsoever. She just wanted what she had worked for. She really needed that $40.00. Thanks for sending it. She'll never know about that Grandmother or not.—Charles

Finally he wrote a letter to his father. Among all of the items Whitman wrote that night, it is the only one never to have been released, undoubtedly because the senior Whitman did not want the world to hear or read the damning things Charles said about him.

At some point while tying up the loose ends of his life, he noticed two cameras that contained rolls of undeveloped film, so he placed both on the dresser next to the rings and watch Kathy had removed before going to bed. With a green felt-tipped pen he printed, "Have the film developed in these cameras. Thank you" and signed his name. They would be discovered shortly after the shooting ended that afternoon, and speculation would run high among both the police and the media about what the photos would reveal. The result was anticlimactic, as they were merely pictures of the excursion to the Alamo, and others taken since the previous March around Austin and at the Whitman home.

It was no longer Sunday. The big day had arrived and he'd already committed himself totally to his plan. He would not hesitate to follow through to the end, and he had a lot of preparation to complete, but first he rewarded himself with a little trip down Memory Lane.

Whitman retrieved his diary from 1964, kept until the end of his Marine Corps enlistment was within sight, and read parts of it, paying particular attention to an entry dated February 23 of that year devoted to Kathy, praising everything about her (except her thighs and knees, which he thought were too chubby) and in which he had stated he was writing about her for the purpose of comparing his thoughts and ideas about her then with those he would have "in the years to come."

The man who read his journal that night was different, internally, from the man who wrote the entries. In early1964, Whitman had been looking forward to climbing the pleasant slope of the future hand in hand with the woman he loved. Now that pleasant slope was a sheer cliff, the end of his "years to come." By early morning on August 1, 1966, he had decided to commit dark and inexcusable crimes drawn from a very short list.

Whether he specifically remembered writing the entry two and a half years earlier and wanted to complete its purpose, or whether he simply happened on it when looking back at his life, he found the entry and commented on it. At the beginning of the entry for February 23, 1964, he wrote "I still mean it. CJW 8-1-66." At its end he wrote "Only time has shown me how right I was in these thoughts over 2 ½ years. My wife was a fine person. CJW." He was careful to use past tense.

He also found a free verse poem he'd written that began, "To maintain sensibility is the greatest effort required" and wrote "8-1-66 Written sometime in early 1964 when I was in a sunken feeling as I have been lately. C.J. Whitman." To another set of maxims he'd written to himself that he'd entitled, "THOUGHTS TO START THE DAY," he appended the comment "8-1-66 I never could quite make it. These thoughts are too much for me. CJW." Those thoughts may have been too much for Charles Whitman that night, but what he intended to do a few hours later would be too much for the rest of the world.

In Vienna, Illinois, a woman named Sylvia woke suddenly at 2 a.m. Something seemed terribly wrong. One of her loved ones was in danger.

Her husband, a veteran of World War II and Korea, was then in Vietnam, and her first thoughts were for him. She and her mother had been driving all day, on their way back to Texas from Tacoma, Washington, and she should have been exhausted, but instead she "had this awful feeling that something bad was gonna happen." She went to the bathroom, hoping not to disturb her mother, and began to pray. She was a devout, lifelong member of the Church of God, and was a firm believer in the power of prayer, but when she began praying for her husband, it did not feel right. She began to cry. Not knowing what else to do she changed her prayer to, "Well Lord, whatever it is, please take care of it and stop whatever it is." She was unable to sleep for the rest of the night.[17]

---

1. Huffman could not recall the caliber of the rifle when he gave his statement on August 2nd, nor when interviewed 49 years later. In fact, his recollection in 2015 was that Whitman took the rifle with him to the Tower, and that is why the FBI (actually DPS) knew to come interview him. This suggests that officials knew to interview Huffman because someone else told them about Charles' and Kathy's trip to Devine, probably Goldie Harris, Johnnie Mike being in New Jersey August 1-3. It may also indicate that the trip to Devine and the trip to San Antonio were on the same day, probably Saturday the 23rd instead of back to back that day and the next. .

Statement of Brock Huffman to DPS, August 2, 1966; AHC; telephone interview of Brock Huffman, May 27, 2015, and email dated June 15, 2015.

2. Texas Dept. of Public Safety report dated August 3, 1966 from Maurice Beckham to O. N. Humphreys; Austin, Texas, Police Department Records of the Charles Whitman Mass Murder Case, AR.2000.002. Austin History Center, Austin Public Library, Texas. The Austin History Center's collection is the single largest depository of primary materials related to the Whitman mass murders in existence, with a guide and table of contents alone numbering 79 pages. Hereafter, while individual reports from that collection will be identified in each note, the collection will be referred to as "AHC."

3. Whitman's friend, F.J. Schuck, theorized that Whitman would not have used anyone's weapons but his own, that being consistent with his personality, but it also suggests strongly that Whitman was not making plans to go up the Tower as much as a week in advance.

4. As part of her divorce proceedings, Margaret Whitman had recently filed a motion to obtain separate maintenance payments from C.A., who objected and claimed she was asking for too much. This may have led to his decision to withhold all payments, at least until the matter was resolved. Memorandum (27 pp.) designated MM 62-5533, August 9, 1966, FBI Miami, AHC.

5. Lavergne at 20, 32, 54.

6. Phone conversation between Francis J. Schuck and Monte Akers, February 7, 2015.

7. Letter dated August 4, 1966 from FBI agent J. Myers Cole; AHC; Lavergne at 108. References to the claim that C. A. Whitman decided to cut off all financial support to Whitman and his mother on July 30, 1966 appear in three or four FBI reports, and stem from the report of a witness who appeared voluntarily at the West Palm Beach, Florida office of the FBI on August 3, 1966. The witness's name is redacted in most of the FBI reports, but the content of the information provided by the witness make it clear that he was a member of Margaret's family who had been around Charles since boyhood, and who was almost certainly her brother, Walter, who lived in West Palm Beach.

8. Lavergne at 87.

9. One might expect them to go to the Americana Theatre, the newest one in the City, and conveniently located in proximity to Wyatt's Cafeteria, but its movie did not begin until 2 p.m. and had a running time of 115 minutes. The State Theater was one of the City's oldest, having been built in 1935, and its proximity to the Paramount might have caused there to be a crowd outside because the movie *Batman* was premiering at the Paramount and its stars, Adam West, Lee Meriwether, Burgess Meredith, and Cesar Romero made an appearance. However, the premier did not begin until 5 p.m., so that crowds should not have been in place when Charles and Kathy were at the State. "ShowWorld" section of the *Austin American Statesman,* pp. 9-11, July 31, 1966.

10. Department of Public Safety memo dated August 2, 1966, to O.N. Humphreys, Jr., Officer in Charge, from Howard W. Smith, Intelligence Section, AHC.

11. Larry Fuess, who saw him typing, or at least saw the typewriter and was told by Whitman that he was typing a letter, said in one account that the typewriter was "on the table" and in another that it "was on the coffee table." Under the theory that he might have called the

coffee table simply a table, but was not likely to call the dining table a coffee table, his latter version is accepted. Interview of Larry Fuess, August 8, 1966; AHC; interview of Larry Fuess by Gary Lavergne on June 6, 1996; Lavergne at 97, note 21.

12. Elaine Fuess, quoted in the *Austin American Statesman,* August 7, 1966.

13. Supplementary Offense Report dated August 7, 1966, by Sgt. R. Kelton, AHC.

14. Report of Sgt. Moody, 4:05, August 4, 1966, AHC.

15. Interview of Judge Jerry Dellana by Sara Ryder, June 2, 1983, Original Tape No. 0511B, AHC; Judge Dellana, who was then a Justice of the Peace and who acted as magistrate for several victims, including Margaret Whitman, said that her fingers were broken at a diagonal, "as if somebody would put it (her hand) in a door jamb and slam the door real hard. I remember the stone had popped out and we never could find the stone."

16. Reports about the number of stab wounds vary from three to five, and the lack of an autopsy of Kathy's body prevents certainty.

17. Interview and hand-written account of Sylvia Walden, June 3, 2015.

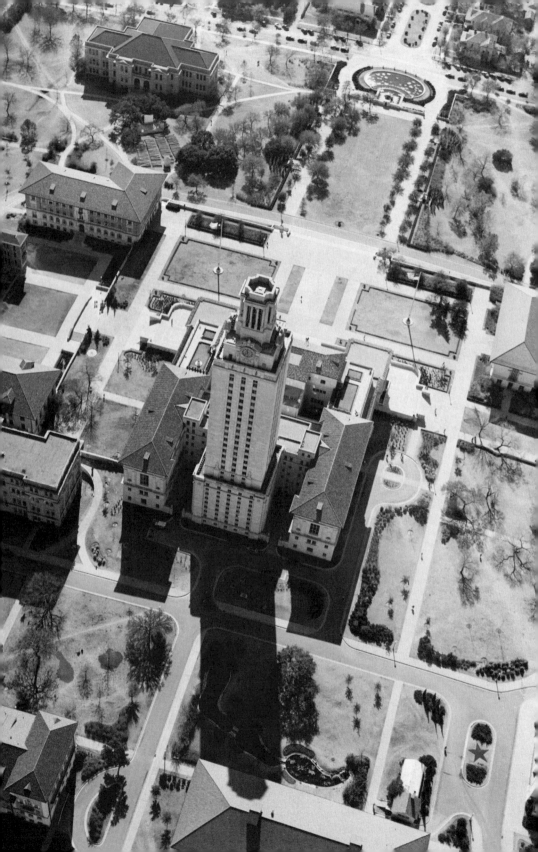

CHAPTER TWO

Time and Place

It is a pleasant city, clean and quiet, with wide rambling walks and elaborate public gardens and elegant old homes faintly ruined in the shadow of arching poplars. Occasionally through the trees, and always from a point of higher ground, one can see the college tower and the Capitol building. On brilliant mornings the white sandstone of the tower and the Capitol's granite dome are joined for an instant, all pink and cream, catching the first light.

-Billy Ray Brammer, The Gay Place

What starts here changes the world.

-University of Texas motto

It was the 1960s in Austin, Texas.

That should be all that needs to be said, all the description necessary, particularly for those who knew the old Austin and understand the 60s.

Every generation believes it is special. Something happens every decade worth remembering forever. Every place has its pride. Yet there was no other city like Austin, not in Texas or most of the country, and there was no decade like the 60s.

Take some San Francisco and some Fort Worth, add some Atlanta and Charleston, a touch of New Orleans, a dash of Nashville, but keep plenty of small town flavor so that everybody still knows everybody else. That comes close to the where.

The 60's don't have a name like the Gay 90's, the Roaring 20's, or the Dust Bowl 30's. The decade doesn't need a name. It was the ten years when every-thing changed.

Aerial view of UT tower and South Mall

25

The 60's were the Cuban Missile Crisis, JFK's assassination, Civil Rights, the Beatles, the British Invasion, the Vietnam War, the assassinations of Malcolm X, Martin Luther King, and Robert Kennedy, first man on the moon, drugs, hippies, the Electric Kool Aid Acid Test, Woodstock, feminism, burning draft cards, burning bras, the Chicano movement, the Stonewall riot, the Watts riot, the Berkeley riot, the Chicago Democratic Convention, Muhammad Ali, the first Superbowl, Charles Manson... did anyone mention the Beatles... or Vietnam?

They were all in the 60's, all of those events and people, and more. Think of it as America's puberty, when innocence was just about gone but not quite, when life was getting complicated and choices were becoming difficult, when a happy child with a tough upbringing was trying to decide which way to go with life, but was getting a lot of mixed messages from inside and outside.

In later years the City of Austin would become known for its many computer and other high tech industries, but not in 1966. As reporter Neil Spelce said, "we did not use the words 'high' and 'tech' in the same sentence together in 1966." The City had black and white television only, one established television station with another just coming on the air to compete, and half a dozen radio stations, almost all AM rather than FM. As Spelce recalled, it was "still a pretty small sleepy state government, state university town."[1]

Then there was the University of Texas, the most progressive, intellectual state university in Texas, maybe the South. There was the football team that took the National Championship in 1963 and which would do it again in 1969. For anyone living in Austin it was THE University. For anyone who attended, being a Longhorn was a lifelong source of pride.

There was Mount Bonnell and the hills to the west still covered in trees. FM 2222 was just a pretty country highway with a fantastic view of the dammed up Colorado River that went nowhere. There was the Legislature coming to town for 140 days every odd-numbered year, so that from early January to late May the City would spill over with odd ideas, or with ideas rushing to catch up with 1955. Then the legislators would leave town with, as folks used to say, all the trash cans tipped over and all the bitch dogs pregnant.

That is the when and the where, but just a little of it. There was so much more.

Seen through the prism of hindsight, the time and place were unique, although even those living in Austin, Texas in 1966 did not, could not, know it. They might have been particularly fond of Austin, hundreds of thousands of people were and are, and they might have understood that the nation was changing, but for most it was just normal life in a normal place. Unique as the place and time may have been, both were about to end.

The degree to which Austin was special was proven a decade later when the great energy crisis of the 1970s hit Texas. The astronomical leap in oil prices caused a great economic boon in the oil-rich Lone Star state, so that millions of dollars were pumped into untutored bank accounts at a remarkable barrel-per-day rate. Hundreds of the owners of those accounts, suddenly able to afford fantasies, decided the place they wanted to live was Austin. Real estate values soared. Homes worth less than $100,000 in 1975 were worth $1,000,000 by 1979.

IBM would open a major facility in the city in 1967, Texas Instruments in 1969, Motorola in 1974, Dell in 1987, 3M in 1988, and Sematech the same year. From 1940 to 1990 Austin's population grew an average of 40 percent per decade. During the 1960s the number of students attending the University of Texas at Austin doubled, and between 1950 and 1970 the number of government employees in Travis County tripled. But most of that was still years away. In 1966, Austin was "the gay place" described by Billy Ray Brammer in times when the description had no sexual connotation.

On a larger scale, the nation was at the end of an era without knowing it. Since its inception, the United States had tip-toed and leap-frogged along a ragged edge of disaster. From revolution to Whiskey Rebellion to slavery to wars with England, Mexico, and Spain, to Civil War, Indian Wars, Prohibition, Great Depression and two world wars, the nascent nation barely had time to catch its breath between crises. Despite all its optimistic primping and promises, it had never been quite able to live up to its potential for greatness... until 20 years before.

With the end of the Second World War and the return of troops from service, the United States finally blossomed into her boasts. It found a halcyon shore and become the nation it believed it could be. Since 1946, despite hiccups and stutters, the USA enjoyed greatness on a worldwide scale. Yes, there were Korean and Cold Wars, McCarthyism, and the struggle for civil rights, but the two decades from 1946 to 1966 were a special time in the minds of most Americans, particularly white Americans, and would be gazed upon with deep fondness for decades to come. It was a period of seeming innocence coupled with xenophobic conceit, punctuated by early rock and roll and infant television, crew cuts, duck tails, poodle skirts, Hollywood, and hot rods. Right and wrong were as distinguishable as black and white.

Then the times changed. Black and white became gray. Right and wrong were not so easy to distinguish, such that G. K. Chesterson's adage of 65 years earlier, "saying 'my country, right or wrong... is like saying 'my mother, drunk or sober,'"[2] gained credence, and perhaps could be accompanied by the additional lament of "what's left in this old world when right is wrong?" That change had begun by 1966, and it would continue.

Austin, Texas, capital of the most conceited of all the states was, and remains, different than the rest of Texas. With a population of about 220,000 on August 1, 1966, it was one of the largest cities in the state, but it had, as a resident of the time recalled, no "big city feel, no sophistication."[3] The Hill Country and the five "highland lakes" were to the west, the dammed up Colorado River split the city, hardshell Baptist Waco was to the north, wide open spaces were to the east, and San Antonio morphed into Laredo and Mexico going south. Like many college towns it had a distinct air of higher learning. Like other state capitals it had a feeling of self-importance and authority. The same combination did not exist in any other Texas city.

The University of Texas opened in Austin in 1883, intent on becoming the flagship university of the state. However, it had an arch-rival in what would become Texas A&M University, founded in 1876. The existence of the University and its rivalry with Texas A&M explains some of Austin's personality. A&M, located in College Station, was by its very name an "agricultural and mechanical" school, but it was also the equivalent of a military academy. The Corps of Cadets was founded in 1876, the college began as an all-male military school. It remained as such, with mandatory membership in the Cadet Corps, until just one year earlier, 1965, when the school began admitting women and Corps membership became voluntary.

Aggies absolutely despised Texas Longhorns and the feeling was mutual. If Aggies were proud of being an all-male bunch of farmers, rednecks, and wannabe soldiers, it was mandatory that Longhorns, or "t-sippers," needed to be co-ed, intellectual, and pacifistic.

So the city, largely because of the University and partly because of the large number of state agencies and their employees, many of whom were professionals, drifted toward a status some people compared to that of Madison, Wisconsin, San Francisco, California, or Boston, Massachusetts. Open-mindeness, love of the arts, and easy-going tolerance were highly-prized without being forced on anyone. Each major Texas city—Dallas, Fort Worth, Houston, San Antonio, El Paso—had its own distinct personality. Austin's was one of intellectual progressivism and free thinking. Inevitably, the rest of Texas was dismissive, so that the future city motto of "Keep Austin Weird," merely meant "keep Austin normal, like cities in other states" to many of its residents.

Something else was happening in Austin in the mid-1960s. Music and a growing counter-culture were moving Austin further from the mainstream. The Beatles, pot, LSD, the civil rights movement, and opposition to the Vietnam War had a place in Austin by 1966, although it would be a couple more years before they were easy to see, and there would always be a healthy seasoning of Bob Wills. Visible on the horizon were Willie Nelson, Janis Joplin, Asleep at the Wheel, the Vulcan Gas Company, Armadillo World Headquarters, the Broken Spoke, Threadgills, T-Bone Walker, Stevie Ray Vaughn, and dozens more, which were percolating into a semi-psychedelic mix of folk, country, blues, and rock music stew guaranteed to make Austin the single "grooviest" place in Texas, ultimately "the music capital of the southwest."

Another resident of the city in the early 60s recalled that:

> The '63 assassination of JFK was the end of an era of innocence in the state and the country, but somehow Austin seemed to shrug it off fairly well. It happened in Dallas, which wasn't really a proper Texas town. No cowboys, no oil wells, bunch of lawyers and bankers. Kennedy was replaced by LBJ, an Austin man.
>
> Austin was weenie shrinking and beautiful Barton Springs, the beautiful cement swimming pool poetically called "Deep Eddy," and Bergstrom AFB where, it was said, B-52s awaited the call to head to Russia for Armageddon. We dutifully practiced "Duck and Cover" drills in our classrooms. It seemed to be just as useful as a standard fire drill, though the naiveté of thinking that ducking under one's desk and covering your head would provide protection from a nearby atomic explosion is somewhere between funny and pathetic.[4]

Looming over it all was the University of Texas Tower, what the same resident of 1960s Austin called "the dome of St. Peters to the football god of Texas. Our Eiffel tower, visible from every street in town," and what J. Frank Dobie once called "the penis of the prairie."[5] Completed in 1937, the tower was officially "the Main Building," having replaced "Old Main," a Victorian, Gothic structure that was essentially the entire college when the school was founded in 1883. At a height of 307 feet tall, it was technically not the tallest building in the City. The State Capitol was 308 feet tall and by then-current legal requirements, no building was allowed to be built higher than the capitol. However, the U.T. Tower's ground elevation was at 606 feet above sea level while grade for the nearby Capitol building was at 599 feet, causing the tower to loom above the Capitol by a strapping six feet.

The Tower had thirty stories, with four sets of elevators. Two of the sets, one in the front and one in the rear, ran from the second floor to the 27th, after which visitors had to climb two flights of stairs to the 28th floor and the observation deck.[6] The elevators could go higher, but not without having an attendant who knew how to do it. A service elevator ran from the basement to the fifth floor, and the other elevator serviced only floors 2 through 17, having been designed as a book elevator for the tower's original purpose as a library. Library stacks occupied the first 14 floors in 1966, while floors 15 through 27 consisted of administrative offices, including the office of the president on the fourth floor, and unique collections such as one devoted to Harry Houdini and another to P. T. Barnum.

It was off-white, constructed of steel with a façade of Indiana limestone in a Spanish Colonial Revival style of architecture. At the top, above the observation deck, were four huge clocks, one facing each direction, each 12 feet in diameter, 14 feet from rim to rim, clad in gold leaf and having been installed in 1936 by the company that later became IBM. Lights installed along the walkway of the 28th floor observation deck and elsewhere permitted the entire tower to be lit up in burnt orange, the University's theme color, when one of the University's sports teams won a victory. For the winning of certain games, such as the national football championship, an eleven-story "1" would be lit on all four sides. Before the observation deck was closed in 1974, the tower was visited by up to 70,000 people a year.

An inscription on the facade above its main entrance at ground level read, "Ye shall know the Truth and the Truth shall make you free," from John, 8:32. At the top was a carillon of 56 bells, the largest in the state and played daily. At 12:50 on Monday, Wednesday, and Friday, a "concert" was played on the carillon, a tradition dating back to 1936. Otherwise the bells chimed on the hour and every 15 minutes. During World War II, an air raid siren was placed on top of the Tower to notify Austin residents of incoming air attacks, but other than for testing, it was never used. The siren was still there on August 1, 1966, but no one thought to sound it.

August could be a bad month for the Tower. On August 10, 1965 it was damaged by an extensive fire on the 20th floor. A decent amount of the building was damaged by water and smoke. Eerily, the fire began about 11:30 a.m. and continued for about 90 minutes, as if to provide a literal fire drill for putting out a different type of fire not quite one year later. Repairs went on for months and the observation deck was closed, probably until May 2, 1966. The chimes and "concert" were banned for a time in order not to startle workers and cause them to fall from the scaffolding., and the Westminster cadence was not reinstated until shortly before May 2. On August 1, 1966, workers were finalizing the application of a water resistant coating to the exterior walls of the upper stories and tall scaffolding was in place on the north side of the Tower that reached nearly to the observation deck.[7]

Austin was a festive place, literally. A month did not go by without some sort of festival celebrating one thing or another, particularly music but also rodeos, art, history, foods, fun, and holidays. The next big one on the horizon as of August 1, 1966 was the Fifth Annual Aqua Fest, a celebration of water activities scheduled to run for ten days along the banks of Town Lake beginning the first week of the month. The Lake, which would later be named Lady Bird Lake in honor of the First Lady, was constructed in 1960.

Started in 1961 as an economy booster during the dog days of summer, Aqua Fest scheduled attractions for everyone, including two parades, a canoe race, fishing contests, drag boat racing, a sailing regatta, an illuminated night time boat parade on the lake, water skiing, kite flying, a Grand Prix sport car race, a beauty contest, a rodeo, a golf tournament, dances, and fireworks. For 1966 the grand marshal of the parade was to be Melody Patterson, the actress who played Wrangler Jane on the television sitcom *F Troop*. Also appearing would be Adam West and Burt

Ward, Batman and Robin in the popular new *Batman* show on television, and Fess Parker, star of *Davy Crockett.*[8] It was hard to imagine that anything else might occur in Austin that week to rival such excitement.

The summer school session was drawing to a close on August 1, 1966, and ahead lay the excitement of the fall semester and the football season. U.T. was not the mega-University it is now. Enrollment was a respectable 27,000, while today it is well over 50,000. As a student named Bob Higley recalled, "the university had always seemed like an idyllic place that was separate from the rest of the world. It was devoted to ideas and learning. You could say whatever you wanted to say; you could be provocative if you wanted to. The campus was smaller then, and the student body was nearly half the size it is now, so there was a real sense of community."[9]

What happened on August 1, 1966 in Austin was not a catalyst for the changes and loss of uniqueness. The Whitman murders that day did not even hurry along the end of the two decades of eminence the U.S. enjoyed after World War II or mark the end of America's two decades of self-satisfaction. If any event deserves that dubious distinction, it is the assassination of JFK just shy of three years earlier.

Instead, the Whitman murders served as a road sign for what lay ahead, including the concept that an American did not have to be the president to fear assassination by a high-powered rifle from an elevated position. The forces that sent the United States down a darkling path toward self-loathing and uncertainty that developed after 1966 were much larger and irresistible than one killer in a sniper's nest.

Nevertheless, history has shown us that the U.T. Tower shootings were a diagnostic symptom of a future American illness, and in the minds of many who experienced the event it was a watershed moment that separated bright days from darker ones that followed.

Brenda Bell was a junior in 1966, and she remembered that "[t]he anti-war movement wasn't very big yet on campus when this happened. The guys still had short haircuts and the girls had flips. We were right at the end of that era, with the Peter Pan collars and the circle pins and the Pappagallo shoes and the fraternity and sorority parties. Random violence and mass murder wasn't something we knew. If this happened now, there would almost be a feeling of having seen it before. But we had no reference point then."[10]

August 1, 1966 would become that reference point.

1. Interview of Neil Spelce (tape recording), AHC.

2. G. K. Chesterson, *The Defendant,* Ch. 16 (London: R. Brimley Johnson, 1901).

3. Paul Stoker, of Dallas, Texas, email dated November 15, 2014.

4. *Ibid.*

5. That name is more often associated with the Nebraska State Capitol building than the U.T. Tower, but a photo that makes the sobriquet appear accurate may be viewed at https://www.flickr.com/photos/atxj2007/2890749909.

6. The exact location and floors serviced by the elevators in the Tower have been described differently in post-incident publications and witness accounts, with some saying the elevator went only as high as the 26th floor instead of the 27th. Currently the main elevators used for guided tours of the Tower run from the ground floor to the 27th floor, and most participants on August 1, 1966 recorded that they rode to that floor. Allen Crum also mentioned riding to the 26th floor instead of to the top, and staff on duty when the authors visited the Tower in March, 2015 were unable to say whether the elevators had been modified since 1966. Because there are multiple flights of stairs between the 27th and the 28th floors, it is understandable how a witness may have recalled the 27th floor as being the 26th. Because the majority of accounts state that the elevator went to the 27th floor in 1966, that version has been incorporated into this book. Similarly, the freight elevator from the tunnels ridden by Houston McCoy and the other police officers who went up the Tower was recorded as having gone to the 5th floor, but a freight elevator in existence today stops at the 4th floor

7. "The Tower Fire," https://www.utexas.edu/tours/mainbuilding/news/index.htm, There is a dramatic photo of the Tower with smoke roiling out of the 20th floor windows at this internet site.

8. Lavergne at 89; Austin Aqua Festival, http://en.wikipedia.org/wiki/Austin_Aqua_Festival

9. 96 Minutes at 106.

10. *Ibid.*

CHAPTER THREE
Charles Whitman Jekyll; Charles Whitman Hyde

I definitely love that young woman. Oh Kathy my little Stinker, I am so very glad that we are man and wife. We have so very much to live for. You are more precious to me than my life itself. This may seem a foolish statement to make, but in the last few months I am really positive that if I were ever faced with the situation of you living or my dying, that I would gladly choose to die for you.

-Charles J. Whitman, March 12, 1964

It was after much thought that I decided to kill my wife, Kathy, tonight after I pick her up from work at the telephone company... [T]he prominent reason in my mind is that I truly do not consider this world worth living in, and am prepared to die, and I do not want to leave her to suffer alone in it. I intend to kill her as painlessly as possible.

-Charles J. Whitman, July 31, 1966

Too much has been written about Charles Whitman. He does not deserve more.

Yet this tale cannot be told or understood without writing more. He is why it all happened. He is a major reason a portion of the public still finds fascination in the events of August 1, 1966 in Austin, Texas. The question "why did he do it?" is still the one most asked by people who learn of the story. The fact that he seemed normal, "all American," was

Charles and Kathy Whitman pose in front of an archway at the Alamo in San Antonio on Sunday, July 24, 1966, a week and a day before the shootings. This was one of the photos from the two Kodak Instamatic cameras Whitman left behind in his bedroom, with a written request that the photos be developed. It is the last photo taken of the pair alive.

handsome, even seemingly superior in some ways but was found after his death to have had a brain tumor, has made him a sympathetic, fascinating character, or cool antihero, in some people's eyes. He has and may yet again inspire copycats. That must stop!

What Charles Whitman did was not something to be admired or emulated. At his worse he was a mass murderer, an executioner of innocents. At his best he was a man with wonderful potential who either threw it away intentionally or did so for emotional and mental reasons that professional help might have prevented. Among the most forgiving of his victims, he is a person to be pitied. Among others he is like Lord Voldemort—"he who must not be named."

In the days following August 1, the governor of Texas and the president of the United States ordered thorough investigations of Whitman. In addition to the Austin Police Department, which began its investigation before Whitman's body cooled, FBI and Texas Department of Public Safety officers fanned out, got on the phone, and beat the brush to find answers, not about who had committed the atrocious crimes, but to find out what caused them.

The last thing the nation and Texas needed was another high profile sniper. Less than three years previously, the assassination of President Kennedy by an ex-Marine shooting from an elevated perch in Dallas put Texas and its law enforcement agencies under the microscope. As of August, 1966, the District Attorney of New Orleans, Jim Garrison, was launching a new investigation into that assassination, claiming some sort of complex, convoluted conspiracy involving the Mafia, Cuba and the CIA. Even without Garrison, book and magazine shelves were filling up with conspiracy theories.[1] Everyone from the President down to the Dallas Police Department was being accused of some sort of nefarious plot, cover-up, or scheme.

This latest incident, by what the world considered another ex-Marine nut case, seemed straightforward. He'd written letters admitting guilt, had been gunned down with a rifle in his hand, and was, as far as anyone could tell, all alone in his aberration. However, the shooter had been stationed at Guantanamo in Cuba in the Marine Corps. He'd been there just before the Cuban Missile Crisis. He'd grown up in Florida. His enlistment in the Marine Corps even overlapped with that of Lee Harvey Oswald by a few months. Who knew what kind of odd links might exist? Who knew what other powder kegs might be hidden?

Nobody from the President down to the Austin Police Department was going to take any chances. This case was going to be investigated from top to bottom, cradle to grave.

President Lyndon Johnson was not a graduate of U.T. but he loved the University and the City of Austin. He'd grown up not far away, and was already making plans to locate his presidential library there. Furthermore, one of those killed was the grandson of a former LBJ staff member and the son of personal friends of the president. Even though the FBI had no jurisdiction over the Whitman crimes, LBJ personally directed J. Edgar Hoover to investigate. Whatever the hell had set Whitman off, the President wanted answers and finality.

Certainly the concern was no less intense in Texas. Governor John Connally, like Johnson, had been there when Kennedy was killed, but Connally's relationship to the killing was more personal. He was within lover's touch of JFK when the shots were fired. He was shot by the shooter. He bore three wounds, supposedly from a single bullet, whereas JFK's body bore only two. John Connally was going to make certain all the stones were flipped over and that whatever crawled beneath each one was fully prodded.

He appointed a large, 32-member panel of experts to do a complete medical and psychological analysis of Whitman. They worked for over a month, interviewing, reconstructing and debating. Law enforcement agencies and the public wanted answers, and needed to know what had gone wrong in order to prevent such a thing from happening again.

The investigations failed on both accounts. No definitive answers were found to satisfactorily explain why Whitman did it, and the dismal record of similar mass shootings since 1966 trumpets the blaring fact that repetition of Whitman's insane acts has not been prevented.

The investigators who conducted their interviews and recorded their findings expected to find witnesses who would recount tales of a troubled youth who tortured animals, bullied classmates, wet the bed, was a teen-aged rebel, was emotionally and mentally unstable, and abused drugs, but if so they were disappointed. What they heard and recorded instead was:

> [H]e was a likeable, intelligent, apparently well-adjusted boy... and (the person interviewed) recalled nothing which, even now, suggested instability on his part or gives any insight into why he did what he did.[2]

Well-balanced, socially conscientious, and self-reliant. (Whitman's) Grade school teacher (and) high school principal described subject as better behaved and (a) better student than most and recalled nothing indicating cruelty, lack of stability or different behavior pattern on part of subject. Neighbors recalled subject as (a) normal boy who showed no lack of stability, cruelty, or odd behavior patterns. Fond of dogs.[3]

Of all the people I know, he was the last person I would ever think would do something like that... He was very devoted to his wife and I never saw or heard any violence from him... Sometimes he took pills to stay awake. He was always studying and took pride in making good grades.[4]

He was an outstanding person, very likeable, neat and nice-looking... of all the people he (the person interviewed) knew, the subject would be the last one to do anything like this.[5]

(He had) "all the standard appellations of a high school yearbook. He was easily the 'Best Looking,' 'Friendliest,' and 'Most Mature.'"[6]

Such a nice young man.[7]

Tall, broad-shouldered, crew-cut, a marine, an architectural engineering student, married to the Queen of the Fair of Needville, Texas, 'a nice, uncomplicated sort of guy,' fond of children, a Scoutmaster. 'Why I remember last summer when he had to go away my son cried because Charles wouldn't be around.'"[8]

I had seen him many times, and I never saw dilation of his pupils. If he did use drugs he didn't use much.[9]

(The person interviewed) cannot think of anything that was bothering the subject enough to drive him out of his mind...(Whitman) was always in good health and took things in stride... [T]he subject (Whitman) must have gone completely out of his mind because (he) was too kind and good hearted to have hurt anyone while he was in his right mind.[10]

He was always kidding and joking and just full of life, and I liked to be around him.[11]

Surprisingly, this dang guy, I thought, had high values.[12]

However, by the time the interviews were completed, the vast majority of the public did not need further explanation. They had heard there was a brain tumor and that satisfied their curiosity. It explained everything, particularly how such a nice guy could have done something so horrible. Only now, as will be explained, can we be confident that the tumor had little or nothing to do with Whitman's actions.

The 25 years and 38 days that comprised the life of Charles Joseph Whitman covered five distinct stages:

1. Birth on June 24, 1941 to July 6, 1959;
2. Marine Corps service to the NESEP program, July 6, 1959 to September 15, 1961;
3. Initial time at the University of Texas, September 15, 1961 to February 12, 1963;
4. Marine Corps service at Camp Lejeune, February 12, 1963 to December 6, 1964;
5. Final time at the University of Texas, December 6, 1964 to August 1, 1966.

Each stage led to the next, of course, and events occurred in each that contributed to what occurred on August 1, 1966. In each he displayed Jekyll-headed and Hyde-bound behavior, but the last two stages, and particularly the fifth, encompassed the most important developments.

The first stage was dominated by his father, Charles Adolphus, "C.A." Whitman. Reduced to the most basic of one-word appellations, C.A. was an asshole. The same neighbors who said glowing things about Charles said of C.A. that he was "a brute," "a quite disagreeable man," "a monumental egotist," "domineering, inconsiderate," with "disgusting" habits, "who dominated everyone he could dominate," "was not as successful or important as he believed himself to be," and who "spiced every conversation with brags about his successes and what he was able to do for other people."[13]

Blaming a man's father for the kind of horror committed by Charles J. Whitman is a cop-out of empyrean dimensions, but C. A. Whitman planted seeds in his son that grew into buds of seeming calm, then blossomed into full hysteria.

Whitman's great-great-grandparents lived in Texas, where his great-grandfather, Charles T. N. Whitman, was born circa 1855, after which the family moved east to Chatham County, Georgia, where Charles T.N. died about the same time his grandson, C.A., was born in 1919.

C.A. had a rough upbringing. One of four children, his mother put him and his brother in an orphanage—the Bethesda Home for Boys in

Savannah—when they were little. Not a lot of detail is known about that childhood, but one can imagine that it was a hardscrabble, mean sort of upbringing that stripped the boy of softness. C.A. married Elizabeth Margaret Hodges on August 17, 1940, avoided military service in World War Two, moved eight times in six years and settled in Lake Worth, Florida in 1947. When she was five months pregnant with their first child, Charles, he hit her in the head with a two by four, fractured her skull and put her in the hospital.[14] She filed charges for assault, but did not leave him.[15]

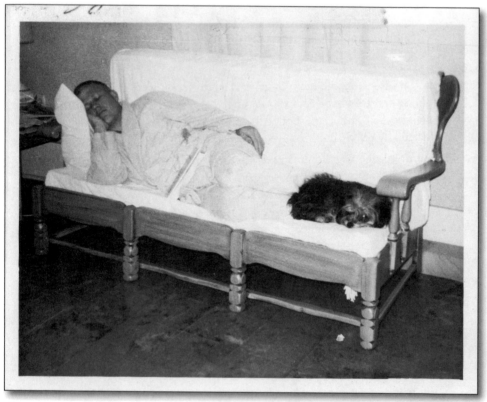

The last photograph taken of Charles Whitman while alive, on Saturday, July 30, 1966, asleep on a couch at his and Kathy's home at 906 Jewel Street in Austin. The couple's dog, Schocie, is curled at his feet and Whitman appears to be wearing a karategi, having probably attended a karate lesson that morning. This was one of the photos from the two Kodak Instamatic cameras Whitman left behind in the Whitman bedroom, with a written request from Charles that the photos be developed.

With little education and only semi-literate, C.A. was the epitome of ambition. Starting as a plumber, then a septic tank installer, then a construction contractor, he eventually became wealthy. By 1963 his company employed 28 workers and had a net worth of $289,463, which equals about $2,250,000 today, and gross annual sales of $308,433.[16] Along the way Margaret gave birth to two more boys, Patrick Grady on April 19, 1945, and John Michael on January 18, 1949. C.A. worked his way into the Lake Worth power grid, becoming president of the Chamber of Commerce, president of the School Board, and Chairman of the local Democratic party. It was an impressive record for a man who seemed universally despised.

He handled his family the same way he did business and politics—by combining iron control and intimidation with the purchase of loyalty. It is not unusual for a man to be too strict and authoritarian in regard to his wife and children. Nor is it unusual for a parent to be too permissive and overly generous with material goods and money, but it is uncommon for a man to be both at the same time. C.A. Whitman was such a husband and father, so much so that neighbors and acquaintances spotted and remembered it, saying that he was simultaneously "overly strict" and "overly permissive."[17] He went out of his way to provide his family with material goods and financial support, and simultaneously reminded them daily that they owed everything to him. They lived in a nice, upper middle class home with a swimming pool in the backyard—quite a status symbol in 1966—drove new cars, had nice clothes and the latest in televisions and appliances, and C.A. provided generous allowances to his three sons.

Money and material possessions drove C.A. Whitman. It was proof of success, and achieving success was the single most essential purpose in life. When he learned that his wife, oldest son, and daughter-in-law had been killed, his first, immediate, and tiresomely repeated concern was not about the tragedy of their loss, but that their homes be locked and secure to prevent anyone from taking the valuables inside. C.A. even bought a house near his home for his mother, the woman who put him in an orphanage, thereby including her in his orbit of control.

When Margaret or the boys did not perform to his satisfaction, he beat them with belts, fists, or any object suitable for the purpose.[18] Following August 1, 1966, he not only admitted but essentially bragged about beating his wife, saying, "I did on many occasions beat my wife, but I loved her... I did and do have an awful temper, but my wife was awful stubborn... (and)... because of my temper, I knocked her around." With regard to the boys he declared "I don't think I spanked them enough, if you want to know the truth about it. I think they should have been punished more than they were punished."[19]

He was also a self-professed "gun fanatic," who covered the walls of the family home with racks of at least sixty firearms.[20] He passed that passion on to his boys, particularly Charles. Hunting and shooting were the one activity in which father and son came closest to bonding, and marksmanship would be an achievement in which Charles took great pride.

Margaret was a devout, practicing Catholic, and she made certain the couple's boys attended mass regularly as well as Catholic schools, and that each became an altar boy. She was sweet, loving, and sympathetic. To the extent Charles received emotional support in his family, it came from his mother rather than C.A.

Charles was quite intelligent, scoring an impressive 138.7 on an Intelligent Quotient test when he was six. His grades in elementary school, Sacred Heart Catholic School in Lake Worth, were good, mostly A's and B's, although not spectacular. He strained to meet his father's demands for perfection and generally succeeded. He began taking piano lessons at the age of five,[21] and became an accomplished pianist. His father not only encouraged the lessons, but placed a bullwhip on the piano to remind the boy to practice regularly.[22] He joined the Cub Scouts at age eight, tried to join the Boy Scouts but was told he had to be 11, but attended meetings "in an unofficial capacity,"[23] until he was old enough. Once in, he accomplished something startling and utterly inconsistent with anyone's perceived pattern for future mass murderers—becoming the youngest Eagle Scout in the world.[24]

Another attribute of the young Charles Whitman was mentioned by at least one boy who was his age: "As a kid, I'd wonder why Charles couldn't come over and play with us. Other kids and me, we'd climb the mulberry and mango trees in back of the house and in the woods, but not Charles. Charles never played with us. He wasn't allowed to have friends; he couldn't have friends over to his house."[25] The issue relevant to that statement is not whether Whitman had friends, but whether he played like a normal boy. He had two younger brothers, plenty of dogs and other pets, was in the Cub Scouts and the Boy Scouts, played baseball, was manager of the football team, was a bit of a daredevil, and liked to pull pranks, so he sounds like a playful boy. However, in addition to the statement above, friends, neighbors, and his scoutmaster stated that when the young Whitman tried to play, it was forced, not natural and never spontaneous, and that he was always nervously looking over his shoulder for fear his father would come after him.[26]

At about the same time he became an Eagle Scout, he took on a paper route for delivery of the *Miami Herald* described as one of the largest routes then existing, and he was a model paper boy. Customers recalled that their paper was usually on their front porch or near their doors, and after two years Charles had saved enough money from the route to purchase a Harley Davidson motorcycle, which he used to deliver more newspapers, and which he wrecked seriously enough to put him in the hospital in February, 1958, when he was 16.

Whitman attended high school at St. Ann's Catholic School. Teachers remembered him as being intelligent and reasonably popular. A friend named Ray Roy recalled that he was a daredevil, and on one occasion dripping with irony he accepted a challenge, while a sophomore, to climb a tower at the school that was there "with some sort of circus act." "He went all the way to the top." It was also remembered that when managing the team at football games, he used the squeeze bottles of water meant for players to squirt friends and classmates in the stands.[27]

He graduated in June, 1959, ranked seventh in a class of 72,[28] and might have been accepted to attend college at the Georgia Institute of Technology.[29] The common story is that there then occurred an incident that altered everything, but the common story has it wrong. The incident occurred, but two years earlier than normally reported.

Charles went out on the town with one or more companions and came home drunk for the first time. At a pool hall he had accepted a challenge to drink an entire pint of gin, and about midnight two Lake Worth police officers brought him to the house, yelling and "acting silly."[30] C.A. Whitman exploded, beat his oldest son, and shoved him into the backyard swimming pool. The police did not file a report, at C. A. Whitman's request, and later publications stated that the incident occurred just after he graduated and was what made him decide to join the Marines. However, both C.A. Whitman and a friend who was with Charles that night said the event occurred while Charles was in the 10th grade.[31]

It is known that he had long wanted to join the Marines, and once he was 18 he did; he told his mother but not his father, and left for duty on July 6, 1959. C.A. was so upset when he found out that he tried to pull strings to have his son's enlistment revoked, even attempting to have the police pick him up.[32] For once, he failed.

So began the second stage of his short life. Charles went through basic training, or boot camp, at Parris Island, South Carolina, then served an 18-month tour of duty at the Guantanamo Naval Base in Cuba. He toed the mark, worked hard, followed orders, prepared for his future, and was an exceptionally good soldier. Captain Joseph Stanton, Executive Officer of the 2nd Marine Division remembered, "He was a good Marine. I was impressed with him. I was certain he'd make a good citizen."[33]

On April 27, 1960, Whitman was in a phone booth at Guantanamo when it was struck by lightning. He was shaken and the door to the booth became jammed so that it required help from fellow Marines to get him out. He was taken to the infirmary, treated and released.[34] If there was a Marvel graphic novel version of his life, the event might explain all that happened later.

Whitman did something else in 1960 that is chilling and which has not been revealed in print until now. While at Guantanamo he told the Marine that was then his roommate that he was "thinking about committing some kind of mass shooting." The roommate went on to become an officer in a Sheriff's department in New York state, and in 2003 he attended a class in risk assessment training being conducted by Dr. Mary Ellen O'Toole, who was then a senior FBI profiler at Quantico. When Dr. O'Toole made reference to Whitman having told the university psychiatrist about wanting to climb the Tower with a deer rifle, the officer raised his hand and shared the story with Dr. O'Toole and the approximate 100 other students in the classroom.[35]

During his service, Whitman was awarded the Marine Corps Good Conduct Medal, the Marine Corps Expeditionary Medal, a Sharpshooter's Badge, and was promoted to Lance Corporal and later to Corporal more promptly than many Marines with his amount of time in service.[36] He scored 215 out of 250 points on shooting tests and, chillingly, was particularly proficient at shooting rapidly over long distances at moving targets. During his tour in Cuba, Whitman applied for acceptance in the Naval Enlisted Science Education Program, which was a scholarship program designed to train engineers who would become Marine Corps officers. If selected, he would be able to earn an engineering degree at a selected college, where the Marine Corps would pay for his tuition, books, plus his normal base pay, a subsistence allowance and a basic allowance for quarters, after which he would go to Officer's Candidate School.

He scored high on the required examination and was approved for enrollment at a preparatory school in Maryland, where he completed courses in mathematics and physics. Acceptance into the program also required him to extend his enlistment by one year, for a total of six.[37] He also met Francis Joseph Schuck, Jr. there, who was destined to become one of Whitman's closest friends.[38] Schuck mentioned that he might apply to the University of Texas at Austin, where Schuck planned to study electrical engineering under his NESEP scholarship, and Whitman did so and was accepted. His major was mechanical engineering.[39]

The third stage of his life began. He was on the road to happiness. The years of harsh discipline from his father had instilled in him a determination to succeed. In fact, failure was completely unknown and unacceptable in his life. He was anxious to prove he was a man and all indications were that he would do so easily.

Charles was admitted to U.T. on September 15, 1961, and immediately received another boost. Francis Schuck located a position as a dormitory counselor at Goodall-Wooten dormitory and was asked if anyone else might be qualified and interested. Schuck suggested Whitman, both were interviewed and both got the jobs, which provided them free rooms. Whitman was assigned to the 7th floor and Schuck the 5th floor, and Charles moved into Room 706 in the Goodall-Wooten Dormitory on campus. His first roommate was John Drolla, a law school student and former dorm advisor.[40]

Life got even better. Schuck got them part time jobs as waiter/bus boys/ bartenders at the Kappa Kappa Gamma sorority house. Not only did they get paid for work surrounded by beautiful college girls, but the job included "11 free (and excellent) meals a week." The only downside of the job was that they were prohibited from commingling with the girls. In what would become a pattern, Whitman quit the job after only a few weeks.[41]

Later, beginning in November, 1963, Whitman kept a diary for a few months, but he did not do so when he was at the University of Texas.

Instead, he kept a record of his finances, detailing every expenditure he made and every financial transaction of any significance, from 26 cents spent for ink to when and where he had checking and savings accounts. Interspersed with the budgetary entries were comments about events of note, such as the first time he had Mexican food (on September 10, 1961 at "El Toro,") to getting a parking ticket (on October 20, "outside Charlie's"). As both this and his later diary would reveal, he was obsessed with finances, although his habit of making careful, complete accounting entries at U.T. began falling off in late October and ended before the year did.

Perhaps surprisingly, he did not drink much. He told Francis Schuck he did not like the taste of beer and alcohol, which various witness investigations confirmed. He would, however, occasionally use alcohol as self-medication, such as the time he took a pint of bourbon to a chemistry exam, hoping it would calm him down. He took a "brace of it while on a 'head call' (bathroom break)" and scored high on the test,[42] but alcohol abuse was not one of his foibles.

Instead, he engaged in high-risk behavior that included pulling pranks, driving like a maniac, getting or nearly getting into fights, and gambling.

The pranks included an attempt, with a dorm resident named David Pratt, to call Nikita Khrushchev and inform him that Whitman did not like him. On another occasion, he arrived at an all-night poker game at the dorm at 5 a.m., dirty, wet, disheveled, and distraught; to announce that a fellow student named Jim had been killed in a wreck. After the stunned poker players called Jim's girlfriend to express their grief, Jim walked through the door and Whitman shouted, "The ghost walks!" then collapsed on the floor and rolled about laughing.[43]

The wild driving included flying down I-35 on a motorcycle at speeds of up to 140 mph with a terrified Francis Schuck behind him.[44] The fights or near fights (which probably occurred in the fifth stage of his life), included one when a friend named Larry Fuess was riding with him and Whitman had an attack of road rage involving the driver in front of them. He jerked off his rings, threw them on the dashboard and jumped out of the car, ready for a fist fight, but the other driver sped away.[45] On another occasion he entered a classroom, found a Saudi Arabian sitting in "his" seat, grabbed the exchange student and threw him into the hall.[46]

In November of his first semester he was arrested, along with Schuck and a friend named James Merritt, for "illegal possession of a deer," and each had to pay a $100 fine and $29.50 in court costs.[47]

With regard to the gambling, despite later telling a friend he put his wife through college playing poker, he was not particularly lucky. A student who played with him, Jeff Robinson, recalled that the game was usually dime, fifty cents, a dollar, and table stakes, meaning those were the chip increments for betting, and players were limited to how much each could lose by the amount in their stacks. Robinson said winning or losing fifty to a hundred dollars was typical, but that the amount could be three or four times that much. He also remembered Whitman as being blond-headed, with a flat top and the aura of an ex-Marine or, in Robinson's own words, "he didn't seem like a lot of fun."[48]

That was because he took poker seriously. It involved money, and he sometimes lost as much as $400 in a night—a respectable month's salary in 1966. He also began failing to satisfy those debts, as much out of stubbornness or pique as inability to pay, and those he stiffed were not always forgiving or harmless. On one occasion he lost $190 in a single hand to a student named Robert Ross. He wrote checks to cover it and the additional $210 he had been beaten out of, but the check to Ross bounced. Ross went to Whitman's dorm room for reimbursement and found him lying on his bed and throwing a hunting knife to stick in a closet door. Charles told the smaller Ross that "my family is loaded. I'll get you your money. Don't worry about it,"[49] and Ross went away. The debt was never paid.

After another all night poker game, Whitman wound up owing $200 to a pair of brothers who were ex-convicts with a seedy reputation. Again he wrote a check but then stopped payment on it, alleging he had been cheated. The brothers visited Goody-Woo room 706 and threatened Whitman with a knife. Charles sought the advice of Francis Schuck and John Drolla, who told him to report the incident to the Travis County District Attorney. Whitman did so, swore out a peace bond against the brothers, and carried a .357 Magnum revolver he purchased in Cuba under his coat until he learned the brothers had been arrested in Dallas for auto theft.

Whitman changed roommates before the end of the fall semester of 1961. An upperclassman named Robert Smalley had a need for a new roommate on the third floor and Charles got the assignment. Smalley was a medical student who had been working at Parkland Hospital on November 22, 1963 when President Kennedy was brought there. Although he was not in the same room with JFK, he saw him, Jackie, LBJ, and the bloodied limousine.[50] Now he would have a second close encounter with history.

Smalley's previous roommate was also a Marine, an ex-MP, and one day he retrieved his MP baton and began climbing from balcony to balcony on the outside of Goodall-Wooten dorm, breaking windows. He was expelled and, irony being what it is, the new roommate assigned to Smalley turned out to be another Marine with temperamental tendencies—Whitman. However, during the time they roomed together, Smalley recalled that he never heard Whitman make an angry remark about anyone, say anything about wanting to shoot, kill, or hurt anyone, or even make a racially-tinged remark. In August, 1966, when a Dallas newspaper reporter tracked him down and interviewed him about Whitman, Smalley described him as "the kind of guy you would take home to introduce to your mother."[51]

During the next semester, Whitman roomed with Francis Schuck on the 7th floor. Schuck recalled that Whitman was "an average Catholic attending services probably more than most," and who retained a close friendship with Father Gileus LeDuc, Whitman's priest in Florida and former scoutmaster.[52]

Despite the partying, pranks, and poker, Whitman was obsessed with making good grades. Francis Schuck recalled that he was "always on edge about his schoolwork and... very conscientious about it."[53] He frequently studied all night, often taking Dexedrine to stay awake, but his grades were lackluster. In his first semester at U.T. he received an "A" in algebra, but an "F" in chemistry, a "D" in economics, and "C"s in three other courses.

He kept up a steady correspondence with his family, sharing discussions about guns and hunting with his father and reporting that once he had his degree in mechanical engineering and was out of the Marine Corps, he planned to return to Lake Worth and join C.A. Whitman's business. Schuck recalled that he never forgot a family birthday or anniversary. He also impressed University administrators. His academic advisor, Professor Leonardt Kreisle described him as "more mature than other students... very, very serious."[54] Schuck helped him with his algebra and trigonometry and described him as well-dressed, well-mannered, good-looking, and personable, although he did have a bad habit of chewing on his fingernails.[55]

In 1961, Whitman was sitting on Francis Schuck's roommate's bed in his dorm room, waiting for Schuck to finish something he was doing so he could help Whitman with an algebra problem, and he made what Schuck described as a "casual aside." Looking out the window at the U.T. Tower, he said "a well-armed man could stand off an army from up there."[56] Schuck did not give the comment any credence. It was the kind of remark any college student, particularly a Marine rifleman who loved firearms and knew about sniper's nests, might make. Schuck said that "[t]he knowledge that I had of Charles though never would have led me to believe that he actually would plot out the fulfillment of such an act."[57] On another occasion Whitman told Schuck that he would like to go to the top of the Tower and shoot people, but Schuck described the statement as being made "in a rather humorous vein."[58] Schuck did not recall exactly how many times he heard Whitman say something similar, but that it was more than twice and that he never heard him say anything of the kind after he got married.[59]

Schuck was not the only person to whom he made such a statement. Professor Barton Riley recalled that in an architectural engineering class one day, almost certainly during the fifth stage of Whitman's life, that another student announced for all to hear that "Charlie is talking about taking a rifle and going up on the Tower and shooting a bunch of people." Riley said he went to Whitman's desk, leaned down and put his elbows on it and told him "now that's just what an old Marine needs to do, just to show that he can shoot." Whitman did not look up. He had "that little bitty smile on his face, and he just kept drawing."[60]

Schuck said that Whitman went to the top of the Tower two or three times, but only on dates for "sightseeing or mood establishment."[61] His trip to the Tower with a rifle was a fantasy, of course, the kind many macho young men consider and some vocalize, not particularly shocking so long as it isn't acted on.

Then he met a girl; not just any girl, but THE girl for Charles Joseph Whitman.

Her name was Kathleen Frances Leissner, and he was introduced to her by Schuck, who was then dating her rooommate, in February, 1962.[62] She was from Needville, Texas, a teaching student who was two years younger than Charles. Pretty, slender, five foot four inches and about 120 pounds, she "mesmerized" Charles. He had dated girls, and was dating one named Carol Conlin when he met Kathy, but she soon became his last and most serious girlfriend.[63] She shared the attraction. He was 21, a handsome, blond-headed Marine, six feet tall and 190 pounds, with a dazzling smile, attending U.T. on a full-ride scholarship, and set to become a Marine officer and an engineer. It isn't difficult to imagine what she saw in him.

The couple courted for only five months before announcing their engagement in July.[64] The date selected for the ceremony was August 17, 1962, which was the 22nd anniversary of C. A. and Margaret's wedding. Kathy was Methodist, but the service was Catholic, held in St. Michael's Catholic Church in Needville. C. A. and Margaret drove from Florida to attend. Charles's close friend and former priest in Lake Worth, Father J. Gileus LeDuc, presided over the ceremony. LeDuc had been Whitman's scoutmaster when he became an Eagle Scout and Charles served as an altar boy at LeDuc's first mass in Lake Worth. By 1962, the priest was assigned to a parish in Houston.

The bride wore "an original gown of white peau de sole and imported lace... (with)... fitted bodice... bateau neckline... scuppoped (sic) alencon lace and butterfly sleeves."[65] Charles wore a white dinner jacket and black bow tie, cummerbund, and black trousers. Schuck was the best man, and the reception was at the home of Kathy's parents. Bob Smalley was supposed to be in the wedding, but he became ill and missed the event. C. A. behaved during the ceremony, but acted atrociously at the reception, letting everyone know that he didn't think the Leissners were good enough for his son and that the family was far below the septic tank-based Whitmans in social standing.

They honeymooned in New Orleans, then drove to Lake Worth so that Kathy could meet friends and other family members. They returned to Austin and took up residence in an apartment. While it is not recorded, it is probable that in October they marveled at Whitman's good fortune to no longer be stationed at Guantanamo, as the Cuban Missile Crisis played out.

His grades improved after he married, but it was too little too late. The Marine Corps decided he was neither demonstrating the academic goals required for the NESEP scholarship program nor conducting himself like a future Marine Corps officer. Early in the spring semester of 1963 he received notice that the scholarship was being revoked and that he was ordered back to active duty to complete the five year hitch for which he had enlisted in 1959.

On February 12, 1963, the fourth stage of his life began. He dropped out of the university and reported to the 2nd Marine Division at Camp Lejeune, North Carolina. The shock and agony of this development was devastating for the young couple and a source of significant shame. It was Whitman's first, genuine, undeniable life failure, something never supposed to happen and totally inconsistent with all his plans and expectations. In March he applied to have the scholarship re-instated, but the request was promptly denied. In July he was promoted to Corporal, but the elevation was small comfort, and was short-lived.

He continued to conduct himself as a model soldier, but he was desperate to be free of the Marine Corps and re-united with Kathy, so he turned to the one source of assistance on which he could always depend—his father. C.A. Whitman prided himself on his connections, and did not hesitate to begin pulling strings to get Charles's enlistment time reduced.

On September 10, 1963, Charles was involved in a jeep accident and was knocked unconscious for several hours, after which he was hospitalized for four days. In November 1963, he was court-martialed for gambling, usury, and unauthorized possession of a non-military pistol. He had threatened a fellow soldier who failed to repay a $30 loan with 50 percent interest in fifteen days. He plead guilty to 14 charges, "including wrongfully possessing ammunition, wrongfully possessing a small caliber pistol, 10 charges of lending money for profit, wrongfully communicating a threat, and gambling."[66] He was sentenced to 30 days confinement and 90 days hard labor, and was busted back to private.

Whitman was stunned and ashamed by the court martial, and probably for good reason. The executive officer of his battalion considered him to still be a model soldier, and wrote an article years later in which he described the acts for which Whitman was court martialed as almost commonplace among Marines.[67] He surmised that Whitman must have seriously alienated his 1st Sergeant or company commander and they were teaching him a lesson.[68] In all likelihood the lesson was being taught because Whitman had started, through his father, to seek an honorable, early discharge, and at the local level someone decided to make him look like a problem soldier who didn't deserve any favors. Whitman suspected as much and speculated about it in his diary, which he began keeping while in the brig.

Added to his mortification, the commander of his battalion, Colonel Bacon, told him on February 6 that he had brought everything on himself, the Marine Corps had fulfilled its obligation merely by assigning him to the NESEP, and that he did not believe Whitman could advance any further in the Corps.[69] It was bitter news for an ambitious young man who had strained to be a model soldier.

On October 8, 1964, he was attacked by four or five other Marines, knocked to the ground and kicked in the head.[70] Whether he suffered severe head trauma from either that incident or the Jeep wreck, and whether mental deterioration followed is anyone's guess.[71]

The diary, or journal, was a great comfort. "I never realized up till now the pleasure of talking to myself in a diary. I believe I will keep one from now on," he wrote on November 11. The entries ranged from upbeat to self-pitying. "The day is beautiful, the sun is radiant and warm but the air has acrispness to it. I wonder what my beautiful wife is doing at this time? I am so in love with her," he also wrote on the 11th. When not writing about Kathy, he wrote about hopes for their future. For a few days he believed Kathy was pregnant, and wrote, "I think into the future trying to picture our child, how wonderful it will be to see Kathy full of life with our baby. When will that day come?" He also revealed gnawing, growing self-doubt and anxiety. "As I look back over my last few adult years they seem so wasted. Will I ever accomplish anything I set forth to do? Oh! but to know the answer to this question."[72] In another entry he wrote that he had "thought very much about the concept 'death.' When it overtakes me someday I must remember to observe it closely and see if it is as I thought it would be."[73]

An issue sometimes raised in connection with Whitman is whether he modeled his actions of August 1, 1966, on those of Lee Harvey Oswald. The answer is apparently no, as he never mentioned the Kennedy assassination in his diary when it occurred. However, following the shootings, on August 5, armed with a judge's blessing if not a warrant, investigators unlocked a chest found in the dining room of Whitman's home in Austin and inside were two "diary type books,... (and) one Time magazine in regards to Oswald killing Kennedy."[74]

C.A. Whitman was a member of the Palm Beach County, Florida Democratic Executive Committee and the man occupying the White House was a Democrat, so C.A. employed an attorney and sent letters to state and federal legislators, with requests that they be forwarded with approval to the Marine commandant. The letters urged that Charles be allowed to return to Austin, where his wife was living, in order to complete his education. More letters followed but the Navy denied the request, ruling that an early discharge solely for the purpose of completing college would be unfair to other Marines, and that Whitman's failure to utilize the opportunities of the NESEP, as well as subsequent infractions, were voluntary acts.

C.A. did not give up, however, and during this time Charles both acknowledged and appreciated his father's efforts and displayed zero hatred or resentment of him. He referred to him as "Daddy," and wrote in his diary such entries as, "[a]fter I talked with Daddy (Mom was asleep in bed. She's been sick) he put me in a better frame of mind then I have been in a long time"[75] and "Daddy definitely put me in a good frame of mind the other night. I have never even thought of letting the Corps get me down physically, but it never occurred to me that they were affecting me mentally until Daddy brought it up."[76]

Just four days after he completed the hard labor, he got in trouble again for failing to take his rifle on a required hike. He explained that he was carrying a pistol holster on the hike, that he didn't have a sling for the rifle and that it was clean, so he made the decision not to take it. The result was that he was charged with "Article 92, Failure to obey a lawful order," and was sentenced to "office hours." It wasn't hard labor but Whitman was mortified. "I can hardly believe it, for something so petty... I guess it is to try and make my record look bad since I am suppose (sic) to see the Sec. of Navy... I called Mom and almost told her but I just can't do it, they are worried enough about me. I am so tired of being a burden to them and Kathy. It seems as though I can find trouble without looking."[77] Of course it doesn't seem like rocket science that a Marine rifleman might be expected to carry his rifle on a military exercise.

One diary entry, for February 23, 1964, is noteworthy both for what he wrote then and for the minor role it would play on August 1, 1966. Usually his journal entries were a half to a full page total with sentences or a paragraph devoted to Kathy. The entry for February 23 was three and a half pages long and was about nothing but her, his feelings for her, and his hopes for their future. He prefaced the entry by saying that he wanted to write down his thoughts about her so that he could compare them with "the ideas and thoughts I have in the years to come."

Most of the entry was praise—"Kathy is one of the most versatile young women I have ever known... her face and her hair are just perfect... her eyes are like twinkling stars... [s]he is an excellent driver... [h]er breasts are more than ample and... are just fabulous... I am constantly amazed at her tiny waist... [s]he is a fabulous cook... is definitely the ultimate in a sex partner... outstanding as a wife and at the same time she is the ultimate in a mistress... she displays an extraordinary amount of common sense... I am a very fortunate person."

Other parts of the entry reveal a critical eye and hopelessly chauvinistic attitude—"By professional standards she is not beautiful, she is too short. And she does not have a model's figure... her only physical fault in my opinion is that her knees and thighs are heavier than they should be... [h]owever I feel that when we live together again, that working together we will be able to trim her legs down to the right proportions... I imagine that part of this complete compatibility is to my own credit..."

He stated that "[s]ince our marriage I have never looked at another woman..." and entries on other days bore that out. When the owner of a clothing store where Charles worked briefly in his spare time told him that one of the girls in the office had mentioned that she wanted to take Whitman to bed, Charles replied that he loved his wife. He said he refrained from trying to explain further because he couldn't convince him how much Kathy meant to him and how little sex with other women meant, adding, "[e]veryone I meet seems to look at me in awh (sic) when they find out I don't run around. This makes me feel very good and superior."

On March 13 he went to town, to a club called "Jazzland," where a "little blond girl" flirted with him, putting her hand on his stomach and telling him that her husband was out of state, and that she was looking for a lover. Charles wrote that he didn't even look at her, "just laughed sort of like 'you don't have what it takes to interest me,' turned around and walked away." He wrote that he felt like another woman's touch violated Kathy's personal property, and that "it disgusts me to be touched by anyone but Kathy." In another entry he wrote that he had a wet dream about Kathy the night before.

The two months of entries in the 1964 record revealed, or confirmed, another critical aspect of Whitman's personality—his obsession with money. Charles seemed unable to let a day go by without taking note of money spent, money owed, money needed, or money considered. The topic dominated his thoughts and, in turn, the entries in the journal. A major reason for his court martial had been for gambling and loaning money to fellow soldiers at exorbitant rates. His father was apparently still financing him, or at least paying his phone bills,[78] but Whitman did not record the amounts of any regular parental subsidies (except for $50 he received from Kathy's mother) and considering how obsessed he was with money there probably were not any coming in from his father so long as he was in the Marines and drawing a soldier's pay.

This certainly does not mean C. A. Whitman was not still working on his son's behalf. On March 12, 1964, he had some "very very good news" to report.

The younger Whitman went to the Camp Lejeune business office after getting permission to depart a day early on leave later in the month, in order to change the paperwork accordingly. There he was given a message to call Florida "immediately," and he did so, afraid there was "something wrong with someone health-wise."[79] When his father came on the line he asked his son how much a year of his life was worth. It registered that "they had received some good news about my discharge," and it was true. Whitman's stint was reduced by a year. His new EAS, or expiration of active service, was to be December 6, 1964, and he would be honorably discharged, as opposed to receiving a general discharge, which had been another issue of contention. Although C.A. took credit, the decision to discharge Whitman was actually for "C.O.G." or "convenience of government," which was common in that time period before the Vietnam War heated up. Despite his troubles, he was recommended for re-enlistment.[80]

On March 23, he wrote "Left to See My Darling Wife 267 DTDIC,"[81] and, despite a declaration on February 7 that he intended to "make daily entries into this book or one similar continually in the future," his daily diary-keeping ended. Doing so was probably not a failure of resolve on his part, however, because he recorded on February 11 that Kathy "doesn't like me writing in my diary."[82]

It is worth noting that Whitman's time at Camp Lejeune can be viewed as a watershed period between a relatively normal life and a life marked by growing irrationality. Neither this book nor others claim that the two head injuries he suffered there, in the jeep accident and when attacked and beaten by other Marines, caused the type of mental and emotional impairment such trauma is capable of causing, but neither should that possibility be dismissed. In addition, it is now known that the water supply at Camp Lejeune which Marines and their families drank and bathed in was seriously contaminated with dangerous chemicals with toxic concentrations up to 3400 times the level considered safe. The condition lasted from at least 1953 through 1985, and involved more than 70 chemicals, including volatile organic compounds, perchloro-ethylene, trichloroethylene, and other chlorinated hydrocarbons. At least 850 former residents have filed claims for nearly $4 billion from the military for problems that include cancer of the esophagus, lung, breast, bladder or kidney; leukemia; multiple myeloma; myleodysplasic syndromes; renal toxicity; hepatic steatosis; female infertility; miscar-riage; scleroderma; and/or neurobehavioral effects or non-Hodgkin's lymphoma, and the federal government is still involved in various law-suits related to the claims.[83] Perhaps the 21 months Whitman spent consuming the water at Camp Lejeune affected him; perhaps not.

The fifth and final stage of Whitman's life began when he mustered out of the Marine Corps on December 6, 1964. Back in Austin, he re-enrolled for the spring semester of 1965, but changed his major from mechanical to architectural engineering. He also found a job at Standard Finance Company in Austin, as a bill collector, then left Standard Finance to take a job as a teller at Austin National Bank, working for $1.25 an hour, which was the minimum wage in 1965.[84] He stayed there only three months, but was remembered by his supervisor as an "out-standing person."[85] He also worked for a short period at Scarborough's department store,[86] but his new solution to money issues, or scheme, was to become a real estate agent.

He believed himself to be conscientious, ambitious, and anxious to improve himself, and he also felt a need to remind himself, in writing, of what was required to continue those attributes. He collected and recorded positive thoughts and advice to himself, such at the following six maxims, which he printed by hand:

1. *Grow up (don't be so quick with an excuse)*

2. *Conduct with superiors (time & place for everything)*

3. *Know your status and position and conduct yourself accordingly*

4. *Courtesy (Generally show respect for seniors but let personal feelings towd. indiv. show).*

5. *Organize yourself and your work so that the insignificant is not a major crisis.*

6. *When time permits exhaust all efforts to find answers before asking the simplest of questions.*

With regard to Kathy, as though he might forget to act appropriately in her presence, he typed the following on a small card and carried it with him:

GOOD POINTS TO REMEMBER:

1. *Don't nag*

2. *Don't try to make your partner over.*

3. *Don't criticize.*

4. *Give honest appreciation*

5. *Pay little attentions*

6. *Be courteous*

7. *BE GENTLE*

On another, full-sized sheet of paper found after August 1, 1966, he typed:

THOUGHTS TO START THE DAY. READ AND THINK ABOUT, EVERY DAY:

STOP *procrastinating (Grasp the nettle)*

CONTROL *your anger (Don't let it prove you a fool)*

SMILE *(Its contagious)*

DON'T *be belligerent*

STOP *cursing, improve your vocabulary*

APPROACH *a pot of gold with exceptional caution (look it over – twice)*

PAY *that compliment*

LISTEN *more than you speak,* THINK *before you speak*

CONTROL *your passion;* DON'T LET IT *lead* YOU - - *Don't let desire make you regret your present actions later (Remember the lad and the man)*

If you want to be better than average, YOU HAVE TO WORK MUCH HARDER THAN THE AVERAGE

NEVER FORGET: when the going gets rough, the ROUGH get going!!!!!

On yet another card he typed:

YESTERDAY IS NOT MINE TO RECOVER BUT TOMORROW IS MINE TO WIN OR TO LOSE. I AM RESOLVED THAT I SHALL WIN THE TOMORROWS BEFORE ME!!!

He began attending the First Methodist Church of Austin, where Kathy was a member, and sang in the choir. Whitman was not, however, either the good Catholic his mother had raised him to be or a devout Protestant like Kathy.[87] He had no confidence in the Pope, in large part because of the Church's stance on birth control, and he rejected the notion of Hell, seeing no purpose in eternal damnation of a person's soul for any reason. In fact, life on Earth, he told a friend named Albert J. Vincik, was the actual hell.

The personal religious belief system he had formulated recognized the existence of God, but not as a Holy Trinity and more in the nature of Pantheism, whereby nature and the universe are identical with divinity. His God was everywhere, made manifest through the movement of molecules and the existence of energy, incapable of either creation or destruction, visited upon each person through the conscience, and not involving concepts of morality, sin, or an anthropomorphic being. Death was a change in the form of energy, and life on Earth, the equivalent of Hell, meant that death was a release from agony and a positive development to be welcomed.[88] The fact that he considered life on Earth to be Hell, when he occupied a position most people would envy and admire, speaks volumes about how Whitman viewed and accepted his lot in life. It very well may have been the product of childhood abuse.

The Methodist Church sponsored a Boy Scout troop, Troop 5, and in January, 1965 he was recruited as an assistant scoutmaster, and by February, he was the scoutmaster. One of the boys in Troop 5 was Toby Hamilton, who was 11 in 1965, and although his association with

Whitman lasted less than a year, it affected his entire life, literally to the day he died. There was a certain "small world" syndrome related to Whitman and what he did, involving odd connections between people both before and after August 1, 1966. The connections between Hamilton and other players in the drama were some of the oddest.

In April, C.A. and Margaret Whitman visited from Florida, and Charles took them to talk to Albert Vincik, whom Whitman met through scouting, about selling real estate and insurance. On May 1, Whitman purchased a two thousand dollar bond in order to become a real estate and insurance agent, but the plan to make money in those endeavors was another bust. He never received either wages or commissions for any sales of either.[89]

During the summer of 1965, he worked as an assistant for NASA, but was contemptuous of the government employees there, remarking that he could "do the work of eight NASA employees in thirty minutes."[90]

In addition to not having a job in which he made good money, he was not an effective scoutmaster. He was impatient with the boys, often treating them like Marine boots, requiring calisthenics, challenging them physically, quarreling with at least one adult about how to handle the troop, and focusing their training on the care and use of firearms. He would demonstrate his shooting prowess to the boys by fastening a clothespin to a line, moving some 75 feet back and shooting the clothespin with a .22 rifle so that it spun on the line until shot to pieces.

Toby Hamilton recalled Whitman as "being all about showing off" as a scout master. He would pull a one dollar bill out, throw it on the floor and tell his scouts "anyone who can do what I can do can have it," after which he would do a hand stand with his feet against a wall, and do pushups in that position. The boys would try to imitate him, but "of course we fell on our faces." Whitman would then snatch the dollar up and laugh.[91]

Hamilton recalled another incident that occurred in June, 1966. A camp-out at Bastrop State Park was planned that would begin on Friday and extend through Sunday. Toby was excited about going, but he had music lessons on Saturday morning that prevented him from leaving on Friday. Whitman was no longer the official scoutmaster, by his own choice, but he planned to drive to the park on Saturday and offered Toby a ride. As he recalled:

Mr. Whitman had a class at UT on Saturday morning and he offered to pick me up and take me to Bastrop State Park to spend some of Saturday and Saturday night with the Scout troop. I thought that was cool so I said I would.

When he arrived at my house, he made me a little nervous because he seemed focused on something far away and seemed angry. On the way to the campout, I tried repeatedly to talk to Mr. Whitman, but he wouldn't respond and acted like I was bothering him. By the time we got to Bastrop State Park, I was really feeling uneasy and couldn't wait to get out of the car, away from him.[92]

Fathers of the scouts remembered him as disorganized, overbearing, and nervous. His habit of chewing on his fingernails persisted and he was gaining weight, so that the boys started calling him "Porky." Fellow scoutmaster Vincik recalled that Whitman was spread too thin and worked too hard. "He was nervous, meticulous and wanted to excel at everything. He also could not stand constructive criticism."[93] The scoutmaster position lasted a little less than a year, and in January 1966 he resigned, citing his studies and part-time employment as the reasons.[94]

During this period Whitman did things that stuck in people's minds as odd. At home he would "inspect" the house for cleanliness, even though Kathy was an immaculate housekeeper, up to and including looking for dust along the top of and behind picture frames. One of his architectural engineering instructors, Barton Riley, recalled that one night Whitman called him about 11:00 p.m. and announced, "I need to see you, now!" and when he arrived at Riley's home he was red in the face, which was something Riley had seen before and which he knew meant Whitman was upset. He was carrying an architectural drawing and Riley figured he wanted to talk about a class assignment. However, when Whitman came inside and saw a baby grand piano, he dropped his drawing, sat down and began playing *Claire de Lune*. Riley described the piece as a "fairly tough little tune to play" and Whitman's playing of it as done "beautifully." Whitman followed that with another song, then stood up, his face calm and relaxed. Riley said "Well, I'll see you in class tomorrow," and Whitman said "Okay," then left.[95]

Sudden outbursts of unnecessary anger occurred. When Whitman received a "C" in Riley's class because he had misunderstood the directions, he hit a desk with his fist and stormed out.[96] On another occasion he became so frustrated with classes and his poor performance that he suddenly and impulsively decided to drop out of school altogether and go live in Japan. Without telling Kathy he sold his books and either withdrew from the University or made arrangements to do so, then went home and began packing to leave. His friend, Larry Fuess, got wind of it and arrived to find the rumor to evidently be true. Whitman was even planning to desert Kathy, and told Fuess, "She'll be okay; she has a job now; she'll be better off." Fuess called Riley, who like Whitman was an ex-Marine. He knew how to put an end to the silliness.

"This is ridiculous. You are not going to do it!" Riley informed Whitman in a drill sergeant's voice. Kathy and Fuess had already begged him to reconsider, to no avail, but upon receiving the order from Riley, Whitman said, "Yessir." The next day he informed Riley that he was back in school, and thanked him for his intervention.[97]

But on at least two occasions, he went too far. As he would admit in March, 1966, he struck Kathy. The date, details and severity of the physical contact are not known, only that they occurred prior to March 29, 1966. There is no record of Kathy displaying bruises, black eyes, or other marks, or of police being summoned to quell domestic violence. However, on one occasion she told their landlady, in connection with securing one or Charles's firearms, that she was afraid "he'll beat me again." She also told her parents that Charles's temper was so explosive that she sometimes feared he would kill her, and there was a period of time during the summer of 1965, while Whitman was working at NASA, that she hinted to a friend, Fran Morgan, about divorce.[98] Otherwise, when it was reported later that he had hit her, acquaintances expressed shock, and said things like, "I just can't believe he ever beat her. If he did, she certainly hid it well."[99] She did not seek counseling or leave home to return to Needville, and neither her family nor Whitman's suspected problems.[100]

Still, Whitman felt tremendous guilt, largely because he was acting like his father. He adored Kathy, depended on her, considered his life incomplete without her, and had always despised his father's violent attacks on his mother, yet he had assaulted her, not once but twice or more. Physical abuse of her was an act impossible to excuse, a bell that could not be unrung, proof to the world and particularly to Charles that he was unworthy.

At some point between his discharge from the Marine Corps in

December, 1964 and March, 1966, the scales finally dropped completely from Whitman's eyes with regard to his father.[101] Prior thereto he'd confided to a few close friends about what he'd suffered at C.A.'s hands and how he felt about him, but by 1965 he'd abandoned all pretense of caring for or being grateful to the man. Perhaps it was in keeping with and coincident with his revised outlook and questioning attitude toward religion, in which the God he'd been trained to believe in and fear since childhood was replaced with a private, indistinct but Pantheistic deity. Perhaps the rage and resentment were harbored for years before being unleashed, but his overwhelming hatred for C.A. Whitman became clearest during the last several months of his life.

A catalytic event probably occurred during a deer hunting expedition taken by Charles, C.A., and Johnnie Mike during the last week of November, 1965. C.A. had ordered a new rifle from an Austin gun dealer that had arrived, but what should have been a joyful outing was marred when C.A. lost his temper and pointed the new rifle at Johnnie Mike. Charles, in turn, pointed his rifle at C.A. and told him that if he ever did such a thing again he would kill him.[102]

A significant source of his outrage at C.A stemmed from the fact that Charles could not stop accepting the older man's money. Whitman told more than one person over the years that it was his dream to someday outdo and outshine his father, not only by his education but by his career and money-making talents. Yet at age 24, Whitman was still receiving a monthly stipend from C. A. His doing so bolstered C.A's own self-image and narcissistic control, but reminded Charles of his shortcomings and lack of independence.

One of Charles's responses to his failings was to work harder, but doing so meant he needed help, and he found it in Dexedrine. Dexedrine, or Dextroamphetamine, is an amphetamine rooted in the military, and it is probable that Whitman was introduced to it in the Marine Corps. It was developed in the late 19th Century, and became popular during World War II when both Axis and Allied forces used it as a treatment for fatigue. The use of amphetamines was particularly common in the Wehrmacht, but American forces used them as well, and continued to do so after the war, not merely as an acceptable type of medication, but as a standard issue necessity. From 1950 and the beginning of the Korean War forward into the Vietnam conflict, the U.S. military purchased mass quantities of Dexedrine and issued them to both enlisted men and officers. In a Congressional inquiry into drug abuse among American forces in Vietnam in 1972 it was revealed that the Navy, Army and Air Force all dispensed their soldiers an average of 800 mg of Dexedrine a year between 1966 and 1969, which is probably a lowball average. One veteran testified that the pills were handed out "like candy" to any soldier who wanted them.[103]

Today, Dexedrine is prescribed as a treatment for Attention Deficit Hyperactivity Disorder, and is closely related to Adderall. On the positive side, therapeutic doses improve cortical network efficiency and can result in higher levels of performance, improved memory retention, motivation, wakefulness, and goal-directed behavior. Use by students was, and is, common, and in the burgeoning drug experimentation and psychedelia of the mid-1960s, it was a pretty low level type of "goofball."[104] But high or sustained intake of Dexedrine has an effect almost opposite the positive, in that it impairs performance, causes muscle breakdown, and elevates body temperature. Common side effects are headaches, nausea, stomach upset, cramps, loss of appetite, diarrhea, dry mouth, nervousness, and trouble sleeping. Whether attributable to Dexedrine or not, Whitman recorded that headaches, nervousness, and insomnia were his constant familiars in 1965 and 1966.

Contributing to Whitman's angst was the fact that Kathy was the principal breadwinner in the family. After graduating in May, 1965, with a degree in Science Education, she first worked as a bookkeeper at Clear Lake Yacht Basin while Charles worked that summer at NASA, and then was hired at Lanier High School as a full-time biology teacher. This provided a salary and health insurance, and with Charles's part time work, it seems as though the couple, with no children and living in a small apartment, should have been financially secure. Nevertheless, the checks he accepted from his father during this period ranged from $180 to $380 per month.[105] Support from the senior Whitman was not limited to monthly checks. For Christmas, 1965, he gave the couple a 1966 black, two-door Chevrolet Impala. It would be the car Whitman drove to the U. T. Tower eight months later, but he let it be known that he despised the automobile, probably because it came from his father.[106]

In March, 1966, an incident pushed him further toward the bizarre decisions of July 31 and August 1. At 9:30 p.m. on the 2nd, an anonymous call came in to the Lake Worth, Florida Police Department. A loud, violent-sounding argument was going on at 820 L Street, the home of C.A. and Margaret Whitman. "They're going to kill each other," or words to that effect, were reported. A patrol car was dispatched but when it arrived nothing was going on and all was quiet at the Whitman home, so the police departed. At 11:30 another call came in. This time it was from Charles J. Whitman, calling from Austin. The dispatcher who received the call wrote that Charles said, "Mr. Charles A. Whitman of 820 L Street has threatened to do bodily harm to his mother. He advises that he is enroute to this city at this time to pick up his mother."[107]

The distance from Austin to Lake Worth is 1,104 miles as the crow flies, and the driving distance is just shy of 1300 miles. Whitman drove non-stop, but it was still the morning of March 4 before he arrived. An ugly family reunion followed.

Margaret had had enough. She called Charles between 9:30 and 11:30 p.m. on March 2 to request that he come to Florida and take her to Texas; no small development after 25½ years of marriage. By mid-afternoon on the 4th she was preparing to leave but C.A. was not cooperating, and Margaret called the local police to ask that a squad car be sent to protect her as she loaded luggage into Charles's Impala. Two officers arrived and stood by for an hour and a quarter.

The exact nature of what caused Margaret and C.A.'s final blow-up, if there was any single event, was not recorded by any of the family participants, but one of the officers nailed it sufficiently in his report by writing that the couple was "giving each other all kinds of trouble for the entire time, all nonsense."[108]

Charles and Margaret made the long drive back to Austin together, during which they undoubtedly conjured up and exorcised every demonic act ever committed by C.A. Whitman, probably interspersed with periodic bouts of crying and regret, followed by more condemnation of the man they had once loved dearly.[109] The 25 or more hours they spent together both strengthened their bond and cemented Charles's conviction that his father was at the root of his problems. Apparently Whitman made the entire round trip without sleeping.

In Austin Margaret may have set up temporary camp at Charles and Kathy's apartment at 1001A, Shelley Avenue, but they soon found her an apartment at 3816 Speedway, Apartment 106.[110] The family migration was not finished. Before March ended, the middle Whitman brother, Patrick, also drove to Austin from Lake Worth, found and moved into his own apartment on 12th Street and found a job as a salesman and truck driver. Charles then located an apartment for Margaret in a high-rise complex called the Penthouse, located on the corner of 13th and Guadalupe, a few blocks from the University and the Texas Capitol. A few weeks later, Patrick returned to Florida. Patrick sided with his father in regard to the separation, and the reason for his time in Austin was probably to try to convince Margaret to return home.

Margaret's new domicile was nice, sometimes described as "swanky." It boasted a doorman and security guards, and Margaret's residence was number 505 on the 5th floor.[111] She went to work as a cashier at Wyatt's cafeteria, beginning on April 8, 1966, at wages close to the minimum of $1.25 an hour. She could afford the apartment, as well as transportation and other necessities, because C. A. continued to finance her, in addition to Charles.

Whitman was adept at covering up his feelings, so most of his friends, acquaintances and professors did not observe behavior they considered unusual. Kathy did, however, and urged him to see a counselor or physician. He finally did on March 29, going to a general practitioner named Dr. Jan D. Cochrum at the University of Texas Health Center. Dr. Cochrum listened to Whitman's description of the bleak life he was experiencing and did two things—prescribed Valium, a sedative, and referred him to a staff psychiatrist, Dr. Maurice D. Heatly. Otherwise, Cochrum considered the visitation routine, and upon being reminded of it and shown a photo in August, remarked that Whitman was "every bit as nice a guy as he looked in the picture."

The appointment with Dr. Heatly, the same day, had more substance. Whitman first completed a form containing questions about past medical procedures and routine information. Two of Whitman's answers are worth noting. First, in response to being asked about the nature of the problem he was experiencing, he wrote "That's why I'm here" in parentheses, indicating he hoped to learn the nature of his problem. Second, when asked about his interests and hobbies, he wrote, "Hunting, Karate, Scuba Diving, Main interest How to make money."[114]

His session with Heatly lasted an hour, and Whitman unloaded. He raged, he cried, he bared his soul and he confessed to the deadly delusion that was calling to him. In all likelihood nobody with the possible exception of Kathy saw the person Dr. Heatly saw, and Whitman hoped for help, a cure, an explanation, and exorcism of his demons. He didn't get it.

Heatly was not the type of miracle worker needed for such work. Another student who sought his help for marital trouble later wrote: "[m]y visit consisted mainly of listening to him talk on the telephone with the driller who was putting in a waterwell on his ranch, after which he gave me a prescription for Librium. My wife came back from her visit crying and said that after pretty much baring her soul, his advice to her was 'Grow up.' I won't hazard a guess as to what comfort and advice he gave Charles Whitman."[115]

Later, Heatly dictated and his secretary typed a double-spaced report covering one and two-thirds pages. It was the only psychiatric report made about Whitman while he was living and represents the most intimate written revelation of its sort other than Whitman's diary.[116] It also became the most significant, or damning, report of Heatly's career.[117]

Some of Heatly's report is off the mark factually, but most resonates like the bell of voiceless reason, and one sentence—"Repeated inquiries attempting to analyze his exact experiences were not too successful with the exception of his vivid reference to 'thinking about going up on the tower with a deer rifle and start shooting people,'"—would be viewed by many, in hindsight, as equal to the shout in the night from Paul Revere. Of greater importance is the fact that Heatly did not simply send him away, but directed Whitman to return in exactly one week and to feel free to contact him "anytime" before then. Charles neither made an appointment nor contacted Heatly, although he would write about the visit later as proof of his mental turmoil, even doubling the length of the session when he did so. He'd probably hoped for a miracle cure from a professional, but the visit was disappointing for him, and thus to the rest of the world.

In April, Charles and Kathy moved from their apartment to a tan brick house at 906 Jewel Street. It was not large, but was significantly roomier than anything they'd had before, and it included a backyard and detached garage. Inside were five rooms—a kitchen, living room, dining room, and two bedrooms—plus a single bath. The front bedroom was Kathy and Charles's and the rear one served as a study.

It was reported that Whitman visited the U.T. Tower with a friend on April 5, 1966,[118] but if so, it means the observation deck re-opened after the 1965 fire nearly a month earlier than the newspaper said it would. Exactly one week earlier he had told Dr. Heatly about the fantasy involving a deer rifle, and one wonders what Heatly would have thought if he knew that Whitman was there instead of his office. Whitman would visit the Tower at least one more time before August 1, for the purpose of showing off the view and campus to his younger brother, but there is no apparent reason for his April visit, assuming it occurred, unless it was to scope out its usefulness as a defensive position. Whether he visited that day or not, one of the three receptionists who worked there, Lydia Gest, said later that Whitman visited the Tower "many times," and would sometimes sit on the couch in the observation deck office and chat with her.[119]

In May, Margaret initiated divorce proceedings and returned to Lake Worth to retrieve more belongings.[120] C.A. had been calling, begging, demanding, and cajoling for her return, but he was neither welcoming nor cooperative when she arrived. They clashed, and he claimed Margaret remarked, "I'm leaving you because you've been too good to us all."[121] Assuming she really said that, she was either being sarcastic or was zeroing in on her husband's narcissistic control tactic of making everyone in the family dependent on him financially. The real reason Margaret left him was because the three boys were grown and no longer at home. She let a selected few know that the welfare of their sons was the only reason she had stayed in the marriage as long as she had, and in June, she wrote a note to her father saying she was divorcing C.A. because she "couldn't take it anymore.[122]

During this brief visit, C.A. attempted to physically remove her wedding ring, but it was too tight on her finger, and Margaret continued wearing it until she died. The divorce proceedings were handled through an attorney in Lake Worth, with Margaret's brother, Walter, who lived in West Palm Beach, on hand to assist. C.A. continued to call Charles throughout May and June, and the elder Whitman stated later that he spent more than a thousand dollars a month trying to get Margaret to come back to him.

With June came new employment for both Charles and Kathy. It was her summer break from teaching, and she found a job as a telephone operator with Southwestern Bell, then the only phone company in Texas. Charles, giving up his plans to sell real estate and insurance, found a position as a laboratory research assistant to study traffic on campus. The job was part time, no more than 25 hours a week at a salary of $160 per month, and was a research project conducted by the University in conjunction with the Texas Highway Department called "Evaluation of Traffic Control at Highway Intersections." He worked there from June 2 to July 29, 1966, and was remembered by his boss, Dr. Clyde Lee, as "a good employee."[123]

As of the end of the Spring semester, 1966, he had completed 98 hours of class work at U.T., plus three hours of credit from East Carolina College, which he'd attended while in the Marines prior to beginning his NESEP program at U.T., and another 3 hours from Alvin Jr. College, which he attended while working for NASA during the summer of 1965. Of the 36 classes he attended at U.T., he had amassed eight "A's", seven "B's," 14 "C's," four "D's," one "F", and two credits for first semester pass/fail introductory courses.

His stated plan was to graduate in May, 1967, then enroll in law school, expecting that degrees in engineering and the law would ensure success and wealth. His grades were not likely to be good enough to get him into law school, but he would not live long enough to find out.

1. For example, in the same issue of *Newsweek* magazine that reported the U. T. Tower killings, August 15, 1966, was an article titled "Again, the Assassination," about growing doubts and conspiracy theories associated with the Warren Commission report.

2. Redacted female Fla. Neighbor, p. 13 in report filed as MM 62-5533, AHC.

3. MM 62-5533, August 9, 1966, FBI Miami, AHC.

4. Brock Huffman (Close friend for three years) interviewed by Fishel of DPS, AHC

5. *Ibid.*

6. Roger C. Williams, English professor at U.T., *Ibid.* at 25.

7. Report of R. Wisian, Austin Police Dept., August 3, 1966; AHC.

8. Unidentified witnesses, apparently from Kathy Whitman's hometown, quoted in *Newsweek*, p. 24, Aug.15, 1966.

9. Leonardt Kreisle (Whitman's academic advisor), quoted in the *Daily Texan*, August 1, 1986.

10. Lt. John C. Drolla, (friend of Whitman's for five years) 25th Transportation Co., interviewed August 4, 1966; Department of Public Safety memo to O.N. Humphreys, Agent in Charge, from Donald R. Fishel, Intelligence Section, AHC.

11. Unidentified friend of Whitman, possibly Kathleen Riley, included in *Deranged Killers: Charles Whitman*, darkdocumentaaries, Discovery Channel,(2009); https://www.youtube.com/watch?v=Jy1B5mfzCBA.

12. Barton Riley, (a professor of Whitman's), quoted in the *Texas Observer*, August 19, 1966; Lavergne p. 73.

13. FBI report MM 62-5533, conducted by Special Agents John R. Barron and Richard B. Kellogg at Lake Worth, Fla. and West Palm Beach Fla., August, 1966, AHC.

14. Telephone interview of Dr. Stuart Brown, April 22, 2015.

15. Brenda Bell, "An Anniversary with No Answers," *Austin American Statesman*, August 1, 2006; FBI interview of witnesses with redacted names who were almost certainly Margaret's brother, Walter Hodges, and his wife, August 3, 1966, AHC.

16. Report of FBI agent John Barron, August 10, 1966, AHC. However successful C.A. was or was not, the IRS imposed a tax lien for $1588.93 on his property in June, 1964 that was paid the following November. Memorandum (27 pp.) designated MM 62-5533, August 9, 1966, FBI Miami, AHC.

17. *Palm Beach Post*, August 3, 1966; FBI Investigation Report of Agents John R. Barron and Richard B. Kellogg, of the Lake Worth, Florida FBI Office, August, 1966, AHC.

18. C.A. claimed he never used anything but his fists and paddles, but the historical record adds other objects, such as sticks, belts, and boards.

19. *Mass Murderers*, 42 (*Time-Life Books*, 1992).

20. *Deranged Killers: Charles Whitman*, darkdocumentaaries, *supra*.

21. Charles J. Whitman, "Autobiography of Charles Joseph Whitman," written when he was 14, AHC.

22. That the item was a bullwhip, rather than a belt or paddle, was confirmed by Francis Schuck, who was told by Whitman that his father used the whip on him, his mother, and brothers on several occasions. Phone conference with Francis Schuck, May 15, 2015.

23. *Ibid.*

24. That record cannot be nailed down with certainty. That same year, 1953, at least one other 12-year-old, George B. Albrecht, of Chicago, became an Eagle Scout in November. But whereas Albrecht had been a Cub Scout for three years and a Boy Scout for nearly two when he won the award, Whitman achieved the rank in September, two months earlier and after being a boy scout for only one year and three months. He earned 21 merit badges in 15 months and reached the coveted rank of Eagle Scout when he was only three months past his 12th birthday. Thirteen years later on August 1, 1966, when Whitman's father discussed his son's ghastly new accomplishments by phone with Captain J.C. Fann of the Austin Police Department, the older man lamented that he could think of no reason for his son to have done what he'd done considering, after all, that "he was a former eagle scout." "Becomes Eagle Scout at 12," *Chicago Tribune*, Part 1, p. 10, Dec. 24, 1953; Report by Capt. J. C. Fann in Offense No. M-968150, Murder of Officer Billy Speed, AHC

25. Dr. Stuart Brown, "Play Deprived; A Tortured Life Explodes," http://www.nifplay.org/vision/early-study/, also citing *The Palm Post*, 2006.

26. Telephone interview of Dr. Stuart Brown, April 22, 2015.

27. Lavergne at 7, citing the *Palm Beach Post*, August 2, 1966.

28. *Mass Murderers*, *supra*. at 40.

29. The association with Georgia Tech was documented when he registered for Selective Service—the draft—on June 9, 1959, and listed his occupation as "Student, Georgia Tech, Atlanta." In addition, an aunt gave a statement to the FBI on August 3, 1966, and said that "following his graduation from high school she seemed to recall that subject enrolled in and possibly attended Georgia Tech, Atlanta, Georgia, for a short time before entering the United States Marine Corps." FBI Investigation Report of Agents John R. Barron and Richard B. Kellogg, of the Lake Worth, Florida FBI Office, August 1966, AHC. However, on August 2, 1966, the FBI contacted Georgia Tech and was advised by its Registrar that "after extensive search of her records, that she could find no information" regarding Whitman being at the college from 1946 to 1966. Teletype dated August 3, 1966 to the Director from the Atlanta FBI office; AHC.

30. Report of FBI agent John S. Barron, Dec. 9, 1966; AHC.

31. The friend who was present but whose name is redacted in the FBI report, told the FBI in December, 1966, that Charlie "yelled something" at a police car as he was driving Whitman home and they were pulled over, after which the police took both boys home, stopping first at the Whitman residence, where Mr. Whitman "proceeded to knock Whitman around' and then "dragged him to the back of the house and apparently threw him into the pool as he heard the yelling and splash." FBI report dated Dec. 8, 1966 from "SAC Miami" to the Director of the FBI regarding "Charles A. Whitman, Jr. – Victim Extortion," AHC; FBI report dated Dec. 15, 1966 from agents John R. Barron and Richard B. Kellogg concerning interview of friend of Whitman's, AHC.

32. "Charles Joseph Whitman," *Murdepedia*, http://murderpedia.org/male.W/w/whitman-charles.htm.

33. Lavergne at 19.

34. Connally Commission report dated September 8, 1966.

35. Dr. O'Toole revealed this startling bit of information to Dr. Roger Friedman in an interview he had with her on June 17, 2015, at her office at George Mason University. She told Dr. Friedman that the officer said that in 1966, when he first heard the news that a mass shooting from the UT Tower was taking place he thought immediately of his conversations with Whitman, and upon learning later in the day that it actually was Whitman, he was not surprised and figured that he had gone ahead finally and carried out his plans. Dr. O'Toole said she regretted not having talked to the officer in more detail or getting his name, but she never forgot what he said. If he should read this book he is encouraged to contact Dr. O'Toole or its authors.

36. Emails from Francis Schuck, May 13 & 14, 2015; John F. Grimm, "Storm Warning," *American Heritage*, September, 1993

37. Telephone interview of Francis J. Schuck, June 7, 2015.

38. On Thursday evening, July 6, 1961, Schuck and Whitman celebrated the end of Charles's second year in the USMC at the Fiddler's Green, the Enlisted Man's Club at Naval Training Center, Bainbridge, MD. He was already a lance corporal, which was rare for a Marine with only two years in sevice. Schuck was then a 3rd Class Missile Technician, and two days earlier they had celebrated his being in the Navy two and a half years. Statement of Francis Joseph Schuck, Jr. (as recorded by the Navy despite Schuck's legal name change), September 13, 1966, Charleston, S.C., AHC; Email from Francis Schuck, May 12, 2015.

39. Whitman was also granted secret security clearance on February 20, 1961. Teletype dated August 3, 1966 from FBI SAC, WFO to Director, FBI and SAC, San Antonio, attention Director De Loach, AHC.

40. Statement of Francis Joseph Schuck, Jr., September 13, 1966, Charleston, S.C., AHC.

41. Email from Francis Schuck, May 12, 2015.

42. *Ibid.*

43. Laverne at 22.

44. Telephone interview of Francis J. Schuck, June 7, 2015.

45. Larry Fuess, *Texas Observer*, August 19, 1966.

46. Lavergne at 75.

47. Like many stories about Whitman, the deer incident has become garbled over the years. Francis Schuck participated in it and many other events involving his friend, and is working on his own book, the working title of which is *The Charlie I Knew*, which should set the record straight.

48. Telephone interview of Jeff Robinson, Austin, Texas, March 11, 2015.

49. *Ibid.*; Lavergne at 21.

50. Interview of Dr. Robert Smalley, La Grange, Texas, March 2, 2015.

51. *Ibid.*

52. Schuck statement, *supra*.

53. *Ibid.*

54. Statement of Leonardt Kreisle, AHC

55. Whitman's habit of chewing on his fingernails was noticed by several people. One of his classmates, James Barnfield, said that he would bring plastic objects to class to bite instead of his fingernails, because they would become sore. Another student who noticed Whitman's fingernail biting, named Shelton Williams, didn't know the big blond student's full name until after August 1, 1966, when he recalled that Whitman always arrived early for the class they shared in the architecture building. There Charles would read his notes while chewing his nails until "I couldn't believe there was anything left to chew," Williams recalled. On one occasion he observed a student approach Whitman and ask him, "Say, Charlie, are you going to go to Vietnam and kill Charlie?" greatly enjoying his own play on names. Whitman replied, "The Marines can kiss my red-white-and-blue ass." Williams later wrote a book about his experiences during the summer of 1966 in which Whitman played only a minor role, and in which the author referred to him as "Charlie Fingernails." Letter dated August 5, 1966 from FBI agent J. Myers Cole to Director Homer Garrison of the Texas D.P.S; AHC; Report dated August 5, 1966 summarizing information received from Agent Deffenbaugh of the San Antonio office, AHC; Shelton Williams, *Summer of '66*. (Denton: Zone Press, 2007); 96 Minutes at 107-08

56. Telephone conference with Francis Schuck, Jr., May 28, 2015.

57. Schuck statement, *supra*.

58. *Ibid.*

59. Telephone conference with Schuck, *supra.*

60. *Deranged Killers: Charles Whitman*, darkdocumentaries, Discovery Channel, (2009), https://www.youtube.com/watch?v=Jy1B5mfzCBA.

61. *Ibid.*

62. Email from Francis Schuck, Jr., May 5, 2015.

63. *Ibid.*

64. Rosenburg Herald-Coaster, July 19, 1962.

65. *Ibid.* August 19, 1962.

66. FBI Report to Marvin Watson, Special Assistant to the President dated August 4, 1966, AHC.

67. The loans and interest were $45 on a $30 loan payable in 15 days; $8 to be paid on a $5 loan; $22 to be paid on a $14 loan; and $32 to be paid on a $20 loan. Letter dated August 4, 1966 to Marvin Watson, Special Assistant to the President, from the FBI; AHC.

68. John F. Grimm, "Storm Warning," *American Heritage*, (September, 1993).

69. "Daily Record of C.J.Whitman" entry for February 6, 1964. AHC.

70. Apparently he and a friend were mistaken for someone else by members of a Military Police Company. Letter dated August 23, 1966 to Marvin Watson, Special Assistant to the President, from "JFC" of the FBI, AHC.

71. FBI report No. CE-3177, p. 2; AHC; "General and Medical Background Information for the Whitman Case," confidential portion of the report of the Connally Commission.

72. Whitman diary of November, 1963. AHC.

73. "Green Memoranda Notebook" in which Whitman recorded his thoughts during November, 1963 to February 3, 1964, located in Group II, Series III, Subseries V, AHC.

74. Report of Sgt. B. Gregory, August 5, 1966, AHC.

75. "Daily Record of C.J.Whitman" entry for February 12, 1964. AHC.

76. These diary entries were written in a notebook with a green cover from the "Federal Supply Service," the cover of which said "DAILY RECORD," below which Whitman wrote "OF C. J. WHITMAN" in matching, inch-high capital letters. He wrote in it only from February 7 to March 23, 1964, his earlier diary entries being in a separate notebook. That period of time was from shortly before he was released from hard labor at Camp Lejeune until the day he left on leave to visit Kathy in Austin. Those two months were a stressful time for Whitman. He was still on hard labor, which continued until February 25, when he began the record, and although many entries were upbeat, some were written by a downhearted, self-pitying young man. *Ibid.*

77. *Ibid.*, entry for February 29, 1964.

78. *Ibid.* entry for March 11, 1964.

79. *Ibid.*, entry for March 12, 1964.

80. Teletype dated August 3, 1966 from FBI SAC, WFO to Director, FBI and SAC, San Antonio, attention Director De Loach, AHC.

81. Shortly after receiving the news about the early discharge, Whitman began writing a number and "DTDIC" across from the date of each journal entry as abbreviation for "Days to Do In Corps." Previously he created a hand-drawn calendar at the end of his "record" titled "Days and Months To Do in the Corps," which contained 30 months of time with a descending day count, beginning at 910, beneath each day of each month—the full amount of time he expected to have to serve before receiving the news on March 12. He intended to mark off each day, as a prisoner might do for a remaining sentence, but he only did so from February 1 until March 22, which was also the last day in which he wrote a complete entry in the record.

82. People have scanned Whitman's diary for clues about his motives for August 1, 1966, and have mostly come away disappointed. One statement that is singled out for notice, however, followed the entry concerning Kathy's dislike for his diary. He wrote, "I definitely feel as though there is something unusual in my mental state. I don't know if it is my imagination or if my feelings are valid. But I notice an unusual uneasiness inside myself." Writers have suggested that the brain tumor that was found on August 2, 1966 was already growing and affecting his outlook on life. It was not.

83. "Camp Lejeune water contamination," http://en.wikipedia.org/wiki/Camp_Lejeune_water_contamination.

84. In a job application to work at NASA the next summer, Whitman stated that he left Standard Finance because the company was cutting expenses. He also listed working for two months, December 1964 and January, 1965, at Scarborough's in Austin as a salesman, and for one month, April, 1965, at Central Freight Lines, which he left because he was "unable to keep up studies." Job application stamped "Security Investigation Data for Sensitive Position," dated May 27, 1965; AHC.

85. *Austin American Statesman*, August 7, 1966.

86. Telephone interview with Brock Huffman, May 27, 2015. Huffman's wife was training manager at Scarborough's and Huffman met Whitman, whom he described as "the nicest guy in the world, very outgoing, handsome, really nice, and never in a bad mood," through her.

87. On January 24, 1964, while in the Marine Corps brig at Camp LaJeune he noted in his journal that "I don't pray anymore." On one occasion when the Methodist minister dropped in to visit, Whitman slipped out the back door to avoid him.

88. Whitman did not confine his philosophical musing to Vincik. John Morgan recalled that he and Whitman "spent hours talking about philosophy, religion, marriage problems, sex, etc. Subject had some way-out beliefs about the above-mentioned subjects. Subject had turned atheistic in his beliefs." Statement of John Fran Morgan to agent O.M. Humphreys, Jr., Texas Department of Public Safety, August 2, 1966, AHC.

89. Report of Sgt. V. McBee, August 1, 1966, AHC.

90. *Austin American Statesman*, August 2, 1966.

91. Hamilton was interviewed for a Discovery channel documentary called *Deranged Killers: Charles Whitman* in 2009 that is online at: https://www.youtube.com/watch?v=Jy1B5mfzCBA

92. Toby Hamilton "Memories of a Smaller Town and a Tragedy That Became Personal," *Austin American Statesman*, August 6, 2006.

93. Statement of Albert J. Vincik, August, 1966, AHC.

94. Lavergne at 48.

95. 96 Minutes at 108.

96. *Ibid.* at 53.

97. *Ibid.* at 69.

98. *Ibid.* at 44, 59.

99. Patricia Barber, quoted in the *Austin American Statesman*, Aug. 7, 1966.

100. Lavergne at 51-52.

101. Whitman's first roommate at U.T., John Drolla, told the DPS that Whitman "did not like his father but had never shown a great deal of anger against him." It is probable Whitman's intense dislike for C.A.Whitman occurred later than 1961. Interview of John Drolla by Agent O.N. Humphreys, Jr., San Antonio, August 4, 1966, AHC.

102. FBI Investigation teletype dated August 4, 1966 from SAC, Albuquerque to SAC, San Antonio, AHC. The information supplied was phoned in by a classmate of Whitman's who met him in September, 1965, and who described Whitman as "his best friend at the University," but whose name was redacted from the FBI report.

103. http://www.ehow.com/about_5541175_history-dexedrine.html

104. Whitman's friend, John Drolla, said Charles once took a No-Doz tablet and so disliked its effect so that he swore never to take another, and that he didn't know how to study and would often stay up all night, but that his tool for staying awake was to splash cold water on his face. The fact that Drolla was Whitman's first U.T. roommate may mean that the Dexedrine habit came later, or that Drolla was simply mistaken. Lt. John C. Drolla, *supra*

105. Lavergne at 54

106. Apparently C. A. made a down payment on the car but Charles was to pay it off. He and Kathy took a loan for $3400, $108/mo./36 months, from the Austin Federal Teachers Credit Union for that purpose. Report of Maurice Beckham to O. N. Humphreys, Agent-in-Charge, Texas Dept. of Public Safety, dated August 2, 1966; AHC.

107. FBI Agent Cole report dated August 17, 1966, AHC.

108. Memorandum (27 pp.) designated MM 62-5533, August 9, 1966, FBI Miami, AHC.

109. An unidentified neighbor told the FBI in early August, 1966, that they took the family dog, Lady, with them from Florida to Texas, but if so the fate of the dog is unknown. FBI report 62-5533, *supra*.

110. Texas Dept. of Public Safety report dated August 4, 1966 from Maruice Beckman to O. N. Humphreys, regarding Margaret Elizabeth Whitman; AHC.

111. The ten-story complex is still in operation, and as of the writing of this book a one bedroom apartment of less than 500 square feet three doors down from Margaret's was available for $1400 per month. Another unit on the 10th floor, twice as large, was $1899. http://www.highrises.com/austin/penthouse-condos/, December 14, 2014.

112. Statement of Goldie Harris, interviewed by Sgt. Rutledge of the Austin P.D., August 4, 1966, AHC.

113. Dr. Jan D. Cochrum, quoted in the *Austin American Statesman*, August 7, 1966.

114. Student Health Center application by C. J. Whitman, AHC.

115. Bill Helmer, "The Madman in the Tower," *Texas Monthly*, August 1966.

116. A story still circulating is that Whitman visited U.T. psychiatrists numerous times in 1966, but U.T. kept reports under wraps. The tale is tantalizing (it was provided to the authors by an archivist at another library and is referenced on the Internet), but Whitman wrote on July 31, 1966, that he consulted only one doctor about his "psychiatric disorders," and had U.T. withheld medical records, it seems unlikely it would have selected Heatly's report to release. Nevertheless, the authors made a request under the Texas Public Information Act for such records, and the University both called to promise thorough review and responded in writing that "the university has conducted a thorough search and has identified no responsive records to your request." Letter dated April 9, 2015 from Margo Iwanski, Assistant to the Vice President, Office of the Vice President and Chief Financial Officer.

117. The entire report read as follows:

MARCH 29, 1966   #8009

This is a new student referred by one of the general practitioners downstairs. This massive, muscular youth seemed to be oozing with hostility as he initiated the hour with the statement that something was happening to him and he didn't seem to be himself.

Past history revealed a youth who was one of two brothers (sic) that grew up in Florida where the father was a very successful plumbing contractor without an education, but who had achieved considerable wealth. He identified his father as being brutal, domineering and extremely demanding of the other three members of the family. The youth married four or five years ago and served a hitch in the Marines during his married life. He expressed himself as being very fond of his wife, but admitted that his tactics were similar to his father's and that he had on two occasions assaulted his wife physically. He referred to several commendable achievements during his Marine Service, but also made reference to a court martial for fighting which resulted only to his being reduced several grades to private. In spite of this he received a scholarship to attend the University for two years, and remain a Marine at the same time. He said that his wife had become more comfortable with him and he says that she really has less fear of him now than in the past because he had made a more intense effort to avoid losing his temper with her.

The real percipitating (sic) factor for this initial visit after being on the campus for several years seemed to stem from the separation of his parents some 30 days ago. Although there has been gross disharmony through the years, his mother summoned him to Florida to bring her to Texas, and she is now living in Austin, but not with her son and daughter-in-law. The youth says his father has averaged calling every 48 hours for several weeks petitioning him to pursuade (sic) his mother to return to him. He alleges to have no intentions of trying to do that and retains his hostility towards his father. Although he identifies with his mother in the matter above, his real concern is with himself at the present time. He readily admits having overwhelming periods of hostility with a very minimum of provocation. Repeated inquiries attempting to analyze his exact experiences were not too successful with the exception of his vivid reference to "thinking about going up on the tower with a deer rifle and start shooting people". (sic) He recognized, or rather feels that he is not achieving in his work at the level of which he is capable and this is very disconcerting to him. The youth could talk for long periods of time and develop overt hostility while talking, and then during the same narration may show signs of weeping.

OBSERVATIONS: The youth told numerous stories of his childhood and of involvement with his father that were not repeated, and it was felt that this relationship together with the genetic feature is largely responsible for his present predicament. Although his father is only semi-literate, he was a perfectionist in other respects and extremely expansive. The youth has lived for the day when he could consider himself a person capable of excelling his father in high society in general. He long ago acknowledged that he had surpassed him in educational fields, but he is seeking that status in versely (sic) all fields of all human endeavor. He has self-centered in egocentric, and at the same time he wants to improve himself. The degenerated state of affairs with his parents plus his repeated recent failures to achieve have become extremely frustrating to him which he (and his father) would express his hostility; thus some of the experiences noted above.

No medication was given to this youth at this time and he was told to make an appointment for the same day next week, and should he feel that he needs to talk to this therapist he could call me at anytime during the interval. M.D. HEATLY, M.D./dms

118. Connally Commission Report, p. 4

119. Lavergne at 81.

120. Margaret and Charles may have made two trips from Austin to Florida in May, 1966. Charles's credit card records show his Gulf credit card was used for a motel room in Fort Pierce, Fla. on May 13, to purchase gas in Quincy, La., and for motel rooms in Biloxi, Miss. on May 31 and Baytown, TX on June 1, 1966; Texas Dept. of Public Safety report dated August 4, 1966 from Maurice Beckham to O. N. Humphreys; AHC.

121. *Ibid.* at 67.

122. Note contained in AHC files, designated "#968150; FBI report to Director and San Antonio Office dated August 15, 1966 from the Anchorage, Alaska FBI office, AHC. This 13 page report, which demonstrates the far-flung nature of the investigation, was based on an interview of a man whose name was redacted, but who served as an altar boy with Whitman in Lake Worth, who was very familiar with the Whitman family, and who stated that Whitman's mother told Whitman that "she would not leave him (C. A. Whitman) while children were young because she wanted to maintain family together until children were old enough to care for themselves."

123. Report of Ben C. Boyd to Agent-in-Charge O. N. Humphreys, Texas Dept. of Public Safety, dated August 3, 1966, AHC.

CHAPTER FOUR

Climbing the Tower

All of us have a tower to climb... to deny that is done at the peril of your heart and mind.

-Harry Crews, *"Climbing the Tower," Esquire, August, 1977*

The sun rose on August 1, 1966, a day larger than a day, not to be measured against any ordinary day with any chance of matching. Charles Whitman had lots to do.

After completing his stroll down Memory Lane, he began preparing. He was a meticulous, detail-oriented individual, always had been, and his planning for the largest day in his life reflected it. He was also happy. His decision and actions of the night and day before had lifted burdens from his mind. Everything that had bothered him was either resolved or no longer relevant. He now had only one job to do and final exams, concerns about money, anger toward his father, concern about his mother, or mooning over Kathy were ancient history. He'd even taken care of the family dog's future.

He was dressed in blue jeans and a white, short-sleeved shirt.

His first task was to call Southwestern Bell, at 5:45 a.m., to report that Kathy was suffering from stomach problems—nausea and diarrhea—and would not be able to come to work for the shift that began at 8:30 a.m. He then retrieved his Marine Corps foot locker from the garage and began packing it with everything he might need for the day, or days, to come. After an hour, he discovered he still needed several things, not the least of which was a method of transporting the foot locker to the top of the Tower. So a little after 7 a.m. he drove to the Austin Rental Company

Stairs leading from elevators on the 27th floor to the 28th floor reception room and observation deck of the U.T. Tower, as they appeared on August 1, 1966.

at 900 W. 10th Street and rented a two-wheeled dolly for 24 hours, paying $2.04. When Austin National Bank opened, he cashed two $125.00 checks, one from his account and one from Margaret's on which he was an authorized signatory.

After driving home and unloading the dolly, he took stock of his supply of weapons and left again, showing up a little after 9 a.m. at Charles P. Davis Hardware at 49th and Burnet. He knew exactly what he wanted. Ted Beard, an employee, helped him with his purchases, consisting of a .30 caliber M-1 Universal carbine, two boxes of .30 caliber ammunition, two extra ammunition clips for the carbine, three boxes of 6 mm. ammunition, two boxes of .35 caliber Remington ammunition, and one box of 9 mm. Luger ammunition. Whitman told Beard he was going to Florida to shoot wild hogs and paid for his purchases with cash.[1]

Next he went to Chuck's Gun Shop on East Avenue, where he had previously purchased the 6 millimeter Remington rifle with a four power scope he would put to use later in the day. He had brought his father with him on that occasion, probably in April, 1965, and father and son had ordered a rifle each, the 6 millimeter Remington for Charles and a .243 caliber Sako for C.A, the new rifle C.A. used for the first time during the tense deer hunt with two of his sons in late November, 1965. Both rifles had to be ordered and paid for in four or five installments, each of which Charles made in person. The owner of the store, Chuck Maretzay, stated later that he never detected anything unusual about Whitman.

He arrived around 9:30 a.m. and Mrs. Maretzay waited on him. Both she and another employee, Irene Miller, said he seemed normal. Once again Whitman knew what he wanted, and bought four carbine clips, four boxes of .30 caliber ammunition, two boxes of 6 millimeter ammunition and one can of Hoppes No.9 gun oil. The total bill was $48.63 and Whitman paid with a check. While filling it out he asked if Mrs. Maretzay needed to call Austin National Bank to verify that it was good and she said she did not, although she did write down his Texas driver's license number, 5308550.[2] Later in the week the check was returned, NSF.[3]

From the Gun Shop he drove to the Sears store at Hancock Shopping Center and arrived there a little before 10 a.m. A clerk named James D. Morehead assisted him and once again he was certain of what he needed—a 12 gauge shotgun. Morehead opened the case and Whitman picked one up, raised it to his shoulder and remarked that it "was light compared to the 21 pound gun I carried in the service," by which he undercut the weight of a Browning Automatic Rifle, which weighs 24 pounds, and which Whitman trained on while in the Marines.[4]

Having plans for the wooden stock of the gun, he asked Morehead if it contained any mechanism and was told it did not. Next he asked if Sears had any carbine clips for sale and was told there were none. Once again he mentioned he was going to Florida to shoot wild hogs. For shotgun shells he selected a box of number 4 shot, which is a large load. Small-sized shot, for quail and dove, is size 8 or 7 ½, with size 6 being for larger birds like geese. Size 4 can bring down a large animal... or a human. He charged the purchase, which totaled $137.95, on his Sears credit card, and left after spending less than fifteen minutes in the store.

From Hancock Shopping Center, Whitman drove south to his house, passing within easy view of the University and the Tower as he did so, and arrived about 10:30 a.m. He then called Wyatt's Cafeteria manager, D. W. Quinney, to report that Margaret was suffering from vomiting and diarrhea and would not be able to report to work for her shift, which began at 11 a.m.

At that point or slightly later, Whitman used the gun oil purchased at Chuck's Gun Shop to clean and lubricate some or all of his fire-arms, and either before or after doing so he took the new shotgun to the garage, tightened it down in a vice, and sawed off the portion of the stock behind the pistol grip. With that done he took a hacksaw and started work on the barrel in order to shorten the 12 gauge into a hand-held scattergun, only to be interrupted by the mail carrier, Chester Arrington, who helpfully advised Whitman that what he was doing was illegal.

Already a double murderer and dead set on a deadly mission, Whitman's response was curt—"It's my gun and I can do what I want with it." Instead of sensing the tension and moving on, Arrington did the opposite and began chatting with him about firearms. Perhaps Whitman softened his tone in order to allay suspicion, realizing that the fed-eral employee might report him for breaking the law. In any event they talked for an incredible twenty-five minutes, mostly about guns. Later Arrington testified that Whitman was "very, very, very calm."[5]

About the time Arrington was leaving, a young boy from the neighbor-hood came along. The local children knew and liked Kathy and Charles, and were drawn by the "army stuff" Whitman had in his garage. This boy's visit was rewarded. Whitman gave him the extra length of barrel he'd just removed from the shotgun.

An inventory that would be conducted later listed nearly 100 items he decided a fellow might need to "stand off an army."[6] While it is probable that some of the items were already in the foot locker, the thoroughness of Whitman's preparation leads one to believe he envisioned a long siege, and his inclusion of some items, such as an alarm clock, snakebite kit, deodorant, and pipe wrench, would be amusing if the purpose of the list was not so chilling.

Charles did not feel it was necessary to take his entire collection of firearms, and left a 410 shotgun, a 25-20 Winchester rifle, and two matching .22 caliber derringers in the house. The Winchester belonged to Francis Schuck, who never got it back.[7] Upon departing the garage, ever meticulous, Whitman locked its front and side doors.[8]

He wrestled the foot locker into the backseat of the two-door Impala, covered it with a quilt, wrapped the longarms in a dark blanket and lay them on the backseat floor, put the dolly in the trunk, the black attaché in the passenger seat, and went back inside the house. There he may have checked for loose ends, and probably took a last look at Kathy. He also pulled a pair of green coveralls on over his jeans and shirt.

At about 11:15 he left his house, driving north. He entered the campus at 21st Street and Speedway and stopped at a security booth at 11:25. The security guard was Jack Rodman. The general public was not allowed to enter the campus simply to drive through or see the sights, but Whitman still had the identification card issued to him for his job as a laboratory assistant, which would not expire until August 31. Showing Rodman the card, he explained that he needed to unload equipment at the Experimental Science Building, and would need a permit for that purpose. Rodman saw the foot locker and Whitman told him there was more in the trunk.

Rodman scribbled a routine 20-minute permit with the times "11:30 a.m.–11:50 a.m." Whitman looked at it and said, "I don't think I can get it unloaded in that length of time. May I have a little longer?" Rodman doubled the time to 40 minutes. Charles thanked him and drove on.[9] He turned left, left again, and dead ahead the Tower soared 307 feet above him. Near the Tower's west door he pulled into one of the reserved parking spaces and stopped, commencing his on-campus crime spree with a parking violation, as his permit was for a loading zone. He removed the dolly, loaded it with the foot locker and firearms, and wheeled it to the door.

Within the next ten minutes, Whitman would encounter 14 people in the Tower and provide them their Warhol-esque 15 minutes. Six would become footnotes in history, two would become heralded as the luckiest people in Austin, two would be seriously wounded, and three would be killed. He would also turn the Tower into the epicenter of human grimness.

Whitman walked inside and turned down a gray-tiled corridor to the elevator foyer. There, Vera M. Palmer sat at a small desk. Her regular job was observation deck receptionist, one of three, but just then was serving as an elevator attendant. Whitman told her that he had items to deliver. Mrs. Palmer didn't question him. He was dressed like a workman and had a parking permit. He retrieved the dolly and wheeled it to the front of elevator number two.

Just then the door to the stairwell opened and the next four people he would encounter emerged. They were two professors, Dr. Antone Jacobson and Dr. J.G. Duncan, and Jacobson's two children, a boy and a girl aged two and six. They saw Whitman and his dolly and assumed he was a workman or janitor. Jacobson said later that the time was 11:35 a.m. Both professors detected the smell of the Hoppe's oil, which is distinctive and which caused Jacobson to "think of guns." He also noticed that the blond-headed man had a long bundle tied to the front of the foot locker, loaded vertically on the dolly, as well as a few items sitting on top.

Whitman backed into the elevator pulling the dolly, with Mrs. Palmer holding the door. When the doors closed, a bit of the blanket became caught in them and Mrs. Palmer poked it inside with her fingers. Whitman pressed the button to go to the 27th floor but nothing happened.

Dr. Jacobson heard Mrs. Palmer tell Whitman, "Your elevator is turned off." She promptly flipped the switch that activated it, and Jacobson heard Whitman mumble, "Thank you ma'am. You don't know how happy that makes me." Jacobson also noticed that the elevator Whitman took was automatic and had no attendant, as did other Tower elevators.[10]

The elevator began to ascend. Horror was scant moments away.

The event would be labeled later by the media as the second most important story of 1966, second only to the Vietnam War.[11] It would affect the lives of thousands of people in different ways, but in particular it would change or end the lives of more than one hundred victims, participants, witnesses, and law enforcement officers. The people affected were not a complete cross-section of Americans, but they were young and old, Caucasian and non-Caucasian, visitors and residents. Those who would be shot ranged in age from unborn to 64 and included Peace Corps volunteers preparing to leave for Iran, at least three military veterans, a funeral director, a professor, two teachers, a writer, a policeman, a life guard, a basketball coach, an electrician, a carpenter, a city employee, a university employee, a reporter, a jeweler, a preacher, a secretary, a receptionist, a housewife, an Air Force Academy cadet, two high school students and, of course, plenty of college students from both the undergrad and graduate schools. They included Democrats, Republicans, independents, conservatives, liberals, and even radicals. They were mostly from Texas, but California, Michigan, Arkansas, Florida, Minnesota, Wisconsin, Bolivia, Mexico, and Iraq were also represented. They met fate that day as individuals, couples, and as a family. What was about to unfold has been compared many times, starting with *Time* magazine's coverage of the incident, to Thornton Wilder's *The Bridge of San Luis Rey*, in which different pesons are drawn from various places, purposes and backgrounds to a common fate, and death, at the scene of the collapse over a bridge in Peru.[12]

When Whitman arrived at the 27th floor, the elevator opened onto a short hallway leading to a set of steps. He wheeled his cargo to the stairs, backed it up 11 steps, then down a corridor to another staircase. He pulled the dolly up another 22 steps, each causing a bumping noise that people in lower floors heard. At the top of the next to last set of steps was a sign reading "Welcome to the observation deck. Please help the University by observing the following practices," with four rules. Shooting people from the observation deck was not mentioned.

He opened the door leading into the observation deck foyer. There he encountered the sixth person, Edna Townsley. She was one of the receptionists who manned the observation deck, the other two being Vera Palmer and Lydia Gest. Lydia would normally have been at the desk that day but she was on vacation. Townsley was 47, the mother of two sons, and divorced. She was a stickler for the rules, and had worked for the University for 12 years, the last four as an observation desk receptionist. She had been at her post since 8 a.m. and was scheduled to be relieved by Vera Palmer at noon.

Nobody knows what was said by Whitman or Townsley, only that he attacked her quickly. He may have taken the time to unwrap one of the firearms and club her with it, but he probably used the foot-long steel bar with which he killed his mother. She may have come over to inspect what he was delivering, knowing that nothing had been ordered, recognizing him as a student rather than a full-time university employee, and possibly telling him he had made a mistake. It is possible there was a struggle and considering the blood she left on the floor, it is possible Edna turned to flee just before Whitman struck. Whatever weapon he used caused a wound very similar to that he inflicted on his mother and in nearly the same place. A blow shattered the upper rear portion of her skull, sending her glasses flying from her face and her crashing to the floor. He hit her again above the left eye. Blood began to pool and flow.

Whitman seized her by the feet and dragged her across the room to a beige sofa against the east wall, pulled it out and put her behind it. He turned, saw there was a long streak of blood leading from where she'd fallen to the couch, but ignored it and began moving furniture in order to barricade the stairs. He placed a chair upside down at the top, pushed the receptionist's desk part way to the stairs, then went to the dolly and removed and unwrapped the longarms.

Just then the seventh and eighth persons encountered by and affected by Whitman's initial actions in the Tower appeared. They were Cheryl Botts and Don Walden, and before the day was over they would be called the luckiest people in Austin. Cheryl was from Rockdale, Texas, a town an hour northeast of Austin. She was 18 and in the big city to visit her grandmother, having arrived by bus the previous day. She had graduated from high school in May but had no plans to attend U.T. Instead she was going to attend Howard Payne College in Brownwood, Texas in the fall.

Don Walden was a student at U.T., majoring in English. He was 22, from San Antonio, and had a job at the Continental Trailways bus station as ticket agent. It was there he'd met Cheryl. Her uncle was supposed to meet her when the bus from Rockdale arrived but he was 45 minutes late. The young couple struck up a conversation and Walden invited

today
The Weather

Increases
By Steel
Denounced

The Austin American
Read by the Decision-Makers of Texas

Probe Due of Spiraling Food Prices
FTC Sets Investigation After Freeman Request, Page A-

Jury Keeps Notes
Of Slayer Secret

Sniper Allowed
To Leave Tower

Viet Need
Escalates
Draft Calls

Back to Work Bill
Passed by Senate

Kick-Off Luncheon
For Festival Today

Austin Aqua Festival
Pre-Festival Events

Writer Threatened
'Don't Let It Be Due To My Book'

her to let him show her around Austin. She accepted and that day they had arrived at the observation deck about 20 minutes before Whitman parked at the foot of the Tower. As she recalled:

> We walked out onto the observation deck and enjoyed the view on all four sides, looking down at the whole city. I grew up in a very small town, so the thing that impressed me was how big everything was. I mean, there were buildings and highways for as far as you could see; it just went on and on, and it was so beautiful. We looked around for at least a half an hour. We didn't know much about each other, so we did a lot of visiting too.
>
> We stepped back inside, and I noticed that the receptionist was not at her desk, but I just assumed she had gone to lunch. The next thing I saw was this reddish-brown swath that we had to step over. My instinct—I mean, I'm a naive small-town girl, okay? I had a rationalization for everything—was that someone was about to varnish the floor. So we stepped over it, and immediately to our right, a blond guy stood up. We had surprised him, apparently. He was bending over the couch, and we found out later that he had put the receptionist's body there and that she was still alive at that time. He turned around to face us, and he had a rifle in each hand. Don thought—I know this sounds crazy—that he was there to shoot pigeons. So I smiled at him and said, "Hello," and he smiled back at me and said, "Hi." All of this took about fifteen seconds; we never stopped walking. We walked to the stairwell and went down one floor to the elevator.[13]

Don Walden, 22, was a student at U.T., majoring in English. He and Cheryl Botts were called "the luckiest people in Austin" after they encountered Whitman in the observation deck reception room between murders and were allowed to leave the Tower unharmed.

In later years people would ask her repeatedly why she was not alarmed when she saw Whitman holding rifles. "But I went to school with guys who went hunting," she explained, "then came to school with their guns still in their pickups."[14]

Walden's recollection was slightly different. He said that Whitman was standing near the center of the room when they walked in and was holding rifles, probably all three, vertically in a sort of bear hug manner. Whitman gave them a smile and Walden noticed the swath of dark liquid running diagonally from southwest to northeast between them and him. He thought the liquid must be floor wax, and he also noticed that the receptionist was gone and the furniture had been moved.[15]

He and Cheryl stepped across the swath of "varnish" and Walden looked back at Whitman, who then said "hello." Walden considered asking if he intended to shoot pigeons but did not, which may have saved the couple's life. They skirted around the upside-down chair at the top of the stairs, walked down to the elevators on the 27th floor, took the one on the left when it came, and rode down.[16]

People have speculated about Whitman's reasons for not killing Botts and Walden. It has been suggested he lacked the nerve to kill them face to face, considering his other victims had been taken from behind or while asleep. More likely he was simply taken off guard and had no need to kill them. He had not known they were on the deck and was

The blood trail on the floor of the reception room at the top of the Tower, left when Whitman dragged Edna Townsley from where he had clubbed her to a place of concealment behind a couch. Seen a few moments later by Cheryl Botts and Don Walden, they assumed it was floor varnish.

holding multiple rifles, none of which may have been loaded, when they walked in. He was intent on his next steps—barricading the stairwell, securing the door to the deck from the outside, and beginning to target people below. Had Botts and Walden acted alarmed at the sight of the blood, suspicious, or inquisitive about what he was doing, he might very well have shot them. Had they been a minute later, so that he had completed barricading the stairs with furniture, he probably would have shot them rather than move chairs and the desk out of the way. Instead they greeted him cordially and promptly exited his life with theirs intact.

As they were descending in one elevator, the last six people Whitman would meet inside the Tower were coming up in the other. Four were from Texarkana, in Austin on vacation, and the other two lived in the city. They consisted of Mr. and Mrs. M. J. Gabour, their sons Mike, 19, and Mark, 15, Gabour's sister, Marguerite, and her husband, William Lamport.

As the elevators were passing each other, Whitman turned Townsley's desk onto its side and shoved it into the stairwell, then placed two chairs and a white, metal trash can on top of it. He could not have expected the makeshift barricade to stop anyone intent on reaching the deck, but it might slow them down enough for him to see or hear, and then shoot, them.

The Gabours exited the elevator, talking and laughing. Mark and Mike were the first ones up the stairs, followed by Mary and Marguerite. The two men brought up the rear. As Mrs. Gabour wrote later, "[a]s we neared the top of the last flight of steps, we saw that an old-fashioned type of desk had been turned on its side down the stairs; a couple of chairs had been piled on top of this. It seemed strange that the janitor could still be cleaning at 11:30 in the morning; but this is what I immediately thought."[17]

As Mike started to edge around the desk to find out what was going on, he saw "a pretty good-sized blonde dude wearing aviator shades running toward me. The barrel of what looked like a sawed-off shotgun was coming up to firing position. In nanoseconds my brain tried to process the images for a response. I had just started to turn toward my family when the first blast caught my left shoulder."[18]

Whitman fired at least three times and possibly as many times as five. Mike was hit in the shoulder, head, down his back, and in his left leg.

Mark apparently tried to duck, because he was hit in the top of his head and was killed instantly. The load of shot that hit Marguerite took her in the chest and she died within seconds. Mary, who had been turning away to speak to the men when Whitman appeared—so that she never saw him—was hit in the back and the face. One of the shots missed entirely and left a round pattern of pockmarks on the metal wall. All four of his victims fell onto and down the hard concrete steps.

One of Whitman's 12 gauge shotgun blasts meant for the Gabour/Lamport families went wild and left this shot pattern in the wall beside the stairs where he killed two and wounded two as they climbed toward the 28th floor.

Mike screamed, writhed, and cursed. Mary, in terrible pain but not understanding what was happening, saw him falling toward her and had the thought that the searing pain in her face was because he was hitting her with his shoes. She remembered thinking, "I can't say anything to him, and he can't help it, but I do wish he would lose his shoes." By the time they landed at the foot of the stairs, both of them had done so.

Mr. Gabour and Mr. Lamport were exiting the elevator when the four bodies tumbled in front of them. "The boys were first and the women were next," Mr. Gabour explained later. "My brother-in-law and I were bringing up the rear. Mark opened the door to the observation deck and a gun started going off. Mike screamed. That's the only voice I remember. They all four came rolling down the stairs."[19]

Mark was lying face down. Mr. Gabour turned him over. The boy's eyes were open and staring, and Gabour knew immediately that his son was dead. Gabour and Lamport pulled Mark's body to the side and saw that Marguerite was also dead. Stunned, in shock, Gabour picked up his wife's white shoes. Lamport picked up his wife's purse and they left to find help.

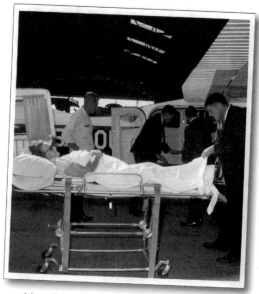

Mary Gabour, who was shot in the face and back by Whitman with his sawed-off 12 gauge shotgun, following surgery and during her recovery. Her wounds caused her to become legally blind, but did not prevent her from writing a book about her family and its experiences.

Mike and Mary faded in and out of consciousness. Not having heard any screams or complaints from Mark or Marguerite, Mary assumed both must be uninjured and okay. Her larger concern was Mike's language. He had distinctly used profanity and she was afraid he would do it again.

"Mom, are you all right?" Mike asked her. "Yes darling, I'm fine. Someone will come to help us soon." Later she thought she may have said it more than once. Mike said something else, but she didn't catch it. "I could hear him saying something, and I hoped it wasn't something bad. I was afraid he might not know how serious this was, and I was trying desperately to ask him not to use any bad language, for goodness sake. I wasn't sure I was making any sound or not."[20]

After emptying the shotgun down the stairwell and seeing the four targets fall away, Whitman turned back, anxious to get started with the business at hand. He either did not see the two men or did not care to go after them. He went to the telephone mounted on the wall in the east window alcove near the couch, lifted the receiver and jerked it violently so that the phone cord was disconnected. Whether he did so to avoid outgoing or incoming calls, possibly including attempted negotiations from the ground, cannot be known.[21]

As he prepared to go out onto the deck, he heard Edna Townsley groan, so he went to where she lay behind the couch and shot her in the head with one of his three pistols. During the next hour and a half he would shoot 40 more people, one of them twice, but Edna would be the only one to whom he delivered a coup de grace. Believing she was dead, Charles Whitman opened the door to the observation deck and stepped outside.

There have been many famous sieges in history—the Alamo, Vicksburg, Bastogne—but what Whitman was planning was a reverse siege, in which an armed force in a surrounded fortification put those on the outside under assault.

He took a white cloth from his pocket and tied it around his head as a sweatband. He had hot work to do beneath the Texas summer sun.

---

1. Report of Sgt. D.L.Moody, Aug. 2, 1966, AHC. Even though Charles purchased the M-1 carbine on August 1, 1966, his father subsequently claimed it was his and he'd loaned it to his son. Memorandum (27 pp.) designated MM 62-5533, August 9, 1966, FBI Miami, AHC.

2. In addition to the one from Texas, Whitman had driving licenses from Florida and North Carolina, as well as a U.S. Government Motor Vehicle Operator's Identification Card set to expire on 8/6/66.

3. Report of Sgt. A.E.Rugledge, Aug. 2, 1966, AHC

4. Report of Officer Morehead, AHC. Whitman kept notes during his Marine Corps training in three small notebooks, each of which is now in the collection of the Austin History Center, and one of which contains basic information about Boeing Automatic Rifles.

5. Lavergne at 119.

6. When finally fully armed and prepared, Whitman had packed the following items and firearms in and with his foot locker:

> A portable Channel Master AM-FM radio in a brown case;
> A blank Robinson Reminder notebook;
> A Paper mate ballpoint pen with black ink;
> A white plastic 3.5 gallon plastic jug filled with water;
> A red plastic 3.5 gallon plastic jug filled with gasoline;
> A canteen filled with water;
> A can of charcoal lighter fluid;
> A green extension cord;
> Several lengths of nylon and cotton ropes of different lengths;
> A length of clothes line wire;
> A length of yellow electric wire;
> A plastic Wonda-scope compass;
> A US Army compass in a canvas case;

A snakebite kit in a canvas case;

An army web belt for the canteen, compass, and snakebite kit;

A hatchet;

A hammer;

A pipe wrench;

A machete in a green scabbard;

A solid steel bar approximately one foot in length;

A cigarette lighter;

A box of kitchen matches;

A Gene brand alarm clock;

A green Tector brand rifle scabbard;

A green Sears brand rifle scabbard;

A shoulder holster for a 357 Magnum;

A cartridge belt for 6 mm. shells;

A Camallus hunting knife in a brown scabbard with a whet stone;

A Randall hunting knife with a bone handle, "Charles J. Whitman" on the blade, in
     brown scabbard with a whet stone;

A large pocket knife with a wooden handle and locking blade;

A pair of gray gloves;

A pair of light brown leather gloves;

A pair of eyeglasses with brown frames in a brown case;

A green and white six volt flashlight;

Four "C" batteries;

Two rolls of white adhesive tape;

A set of ear plugs;

A Deer bag;

A green rubber army duffle bag;

A pair of Kirby, 7 x 35 field glasses;

Twelve containers of food, including Spam, fruit cocktail, Planters peanuts, and a
     box of raisins;

Two cans of Sego;

One jar of honey;

A package of sweet rolls;

Sandwiches;

A knapsack containing the following:

     a package of toilet paper;

     a can opener'

     a soap dish with assorted pills;

     a queen brand pocket knife;

     a pair of sunglasses;

     a can of foot paper (powder?)

     a Gillette razor;

     Mennen spray deodorant.

The sales slip from Davis Hardware dated August 1, 1966;

A box of 6 MM Remington shells;

Four boxes of 35 Caliber Remington shells;

Three boxes of 357 Magnum shells;

Two boxes of .30 caliber shells;

A box of .25 caliber automatic shells;

A box of Remington 9 mm Luger shells;

A box of Winchester 12 gauge shotgun shells, #4 buckshot

A 15 round .30 caliber carbine clip;

Two 30 round .30 caliber carbine clips;

Two 9mm Luger pistol clips;

A .25 caliber clip;

A Remington Model 700, 6 millimeter, bolt action rifle, serial number 149037, with Leopold, four power scope, serial number 61384; with leather strap; to which Whitman had attached a piece of tape with handwritten scope sightings;

A U.S. M-1 Universal Carbine, .30 caliber, semi-automatic, serial number 69799, with a web sling;

A Remington .35 caliber pump rifle, serial number 1859;

A Sears 12 gauge shotgun with barrel and stock shortened;

A .357 Magnum Smith &Wesson Model 19 revolver, chrome, with a 4 ½ inch barrel, serial number K391583;

A 6.35 millimeter Galesi-Brescia semi-automatic pistol, serial number 366869; and

A 9 millimeter Luger pistol, serial number 2010.

7. Telephone conversation with Francis Schuck, February 7, 2015.

8. Report of Sgt. B. Gregory, Aug. 2, 1966, p.2, AHC

9. Saul Pett, Jules Loe "Trail Through the Sniper's Mind: What Made Charley Whitman Tick?" *The San Antonio Express*, August 27, 1966.

10. Statement of Anton Jacobson to Lt.George Phifer, Austin P.D., August 4, 1966. AHC

11. 96 Minutes at 104.

12. "The Madman in the Tower," p. 14, Time, August 12, 1966; *Ibid.*; Roger Friedman in a phone conversation with Monte Akers, January 30, 2015.

13. 96 Minutes at 176.

14. "Surviving History - For 48 Years: In the UT tower with Sniper-Killer Aug. 1, 1966," *Rockdale Reporter*, May 22, 2014

15. Interview of Dr. Don Walden, June 3, 2015.

16. When the couple arrived at the ground floor they went outside and across to the nearby Academic Center, where they stayed for what Walden said was only two minutes. When they came outside again they walked back toward the Tower intending to ask someone why the flags on the University campus were flying at half mast. It had nothing to do with what was about to happen, but was in honor of the passing of Lt. Col. Richard B. Pelton, a university professor who died on July 29, 1966 at the age of 56. By that time the shooting had started. Walden and Botts saw two people crouching beneath a tree and a man lying on the ground, either dead or wounded. A shot rang out and Walden grabbed Cheryl's hand and they ran into a building where they stayed for the next hour and a half. Affidavit of Don W. Walden, made August 4, 1966, AHC.

17. Mary Gabour Lamport, *The Impossible Tree*, 108-09 (Austin: Ginny's Copying Service, 1972).

18. 96 Minutes at 176.

19. "Deranged tower sniper rained death on UT campus," *Houston Chronicle*, July 8, 2001.

20. Mary Gabour Lamport, *supra* at 110.

21. One theory was that Edna Townsley, either suspecting Whitman's intentions or planning to call to verify whether he was supposed to be delivering anything to the observation deck, was on the phone when Whitman hit her from behind. However, that theory is inconsistent with the location of the swath of blood leading from where she was struck to the couch. A somewhat similar report was made by the FBI on August 2, 1966, in which it was stated that Mrs. Townsley "prior to being killed, supposedly notified security police subject was on floor and acting strangely." However, the same report contains various errors, and there is no other record of Whitman having done anything before arriving at the 28th floor that might have attracted Mrs. Townsley's attention. FBI Teletype Report dated August 2, 1966, 1:37 a.m., to Assistant to the Director DeLoach, AHC.

CHAPTER FIVE
Adhesive Tape and Rock Squirrels

"He could plug the eye out of a squirrel by the time he was sixteen."
-C.A. Whitman, commenting on his son's shooting ability, August, 1966

Everyone knows that Charles Whitman was a superior marksman. It is his legacy. When the worthwhile accomplishments of his life are boiled down, the grease at the bottom of the kettle consists only of that—he was a damned fine shot.

Good marksmanship consists of a lot more than the ability to place crosshairs or open sights on a target, hold steady and squeeze a trigger. It is nearly a science, and the nature of Whitman's exercise of that science on August 1, 1966 has given rise to at least three theories that are almost certainly myth—that he used multiple rifles because he wanted to create the impression there were multiple shooters, that he selected Claire Wilson as his first target because she was pregnant, and that he intentionally shot her in the abdomen because he intended to kill the baby. Additionally, a miniscule scrap of evidence connected to his employment of the science exists that speaks volumes about his plans for that day.

In addition to being able to see and aim at a target, a shooter must consider the effect of "meso variables" such as bullet shape (spherical or non-spherical), bullet drop (gravity), drag resistance, wind, spin drift, vertical angle, ambient air density, and equipment issues such as lateral jump and lateral throw-off. Each, as well as human conduct, affects the path of the projectile and determines where it will strike. Additionally, thermal expansion—the increase in barrel temperature resulting from firing multiple rounds—greatly affects accuracy. It is thermal expansion that explains away the first and third of the three myths described above.

View of South Mall toward downtown from UT Tower.

Thermal expansion causes improper seating of a round in the chamber, which causes dirty gas to flow around the bullet, which causes fouling of the barrel. Fouling of the barrel increases friction in an uneven way, and the round will not stabilize in the air in a predictable manner. As heating increases the barrel expands, causing loss of muzzle velocity and giving an irregular spin to the bullet. The gas and fouling also result in positive pressure, or resistance, in front of the round. Generally speaking, firing only one round every four to five minutes can cause an elevation in barrel temperature of up to 150 degrees Fahrenheit after nine rounds, and at the actual instant of firing, barrel temperature can reach 1200 degrees for a fraction of a second.

If the barrel of Whitman's 6 mm. rifle had a temperature of 100 degrees Fahrenheit before he began shooting on August 1, 1966, based on the ambient air temperature, and if he fired three rounds per minute, the barrel temperature would have been 147 degrees after the first minute, 177 degrees after the second minute, 242 degrees after the third minute, and 278 degrees after the fourth minute. Tests have shown that for every 11 degrees of change in temperature, the accuracy of a bullet changes by a ¼ "minute of angle," or MOA, which is 1/60th of a degree.[1]

As the distance to the target increases, the size of a single MOA also increases. Accordingly, the accuracy of his shots would have changed in the following manner if he continued firing the same rifle: at the end of the first minute, a change of 1.07 MOA occurred, meaning the bullet's point of impact was 1.07 inches off of dead center at 100 yards, 2.14 inches at 200 yards, 3.21 inches at 300 yards, 4.28 inches at 400 yards, and 5.35 inches at 500 yards. During the second minute the amount of change was 1.75 MOA, so that the bullet strike changes were 1.75 inches at 100 yards, 3.5 inches at 200 yards, 5.25 inches at 300 yards, 7 inches at 400 yards, and 8.75 inches at 500 yards. Assuming he kept firing the same rifle at the same speed after two minutes, the change in the MOA and the corresponding change in point of impact would continue until, during the fourth minute, the bullet strike would be considerably further from dead center—4.04 inches at 100 yards and 20.2 inches, or nearly two feet, at 500 yards.

Accordingly, Whitman took three rifles to the top of the Tower instead of just one. He intended to do a lot of shooting in a short period, and knew all about thermal expansion. Although he began by shooting the 6 mm. Remington, he switched quickly to the other two, and was heard

Photographed on August 1, 1966 are the four "longarms" Whitman carried to the top of the Tower and used that day. Note the piece of white tape on the butt of the scoped Remington rifle, second from the right, on which he wrote the three numbers he needed to achieve accurate shots from an elevated position. Also note the damage to the pump rifle on the left, where a shot from Austin Police Officer Gerding, on the ground, hit the rifle as it was lying on the ledge of the Tower beneath the south face of the clock. It was this rifle that Allen Crum picked up from the floor of the south side of the Tower walkway shortly before Whitman was killed.

firing the semi-automatic M-1 carbine, which was designed to be fired rapidly and to withstand the stresses of sustained fire, within four to seven minutes of his first shot.[2] He had neither reason nor desire to make people on the ground think there were multiple shooters. The thought might have amused him had he known what they were thinking and had there been room left in his brain for amusement, but sharing the credit for living out his delusional fantasy was the opposite of what Charles Whitman desired and intended. He used multiple rifles and dashed from one to another in order to let each rifle cool between shots, as well as to hit as many targets as possible in different places.

Additionally, just as increased barrel temperature affects accuracy, so does reduced barrel temperature. A shooter's first shot through a "cold bore" is less accurate than those that follow immediately, and invariably that first bullet strikes low on the intended target. Another outburst of technical information might be offered to explain the phenomenon, but let it suffice to say that the accuracy of cold bore shots varies with each rifle, and Brandon Webb, a member of Seal Team Three and a trained sniper, described the standing cold bore shot as being one of the most difficult parts of his specialized, very challenging training to master.[3]

Which means that when Whitman selected and targeted his first victim, the very pregnant Claire Wilson, he almost certainly aimed at her chest—a typical "main mass" shot—but the bullet fired from his standing cold bore shot dropped and hit low, in her abdomen.

If the barrel temperature, a factor unrelated to wind, drag, gravity and so forth was not enough, the high elevation imposed another set of variables. When shooting from high angles a shooter must know the basics of physics in relation to the arc of each bullet's path. Otherwise, the bullet will fly over the head of a target below and near. This fact explains why Claire Wilson was selected as his first target. As will be explained, she literally ambled into his gunsights.

Consider this analogy. If two people play catch on a flat plane, each knows from experience how to toss the ball with the right arc and force to land in or near the other's hands. If, however, one person is on a hill 250 feet higher and holds the same point of aim as on the flat plane, the ball will soar over the head of the intended target. The elevated player must adjust, perhaps aiming at the lower player's feet, in order to throw a catchable ball.

The same situation exists for an elevated shooter, but moreso. Whitman, being a Marine rifleman, trained to shoot from high angles, and in order to make an accurate shot at any given target from the Tower, he needed to know the general distance to it from his shooting position, and he then needed to apply a formula to that distance based on his elevation.

He didn't have time to do that for each shot, of course, and he knew exactly which shots were going to not only be the most challenging but also the most common, so he prepared before he climbed the Tower in his typical meticulous way, and left behind a small artifact that explains how he did so. It is that artifact that dispels the myth of his selecting Claire Wilson as his first target because she was pregnant.

100

Whitman's 6 mm., scoped rifle is now on display at the Crime Museum in Washington, D. C., and the evidence of his preparation is still there in the form of a small piece of white fiber, or adhesive tape, perhaps two inches long, affixed to the butt of the rifle. It was there on August 1, 1966, and can be seen in some of the photos of his arsenal. It contains only three numbers, handwritten vertically: "41.6, -6.5, 89." The last number is smudged, and could say "39," but that would make absolutely no sense, whereas "89" is chillingly appropriate.[4]

The meaning of the three numbers does not jump out at a trained marksman, and is nearly indecipherable to everyone else, but once their purpose becomes clear the result is quite interesting. They mean that when Whitman was firing from the observation deck of the Tower at people on the upper terrace of the South Mall, he accurately calculated that he was shooting at a 41.6 degree angle at targets an average of 89 yards in horizontal distance from where he stood, which required him to make a sighting adjustment of negative 6.5 MOA, or mill dots, within his telescopic sight in order to hit his targets.

It took an expert in shooting and ballistics a couple of days and a long conversation with a former sniper in the Vietnam War to be certain of that meaning, but at the end of the day there was no room for doubt.

One might think that if Whitman needed a written reminder for sighting his rifle, it was for long range shots like the two he made that brought down victims at 500 yards that day. Not so. He knew all he needed to know to make a long range shot, and while the elevated shooting perch figured into his aiming technique, what was unusual about his plans for August 1, 1966 is that he expected to do a lot of shooting at targets almost immediately below him, particularly on the South Mall within less than 100 yards from the base of the Tower. He knew that making such shots at such a sharp angle required him to aim low, just like the ball player on the hill.

He arrived at the three numbers in a process like this: he learned the distance he expected to fire and his elevation in relation to the targets. With that information and the height of the Tower he could find the hypotenuse and then the cosine of the angle at which he would be firing, and from that he applied a formula to the ballistics of the bullet in order to know how to aim.

If, for example, the target was at 100 yards (300 feet) and the shooter was standing approximately 231 feet higher, plus six feet for his height,

those numbers provide sides A and B of a triangle. Then the formula, A squared + B squared = C squared, provides the hypotenuse. Knowing the hypotenuse allows one to apply the formula and find the cosine, which is the adjacent side. Then the cosine is multiplied by the distance to the target to find the point of aim.[5]

The rifle scope Whitman was using was a Leopold M8-4X model. Looking through it, the shooter sees cross hairs, and on each of the horizontal and vertical arms of the cross are hash marks. Each hash mark represents a mill dot, or one MOA. Whitman's calculations told him that in order to hit a person approximately 89 yards from where he was on the observation deck, his point of aim needed to be 6½ mill dots below the cross hairs in the scope.

Why 89 yards? Because that is at or very near the center point of the upper terrace of the South Mall, and within a few feet of where Claire Wilson and Thomas Eckman were when Whitman shot them, as well as Dr. Boyer, Maitlin Huffman, and David Gunby. By selecting the

Whitman's victims were hit on all sides of the Tower and at widespread locations and distances. This image depicts the locations of 25 of 46 of his victims on August 1, 1966, and illustrates the extent to which no person on or near the University campus was safe if in view of the observation deck of the Tower.

midpoint of the upper terrace as his constant, Whitman could quickly and accurately adjust his aim according to the approximate distance each target was from that midpoint.

Assuming "Betty" did encounter him on the Drag on July 29 and 30, he was probably there to step off distances in anticipation of the work he was planning. The selection of 89 yards—not 85 or 90 or 100—was intentional, but he probably did some additional measuring and stepping off, as well as determining lines of sight, in order to know where to look for targets at other places, and how to aim to hit them, during his hurried work on the coming Monday.

But would anyone as meticulous as Charles Whitman be satisfied with just mathematical calculations and measuring distances by counting paces? Wouldn't he have wanted to verify by actually firing the 6 mm. rifle from an elevation of 250 to 300 feet at targets almost directly below him? Hard to say, but the answer to the question could shed light on the answer to another—how long in advance of August 1 did he make specific plans and preparations?

Assuming he did prepare, where could he possibly have gone to replicate shooting from the Tower? Where in the vicinity of Austin is there a site suitable for such verification and practice?

Rock squirrels are moderately bushy-tailed rodents with mottled grayish brown fur that make their homes in rocky areas. As large or larger than a tree squirrel, they can cause damage by burrowing, feeding on crop seeds, tunneling beneath structures, and making holes in playgrounds and parks, such that groundskeepers and others charged with maintenance responsibilities welcome their elimination.[6]

There is a colony of rock squirrels that inhabits the rocks and rip-rap at the base of Mansfield Dam (Lake Travis) on the spillway side.[7] The height of Mansfield Dam is 278 feet, and when Whitman's old friend, Francis Schuck, was asked where Charles might have gone to simulate shooting from the Tower, Schuck's unhesitant suggestion was that he might have gotten permission to shoot rock squirrels from Mansfield Dam. He admitted not knowing if Whitman actually did so, but he also said there was a lot that Whitman did in that category.[8] Besides, the timing for doing so in preparation for August 1, 1966 would have been in the fifth stage of Whitman's life, and Schuck was closest to him during the second and third stages.

A man who grew up near the dam and then worked in LCRA's hydro-electric division for 36 years recalled that it was common for young men to shoot rock squirrels and other things from the dam in the 50s and early 60s. There were no houses nearby, and it was unlikely that anyone who did it bothered to get permission. His only proviso was that whereas shooting with a .22 probably wouldn't have been noticed, that prolonged shooting with a high-powered rifle would have been heard and the shooter would have been asked to stop.[9]

It is all speculation, of course, but Whitman acquired the 6 mm. rifle in late 1965, the rock squirrels went into hibernation for the winter and did not come out until spring, the observation deck was closed after the August, 1965 fire and did not open until April or May, and Whitman would not have known when it would open until it did. That suggests that on some day or days between early May and late July that Whitman might have gone to Mansfield Dam, possibly with permission from an LCRA administration happy to be rid of the burrowing rodents, to pick off rock squirrels while pretending they were students on the South Mall. Based on the experience, he could have verified that for shots at or near 89 yards of the base of the dam, a visual adjustment of his aim within the Leopold scope of negative 6.5 mill dots spelled bad news for rock squirrels, as well as innocent people who meant him no greater harm than the squirrels.

The foregoing, when combined with $3.65, gets one a cup of coffee at Starbucks, but for those who want to speculate, it supports the argument that Charles Whitman began working seriously toward fulfillment of his delusional fantasy weeks or months before he implemented it.

That is not the premise of this book. Its authors believe he did not decide to actually climb the Tower until July 30, and the fact that he needed to slap a little piece of adhesive tape on the butt of his rifle to remind him where to aim, as opposed to having the information well-entrenched in his brain based on careful preparation, supports that opinion. Still, he obviously fantasized about climbing the Tower for years in advance, he loved to shoot, and it would have been totally in keeping with his personality to practice fulfilling his private little dream, just in case it ever became reality.

---

1. Calculations performed by Kyle Wineman, firearms consultant, May 15-20, 2015. Mr. Wineman is an experienced shooter familiar with the intricacies of ballistics, and his grandfather was a sniper in the Vietnam War who helped him analyze and verify the numbers on Whitman's piece of adhesive tape.

2. Bill Helmer, "The Madman in the Tower, *Texas Monthly*, August 1966.

3. To quote Webb: "The unique conditions of a cold bore shot are not simply a matter of human factors. Yes, that's part of it: we had to learn how to be at the top of our game instantly, with no opportunity to warm up and shake it out with a few practice shots. But there's also pure physics involved, because the bullet itself behaves very differently when the rifle itself is cold. As you start shooting rounds through a metal chamber it starts heating up, creating an increase in chamber pressure, which translates into a change in the bullet's trajectory. Put a bullet through a hot chamber and it may travel as much as a few hundred feet per second faster than when you put it through a cold chamber. Elevation—how far the bullet travels before succumbing to gravity and beginning its inevitable downward arc—is profoundly affected. This is why snipers are careful to track and log our cold bore data." Brandon Webb, *The Red Circle*, excerpted at http://navyseals.com/2030/navy-seal-sniper-school-by-brandon-webb/ (March 20, 2013).

4. Emails from Rachael Penman, Exhibits Manager, Crime Museum, Washington, DC, May 18 & 19, June 23, 2015.

5. If one applies the previously described formula and adds Whitman's height into the equation it reveals that he shot from 237 feet at an estimated range of 89 yards, or 267 feet, which yields a cosine of .7477 and an angle of 41.6 degrees and makes the point of aim 199 feet. Considering this result one would need to adjust -6.5 MOA to accurately hit a target at that range from that elevation. Wineman, *supra*.

6. Jon Boren and Byron Wright, "Controlling Rock Squirrel Damage in New Mexico," New Mexico State University, March 2003, http://aces.nmsu.edu/pubs/_circulars/CR574.pdf

7. E.g., Jean W. Saile, "History of Apache Shores, " http://www.apacheshorespoa.com/web124/news24_Histoyofapacheshoresbyjeansaile.asp.

8. Emails from Francis Schuck, May 20 & 21, 2015.

9. Telephone interview of Keith Hamilton, May 29, 2015.

CHAPTER SIX

The First 30 Minutes

"Oh Monday morning, you gave me no warning, of what was to be."
-from Monday Monday, by the Mamas and the Papas, 1966

"[O]n that day I came to know, with absolute certainty, that I have the capacity to kill someone. That is how outraged I became. That is the stain the shooter tattooed on me."

-Bob Higley, U.T. student on August 1, 1966

Charles Whitman peered over the edge of the Tower. Beneath him, lives were spread out like tablecloths at a picnic, lives that were leaves on the story tree, lives that were an interruption of death of very short duration, lives that were no business of his.

Although most victims and participants did not know each other, some did or had a connection in the nature of six degrees of separation. One whose experience was particularly remarkable was Alfred McAlister. He was a member of the Austin High Class of '66, which meant he knew several of the people who would be involved in the day's events. In particular he was a good friend of Paul Sonntag's, had been on the high school swim team with him and was a fellow surfer. He was taking a couple of courses at U.T. that summer but instead of being on campus to go to class, he was there to hang out playing nine ball pool with friends.

Law enforcement officers firing at the sniper on the Tower from the roof of a campus building.

McAlister had ridden his Honda motorcycle to the campus that morning, parked it near the Student Union, and went inside, about 11:15, to the Chuck Wagon, which was the snack bar, coffee shop, and a gathering place for various groups of students.[1] One of those consisted of students who were beginning to let their hair grow, who were opposed to the Vietnam War, and some of whom were members of the Students for Democratic Society, or SDS. Alfred considered them to be the coolest kids on campus, and had, of course, heard them called "hippies."

There was a crowd that day, and amongst the crowd was a woman Alfred considered the "belle of the ball," the most beautiful, most well-spoken, most opinionated, and most influential. She was drop dead gorgeous, even though pregnant, or maybe because she was pregnant. She was PROUD of her condition, and she had an aura about her. Alfred recalled that when she walked around a table, everyone there, and at the next table too, would follow her with their eyes and when she started talking everybody would get quiet. Her name was Claire Wilson.

Alfred McAlister (formerly Alfred Gallessich) was a freshman at the university on August 1, 1966, a friend of two of those killed, and an admirer of Claire Wilson, Whitman's first victim. A future professor at U.T., McAlister was waiting on one of the two friends, Thomas Eckman, when Eckman was killed, and then ran to the aid of the other, not knowing it was Paul Sonntag until later. Like both Whitman and Houston McCoy, McAlister was an Eagle Scout.

Alfred did not know her, had never gotten within ten feet of her, and he'd only intended to stop by for a few moments, grab a Dr. Pepper and donut, and then head downstairs to the basement floor of the Student Union for a few hours of nine ball. There was a bowling alley down there too, but he and his friends only cared about playing pool, and chances are they would tie the table up for the rest of the day.

Then he saw something that stopped him in his tracks. Standing next to the pregnant woman was Thomas Eckman. He and Tom had been in Boy Scouts together. Alfred had become an Eagle

Scout, and when he was 12 and Tom was 13 they had attended St. Edwards University, which had a junior and senior high school back then. Alfred and Tom had been at school together, had attended scout meetings and gone on campouts, and had been buddies, but they'd not seen each other for nearly five years. Now Eckman was back and he was with the woman Alfred most wanted to meet. They were together and had just stood up as if to leave.

Alfred made a beeline for Thomas, who recognized him immediately, and they quickly agreed that they needed to spend some time together and catch up. Thomas did not introduce Alfred to Claire, who was busy assuring her friends that she'd soon return. Instead, he said "I'm about to walk my girlfriend out, but I'll be right back. Are you going to be around?"

Alfred said yes, that he would be in the pool room. Tom promised to be back in no more than 15 minutes. He and Claire left the Chuck Wagon and exited the Student Union onto the South Mall. Alfred headed downstairs. His friends were already there and playing.

Five minutes passed, then ten, then fifteen. Alfred was still slightly aglow with the excitement of running into Thomas, but what was taking him so long? Someone came dashing down the stairs. Alfred looked up hopefully but it wasn't Tom. It was a kid Alfred didn't know and he was shouting, "There's a shooter on campus, in the Tower, he's shooting people, swear to God!" What Alfred would not learn until later was that Eckman was already dead, Claire was wounded, and Paul Sonntag had just moments to live.

Claire was Whitman's first target, and she was, of course, actually two lives.

Claire Wilson may have personified the 1960s and Austin, Texas. Only 18 but harboring political views that ran counter to conservative tradition, with civil rights activism, life in a commune, opposition to the Vietnam War, gun control advocacy, spiritual awakening, and teaching on her dance card, she might have been a poster child for the nascent counter culture movement with which the decade, and to a lesser degree, the City, have since been branded. She was also unwed and cohabitating with a man who was not the father of her child. However, her immediate destiny was for different symbolism and a different, literally embryonic, notoriety.

Strolling across the campus with Thomas Eckman that morning, her thoughts were light-years away from danger and threat. The day was particularly hot, the temperature close to 100, unpleasant for most folks and brutal for a pregnant woman nearing term. They were walking on the "upper terrace" of the "South Mall," a cemented area of the University of Texas campus just south of the Main Building, or Tower, near Inner Upper Campus Drive.

Both opposed the Vietnam War, and both were members of the SDS, which had roots stretching back to the early part of the century, although its image was just beginning to be considered radical. The University of Texas chapter had existed since 1964, and until recently the organization's primary concern had been civil rights and opposition to segregation, but within the last year its focus had shifted to opposition to the war.

Predictably, SDS-like attitudes attracted negative press in Texas. Reporting on an anti-war rally the previous October, a *Dallas Morning News* article described the protesters as "shaggy-maned" and "homegrown leftists," with "shoulder-length hair," "T-shirts, sandals, leotards and dirty jeans."[2] If that was the SDS image, it had not been adopted by either Claire Wilson or Tom Eckman. She was wearing a plain maternity dress with a wide white collar and sensible shoes. He had hair just barely over the top of his ears, sported black horn-rimmed glasses and was clad in a short-sleeved plaid shirt and light trousers. His only mark of allegiance to left-wing fashion was a wispy moustache.

Claire and Tom had classes in the afternoon, and although they lived in an apartment not far from campus, Claire's condition caused them to drive to campus and park. Now they needed to return to their car and feed the parking meter. They were holding hands as they walked. Tom was concerned that she was not getting enough nutrition for the baby and she had just told him that she had had a glass of orange juice that morning.

They did not know that there was a man staring through a telescopic sight at them, or that they had an indirect connection with him. Earlier that summer they had taken care of the son and the house of a husband and wife named Hamilton for a few weeks while the couple was out of the country. It was an ideal arrangement for everyone—a place to stay near campus, rent free, while getting paid to boot. The son, Toby, turned out to be a joy to be around, and he wrote later that "By the time my parents came back, I wished I lived with Tom and Claire."[3] Toby was a boy scout, a member of Troop 5, which was sponsored by an Austin Methodist Church. His scoutmaster for most of 1965 had been the man now peering through the telescopic sights.

At 11:48 a.m. Claire and Tom stepped into the brilliant, butter-colored sunshine and walked toward the center of the upper terrace of the South Mall. Nearby, from high up on the biscuit-colored tower, a loud noise rang out.

The shot was low but true, more than true. Claire Wilson dropped to the sidewalk.

Tom Eckman stared in disbelief. "Baby, what's wrong?" he asked, reaching toward her. They were his last words. A second shot hit Eckman in the shoulder. The bullet passed through muscle and into his heart. He fell beside Claire.

"Tom!" she cried out. She was not in pain, not yet, but felt as though she had stepped on a live electric wire, and now a heavy force seemed to be pressing her down. Tom did not answer. Claire did not understand what was happening, but she suspected that Tom was dying if not already dead. She would later state, "I knew immediately that I'd lost the baby. By the eighth month, your baby's moving a lot. And after I got shot, the baby never moved."[4]

A man in a gray suit walked by. "Please," Claire shouted, "get a doctor, please!" The man stared at her with a look of disgust. "Get up," he said, "what do you think you're doing?"

A sign of the times. The man thought she was protesting the Vietnam War, participating in guerrilla theater. As if intuiting her political beliefs and punishing her, he walked on.

As the man did so the cross hairs of Whitman's four-power telescopic sight mounted on the bolt action deer rifle located some 250 feet away and above settled on Dr. Robert Boyer, a 33 year old physics professor and Rhodes scholar, possibly the man who had just dismissed Claire Wilson and her plea for help. Boyer had taught applied mathematics at U.T. the previous year, had just completed a teaching assignment in Mexico, and was about to leave for a teaching job in Liverpool, England, where his pregnant wife and two children were awaiting him. He had arrived on campus ten minutes before, at 11:40. He was a brilliant man with a brilliant future, but the world would be denied what that brilliance might have delivered.

He had a 12:30 lunch engagement with the man who had driven him to the university, Robert Palter, and had just tended to some business in the Main Building and was on the upper-terrace of the South Mall only a few feet from Claire Wilson and Tom Eckman, walking south toward the steps from the upper terrace next to the statue of Jeff Davis. Whether he was the man to whom Ms. Wilson cried out to for help is lost to history, but both were wearing a suit and tie.[5]

The shot hit him in the lower back, destroying a kidney. He fell down the steps, which made it possible for others to reach his body and get him to an ambulance driven by Morris Hohmann, who got him to Brackenridge Hospital at 12:12, the first victim to arrive.

The game was on, but only one player knew the rules. Other players could only react. Their fight or flight adrenaline molecules stopped and stared at each other in confused disbelief.

There is some small debate about the exact moment when Whitman opened fire. The consensus is 11:48, and the non-quintuple nature of that figure tends to make it credible. However, Cheryl Botts was certain the clock on the tower was at 11:50 when she and Don Walden left the observation deck to step inside.[6] If that was so, then Whitman would not have had time to start shooting at people below—after moving the desk, loading his shotgun, shooting the Gabours, and shooting Edna Townsley—until close to 11:55. There were also police officers and U.T. Security guards whose post-action reports indicate that they first received reports about the shootings at or within a couple of minutes after 11:48, and although the first reports went out quickly, they did not go out immediately. All of the radio messages and "chatter," beginning with Professor Michael Hall's call to the APD at 11:52 a.m. have been preserved, and the first officer summoned by the APD dispatcher was Officer Houston McCoy in unit 219, also at 11:52.[7] He was the first summoned, and he would be the one who would end it all.

Nailing down the exact time of the first shot from the Tower is not critically important, but it establishes the duration of the siege, considering that the time of its conclusion is not in doubt, and it helps determine the order in which Whitman's victims were killed and wounded.

Whitman was living out a fantasy, different from the thousands of modern video gamers who play *Grand Theft Auto, Call of Duty,* and dozens of other electronic shooting games only in its reality. The first 30 minutes of that fantasy were the best from his twisted perspective, because he had a target-rich field of view and no return fire. That would change significantly by 12:15, but before then he dashed from place to place along the narrow observation deck walkway with no challenge other than selecting victims. He had placed his three rifles at different locations along the observation deck wall, and the different sounding reports from different locations caused nearly everyone to believe there were two or more snipers.

He may have chosen to initially stay on the south and west sides of the Tower because in earlier trips to the observation deck he reconnoitered shooting positions from the different sides and decided the south and west sides were best for his purposes. Those two sides looked down on the open South and West Malls, whereas the East Mall is smaller and shaded by trees. The south and west sides also provided the best view of the doors from outside that police would use. Also, not only did the north and east sides offer less inviting targets, but once return fire commenced, those sides offered good cover to the police officers and others who fired back. Still, Whitman worked his way around the entire tower during his reverse siege because people on all four sides reported seeing him in their respective areas at one time or several.

Next to fall was David Gunby, a 23-year-old electrical engineering student from Dallas. Wearing Bermuda shorts and a sports shirt, he'd exited the library moments before, but left a book behind—a small incident in life that made all the difference—so he turned around to retrieve it and was walking across the upper terrace, directly below the Tower. Whitman had to lean out and shoot almost straight down. The projectile entered Gunby's left arm, went into his back and down, severed his small intestine and scattered bullet fragments into his kidney. He would be taken to Brackenridge where doctors would make a surprising discovery. For the rest of his life he would have a lot of reasons to remember what Whitman did to him, although he would rarely speak of it. Technically he would become the last person Whitman killed.

The next victim was Deaverau "Matlin" Huffman, a 31-year-old graduate student working on his doctorate in psychology. He was wearing a black suit with a white shirt and tie because he had taught a course that morning. He had just left the Psychology Building and was walking across the South Mall when Whitman saw him and put a bullet into his right arm, breaking it and causing it to bleed steadily. Although not a

David Gunby lying wounded on the upper terrace of the South Mall. Gunby was shot after exiting the library, where he'd gone to retrieve a book he left behind after studying. His wounds were not immediately fatal, but they required a kidney transplant and dialysis three times a week. He died on November 12, 2001, after declining further treatment. His cause of death was listed as homicide and he is considered Whitman's 17th fatality.

serious wound, he would lie face down near bushes on the upper terrace for more than half an hour, losing two pints of blood.[8]

The Office of the Dean of the Graduate School was located in the Main Building and had windows that looked onto the South Mall. Air conditioning in the office meant the windows were closed and the ambient noise prevented its occupants from hearing the sound of gunshots outside and above. One of the office's secretaries, Charlotte Darehshori, had been working there only a month. When she looked out a window and either saw three people lying on the ground or actually saw them fall—reports differ—she immediately ran outside to assist them.

She was 24, married with a three-year-old daughter. Slender and attractive, dressed in a blue sleeveless shift, wearing her brown hair in the puffy style that was popular in the mid-60s, she did not know why three people were on the ground, only that she should help. When she was nearly to the first body, either Gunby or Huffman, she heard and saw shots being fired from above. She headed for the nearest cover, a huge concrete and steel base of a large flagpole. The concrete apron was two feet tall and the tapering metal base provided another foot of protection. She sat down on its south side, out of Whitman's view, and tucked her legs beneath her demurely. There she would remain for the next hour and a half, unable to help or be helped, but a photo taken of her by a UPI photographer became one of the iconic images of the day.

It was still not 12:00. The first phone call to the Austin Police Department came in at 11:52 from History professor Michael Hall. He'd heard a loud crack and stepped outside to see what was happening. Seeing a body in a pool of blood, either Gunby or Huffman, and another student cringing behind a tree and looking toward the top of the Tower, he ran to a phone.

U.T. Traffic Control Officer Allen R. Hamilton reported later that he received the first call about shootings inside the Tower at 11:48, and by 11:55, U.T. Security officers L. W. Gebert and Jack O. Rodman were on the way up, although unarmed. University security officers were not sworn peace officers and did not carry firearms. Their principal duty was traffic control and campus access. Rodman had given Whitman his parking permit. Just then their principal concern was to evacuate the Tower, lock it down and assist any wounded who were inside.

Shelton Williams, U.T. senior and classmate of Whitman's, was driving on Guadalupe in his brand-new, red 1966 Mustang. He was from West Texas and was showing his sister-in-law, who was visiting from Midland, the City of Austin. He stopped at a red light outside the University Co-op, The song *Monday, Monday*, by the Mamas and the Papas, was playing on the radio when he heard the first gunshots and knew immediately what they were.[9]

It was then 11:56, and Whitman shifted his position from the south central part of the Tower walkway to the southeast corner. His next two victims shared a name that was prominent on the U.T. campus. Major George W. Littlefield, a Confederate veteran of the 8th Texas Cavalry, lived in a Victorian home built in 1893 located beside the campus at 24th and Whitis Streets. Despite being wounded so severely in 1863 that he could not walk without crutches, Littlefield became a successful businessman, banker and cattleman, as well as a philanthropist who made numerous significant contributions to the University before he died in 1920.[10]

Adrian and Brenda Littlefield were a young married couple, aged only 19 and 17 respectively. He was about to become an evangelist for the

United Pentecostal Church, and she worked on campus. Like other University employees, she'd come to campus to pick up her paycheck, and they were walking away from the Main Building and were on the east side of the quadrangle, about 25 yards from the base of the Tower, when Whitman targeted them and fired three times. Adrian was hit in the back and the bullet entered his stomach. Brenda was shot in the left hip. His wound was serious but hers was not. It would be half an hour before he could be evacuated and taken to Brackenridge Hospital.

Thomas Ashton was 22 and from Redlands, California. He and 26 other Peace Corps volunteers had arrived in Austin on June 20 for training at the University before they went overseas. Ashton was going to teach English in Iran, then a stable, friendly nation under the rule of the Shah, and was scheduled to ship out on September 14. He had just finished a class and was planning to meet other Peace Corps members for lunch in the Student Union, but was then on the roof of a University building called the Computation Center, probably to meet a girl. He heard shots and looked west, trying to ascertain what was going on higher up on the campus. A bullet ripped into the left side of his chest, near his heart. It did not kill him instantly, but he died a little more than an hour and a half later at Brackenridge at 1:35 p.m.

It had taken two minutes for Whitman to shoot the Littlefields and Ashton. He then dashed from the southeast corner to the southwest corner of the Tower and looked down. He saw two young ladies, both University employees who worked in the Main Building, Nancy Harvey and Ellen Evganides. They had seen a University security officer enter the building and rush up the stairs before they walked out the door, and just as they exited the building they heard the shots that hit the Littlefields. A security guard also heard the shots, but believed they came from inside the Tower. He told them it was safe to go outside, so they did and began walking west toward the Drag, planning to go to lunch.

Like Claire Wilson, Nancy Harvey was pregnant, but was only four and half months along and her back was to Whitman so he could not have known. Similarly, he did not know that she, like him, was from Lake Worth, Florida. As they walked, Whitman was taking up position in the southwest corner and the pair was almost 100 yards from the base of the Tower when someone shouted "Hey, you shouldn't be out there!" Puzzled, they looked in the direction of the caller. Whitman fired. The bullet hit Nancy in the hip. A second shot missed, but ricocheted into

Ellen's left leg. Neither woman fell. Instead they hobbled for cover between the Student Union building and the Academic Center. One of them, almost certainly Ellen, ran into the Student Union, crying and terrified, and past Don Vandiver.

Don was a student but also a reporter for the *Austin American Statesman*. He'd started school at Amarillo College, and had been awarded a scholarship and a job with the Amarillo *Globe News* when his theme, one required of all freshmen, was selected as the best of his class. He hadn't even known he was in a competition, but he wasn't the least hesitant to quit his "wonderful" job at a sheet metal fabrication shop to become a reporter. The next year he won another journalism scholarship that paid his tuition, books and fees, plus a monthly stipend, at the University of Texas so long as he could maintain a B average or better. He transferred to U.T. in the fall of 1965 as a junior, and an editor at the *Globe News*, Bonnie Merriman, put in a good word for him at the *Statesman*. The next thing he knew he was a reporter there.

He didn't have the greatest working schedule available—3 p.m. until midnight on Friday, Saturday, and Sunday nights—but it was an ideal arrangement for a student and he sometimes worked on weekdays when other reporters were on vacation or absent. He was not working that Monday, but had an 8 a.m. class, after which he went back home, then returned to meet a friend for lunch at the Chuck Wagon. When he didn't see the friend, about a quarter of 12, he made use of the time by walking to the bulletin board in the hall leading to the door to the South Mall and scanning it for ads for apartments for rent or roommates wanted. Don lived too far from campus to walk to class, and often there was no parking available closer than eight or ten blocks away. He was hoping to find something nearer to campus for the fall semester.

He was reading the various notices on the bulletin board when a girl dashed in from the South Mall, screaming, crying, and running as fast as she could. The lighting in the hallway was not bright, so it did not register on Don that the black stains on her dress might be blood. His immediate impression was that she or someone had spilled ink on her, ruining the dress, which was why she was so upset. The possibility of a fraternity prank also crossed his mind. She did not pause to explain, but kept running and crying.

Don's curiosity was aroused, so he went outside to see what was happening. There was a crash bar exit door near the bulletin board that gave out into a triangular-shaped area between the Student Union and the Academic Center, and he went through it. Outside he saw an odd sight. There were a few trees on the West Mall, and two boys were crouching—obviously hiding—on opposite sides of the same tree. Don stared at them, wondering, when he heard a shot. Rather than suggest the irrational truth, the sound supported his suspicion that one of the fraternities—Kappa Alpha—was up to something. Kappa Alpha was the "Old South" fraternity, famous for honoring the Confederacy, staging antebellum-style balls and for firing a black powder cannon the U.T. chapter owned. The thought that skipped across Don's mind was "the Kappa Alphas have got their cannon out and they're scaring people to death."

Then he heard another shot. Like most young men in Texas, Don grew up around firearms and hunting, and the thought that followed the shot was "that crack, that doesn't sound like that old cannon. That sounds like my deer rifle." A third shot eliminated all doubt. It hit the window of the second floor landing of the Student Union, scattering shards near where Don was standing. He still didn't know where the shots were

The bodies of Thomas Eckman, Claire Wilson, David Gunby, Maitlin Huffman, and Rita Jones lying on the upper terrace of the South Mall during the shooting spree. Eckman was dead and Jones was unhurt. The others were wounded and survived, although Gunby's death in 2001 was caused by the wounds inflicted by Whitman and was recorded as a homicide.

coming from, but he knew he wasn't in a safe place. Rather than return to the Student Union, he dashed to the Academic Center, through a door into its basement and then up to the first floor, from which he could see through large glass doors onto the West and Main Malls. He saw bodies on the ground, people hiding, and others shouting to or restraining fellow students from stepping into the open.

Not merely "the open." The U.T. campus had become a killing field.[11]

Don Vandiver was the only newspaper reporter in Austin who was on the U.T. campus from the beginning to the end of Whitman's shooting spree, and who then played a role in the events of the immediate aftermath. However, due to a collection of factors beyond his control, he did not receive the credit that his actions and reporting merited, and was even overlooked and treated unfairly in a couple of ways. The whole experience caused him to turn away from a promising career as a journalist and toward becoming an attorney.

Whitman's shot through the Student Union window was his next after he wounded Harvey and Evgenides. The window was open and he probably saw a thirty-year-old student, Dolores Ortega, standing on the right side. Three others, students named John Scott Allen and Bill Helmer, plus another girl, were observing as though the window was an IMAX screen. Whitman added the ultimate in 3-D effect.

Helmer had been outside when the shooting started, had seen the shooter, and had thought "Just look at that! There's some fool up there with a rifle, trying to get himself in one hell of a lot of trouble!" Then he heard others yelling about students being shot and joined in, shouting at a student on the sidewalk near the Littlefield Home to take cover, which caused the student to stop and look in puzzlement until Whitman opened up on him with the semiautomatic M-1 carbine. He dashed to the protection of an alley with bullets snapping about.

Helmer then went to the Student Union and the stairwell window that afforded a good and, he thought, safe view of the Tower. A girl in a white blouse, Ortega, was on the right-hand side with the other girl, so he went to the left where Allen was standing and looked over his shoulder. They could see the sniper, who would lean out over the parapet, aim, fire, tip the weapon up to work the action, then walk calmly to another point and do the same thing. The Tower clock started chiming the noon hour.

Pom-pom-pom-pom... 16 notes, high and sweet. Some say the chimes say a poem:

Lord, through this hour
Be Thou my guide,
For in Thy power
I do confide.

After the chimes, there is a long pause—23 seconds if you hold a wrist-watch on it... Then the hammer gathers itself and bongs 12 times against the 3 1/2-ton bell in stately cadence—measured tones, but soft and mellow. A practiced man could aim down campus and fire numerous times during its swell of sound.[12]

Seconds after the echoes died Whitman put a shot through the open window where the four students were watching. The bullet struck the outside edge of the window near Ortega's face, filling the stairwell with glass, splinters, bullet fragments, and concrete dust. All four dropped to the floor, Dolores flat on her back, hands to her face, screaming. Helmer thought "Son of a bitch! This guy is *good*,"[13] and started crawling to her on hands and knees. His left hand slipped on blood and he nearly fell on his face. It was coming from the right forearm of Allen, which was pumping it out in rapid squirts about three inches high.

The upper terrace of the South Mall as it appeared in 2015

Helmer turned back to Allen and shouted for someone to give him a handkerchief. Allen used his good arm to pull one from his back pocket and hand it to him and he used it as a tourniquet. Ortega had debris in her eyes and was cut by glass but was okay. Other students ran up the stairs, one of whom needed convincing by Helmer that the blood with which he was spattered was not his own. While washing up in the basement men's room, Helmer discovered what looked like a shaving cut on his neck that held a tiny piece of copper jacket from the bullet. The realization that it could have been a larger chunk made it hard for him to breathe.[14]

A different pair attracted Whitman's attention. Oscar Royvela was a 21-year-old from Bolivia attending the University on a "Good Neighbor Scholarship." The GNS was a program sponsored by Texas and offered to students born in and a resident of a nation in the Western Hemisphere other than Cuba or the United States who did not have dual citizenship and who planned to return to their native country after completing their studies. After considering 40 colleges, Oscar chose U.T. because it was economical and had a good engineering program.

He met his girlfriend, Irma Garcia, also 21, for lunch that day. She was from Harlingen, and when they heard shots, they walked out to see and were standing between Hogg Auditorium and the Biology Lab when a shot hit near them. As Oscar explained later that day:

> I grabbed Irma's hand and said 'Let's start running,' At that time, she got hit. Her flesh opened like a flower. Her back was torn open. I couldn't believe what I was seeing. So, I fell to the ground. I was asking people to help Irma. No one was coming. I stood up again. A blast hit me in the back. It just missed my lung, broke two ribs and went through my left arm. I started vomiting blood. I thought I was going to die. Then this boy with a beard dragged us back.[15]

The boy with the beard was either Jack Pennington or Jack Stephens. Both were nearby and immediately dashed to help. One of the Jacks grabbed Oscar by his feet, the other grabbed Irma's, and they dragged them unceremoniously out of the open and behind cover to safety.

Whitman shifted positions. His new field of fire was Guadalupe Street, "The Drag," which borders the campus on the west. He moved from the

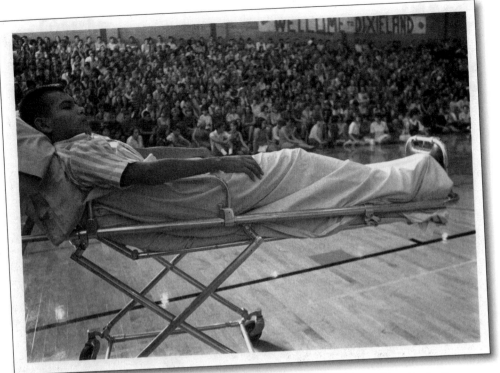

southeast corner to the center of the west side of the walkway, from which he could focus on pedestrians along Guadalupe and have a clear field of view along 23rd and 24th streets. He then began what would be the deadliest seven minutes of the day, the first target of which may have been his favorite.

Alex Hernandez[16] was 17, the oldest of eleven children, and he earned money for the family by selling the *Austin American Statesman*. He did not usually sell papers along the Drag, but that day he was standing in for a boy who was on vacation. Alex and an 11-year-old cousin were riding together on a bicycle, the bag of newspapers thrown over both their shoulders in order to reduce the weight on one, but which caused them to be harnessed together.

Here was a moving target, Whitman's specialty. He took aim, led the boys just enough, and squeezed the trigger. The bullet smashed into Alex's hip and blew out the top of his leg, breaking the femur bone and exiting into the bicycle seat. The boys flew together, away from the toppling bike and onto the hard pavement.

Alex lay back, going slowly into shock. His little cousin tried to help him, tears running down his cheeks, but Alex mumbled "you can't help me, go and hide," before slipping into unconsciousness. Bystanders ran forward and pulled the boy out of the street and into a shaded area across the Drag from the University Co-op and out of the line of Whitman's shots.

Whitman had many targets to choose from and he fired rapidly, zeroing in on an area near the corner of 24th and Guadalupe. Furthermore, traffic on the Drag and the bustle on the sidewalks at the noon hour masked the sounds of his shooting. It was heard, but was not loud enough to be instantly alarming. He fired brazenly from the top of the wall, rarely missing, his white head band visible to those who saw him. Between shots he took cover along the observation deck, ran along the walkway, then popped up to aim and fire again.

Karen Griffith was next. She was about to begin her senior year at Lanier High School, where Kathy Whitman had taught for a year and at which she was scheduled to teach again. If Karen had not had a class under Mrs. Whitman, she certainly knew who she was. She had probably seen Kathy's handsome, blond-headed hunk of a husband pick her up from school, had probably gossiped and giggled about him with other girls her age. Good-looking young ladies like Karen noticed good-looking young men like Charlie, particularly one married to an attractive female teacher. Never in any thought she had ever had

Beautiful, 17-year-old Karen Griffith was a senior at Lanier High School, where Whitman's wife, Kathy, taught. She was shot while walking on "The Drag" and died on August 8, 1966

about Mr. Whitman did she muse about him killing her from somewhere in the sky.

She was walking north, unaware she was in danger. A bullet smashed into her chest, destroyed her right lung, and seriously damaged the left one. At Brackenridge, surgeons removed what remained of the right lung and tried desperately to keep her alive. She held on for a week, and was the last to die immediately after the shooting, on August 8.

Thomas Karr was supposed to be in class, but he had decided to cut. The 24-year-old student and ex-serviceman from Spur, Texas had just taken a Spanish test for which he'd studied all night, and he was walking toward his apartment on 28th Street. He was an honor student at Arlington State College and was attending U.T. just for the summer. He was walking south on the Drag and saw Karen Griffith get shot. He started toward her to help, but a bullet from Whitman intervened. It caught him on the left side of his back, traveled through his body and exited on the right side, dropping him instantly. It was a major wound but he hung on through an ambulance ride to Brackenridge, then died during surgery an hour and ten minutes later.

Karr was a large, muscular man who was an easier target than the moving Hernandez or the petite Griffith, and so was Whitman's next target. Harry Walchuk stood six feet tall and weighed 186 pounds. He was 38, a navy veteran, the father of six, and employed as a political science teacher at Alpena Community College in Michigan. He had graduated from U.T. 12 years earlier and returned to work on his doctorate, for which he had been studying at the library before walking to the Drag for lunch. He'd stopped at a newsstand along the sidewalk to ask for a magazine that was not available, and was wearing a white shirt. A pipe was in his mouth.

Either when he heard the shots that took Griffith and Karr or saw them prone on the sidewalk, he turned in their direction, presenting a full frontal, stationary target, an easy shot for Whitman. The bullet hit him in the chest and traveled at a downward angle. Blood blossomed on his shirt, and as he fell his pipe dropped first and made a clinking, musical sound on the sidewalk, so loud that multiple by-standers mentioned it. The bullet seemed to have taken lessons in deadliness. It hit his lungs, heart, stomach, and spleen. Walchuk's death made three in a row for Whitman, his version of a hat trick, the only one of the day.

David Mattson, Roland Ehlke, and Tom Herman were three more Peace Corps volunteers, and they were walking on the Drag intending to go the

Student Union and have lunch with Thomas Ashe, having no idea that their friend was already dying. All four were scheduled to go to Iran in another six weeks. Mattson was from Minneapolis and Ehlke was from Milwaukee. Whitman drew a bead on the trio, hoping perhaps to score a trifecta and get all three with one shot. If so he was partially successful. His bullet hit Matson in the right wrist and Ehlke in the right arm and both legs. Herman was not harmed.

The nearest store was Sheftall's Jewelry Store, and the boys hobbled and crawled toward its open door. A 64-year-old employee named Homer Kelley stepped outside and helped them get inside as Whitman targeted the store. At least two rounds came through the large plate glass door, which stayed intact but from which slivers of glass flew, nearly as deadly as the bullets. One of the bullets hit Kelley in the leg, making him Whitman's oldest victim of the day. Ehlke, despite his three wounds, later insisted on going out to help others on the sidewalk, and was shot again, this time in the right arm, thereby gaining the distinctions of being the only victim shot twice, as well as the victim with the most wounds.[17]

About that time, shortly after Alex Hernandez was shot, the floor manager of the University Co-op began what would be one of the most heroic actions by a citizen that day. Allen Crum was no stranger to gunfire or duty. He had served 22 years in the Air Force, starting as an 18-year-old B-52 tail gunner during World War Two and working his way up to master sergeant. Now he was set to become Gettysburg's John Burns of the U.T. Tower shootings.

At first he thought the commotion around Hernandez was a fight, and he started to go across the street to break it up. Then he heard shots and began shouting for people to take cover. He reached Hernandez and directed that the boy be moved to a safer area near the entrance of the West Mall. He instructed some students about what to do to staunch the youngster's bleeding, which might have saved his life, then ran back across the street to the Co-op, where he told customers inside what was happening and that they should stay inside away from the windows.

One of those he instructed was a freshman named Saralynn Lankford, who had graduated from Austin High School in May and who was registered to begin classes at Smith in September. The daughter of a U.T. professor, Dr. Charles Lankford, she was also a friend of Paul Sonntag, Carla Sue Wheeler, and Claudia Rutt, classmates who were then chatting on the sidewalk. Instead of joining them, she spent the next hour and a half safe, hiding behind a book shelf.

From the Co-op, Crum went to the intersection of Guadalupe and 23rd to direct traffic away from the Drag, and after getting others to continue that effort, he found a phone and tried unsuccessfully to call his wife to assure her he was safe, which was not exactly true. He had decided to storm the Tower. He ran as far as the Academic Building and hid behind a pillar until Whitman shifted his fire from the Drag to the east side of the Tower. He crossed a driveway and entered the Tower through a west door, prepared to be in on the kill.[18]

Back on the Drag everyone had stopped what they were doing and were in the process of finding cover. Still, for most it simply did not register that evil was in the air and taking names. One of those was Paul Sonntag.

The tragedy of the Tower murders is personified in the handsome face of 18 year-old Paul Sonntag. A graduate of Austin High School, Paul was the son of a prominent Austin family. His grandfather, for whom he was named, was a speechwriter for LBJ and was KTBC TV's news director. Killed on the cusp of a bright future, his death continues to affect people discussed in this book after 50 years.

Among Whitman's many victims, Paul's death would touch off the most far-reaching grief. Paul's grandfather, for whom he had been named, was Paul Bolton, a former speech writer for LBJ. Paul's family knew the president, and Bolton was director of the news staff for the local radio and television stations Johnson had started. Many Austinites knew of Bolton from television and the radio, which added a touch of celebrity to Paul's life.

He was 18 and a member of the high school class best-represented and hit hardest by Whitman's shooting spree, being the 1966 senior class of Stephen F. Austin High School. Standing five foot nine and weighing 140, his charm was not his physical size but his charisma.

128

Acquaintances remembered him as always cheerful and upbeat, almost to the point of being bubbly, and being a leader rather than a follower.[19] He was devoted to the Beach Boys and to exuding a surfer image, which was more than mere facade. As did his friend, Alfred McAlister, he would make trips to the Gulf Coast, particularly after a storm, when he could. In fact, he was rarely seen wearing anything but a "surfer shirt" with broad alternating stripes of either white and red or white and blue, depending on which was clean and available. The shirts were intended to make a surfer easier to see among the waves. He was wearing the red and white one that day.

A lot of Paul's life centered around the water. In addition to surfing, he had been on the Austin High swim team until senior year, and had worked as a life guard at Reed Park, near his home on Pecos Street, for three summers. Now, one of the reasons he was on the Drag was because he had needed to come downtown to the City's Parks and Recreation office to pick up his last paycheck—$75.12 for two weeks' work. The other reason was to give his girlfriend, Claudia Rutt, a ride to a health clinic to get a polio shot.

Claudia was the love of Paul's life, but he was about to leave for school at the University of Colorado in Boulder, whereas she was going to attend Texas Christian University in Fort Worth. Claudia's dream was to become a ballet dancer, and in 1949, TCU had become the first university in the United States to offer a bachelor's degree in ballet. The School for Classical and Contemporary Dance at TCU was THE place to go for anyone serious about ballet, and Claudia was very serious.

Claudia was Jewish and Paul was a Methodist, which made their bond more significant. Paul was no stranger to Jewish customs and people. His all-around best friend in grade school, Roger Friedman, was Jewish. They were each other's first good friend from outside their respective religious communities, and even though the Sonntag and the Friedman families did not socialize, both sets of parents encouraged their sons to think progressively, to welcome diversity, and to have open minds. Roger had gone to McAllum High when Paul went to Austin High, so they had not seen each other much recently, but they were still tight.

After completing their two errands, Paul and Claudia had decided to go to the University Co-op to shop for records. They found a parking spot on the east side of the Drag, not far from the Co-op, which was a primary campus bookstore, so nearly every student at U.T. went there at least once. In addition to text books the Co-op sold school supplies, Longhorn souvenirs, clothes, practically anything a student might want to show his school pride, plus anything a student could use in his or her dorm room. That meant nothing to Claudia and Paul, of course, but the Co-op also had one of the best, most complete record album selections in the City.

They parked, dashed across the street, and immediately ran into an old friend, Hildy Griffith, who was in their graduating class at Austin High. She was going to go to U.T. In fact, she was already staying on campus at Kinsolving Dorm—THE dorm for young ladies from west Austin—and was attending freshman orientation. They chatted. The senior class of 1966 had been tight, and the feelings of camraderie had not dimmed since graduation. The class had left its mark, literally, although few outside the most popular, in-crowd members of the class knew about it. That mark was on the cover of the 1966 yearbook.

Austin High's mascot, or talisman, was the comet. They were the Austin High Comets just as the new pro football team in Dallas was the Cowboys, and each yearbook was called the Comet. Students, many seniors, made up the yearbook staff and controlled its design and artwork. So it was that the editor in chief, aided by some co-conspirators, designed the cover to include the word "Comet" with the vertical stem of the "t" consisting of a vertical, round-headed object streaking upward and leaving a trail of dripping residue as its tail—obviously an ascending coment. The crossbar of the "t" was a horizontal banner reading "Nineteen Sixty-Six" in capital letters. A cursory glance at the yearbook cover did not arouse any suspicion. On the other hand, anyone who bothered to study it would realize that the first four letters of the title were set back a little too far from the stem of the "t" so that the cover could also be interpreted as saying "Come" followed by a phallic symbol that was dripping ejaculate.

The yearbook staff slipped the cover design past the critical eyes of the faculty and into Austin High legend. The yearbook had been out for such a short period of time that there was still concern that their coup would be discovered and recalled, but members of the in-crowd of the class knew of the secret, and that included Paul, Claudia, and Hildy.[20]

Paul asked Hildy to go with them to the Co-op but she declined, saying she needed to get back to the dorm. She walked away, heading north past the Varsity Theatre. There was construction going on along the

Drag, and barriers were placed along the sidewalk. Paul and Claudia skirted around one and ran into another friend and former classmate, Carla Sue Wheeler, so they paused to talk about their respective plans and futures.

There was a noise, a sharp, loud crack. Paul looked at the cars on the Drag. One of them must have backfired. The trio looked around, puzzled. Down the street they saw a knot of people gathering on the other side of the Drag. It looked like a boy had fallen from his bicycle.

There were two more shots, not rapid and close together, but about five seconds apart and deliberate. A woman gave a shout... or a scream. Another bullet came in, striking closer to the three friends, and they dove for cover, selecting the nearest construction barricade. They huddled there a few seconds and another shot was fired. It was coming from high up.

"Someone is shooting from the Tower," a nearby student called out from the open doorway of a shop. This announcement was followed by the buzz of several voices. The construction barricade had a door in it, and Paul opened it, stood up and gazed toward the Tower. Carla was nearest him, Claudia on her other side. Then he saw it, a man's head high up on the Tower's observation deck. He had something white wrapped around his forehead and was pointing something toward the Drag.

"Carla, come look," Paul said. "I can see him. This is for real." Those were his last words. Whitman's bullet hit him in the mouth and killed him instantly. Claudia stood, moved toward her lover, and Carla reached to hold her back. The next shot hit them both, Carla in her restraining hand and Claudia in the chest, damaging three of Carla's fingers and killing Claudia. The trio fell close together. Seeing there was nothing she could do for her friends, Carla ducked back behind the barricade. She was, or had been, an accomplished piano player.

Across the street Alfred McAlister came out of the Student Union. After the student ran down the stairs to the pool room shouting about a shooter, he had dashed upstairs intending to look out of the window on the landing between the first and second floors of the Student Union, knowing it offered a clear view of the Tower. Before he got there, he saw glass on the stairs, a splash of blood, and students who'd been injured. He turned around and exited the building by a door, no longer existing today, that let out on the Drag.

A small crowd had gathered, sheltered behind the west side of the building, some occasionally peering around the corner to look at the Tower. Someone pointed at a pair of feet visible between two parked cars and Alfred acted almost by reflex. He knew first aid from his Eagle Scout training, and nobody else was helping whoever was lying across the street. At the same time he reasoned that if he ran fast and in a zig-zagging pattern, it was highly unlikely the shooter could draw a bead and hit him as he dashed across two lanes of traffic.

The time it took him to think it through and act was less than it takes to describe it. No more than 20 seconds passed from the time Alfred came out of the door of the Student Union, joined the crowd, saw the feet, and began running. He "blasted across the street and jumped down behind a car, didn't really look at the body," until he was certain he was not being fired on. He felt confident that if he exposed himself even a little bit the shooter would zero in on him.

After a few seconds he looked at the person lying next to him. The young man's face was turned away from Alfred and his head lay in a large pool of blood. Alfred reached out and touched the body, enough to move it a little and to get a better view of the wound. He too was a hunter. Not only was he familiar with guns and shooting, he knew what happens when a hollow point bullet strikes, and that it makes a large, nasty exit wound. That was what he was seeing now. As he recalled, "a hollow point comes in and just explodes, and it was like hamburger and bone. That guy was dead."

There was blond hair involved, and there was a red and white shirt like the one Alfred's good friend Paul Sonntag liked to wear, but the point was that there was nothing McAlister could do for this fellow, whereas there were others he might still be able to help. As he recalled:

> In terms of what's happening is that he's dead, and then there's a woman over there, not very... maybe ten feet away that I didn't see before and she's WAY in the line of fire to go over and mess with her, and she really looked dead. And so I just made a judgment not to render aid. I mean, the amount of blood and the risk to myself, quite frankly, I just made a calculation to just stay pinned behind the car so I just blew off these dead bodies and didn't look at them again because I became attuned to... you know, I need to get out of here and am I going to get shot next,

and it's weird but between the passenger side window and the rear window of one of those cars I had a view where I could see the top of the Tower. Looking through the side window and the rear window I had a partial view of the Tower so I could see a lot. I would see the gun come up and see the puff of smoke when he took a shot. He didn't take a shot directly at me, you know. He took a shot a little to the south on Guadalupe, I saw, but like 45 degrees off of me that direction so I didn't think he was about to shoot me or anything but I was just going to stay behind cover.[21]

The shooter in the Tower was now firing from its southwest corner.

Two other students, Clif Drummond and Bob Higley, were also focusing on Sonntag. Drummond was the president of the U.T. Student Body and Higley was a friend who described himself as Drummond's Aide-de Camp. They had been in Drummond's office on the third floor of the Student Union when the shooting began. Drummond, a pharmacy major, grabbed a white lab coat hanging on the door to use for bandages, and the pair dashed out to help. They passed the blown out window on the stairwell landing and exited onto the Drag, probably just seconds after, but possibly before, McAlister. They saw Sonntag. Higley recalled that "Drummond said something to the effect of 'Let's go get him.' We looked each other in the eye and had a *Butch Cassidy and the Sundance Kid* kind of moment. I said, 'Are you going first or am I?'"

Bob Higley, active participant, with his close friend Clif Drummond, in assisting victims shot by Whitman on August 1, 1966.

Drummond was wearing a pair of new loafers with leather soles he'd purchased at the Co-op a couple of days earlier, and while coming down the stairs in the Student Union it occurred to him that they would not be good shoes to run in, so he kicked them off before running into the street.[22] They zigzagged, Drummond leading, and Whitman spotted them. Bullets began thudding into the soft, sunbaked asphalt near them and Drummond dashed between two parked cars and went right.

The shots stopped for an instant and Higley had a quick thought that saved his life. It was possible the shooter, who was obviously good, had run out of ammunition, but Bob did not think so. He reasoned that the sight of Drummond dashing between the cars convinced the shooter that Higley would do the same, and so he put his sights on the gap and intended to pick the second runner off the instant he entered it.

As with McAlister, his actions took less time than it takes to describe them. Instead of following Clif into the kill zone, Higley cut right and slid across the hood of one of the cars. In doing so the metal button on his Levi's left a long, screeching scar in the hood's finish, but the cause of that loss to the owner, whom Higley suspects is still looking for him, ensured Bob Higley's life. Whitman, apparently outraged that he'd been out-witted, sent three quick, tightly-patterned shots that hit a stack of red bricks on the sidewalk placed there to be added to the façade of a little boutique store called The Cadeau.[23]

Clif Drummond, University of Texas student body president who, with his friend Bob Higley, was instrumental in aiding several of Whitman's victims on August 1, 1966.

McAlister was focusing on his view of the Tower, but he

became aware of the other two students being nearby. "My eyes were on the Tower. I wasn't looking around. I wasn't thinking anything, but I became aware that there were other people there, you know. There were a couple of guys somehow that were there, I don't know if they just got there or were already there, I don't know." He also did not know that the two bodies nearby were his close friend and Claudia Rutt, a classmate on whom McAlister had once had a crush.

One of many inexplicable differences in eyewitness recollections of the day is that although McAlister, Higley, and Drummond focused their attention on Paul Sonntag, the scenes seared into their memories did not match. McAlister saw two feet sticking out into the street between two parked cars belonging to the young man he ran to, but Drummond and Higley saw a young man leaning against a parking meter, his feet pointing away from the street, and his head lolling to one side. When Higley and Drummond reached the student, whom Drummond said had been shot in the mouth, Higley pulled the body toward him and laid him over, which might have put him in the position McAlister saw, assuming he crossed the Drag after, instead of before, the other two students.

Higley hoped and believed the young man was still alive, and asked Drummond "what do you think?" Clif saw that his fingers were turning blue and told Bob, "look at his fingernails, he's cyanotic," then checked for a pulse. He found none, but said later "I've gotta tell you, checking for a pulse when your adrenaline is pumping is a useless exercise."

A Chevrolet station wagon came peeling around from 24th, onto the Drag, tires squealing, and roared to a stop. The vehicle had no lights, siren or markings and the driver, who wore no uniform, jumped out, opened the back, and said, "get him in here." Bob and Clif picked Sonntag up. Alfred asked, "do y'all need any help?" and one of the three replied, "no, we got it." Alfred considered it "my role as I'm watching and if I see that gun come around this direction I'm going to say "!#%#!" to warn them." Sonntag's body was unwieldy and hard to move, so it took a minute or two to get him in the back of the station wagon, during which time they would have been sitting ducks if Whitman had seen them. The driver slammed the door and took off.

Higley and Drummond went through The Cadeau to the alley, and within seconds Clif stepped on a broken beer bottle and cut his feet, which also had second degree burns on the soles from the hot asphalt. Higley removed his desert boots and gave Drummond his socks to wear, and his fear gave way to pure anger. "The whole thing was so unfair. I was still thinking that Sonntag had been badly wounded, that he was capable of being resuscitated. I couldn't have gone on if I'd thought, 'Gee, we just recovered the body of a dead student.' I couldn't allow myself to believe that this kid was dead."[24] Afterwards they assisted three other wounded students, two girls and a boy, from the sidewalk and into stores, one probably being Sheftall's.

McAlister remembered someone, possibly a motorcycle cop, telling him to get the hell out of there. He felt shell-shocked, and moved carefully away, going down the Drag to another street, then over and back to the safety of the Student Union.[25] He had no idea he had known the identity of the dead bodies with which he had just been involved, or that another boyhood friend, Tom Eckman, was also dead, another classmate was wounded in the hand, or that the woman who, just half an hour earlier, had been a goddess on his private pedestal was lying wounded in the hot sun. It was the kind of "small world" experience that no one should endure.

It was then 12:07. Whitman's seven minute assault on the Drag had yielded ten casualties, five of them fatal. He decided to move again, and shifted back to the south side of the Tower, where some people were trying to aid his earlier victims and others were looking for a way to put a stop to the madness.

One of the latter was Austin Police Officer Billy Speed. He was 23, a former paratrooper, married with a one year old daughter, and had been on the force for 13 months, pulling down $360 each one. Earlier in the day he'd told his good friend and fellow officer, Houston McCoy, that he couldn't live on that amount and hoped to have more in his future, and that he had decided to go back to college. At the moment he had a grand total of 50 cents in his pocket.

He had not, however, revealed the full depth of his concern to McCoy. Something was eating at him, telling him to get out of police work quickly or "something bad" was going to happen. He told Officer Jerry Day about it earlier, before talking to McCoy. He was afraid he might be killed and would not be around for his baby daughter. The feeling was so strong that he had decided he would hand in his resignation that very evening when he completed his shift, not just so he could start working on a new career, but because whatever it was that was making him feel uneasy seemed as threatening as anything could be.[26]

He was investigating a minor traffic accident when radio calls went out to all units to proceed immediately to the University. Dispatch did not try to direct any of the officers about where exactly to go or what exactly to do. Every officer was on his own and Speed, in Unit no. 353, drove onto the campus and parked near the Littlefield Fountain. He got out and began working his way north toward the Tower, staying under the

Austin police officer Billy Speed, killed by Whitman on August 1, 1966.

cover of trees, passing the statues of Confederate heroes Albert Sydney Johnston and Robert E. Lee, then across Inner Campus Drive to the wall that ran behind the statue of Jefferson Davis and beside the steps from the lower to the upper terrace of the South Mall. Officer Robert Culp was already there, having taken the same general route toward the Tower. Six or eight civilians were hiding nearby along with a KTBC television newsman named Phil Miller. Another APD officer, Robert Still, arrived.

The wall at the Davis statue was over seven feet high to anyone standing on its south, or lower side, the lower four-plus feet being the solid base of the upper terrace on which the statute was constructed, and the upper three feet being concrete balusters supporting a top concrete rail. The shape of the balusters created open spaces four to six inches apart. Culp and Speed were armed with shotguns and revolvers, neither of which was of any use at their present distance. They would have to get to the top of the Tower and within yards of the shooter in order to bring him down. The question was how to do that without being killed in the process.

Whitman's new position on the Tower placed him directly below the Roman numeral VI on the clock in middle of south side.[27] He had fired some shots since shifting his position but none at the officers, and Culp, Still, and Speed stood up, which meant that their faces came even with the balusters and they could see the observation deck through the gaps. The officers thought they were safe, but a bullet from the Tower dissuaded them of such a notion. It hit between two of the balusters, showering bits of concrete in all directions and leaving a hole that is still there today. Everyone ducked and Speed turned his face to the side to avoid the flying dust and stones. He was then just barely visible in Whitman's scope through two of the balusters, and Whitman's next shot was his most accurate of the day. It passed through the narrow opening between the balusters and hit Speed in the right shoulder, then continued into his chest. He fell forward, mortally wounded.

Still and Culp pulled him back, out of the line of fire. He was unconscious. Blood was soaking his uniform shirt, and Culp dashed away to a building to find a phone and call in an "officer down" alert. A woman came forward to attend Speed, saying she was a nurse. A student ran to another building and returned with a little tin cup of water and another, Judith Parsons, removed her slip, soaked it in the water and placed it on Speed's forehead.

The scar left by one of Whitman's bullets on the top of the wall along the south end of the upper terrace of the South Mall, below which Austin Officer Billy Speed was killed.

A student named Brenda Bell watched from nearby Parlin Hall, close enough to Speed "that I could have thrown my pencil on him." She watched the nurse, the boy with the cup of water, and Judith Parsons and decided she was experiencing a self-awareness moment. "I realized that there was no way that I was going out there to help him. I didn't want to get shot. That was a defining moment, because I realized I was a coward."[28]

None of it made any difference for Billy Speed. Whitman had killed a policeman. Throughout the next two days, each of dozens of police reports submitted by officers of the Austin Police Department would be filed under the heading "Offense Number: M-968150, "Offense: Murder," "Victim: Officer Billy Speed," "Address: APD."

As if satisfied, Whitman took a short break. For five minutes he did not fire, and probably tuned his portable radio to a local station with breaking news about himself. It is certain, though, that he was not "munching on peanuts and drinking gasoline," as suggested in a 2011 satirical blog called "Charlie Whitman's Tumor."[29] About 12:14 he went back to work.

Roy Dell Schmidt was a 29-year-old electrician who had been an Austin City employee since 1954. He and a fellow employee, Solon McCown, were eating lunch at the electric distribution department on West Avenue when they got a service call at 12:05. They drove to the campus, saw the commotion and thought there might be a fire, so they pulled in and parked their truck in a parking space being vacated by television reporter Joe Roddy. Another City employee who was there, Don Carlson, told them what was happening and that they had better take cover.

The three men crouched behind a Chevrolet for a few moments talking about what was going on. Then Schmidt stood up and said "It's okay, we're out of range" or words to that effect. They were, in fact, more than 500 yards from the Tower, and should have been safe. They were not. The shot that killed Schmidt was Whitman's second longest of the day.

Schmidt grabbed his stomach, shouted, "I'm hit. I'm hit." and fell. A patrolman named Jim Cooney attempted to get to him but Whitman kept him pinned down. When an ambulance was able to carry him to Brackenridge, Schmidt was dead on arrival.

The shot that killed the electrician was fired at about 12:18, which was 30 minutes into Whitman's killing spree. It marked a watershed in the reverse siege being carried out by the shooter. Schmidt would be the last of his victims to die that day, and he would be Whitman's last "easy" shot of the day.

Much more had been happening during that half hour than just people getting shot. People were responding to the crisis in different ways, many of which were heroic. Claire Wilson, Whitman's first victim, recalled that within moments of being wounded that "a really lovely young woman with red hair ran up to me and said, 'Please, let me help you.' I told her to get down so she wouldn't attract attention, and she lay down next to me. It was a beautiful, selfless act. I told her my name and my blood type, and she made sure to keep me talking so I wouldn't lose consciousness. She stayed with me for at least an hour, until people came and carried me away."[30] The woman's name was Rita Jones.

Nearby, numerous people could see the dead and wounded lying in the open on the South Mall. They consisted of Claire Wilson, Tom Eckman, Maitlin Huffman, and David Gunby, all lying within a few yards of each other. Rita's presence brought the number to five. Occasional movement by Claire, Huffman, or Gunby, and particularly the fact that

Claire was obviously pregnant, made more than one onlooker anxious to do something to help her, but others, including police officers, warned them not to venture into the open.

One of those watching was David Orton, a mortician for Cook Funeral Home. That day had been a rare day off, but he'd gone to the Home to meet some friends and upon hearing about the shootings, had taken one of the Cook ambulances—a 1965 Ford Station Wagon—to do what he could, even though he was alone. He drove down Lavaca to 19th Street (now MLK Blvd.) and turned onto University Drive, stopped, and saw a police car parked under a tree and an officer waving at him. He also realized that the "pings" he was hearing and seeing were from bullets being fired from the Tower.

When he parked beside the squad car, he was directed to go pick up an officer who was down, which was Billy Speed. Another police officer helped him load Speed into the ambu-lance, who was dead on arrival at Brackenridge. He then returned and ran into a friend named Bill Morris, who agreed to help him. They parked the ambulance, removed the portable cot from its rear and wheeled it to where he could see the group of bodies lying in the open on the South Mall. He wanted to pull the cot out and load Claire Wilson onto it, but a police officer told him not to do so, and he left to find other victims whom he could assist. Before the day was over he picked up four, including Speed, the last of whom was Claudia Rutt.[31]

Rita Jones, who bravely ran to and lay down beside the wounded, pregnant Claire Wilson on the Upper Terrace of the South Mall. She remained with her under a blazing sun for approximately an hour, until other students were able to carry Claire out of danger.

Two other onlookers at the South Mall were John Fox and James Love. Fox would later enjoy considerable celebrity in Austin under the pseudonym "Artley Snuff," with a band called the Uranium Savages, was another member of the Austin High Class of '66, and was a friend of both Alfred McAlister and Paul Sonntag. He was 17 and taking Freshman English that summer at U.T., and he and Love had been at Love's room at the Stag Coop on the southwest corner of Rio Grande and 21st, playing chess and listening to 1490 am radio, or KNOW, which was the local station most popular with young people. Just before noon, the DJ came on and reported that someone was on the Tower with an air rifle, so John and James went to the campus to see what was going on.

They entered on foot at Inner Campus Drive at 22nd Street and walked down the street heading east, early enough that police had not yet erected barricades. When a man waved and told them to get out of the street, they went to Sutton Hall, on their right, and climbed to the third floor, from where they saw bodies lying on the mall and realized that things were more serious than someone shooting an air rifle. They went downstairs and walked to the statue of Jefferson Davis, where Officer Speed had been killed, but his body had already been removed. From there, looking around the base of the statue, they could see the five bodies lying in the open.

Fox and   would remain there for an hour, and he would later recall what he described as a "strange auditory memory," unique to urban warfare. The sound of shots bouncing off different buildings at different angles created an odd echoing effect, and in later years when he saw television coverage of Sarajevo, Beirut, or other hot spots, the same sound would produce memories of that long hour. There was also blood, Robert Boyer's and Billy Speed's, near where they were crouching, and even though nearly half a century had passed when Fox told of it, the memory caused him to choke up and become emotional. His feelings at the time would also become more intense, and would cause him to act courageously.[32]

Others, most, could only observe, marvel, cringe, or gather isolated memories they would carry for the rest of their lives. Brenda Bell remembered that "[w]e weren't even scared at first. We were just wildly curious. I was in Shakespeare class when it started, and we all ran to the windows of the English building, which is now Parlin Hall, and stood there peering out over each other's shoulders." A freshman named David Bayless, Jr. was outside when the shooting began, and as soon as he realized what was happening he ran to Batts Hall, a classroom building, and arrived as the noon bell rang for classes to let out. "I held my arms out and tried to block the doors that led out onto the South Mall. I didn't scream or holler. I just said, 'Don't go out there. Someone's shooting people.' But no one believed me. They looked at me like I was a dumb kid and pushed right past." Gayle Ross, a junior, recalled that the event "had that same feeling of time isolated, of before and after, that the Kennedy assassination had," and her thought, once she realized what was happening, was "Oh, no, not again. You knew that after this day, this moment, nothing would ever be quite the same again. There was a quality of suspended animation. Normal life had stopped, and for this little space of time, everything revolved around the Tower and that man."[33]

A few blocks from campus, 12-year-old Toby Hamilton, who'd had Whitman as a scoutmaster and who loved Claire Wilson and Tom Eckman, was watching the Tower through a telescope he used for star gazing. He could hear the shots and could see the puffs of limestone

The view from the observation deck of the Tower toward The Drag (Guadalupe Street) as it appeared in 2007.

dust along the observation deck. Later, when he learned that the man doing the shooting was Charles Whitman he was "not surprised."[34]

John Pipkin, a senior, went to Scholz's Beer Garten, an Austin landmark near the Capitol, for lunch. He and two friends were starting on sandwiches when a young man burst in the door, climbed onto the bar and shouted "You gotta hear what I'm saying! There's a sniper up on the Tower and he's shooting people!" Pipkin recalled that "Everybody in the place starts laughing and saying, 'Yeah, right—a sniper on the Tower. Let's drink to the sniper!' So everybody raises their beers and makes a big joke out of it. The guy says, 'No, I'm serious. There's a sniper up on the Tower and he's shooting people!' And about that time, we started to hear sirens."

Another student, a junior named Harper Scott Clark arrived at Scholz's at 12:10 and found it devoid of joking and filled to overflowing with people watching a black and white TV in a corner. "Everyone was standing around with their mugs and pitchers because there was nowhere to sit. There was a businessman standing near me—your typical good old boy in cowboy boots and pressed jeans and Western-style shirt—and he said, 'Well, I hope they get him off that Tower pretty quick, because the anti-gun people are going to go crazy over this.'"

In the Academic Center, Don Vandiver was doing his job. He didn't have a notebook or a camera, but he gathered up several sheets of paper providing directions to the location of books in the undergraduate library, which was in the Academic Center, and used their blank backs to record notes from interviews. He wanted to call the *American Statesman* office to report what was happening, but

Don Vandiver in 1963. The only reporter for the Austin American Statesman *who was on campus from the beginning of the shootings until the end, he was also the first to go to the Whitman residence, before police arrived and found the body of Kathy Whitman inside*

144

the phones in the building each had a line of 30 or 40 people queued up to call out so, as he recalled, he "started acting like a reporter and started interviewing people who were involved in it who were caught there." The first girl he talked to was named Phoebe Reading, and her comment was, "I think I'm going to go back to SMU. Dallas is a lot quieter." The next was a senior math major named Don Bynum. He told Don that he had been sleeping on the patio on the roof of the Academic Center—a popular place for sunbathing and relaxing—when the shooting began. He had seen the shooter on the outer rim of the Tower, and said he appeared to be using two different rifles.

Hoping to get a similar view, Don went upstairs and tried to access the roof, but the door had already been locked. He went downstairs again and out the door he had come in, which put him on the south porch of the Academic Center. There he encountered a graduate student named James Damon. He told Vandiver that his wife worked in the Tower on the 12th floor and he didn't know if she was okay, but that he had gone home and retrieved his rifle. He had been on the fourth floor of the Tower when the shooting began, his wife was pregnant, and he ran a distinct risk of being gunned down when he tried to escape the building, but priorities were priorities. "I went home and got my gun. It was an M1 carbine, which I'd bought for $15 when I was discharged from the Army. I went to the top of the new Academic Center and tried to keep out of sight. That was the closest I could get. I only saw him once, long enough to take aim, but from time to time I would shoot over the ledge of the observation deck and try to hit him."[35] Damon may have been the first to do so, and he stopped only when he ran out of ammunition. He was on his way back to his car to get more when Vandiver encountered him.

Vandiver interviewed a building mechanic named Lou Gorman who was in the process of locking doors to keep people from exposing themselves. Gorman's observation was, "it's going to be where a person isn't safe anywhere." Two men wearing cowboy hats, coats and ties, carrying rifles and with handguns at their waists, appeared. They were Texas Rangers. Vandiver produced his credentials, which included a card that entitled him, as a reporter, access to a crime scene, and the two Rangers said he could accompany them. After directing Gorman to unlock the door to the roof, the three men went outside onto the patio area used for sunbathing, where Don Bynum had been napping. Towels and at least one portable radio, still turned on, were scattered about, left behind by students who had been relaxing when Hell broke loose.

They dashed to a retaining wall about 50 feet from the door to the roof and ducked down. The Ranger nearest Vandiver removed his 1911 Colt .45 automatic pistol from its holster and offered it to Vandiver, asking him if he wanted to help them keep the shooter's head down. Vandiver was quite familiar with firearms, but he declined, saying, "no, I'd pro-bably shoot myself in the foot." He peered over the wall and could see two girls and three boys pinned down at the corner of the West Mall. "I could see another boy under a tree, another behind a statue, and I could see a girl,"—Charlotte Dareshori—"crouching behind a flagpole."[36]

Inside the Tower, people on the floors beneath the observation deck spread the word about what was happening above and began barri-cading themselves into classrooms and offices. Immediately after hearing the shots that cut down the Gabour family, a man was heard shouting for help, and four men, an instructor, his assistant, an assistant to the director of admissions, and the husband of a receptionist, went upstairs to investigate. They encountered M.J. Gabour, in shock, still carrying his wife's blood-stained shoes, then proceeded further until they came to the Little Bighorn scene at the foot of the stairs on the 27th floor. One of them tried to call for help but was unable to oper-ate the University PBX system. Shots could be heard from above and another in the group looked out a window and saw bodies lying on the ground below.

Nobody knew what they were dealing with—a single gunman, multiple gunmen, some sort of military or terrorist invasion? Those were days of the Cold War, civil rights, the Vietnam War and growing opposition to that war. Practically anything might be going on, including something that made more sense than what was motivating Charles Whitman.

"Get back. There are bodies all over," one of the four men yelled, and the group fell back to where five others, including two nuns who were studying the Greek Classics, were waiting. All but one went into an empty room, number 2608, where they barricaded the door with filing cabinets. The other ran downstairs warning people on every floor about what was happening.[37] Knowing only that death lurked above outside, they locked doors and built breastworks.

Outside, police officers moved steadily toward the Tower. Some were already inside.

1. One publication referred to the Chuck Wagon as the "radical hangout in the Student Union," but at most there was an area where the so-called "counter-culture" students congregated. Bob Feldman, "Civil Rights:, SDS, and Student Activism in Austin, Texas, 1954-1973," http://www.theragblog.com/bob-feldman-civil-rights-sds-and-student-activism-in-austin-texas-1954-1973/

2. Burr, Beverly, "History of Student Activism at the University of Texas at Austin (1960-1988)," TC 660H, Spring 1988, Supervising Professor: Harry Cleaver, Economics. http://www.campusactivism.org/server-new/uploads/burrthesis.pdf

3. Brenda Bell, "Man Entwined with Shooting at UT Tower in Life, Death," *Austin American Statesman*, Dec. 21, 2011

4. 96 Minutes at 195.

5. Claire Wilson James recalled, as recorded by Toby Hamilton, that the man was wearing a gray suit. The morgue photograph of Dr. Boyer is black and white, and while his suit coat appears to be gray, it could also be dark brown or another color. Ms. Wilson has never asserted that Dr. Boyer was the man who spoke to her, but his closeness in time and location makes him a logical candidate.

6. Statement of Cheryl Botts to the APD, August 1, 1966, AHC.

7. Recordings of all radio dispatches related to the Whitman mass murders on 8/1/66, provided by Monika McCoy, March 15, 2015; Houston McCoy's annotated transcript of same, provided the same day.

8. "Deranged tower sniper rained death on UT campus," *Houston Chronicle*, July 8, 2001.

9. Shelton L. Williams, *Summer of '66*, pp. 106-07 (Denton: Zone Press, 2007).

10. The home was left to U.T. in 1935. Additionally, the Littlefield Fountain is on the main campus, the Littlefield Residence Hall is a women's dormitory, the Littlefield Society is an organization of donors who have contributed at least $25,000 to the University, one of Austin's downtown business high-rises is the Littlefield Building, and the Austin Chapter of the Sons of Confederate Veterans is named for Littlefield.

11. Telephone interview of Don Vandiver, Lubbock, Texas, January 30, 2015.

12. H.D. "Doc" Quigg, *Doc Quigg's Report on Texas Tower Shooting*, UPI, 1966, http://www.downhold.org/lowry/doc.html

13. 96 Minutes at 177.

14. Bill Helmer, "The Madman in the Tower, *Texas Monthly*, August 1966.

15. Statement of Oscar Royvela to the APD, August 1, 1966, AHC.

16. Hernandez's first name is alternately spelled "Alex," "Alek," and "Alec" in different reports.

17. Assault with Intent to Murder Report filed by Sgt. D. Kidd, APD, regarding Ehlke, August 2, 1966, AHC.

18. Affidavit of Allen Crum dated August 2, 1966, AHC.

19. Interview of John Fox, April 25, 2015.

20. As well as John Fox, George Cofer, Alfred McAlister and other members of the senior class interviewed for this book.

21. Interview of Alfred McAlister, Austin, Texas, January 20, 2015.

22. Higley's recollection was that they both removed their shoes, so that he could give Drummond his socks to wear, and that Drummond was wearing cheap Mexican sandals called Huaraches, but Drummond recalled it differently. Interview with Clif Drummond and Bob Higley, May 8, 2015; email from Clif Drummond dated May 15, 2015.

23. *Ibid.*

24. 96 Minutes at 182.

25. McAlister interview, *supra*.

26. Radio dispatches of 8/1/66 annotated by Houston McCoy, provided to author by Monika McCoy, March 15, 2015; email from Monika McCoy, Kyle, Texas, March 18, 2015; Jerry Day, interviewed in *Deranged Killers: Charles Whitman*, darkdocumentaries, Discovery Channel, (2006). https://www.youtube.com/watch?v=Jy1B5mfzCBA.

27. http://www.downhold.org/lowry/doc.html.

28. 96 Minutes at 180.

29. *Encyclopedia Dramatica*, "Charlie Whitman's Tumor," https://encyclopediadramatica.se/index.php?title=Charles_Whitman's_Tumor&diff=next&oldid=227497.

30. 96 Minutes at 177.

31. Interview of David Orton, April 22, 2015.

32. Interview of John Fox, April 25, 2015.

33. 96 Minutes at 106-07.

34. Interview of Monika McCoy, March 12, 2015.

35. 96 Minutes at 106, 179,

36. Interview of Don Vandiver, *supra*.

37. Lavergne at 134-35

CHAPTER SEVEN
The Next Hour

Not every shot went in but most went in;
in just over an hour with the tumor thudding in his brain he killed 13 hit
33. His empty father taught him to respect guns (not persons).
-John Berryman, Dream Song 135

Approximately 20 minutes after his first shot from the observation deck, Whitman began to encounter return fire, not only from the police but from armed citizens.

Whitman had no monopoly on pride of marksmanship. Many students had been picking off bunnies, bambies and varmints since before puberty. For macho young Texas men, the opportunity to grab a rifle and start shooting at a bad guy was a dream come true, an incident they would cherish and brag about to their grandchildren. Not only was it great fun, but was clearly a public service, a demonstration of civic responsibility and a chance to go down in history alongside David Crockett. It was the Irish Sweepstakes, the French Repechage, the Powerball Lottery of shooting contests.

Ann Major, a senior, described it as "a sort of cowboy atmosphere, this 'Let's get him' spirit." In the San Jacinto Café, located near campus, students and citizens were watching events play out on a television when a young man ran in carrying a deer rifle. He hurriedly purchased a six pack of beer and ran out again, anxious to join the good times guaranteed by combining bullets and beer. Clif Drummond recalled that "[s]tudents with deer rifles were leaning up against telephone poles, using the pole, which is rather narrow, as their

Vietnam veteran Brehan Wilson carrying the dead body of Thomas Eckman from the upper terrace of the South Mall, where Eckman was killed by Whitman immediately after the shooting of Eckman's girlfriend, Claire Wilson.

151

shield. And they were firing like crazy back at the Tower."[1] Some students had only .22 caliber rifles, but one recalled hearing what he called "an elephant gun," the blast from which was louder than any other weapon on campus.[2] This was almost certainly Officer Cooney of the APD, who fired a box and a half of ammo from his own rifle, a 400 Magnum Weatherbee.[3]

Forrest Preece, a junior, "saw two guys in white shirts and slacks running across the lawn of the Pi Phi house, hustling up to its porch with rifles at the ready. Someone was yelling, 'Keep down, man. Keep down!'" J. M. Coetzee, a doctoral candidate in English literature and linguistics who would win the 2003 Nobel Prize for literature, recalled that "I hadn't fully comprehended that lots of people around me in Austin not only owned guns but had them close at hand and regarded themselves as free to use them." Brenda Bell, a junior, said "I don't know where these vigilantes came from, but they took over Parlin Hall and were crashing around, firing guns. There was massive testosterone."[4] Nobody knows how many were shooting from the ground, but witnesses guessed it was "several dozen."[5]

Bill Helmer, a graduate student in history, captured the situation best, recognizing the yin and yang of the situation: "I remember thinking, 'All we need is a bunch of idiots running around with rifles.' But what they did turned out to be brilliant. Once he (Whitman) could no longer lean over the edge and fire, he was much more limited in what he could do. He had to shoot through those drain spouts, or he had to pop up real fast and then dive down again. That's why he did most of his damage in the first twenty minutes."[6]

The drain spouts were twelve openings along the floor of the observation deck, three on each side, located 12 feet apart and measuring four inches wide by 18 inches high. From the ground they were small, pencil-tip sized targets with concrete drain spouts extending nearly three feet from each that served as a partial screen from marksmen below. From Whitman's vantage they were ideal gunports. He could kneel, sit, or lie down at one and have an approximate 30 degree slice of the panorama in which to locate targets. Doing so was not nearly as satisfying as leaning over the top of the parapet, but it offered good cover and he fired dozens of shots from them. One of the films taken by a television cameraman during the shooting captures him behind one of the spouts, but he is no more than a dot moving within a slightly larger dot.[7]

The action of citizens in returning fire was controversial then and now. It wasn't the image anyone associated with the City or the University wanted to project, but there can be little doubt that it prevented Whitman from being able to draw a bead on more targets than he did. Not quite 50 years later, a bill was filed in the Texas Senate to authorize the carrying of firearms on any public college campus in Texas, and the committee hearing before the Senate

The view through one of the 12 drain spouts along the floor of the U.T. Tower observation deck, through which Whitman fired after gunfire from the ground forced him to keep his head low.

State Affairs Committee drew testimony from dozens of people, including Claire Wilson James, the first of Whitman's victims on the ground, plus Alfred McAlister and James Bryce, who were on campus during the shootings. One of the senators on the Committee, Judith Zaffarini, was also on campus, and it was her recollection, along with that of Ms. James, that the return fire was thought at first to be coming from other shooters who were in league with the one in the Tower. Mr. Bryce presented an additional piece of information—that the Austin Police Chief notified radio stations to request that citizens bring high-powered rifles with scopes to the police department for officers to use, but the request became garbled in being broadcast, and was understood as an invitation for citizens to bring their rifles and join in the firefight.[8]

John Pipkin left Scholz's and walked across the street to the Chi Omega sorority house, where some friends were sitting, watching the action, and talking. A Texas Ranger approached carrying a pair of binoculars and a scoped rifle. He looked at the young men and motioned to Pipkin. "Son, you ever done any hunting?" he asked, and Pipkin replied, "Yes, sir, I've been hunting all my life." "Well, take these binoculars," the Ranger said. "I need for you to calibrate me." Without knowing exactly what was expected of him, Pipkin said "Okay."

47 minutes into the reverse siege, a bullet fired from the ground at Whitman kicks up limestone dust on the south side of the Tower.

What the Ranger needed was a spotter. Calibrating means to adjust an instrument until it is accurate, and the instrument in this case was the peace officer's marksmanship. Pipkin remembered that "Whitman would stick his rifle out through one of these drainpipes on the observation deck every once in a while and shoot at someone. The Ranger would shoot back, and I'd say, 'You're an inch too high,' or 'Bring it over to the left a couple inches.'"

It was definitely a tale to tell grandkids—about when the West was wild and Texas was wooly, way back in 19 ought 66 when outlaws blazed away at townsfolk and young men were needed to blaze back and help Texas Rangers bring them to justice. Nobody could know that Pipkin's grandkids and those of the other students around him would occupy a time when such shootouts border on the commonplace.

Pipkin continued: "I was looking through the binoculars when all of a sudden I thought to myself, 'Gosh, he's pointing that rifle at me.' It was like I could see up inside the barrel of the rifle, from four hundred yards away. The next thing I knew, I could feel bullets grazing the top of the hair on my head. The ranger said, 'Boy, we got his attention now.'"

Pipkin dropped the binoculars and scurried to a nearby tree, then decided it was too insubstantial and selected a car to hide behind. He sat there panting and the Ranger called "You okay, son?" "I guess," Pipkin said. "I'm alive." "Yeah, that was pretty close," the Ranger acknowledged. "Yes, sir," Pipkins said, "it was too close. I think I'm done with my spotting."[9]

After shooting Schmidt, Whitman decided that targets were becoming sparse on the south and west sides. None of the shots he'd just fired from rain spouts hit anyone, and the irritating return fire was interfering with his mission. At about 12:20 he shifted to the north side of the Tower and its northwest corner to look for new targets.

On the northeast side of the Tower, but well away from it, was the U.T. Law School. Inside, third year law student Otis Shearer was attending a summer term law class during the noon hour. He was 25, from Booker, Texas, and had served a stint in the Air Force. Around the time that Whitman was shifting to the north side of the Tower to shoot from, a school official interrupted the class to make an announcement—a shooter was in the Tower firing at people; class was going to be dismissed but students were directed to avoid the main campus.

Air conditioning and closed windows had prevented the shots from being heard inside the law school, but once outside Shearer recognized them immediately as coming from one or more rifles. They were sporadic, but continuous. He listened for a few moments and then headed for the Delta Theta Phi law fraternity house to watch the television there and get more details. Later he learned that a female acquaintance had been wounded in the arm, but he never had a chance to talk to her about it.[10]

Another law student in class when the shooting began was future United States Senator Kay Bailey Hutchinson. She was a second year student from Galveston, and would be elected to the House of Representatives six years later at age 29. She also recalled the announcement about there being a shooter in the Tower, and she and some friends went outside to where they could see the Tower. She recalled that "[w]e could see the smoke (i.e. limestone dust) from the gun each time it fired, although we did not know at the time that he was marking innocent people."[11]

Another of the well-represented Austin High School senior class of 1966, in addition to Paul Sonntag, Claudia Rutt, Carla Sue Wheeler, Hildy Griffith, Alfred McAlister, John Fox, and Saralynn Lankford, was George Cofer, who was working as a clerk for the Texas House of Representatives, in the Capitol. Shortly after the shooting started there was a commotion as Texas Department of Safety (Highway Patrol) officers normally assigned to work at the Capitol began hustling about and heading for the campus. George, not knowing exactly what was going on, did what Alfred McAlister and many people did—rushed to see what was happening. He jumped in his 1960 Volkswagen bug, turned onto 19th Street and then onto University Drive and charged toward the Tower. As he got near he began to see people crouching behind parked cars, hiding behind trees, and generally huddling behind whatever cover was available. He also began hearing a fairly steady "pop, pop, pop" that he recognized immediately as rifle fire. Unceremoniously, George made a quick U-turn and left the campus at a slightly faster clip than he had entered, returning to the Capitol and becoming one of the few, fortunate members of his senior class who was present but who would not retain a tragic recollection of the day's events.[12]

Claire Wilson, lying beneath a blazing sun, was unable to move and uncertain whether she should even try. Then Rita Jones ran out to lie down beside her. Rita was an art major who was also studying Spanish and Portuguese. She was married to Jeff Jones, a radical campus political figure, on the staff of the underground newspaper, *The Rag*, who would become the U.T. student body president in 1970. When the shooting began she had been on the east side of the Main Building, trapped because she would be in the open and exposed to Whitman's fire if she tried to go anywhere else. However, when she saw Claire, obviously pregnant, obviously wounded, lying in the open on the South Mall, she abandoned any concern for her own safety.

In response to Claire's directive, Rita lay down beside her. Claire was straining to retain consciousness, and Rita did all she could to assist. She asked her name, blood type, and once she had gathered personal information that might be useful once Claire was delivered to medical personnel, she began chatting with her about, as Claire recalled, "all kinds of things."[13]

Tom's arms were lying across Claire and she tried to move to get out from under them, but Rita told her to lie still and not give the shooter any reason to focus on her again. She told Claire about the A-line dress

156

A dramatic still from a film depicting heroism during Whitman's shooting spree. On the left Rita Jones and an unidentified student flee the upper terrace of the South Mall. In the center Brehan Wilson leans down to pick up the body of Thomas Eckman as John Fox prepares to pick up Clair Wilson and James Love, wearing shorts, approaches. The student at the right is unidentified. A victim's shoe is in the foreground.

she was wearing, saying her mother had sewn it for her but that she really didn't like it. However, she needed to do her laundry and was wearing it that day because it was clean. The dress had a large square of colorful quilt work on the front, but the rest of it was beige that blended into the concrete surface of the Mall. Rita worried that the quilt work might make an inviting target, so she lay on her stomach next to Claire, hoping the color of the dress reduced the likelihood of being shot.

Rita remained there for an hour, until genuine help arrived that could carry Claire to safety, being James Love and John Fox. They were still crouching behind the Jeff Davis statue, but two things were gnawing at Fox. The first was Claire Wilson's situation. Her pregnancy and occasional movement, confirming she was alive, ate at him. He wanted, needed, to do something to help her. The other thing was more physical—he began to suffer from heat exhaustion.

He was wearing dark clothing, and the combination of excitement and heat began to make him feel light-headed and nauseous, so he stepped away from the statute base, which was then in the sun, and sat down beneath a nearby bush. In a few moments the unpleasant feelings went away and he stood up again, but a new thought occurred to him. If he could be made to feel ill in his situation, how must the wounded, pregnant woman lying on the searing concrete in the hot sun feel? He could simply step away and sit down in the shade, but she could do nothing but lie there and endure. He had to do something.

It was as if the same thought affected others at the same time. Students began to move. A large Vietnam vet named Brehan Ellison ran to Maitlin Huffman. Another student came close behind and ran to the group consisting of Wilson, Eckman, Gunby and Jones. Huffman got up and ran with Ellison toward the steps located immediately east of the Jeff Davis statue, but he had lost a lot of blood and just as they reached them, he collapsed and fell face first down the steps, leaving splashes of blood. Gunby also stood up and ran west with his rescuer. A few quick seconds passed and Ellison ran out again, quickly followed by an unknown student, then Fox, Love, and another student. As Ellison struggled to try to pick up Eckman's limp body, Rita Jones jumped up, grabbed her purse and ran off the mall heading east, followed by the first of the two unknown students.[14] Love and Fox picked up Claire Wilson, Fox by her feet and Love by her arms, and they carried her awkwardly off the mall to the steps beside the Jeff Davis statue. The other student, apparently seeing no one else to assist, ran ahead of them.[15] Ellison was the last to get off the mall, carrying Eckman. John Fox saw Eckman and said that his face was as white as marble, paler than any person he'd ever seen.

In the meantime, Whitman found a target on the north side of the Tower.

Robert Heard was a reporter for the Associated Press. When he got word of what was happening , he and Ernie Stromberger, a reporter for the Dallas *Times Herald*, drove to the campus and found a place to park behind two highway patrolmen who were preparing to assault the Tower at about 12:15. Rather than getting rifles they were assembling shotguns, apparently in order to confront the shooter face to face. Figuring they might be on the trail of a story, Heard and Stromberger decided to follow them. The story turned out to be different than anticipated.

"When they (the officers) ran across Twenty-fourth Street, Ernie stayed put; I followed, a few seconds behind them," Heard recalled. He'd had an operation on his knee the previous June and it slowed him down. Countering that disability was the fact that once he got across the street,

James Love and John Fox carry the severely wounded Claire Wilson from the scene of her wounding and the death of her unborn son on the upper terrace of the South Mall.

26 yards from where he'd stopped, the roof of the Biological Sciences Building would be between him and the Tower, shielding him from the shooter. Unfortunately for Heard, the knee operation trumped the protection of the roof. Besides, Whitman loved moving targets.

"Just before I reached the curb, I was shot down. I'd forgotten my Marine training; I hadn't zigzagged. It felt like someone had hit my shoulder with a brick. I staggered another three yards and fell in the street." Like any good guy on any television Western, he shouted, "He got me." The bullet shattered his left arm just below the shoulder joint, causing it to flap uselessly at his side. He was wearing a white shirt that quickly began turning red.

"As soon as I hit the pavement, I sat up... Some people in the Biological Sciences Building yelled, 'Lie down! Lie down!' Either they or another group of students—I never knew who they were—ran out into the street, knowing they could be shot, and dragged me under the trunk of a Studebaker."

Police officers nearby, other than the two Heard and Stromberger were following, saw Whitman. He was scanning the area with his binoculars.

The white headband was visible. The officers fired at him and Whitman ducked, then moved to the northwest corner of the Tower.

Ernie Stromberger helpfully phoned the *Times Herald* and told his co-workers to "[t]ell the people at the AP that they no longer have a man on the job."[16]

Focusing his attention on the northern part of the Drag, Whitman initially did not see any targets. There were students and others crouching behind parked cars and peeking over fenders at the Tower, but even with a four power scope the target each presented was negligible. Whitman peered through each drain pipe on that side searching for a victim.

The A&E Barbershop was located at 2535 Guadalupe, more than 500 yards northwest of the Tower. Inside, 35-year-old Billy Snowden was getting a haircut. He was the basketball coach at the Texas School for the Deaf. The television was on with news of what was going on outside, but Snowden and the barber decided to go to the door and look out anyway. They were at least three blocks from the Tower and certainly safe.

"We thought at first that we better get back inside," Snowden said later, "but then we decided we were too far away to get hit. I was standing

Students on the Drag scatter as Whitman finds their range. The student at the far right has just been hit with a either a piece of a bullet or a small chunk of concrete from a near miss and is grabbing at his back. He is probably one of those slightly wounded on August 1, 1966 whose identity is unknown.

in the door and had it about half open. The barber was standing beside me."[17]

It was Whitman's longest shot of the day. The bullet hit Snowden in the left shoulder, destroying three nerves, causing it to go partially and permanently numb.[18] Snowden's wounding, like the killing of Schmidt, was an extremely long shot, even for a skilled marksman.

Whitman ran from the northwest corner of the Tower to where he had leaned his new M-1 carbine against the wall near the door into the reception area. He retrieved it, made certain it was loaded and hustled back to a central drain spout on the west side. He peered out and had a nice surprise. There, at the corner of 24th and Guadalupe, outside Rae Ann's Dress Shop and near the Varsity Theatre, a knot of perhaps a dozen people had gathered and were peering upward, trying to get a glimpse of the shooter. He got a glimpse of them instead.

Among the group were Lana Phillips, Sandra Wilson, Abdul Khashab, and Janet Paulos. Lana was a 21-year-old music major who worked part time in Rae Ann's. She was there when the shooting started, and had periodically stepped outside to see what was happening. Sandra Wilson

Students crouch behind automobiles parked along the Drag and gaze toward the Tower as the shooting continues.

was a 21-year-old who lived at 2208 Rio Grande. Abdul Khashab was a 25-year-old graduate student in chemistry from Iraq, attending the University on a scholarship from the Iraqi government. Janet Paulos was his fiancée. She was 21, from Garland, Texas, a senior majoring in English. They were planning to be married in just 26 days.

Whitman aimed the carbine and fanned the trigger, sending multiple rounds into the group nearly as quickly as he might with a machine gun. The result was as satisfying as he'd hoped. At least three fell and the rest scattered. He paused a couple of seconds, either to appreciate what he'd just done or to change out clips in the rifle, then saw that one of the group was still visible. He fired another burst.

The three he hit with the first burst were Phillips in the right shoulder, Khashab in the right elbow and hip, and Paulos in the chest. The second burst got Sandra Wilson.

Khashab and Paulos would keep their wedding date, even though he would wear his right arm in a sling and neither one of them were spry. Later they would move to Iraq, and Khashab would cite one reason for doing so as his disgust for what the United States had allowed to happen to him. "There must be something wrong somewhere when in a civilized country like this a guy can get guns like he did and do what he did," Khashab would declare.[19]

Lana Phillips' comment on her own shooting was less ironic. "I wasn't scared until I got shot. I was watching the Tower and watching people get shot. I didn't think I was within range, plus, I was standing behind some other people and I thought they would get shot before I would. I was wrong."[20]

The shooting of the group caused everyone else nearby, most of them young men wearing white shirts and dark trousers, to dash down the sidewalk to find cover. A newsman captured their flight on film, and just before disappearing from view, the student at the end of the line jerked, twisted, and grabbed at his back, having been nicked with flying concrete or a piece of lead.

In the block south of where the group had been fired into, a construction crew was working on the façade of the Texas Theatre, one of whom was 18-year-old Orville "Chip" Jansen. He'd gone into the Co-op to get lunch and after coming back outside saw Alex Hernandez get shot from his bicycle. When, a few moments later, he saw a young woman get shot near the corner of the Drag and 24th, he "went on automatic, just acted, saw someone injured and knew I had to help."

To avoid exposure to the Tower, he ran through a store to the alley, then up to 24th and over to where she was lying. An electrician from the same work crew came with him, and they saw a young man, almost certainly Khashab, and thought he was dead. The girl, who would prove to be Sandra Wilson, was not, although she was in shock, and they picked her up and carried her to the alley.

She latched onto his stomach, holding so hard that he had bruises on his stomach for a week, and when the ambulance came, the driver saw the situation and said, "why don't you come with us," which he did. The bullet had hit her in the corner of the shoulder, come out under her arm and went into her chest, hitting ribs. It severed an artery that was spurting blood, so he pinched it off and held the wound to slow the bleeding, which almost certainly saved her life. They went to Brackenridge and he stayed with her until she went into surgery, then rode back with the same or a different ambulance driver, who dropped him off at the University. Not quite fifty years later, Jansen insisted repeatedly that he'd not done anything courageous or heroic, but of course he had.[21]

It was then about 12:30. The reverse siege was not quite 45 minutes old, and the scene at Brackenridge Hospital was chaos. There were six funeral homes in Austin, four Caucasian, one African-American, and one Hispanic, and all put their emergency vehicles on the streets.[22] The ambulances were pulling up to the single emergency entrance at Brackenridge more quickly than hospital personnel could admit them.

At 12:15 the hospital's administrator activated the institution's disaster plan, and the Brackenridge Emergency Room Supervisor, Leeda Lee "The General" Bryce arrived moments later, called in from sick leave. Sirens from approaching ambulances were blaring and the cars began backing up. Ten nurses and twenty student nurses rushed to the ER and began helping unload, wheel wounded and dead inside, and send the ambulances back into the fray. Robert Heard recalled that after he arrived and woke up inside the ER on a cot, there was so much blood on the floor that doctors and nurses were slipping in it.

Ambulances continued to pull in. Instead of turning sirens off as soon as the emergency vehicle was out of traffic, which was customary, many drivers let them blare all the way to the ER entrance. Anyone available pitched in, including local television newsman Joe Roddy. All stretchers available were pressed into service, and Roddy recalled "two or three dozen, just piled up, waiting."[23] The line of ambulances stretched out of the ER entrance and onto the street. Doctors from all over the hospital were on hand, some assisting with the unloading, some examining, and some preparing to operate. Soon the word was sent out the less severely wounded should be taken to Seton Hospital, which was further away, and those with flesh wounds, such as Brenda Gail Littlefield, were carried there.

Camille Clay, a nursing supervisor, described the emergency room as "something you'd see in Vietnam. I had never seen anything like it in my life, and I never want to see anything like it again."[24] Some of the incoming wounded, those who had been lying on cement beneath the broiling sun, had first and second degree burns in addition to their gunshot injuries.

Howard Hughes, an intern at Brackenridge, recalled that "[t]he casualties came pouring in. Initially there were only ten interns, two surgical residents, and our supervisor. Many of the wounds were bleeding out quickly, so we shouted back and forth, trying to decide which patients should go to the operating rooms first and doing whatever we could to stabilize the gunshot victims. There was blood everywhere, patients in the halls, not enough operating tables or available doctors."

They quickly ran out of room in the ER for all of the injured, but there were several casualties who could no longer benefit from medical attention. "We put the victims who we believed to be deceased in one room, on the floor," Camille Clay recalled. "You just couldn't believe it, all those dead teenagers lying on the floor. They were shoulder to shoulder, with just enough room to step between them. We started trying to identify them. You see, they didn't come in with their wallets and purses and things. One in particular I remember was a boy who was wearing a class ring from Austin High School that was engraved with his initials. I called the principal and asked him to pull the records for the class of 1966." The young man was Paul Sonntag, whose handsome, boyish face would have broken the heart of any observer.

The hospital's director of medical education, Robert Pape, said later that "[d]octors who were experienced in trauma started arriving at the hospital and offering to do whatever needed to be done. General practitioners, psychiatrists, dermatologists came too. Fifty-eight doctors signed the ledger in the emergency room and volunteered their help."

Also on hand were Justice of the Peace Jerry Dellana and Friar John Payne, of St. Ignatius Church, but not to render aid to the wounded. Dellana was serving as coroner, and was there to hold inquests for the dead. Father Payne was there to give them last rites.[25]

Family members of the dead and injured, as well as people who were unable to locate loved ones and feared they were at the hospital, forced their way in and moved from bed to bed and gurney to gurney, demanding of staff to know if a particular person had been admitted, getting in the way, and in some cases becoming overwhelmed with grief at what they discovered. The situation was made worse when Paul Sonntag's family arrived and it was discovered that someone had misplaced the key to the room where his body had been placed.[26] "There were a lot of hysterical people trying to get into the emergency room," Camille Clay said. "Finally the police had to go outside and put up a barricade."[27]

Seven of those brought to Brackenridge were DOA. Four more died in the Emergency Room and one died during surgery.[28] A young girl wearing a short-sleeved sweater was tended to by Dr. Albert Lalonde. At first, he could see no obvious injury. She was barely conscious and said, "I can't breathe, I can't breathe, I can't breathe." Dr. Lalonde spotted a blood stain and lifted her sweater. The tip of her lung was protruding from a bullet hole and her chest cavity was filling with blood. Within another minute she was unconscious and Lalonde stated that she then died. The girl was almost certainly Karen Griffith, but she did not die for another week.[29]

Another was a young man who was taken to Intensive Care because they had run out of room in the ER. Dr. Lalonde saw he badly needed blood and told a lady who had volunteered at Brackenridge for several years to go to the blood bank and get some. She did, hurrying as fast as she could, but by the time she returned the young man was dead. Without thinking, Dr. Lalonde said, "you're too late." The woman's face fell, believing she was the cause of the patient dying. Dr. Lalonde acknowledged that "it was a terrible thing to say."[30]

After dropping off a body, mortician/ambulance driver Morris Hohmann and his assistant, Turner Bratton, drove back to the Drag to retrieve more victims, and about 12:30 they pulled up outside Sheftall's Jewelry Store at 2268 Guadalupe. It was in front of the store that the three Peace Corps volunteers, Ehlke, Matson and Herman, had been

A. Main Building "The Tower"

B. Student Union

C. Academic Center

D. Jeff Davis Statue

    Stairs leading to South Mall Upper Terrace

E. East Mall Terrace, Computation Center Roof

F. Batts Hall

G. Radio/TV Building

    Underground entrance to UT Tower Basement

H. Littlefield Fountain

I. West Mall

J. Hogg Auditorium

K. Biology Building

L. Goodall Wooten Dormitory

M. Texas Theater

N. Left to Right: Sheftall's Jewelry, UT Co-op, Hemphills Bookstore

O. Sommer's Drugstore

    Snyder-Chenard's dress shop to the left

P. Varsity Theater

Q. A & E Barbershop

R. Speech Building

Victims

IN TOWER
1. Edna Townsley
2. Mark Gabour
3. Marguerite Lamport

4. Claire Wilson's baby boy
5. Thomas Eckman
6. Dr. Robert Boyer
7. David Gunby
8. Thomas Ashton

9. Harry Walchuk
10. Karen Griffith
11. Thomas Karr
12. Paul Sonntag
13. Claudia Rutt
14. Billy Speed
15. Roy Schmidt

The University of Texas campus as it existed on August 1, 1966, The location of major buildings and the site where each of the 15 people killed by Whitman in the Tower, on campus, and along Guadalupe Street, or "The Drag" were hit. His other two victims, Kathy and Margaret Whitman, were killed the night before.

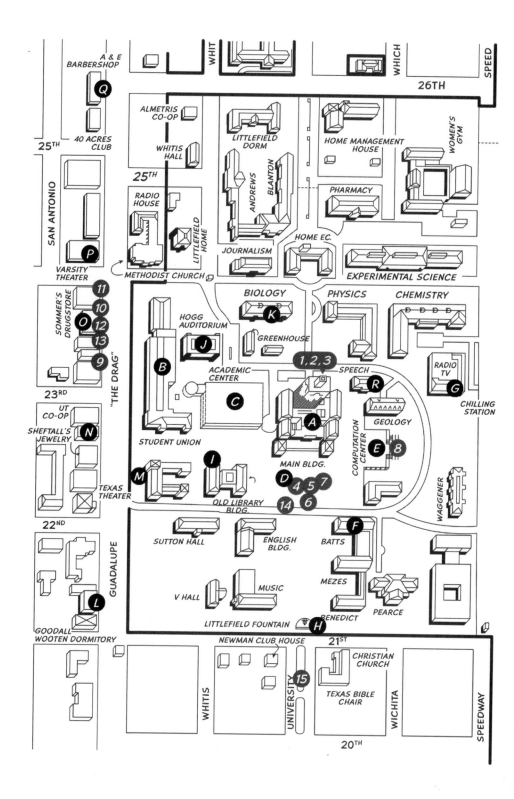

fired on some 20 minutes earlier. By the time Hohmann arrived, the store had become a sort of triage-on-the-Drag. He reported that seven wounded were inside. Although the identity of all is not certain, Matson, Ehlke, and Kelley were definitely there, and they might have been joined by Wheeler, Paulos, Phillips, and Khashab. There was a foot-wide swath of blood where one of the victims had been dragged across the floor, bullet holes were in the front door, and the carpet was ripped by incoming bullets. The store was well inside the shooter's red zone, but that did not dissuade Hohmann from parking and rushing inside.

There he was told that it would be safer to move the ambulance to the rear entrance in the alley, so Hohmann ran back outside, told Turner to pull around back, and then trotted alongside the vehicle as it turned left onto 23rd Street heading for the alley. Hohmann was shielded by the ambulance until the turn, but then Whitman had him in his sights. He put a bullet into Hohmann's right thigh with the 6 mm. Remington. The wounded ambulance driver rolled under a parked car, saw that his leg was pumping blood onto the pavement, and removed his belt to use as a tourniquet. It did the job but he pulled it too tight and caused the leg to swell.

Two construction workers, Bill Davis and Phil Ward, were hiding behind the construction barricade where Sonntag, Rutt, and Wheeler had been shot. Obviously they were in a spot well covered by killing fire, and neither was anxious to become the next victim. As a result, Hohmann lay under the car for 15 to 20 minutes, during which he could hear Davis and Ward arguing with each other about which one of them should try to pull him to safety. They finally did, and he insisted on hobbling to his own ambulance, which was full but still there.[31] At Brackenridge he received eight pints of blood.[32]

Inside Sheftall's, Peace Corps Volunteers Tom Herman and David Mattson concluded that they had wound up in a place that was doubly dangerous. Not only were bullets flying outside, they were inside a top priority business for robbery, which might either be the reason for the shooting or an opportunity that would occur to someone. "We thought that perhaps Sheftall's was being robbed," Mattson said later, "so Tom Herman and I locked ourselves in the back lavatory. It was sheer terror not knowing if we would be able to escape or if someone was going to come back there and finish us off. A policeman finally pounded on the

Ambulance driver Morris Hohmann is believed to have been Whitman's last shooting victim. At Sheftall's Jewelry Store on The Drag to pick up wounded who were inside, he was shot in the right thigh while directing the movement of his ambulance and was forced to crawl beneath a parked car to avoid being shot again."

back door and said, 'There's an ambulance just a couple of doors down, so make a run for it.'"

They came out of the bathroom and learned that the ambulance was now behind the store but that the driver had been shot. "We squeezed in beside him, and the policeman took us to the hospital, driving down alleys and using buildings for cover."[33]

Hohmann was probably Whitman's last victim and if not, then anyone shot later was one of the handful who was wounded so slightly that the details of their injuries have been lost. Targets were getting harder for him to find and return fire more intense. Hundreds of eyes, scopes, and television cameras were trained on the Tower, waiting for a glimpse or a kill shot. Had Whitman's entire spree been a wind-up toy, it would have begun to run down. He continued to fire, but quickly and without taking careful aim. The drain spouts were risky to fire from, as any movement inside one of them set off a flurry of shots from the ground. Then something new attracted his attention.

Shortly after learning there was a shooter on the Tower, the Austin Police discussed the feasibility of going after him with a helicopter. After discussion the idea was rejected. Whoever was shooting was a marksman and a helicopter offered too easy a target. Somebody suggested an airplane and pointed out that Williamson County Deputy Sheriff Jim Boutwell was both a pilot and a flight instructor. Police Chief Bob Miles gave the plan a green light.

Boutwell and an APD Lt. Marion Lee took off in a small Champion Citabria airplane from the airport at Pflugerville, just northeast of Austin. As they were preparing to do so, Boutwell cheerfully asked Lee, "In case I got hit could you land this airplane?" Lee, who had never flown a plane but knew about gravity, replied just as cheerfully, "Sure I could. Let's go."[34]

Austin police lieutenant Marion Lee, who accompanied Williamson County Deputy Sheriff Jim Boutwell in a small Champion Citabria airplane that flew over the Tower during Whitman's shooting spree. Lee, a marksman, hoped to be able to shoot Whitman but air turbulence created too much risk that his shots would hit people on the ground.

They ascended to 1200 feet and flew to the University. Circling, they studied the observation deck and spotted Whitman. He was alone, putting an end to speculation that there might be two or more snipers. Lee brought his rifle up and tried to get the shooter in his sights, but there was too much turbulence. Despite being a calm day the heat caused thermal lift and made the little plane bounce. Lee did not want to risk a shot unless he was certain it would damage only the sniper rather than people on the ground below.

Whitman saw the plane circling— another moving target—took aim and fired at least twice. That is the number of times he punched holes in the fabric skin of the Citabria. "Back away," Lee told Boutwell, "but stay close enough to offer him a target and keep him worried." Boutwell flew out of range,

The Champion Citabria airplane piloted by Jim Boutwell and manned by marksman Marion Lee flying toward the Tower and above a flag flying at half-mast. Flags were at half-mast on campus on August 1, 1966 to honor Lt. Col. Richard B. Pelton, a university professor who died on July 29, 1966 at the age of 56.

probably to Whitman's disappointment, but continued to circle until the incident ended. As the pilot said later, the only protection he had was "the fabric side of the airplane and a blue shirt." Shooting a plane out of the sky would have added considerably to Whitman's marksmanship credentials and the drama of the day, but it was not to be.

It isn't possible to calculate how many bullets were fired by or at Whitman that day. Even though the investigative reports made afterward were very detailed, nobody swept and counted the shell cases atop the Tower, and Officer Shoquist recalled seeing various people picking up the brass empties. Various Texas Exes—alumni—around the country have one or more brass hulls picked up on the ground mixed in with their other detritus from college, but nobody saw any reason to get after-battle ammunition supply reports from students. Whitman took at least 700 rounds to the top of the Tower with him, but if a count of how many bullets remained after he was killed exists, the number has been lost. He may have fired as few as 100 times, hitting a target 45 times (Ehlke twice), or he may have fired five times that number.[35]

Each of Austin's finest was required to file a report at the end of their shift or extra duty, and SOP for an incident in which an officer discharged a weapon at a citizen might normally have resulted in a temporary suspension, an investigation, and a hearing. In the case of Charles Whitman, a rough count of the number of shots fired was all that was required.[36] Adding that from citizens, more lead was put into the air than in a few well-remembered Civil War battles, and it is somewhat amazing that none of it fell out of the sky onto citizens, automobiles, or family pets. Perhaps relic hunters with metal detectors will scavenge a few from front yards to sell on eBay. Perhaps it has already been done.

The story was dominating local and national news. Major networks, newspapers and periodicals that did not already have a reporter in Austin were dispatching representatives to the city as fast as they could. The names of the dead and wounded were being compiled at Brackenridge, and even though it was customary to not release the name of anyone killed before their family was notified, KTBC decided to do so in order to provide reassurance to lucky but terrified families whose loved

Paul Bolton, grandfather and namesake of shooting victim Paul Bolton Sonntag, a speech writer for LBJ and director of KTBC News of Austin, was at his desk in the news office when he heard the name of his grandson read on the air by newscaster Joe Roddy.

ones were actually safe.[37] Newscaster Joe Roddy began reading a list of those who were confirmed to be dead during a live broadcast from the hospital. As he was doing so, the director of the KTBC news staff, Paul Bolton, interrupted him.

"Joe, hold it a minute, this is Paul over at the newsroom. Everyone is interested in that list of names. I think you have my grandson there. Go over that list of names again, please." Roddy read the list again and Bolton listened. When Roddy was finished, Bolton removed his headphones, stood slowly, and walked out of the newsroom. The name could not have helped but leap out at him—Paul Bolton Sonntag—his namesake, his beloved grandson, was dead.[38]

The reverse siege was now over an hour old and had less than half an hour to go. Over the full 96 minutes at least six victims were wounded who cannot be placed in a reliable time line. Furthermore, although the number of wounded is often cited by reports as being precisely 32, that number is probably low. The figure is based on the names that made it into the police investigation which in turn was based on lists of those who went to Brackenridge, the U.T. Student Health Center, St. David's, or Seton Hospital to be treated for injuries. A number of those had fairly minor wounds, such as from flying glass or small bullet shards. They were quickly treated and released, and by the time the police arrived were no longer available to be interviewed. Their names made it into the hospital records and a report was filed for the police investigation, but no information was collected outside of a slight explanation of their wounds. Also among the records are hurried notes kept by either hospital personnel or police officers, listing known victims, including at least two, Miguel Solis and Brenda Wilkenson, not subsequently listed with the wounded. Undoubtedly there were others even more "lightly wounded" who didn't seek treatment at these locations or at all, such as the unidentified man whose minor wounding was caught on film, and so were not included among the number injured.

One might think that all of the publicity given the event, its historical standing, and the passage of fifty years would have filled in all of the blanks. Yet for many people the events of that "Monday Monday, can't trust that day" were something they forced out of their minds as quickly as possible. They took no pride in being scared silly or hurt badly, and did not consider it something to brag about later. Among the wounded, many developed the attitude expressed 17 years later by

Morris Hohmann when he told an interviewer, "I frankly would like to see the issue put to rest and not brought up on an annual basis."[39]

The six victims whose time and place of wounding cannot be verified are C.A. Stewart, Robert Frede, F.L Foster, Billy Bedford, Mariana Martinez, and Della Martinez. The last two were mother and daughter, respectively, visiting from Monterrey, Mexico, and were treated for injuries from shell fragments and released. They were visiting family or friends who lived at 2515 Rio Grande in Austin, and they returned to Monterrey with an interesting tale to tell.

C.A. Stewart was from Baytown. He was treated at Brackenridge and released, but the nature of his injury was not recorded. F. L. Foster lived at 5702 Mojave Drive and had the same experience. Robert Frede was treated at Brackenridge for "gunshot" and released with no record of his address. Billy Bedford managed to stay so far below the radar that there is no police report or medical report about him; only that he left before being treated.

Various stories of miraculous shots or interesting wounds circulated that may be accurate but are not supported by good records, such as John Pipkin's recollection that "[h]e was picking people off at incredible distances and hitting them where he could do the most damage. I heard about a guy who was eating a sandwich in the front yard of the Kappa house, minding his own business, when he was shot through the chest."[40]

A verifiable truth was looming for Charles Whitman. He had only moments left to live.

---

1. 96 Minutes at 179

2. Interview of George Russell, Mayor of Marble Falls, April 7, 2015.

3. Report of Officer Cooney, APD, Aug. 1, 1966, AHC.

4. *Ibid.*; Forrest Preece *Westside Stories*, http://trysomethingmore.com/westside-stories-by-forrest-preece/.

5. Interview of Clif Drummond and Bob Higley, May 8, 2015.

6. 96 Minutes at 179.

7. *Sniper 66; The Charles Whitman Murders,* Part 2, https://www.youtube.com/watch?v=t-3dAaV9R3IU, at 6.00-.02 minutes of 14.11 minutes.

8. Testimony of James Bryce, Claire James Wilson, Alfred McAlister regarding Senate Bill 11, before the Senate State Affairs Committee, Austin, Texas, February 12, 2015.

9. 96 minutes at 180.

10. E-mail exchange between Monte Akers and Otis Shearer, December, 2014.

11. 96 Minutes at 177.

12. Interview of George Cofer, Austin, Texas, March 19, 2015.

13. *Ibid.*

14. She was badly sunburned and slightly stunned. She returned to her apartment, made lunch, ate, and returned to her studies. Laurel Butler, life partner of Rita Starpattern, quoted by Forrest Preece *supra*.

15. Interview of John Fox, April 24, 2015, and exchange of email messages with him on April 25, 2015. The dramatic, multiple rescue was caught on film by at least two photographers, and can be viewed online at http://www.texasarchive.org/library/index.php/Special:GSM-SearchPage?fulltext, and at https://www.youtube.com/watch?v=MAET3gFy5E8.

16. 96 Minutes at 178.

17. Lavergne at 178.

18. Report for Offense No. 968193, Assault with Intent to Commit Murder, dated August 1, 1966 by Sgt. D. Kidd, Austin P.D., AHC

19. Lavergne at 245.

20. *Ibid.* at 178

21. Telephone interview with Orville, "Chip" Jansen, May 15, 2015.

22. DVD of David Orton, March 9, 2012, provided the authors by David Orton. An armored car was also used to rescue wounded,. It was used to pick up Adrian Littlefield and David Gunby, and at least one source reported that Whitman peppered it with bullets, although other accounts say that the only vehicle he fired at was Alex Hernandez's bicycle. *Sniper 66*, https://www.youtube.com/watch?v=hRDHYeH82OA

23. *Ibid.* at 183.

24. 96 Minutes at 182, 195.

25. Interview of Judge Jerry Dellana by Sara Rider, June 2, 1983, Original Tape No. 0511B, AHC. Misunderstandings also occurred. An elderly, obese man was brought in who was believed to be one of Whitman's victims. No wounds were visible and it was thought he died of a heart attack until he was turned on his stomach. A small spot of blood was seen in the small of his back, and Dellana said it was decided the man had been shot in the back with a 6 mm bullet that had not exited. Dellana remembered the incident clearly, only to find out in 1983 that the patient's name was A.G. Harris, and he actually had died of a heart attack with no connection to Whitman.

26. Interview of Dr. Ada Simond by T. Galyen, 1986; Tape recording at the AHC.

27. 96 Minutes at 195.

28. Interview of Dr. Albert Lalonde by Sara Rider, June 2, 1983, Original Tape No. 0511A, AHC.

29. Only two of Whitman's female fatalities were shot in the chest, Claudia Rutt and Karen Griffith, and whereas the authors of *Admissions: The Extraordinary History of Brackenridge Hospital* identified the girl described in Lalonde as Rutt, it is well established that Claudia Rutt was DOA when she reached Brackenridge after being the last victim taken to the hospital by Cook

Funeral Home ambulance driver and mortician, David Orton; Interview of David Orton, *supra*; Neal Spelce, *The Neal Spelce Collection, No. 3 - UT Tower Shooting*, http://www.texasarchive. org/library/index.php?title=The_Neal_Spelce_Collection,_No._3_-_UT_Tower_Shooting.

30. Dr. Lalonde, supra.

31. Interview of Morris Hohmann by Sara Rider, May 31, 1983, Original Tape No. 0513, AHC.

32. Lavergne at 190

33. 96 Minutes at 178.

34. Lavergne at 207.

35. Several of Whitman's shots that missed were recorded by police officers. Officer Culp saw two shots, the second of which killed Speed. Officer Day was at the west doorway of Batts Building when two shots hit ten yard west of him. Running across South Mall and zig-zagging, a bullet hit six feet to his right, and another on his left. Officer Moody said a bullet struck in front of his motorcycle on Speedway, a second hit a tree, and a third was fired straight down at him. Officer Simpson reported that one shot "nearly hit him" and was followed by two more "even closer."

36. For example: Officer Baylor: had two boxes of ammunition and fired approx. 50 rounds, saw Officer Garrett open fire. Returned more fire later;

Officer Cooney—fired one and half boxes of ammunition from his personal rifle, a 400 Mag. Weatherbee

Officer Day: Day—inside the tower he tore the screen off a window on the third floor and fired his .38 pistol toward the observation deck until he ran out of ammunition;

Officer Estepp—fired two shots from his personal .243 Remington, Model 700 with a four power scope from the top floor of the Administration Building;

Officer Fraser—fired several shots to no avail from the biology lab and greenhouse;

Officer Gann: fired six to eight times from the BAE building;

Officer Gerding: fired 20-25 rounds from the top of the business economics building. Hit what he believed was a box of ammo or field glasses case (actually one of Whitman's rifles) sitting on ledge near south face of clock;

Officer McCullough: fired one rifle shot from the observatory of the Physics building when he saw Whitman fire a round almost straight down at 12:10;

Officer Moody: fired ten rounds from the university observatory;

Officer Petri: fired eight shots from 21st and Wichita at the "port holes" on the south side of the tower;

Officer Olsen: observed from the top of the B.A.E. (business administration and economics) building while Estepp and Woody fired their rifles at the drain holes;

Officer McCullough—fired one shot about 12 o'clock, and then with Sgt. Moody fired four shots about 12:45;

Officer Rigby: fired one shot at what he thought was a man behind the clock (but wasn't) that hit below the clock on south side, then fired six shots from the 4th floor of a building;

Officer Schulle—fired eight to ten shots from the SE corner of the Engineering building at 26th & San Jacinto;

Officer Simpson: obtained a rifle and fired from the SW corner of the 2nd building north of 21st and University Ave. and fired repeatedly until radio report came in that the sniper had been apprehended;

Officer Wilson—fired two shots, one at the south most drainage hole on the east side and one when the sniper stood up at the same location; and

Officer Woody—fired three shots.

37. Neal Spelce in *Sniper 66*

38. Lavergne at 188.

39. Interview of Morris Hohmann by Sara Rider, May 31, 1983, Original Tape No. 0513, AHC.

40. 96 Minutes at 177.

CHAPTER EIGHT

Over the Edge

We get to the landing and I look out and I can see the face of a small boy with his tongue protruding out, he's dead you know, he's facing me.

-Ramiro Martinez, 1999

With tunnel vision I aimed at a white headband around his forehead, fired .00 buck round and observed his head bouncing back and forth.

-Houston McCoy, 2010

After an hour of reverse siege, there were dozens of law enforcement officers closing in on Whitman. His casual asides to Francis Schuck in 1961 and 1962 that "a well-armed man could stand off an army" from atop the Tower was purest fantasy, and his overpacking for the duration of the standoff was total. He could have saved himself the $2.04 for the dolly, carried up longarms and scatter gun in a blanket, with ammo in his black attaché, and had all he needed.

Like the Navy Seas who killed Osama Bin Laden, it was a team effort that finally brought him down, albeit a hell of a lot less planned out, and the madding public has insisted on singling out one trigger puller for credit and hero worship when it might have been any of nearly a dozen officers or one civilian who finally carried out Whitman's suicide-by-cop finale.

One of dozens of students and bystanders who seized rifles to fire at the sniper in the Tower from the ground, helping to direct traffic at the base of the Tower after Whitman had been killed and bodies of his victims were being removed from the Tower. Note in this photo and others that the wearing of white or light-colored short-sleeved shirts and dark trousers was so common for young men on campus during the summer of 1966 that the fashion could be mistaken for a school uniform.

179

Novelist Harry Crews visited the U.T. Campus in the 1970s, while memory of the shootings was fresh, and became haunted by the Whitman story. Both were former Marines, but that was not what caused Crews' empathy and angst. He later wrote an essay called "Climbing the Tower," that was published in *Esquire* magazine in 1977 in which he wondered how many times Whitman must have considered going up the Tower and unleashing his demons before he finally did so. "How long must he have resisted the temptation! What battles must he have fought in himself before he finally lost it all forever."[1] That was what drew Crews to Whitman—the inner turmoil—something the author had known all his life and with which some of his stories fairly squirm. He wrote that "[a]ll of us have our towers to climb. Some are worse than others, but to deny that you have your tower to climb and that you must resist it or succumb to the temptation to do it, to deny that is done at the peril of your heart and mind."[2]

The eight peace officers and single civilian who chose to climb the Tower around 1 p.m. on August 1, 1966, neither denied, resisted, nor succumbed. They certainly had a tower—the Tower—to climb, but to deny doing so would have been at the peril of the lives and welfare of untold innocents rather than themselves. Those who did so were Phillip Conner, W.A. "Dub" Cowan, Jerry Day, Ramiro Martinez, Houston McCoy, Harold Moe, George Shepard, and Milton Shoquist. The civilian was Allen Crum.

W.A. "Dub" Cowan, Department of Public Safety intelligence officer who was one of the first inside the Tower on August 1, 1966.

Cowan was a Department of Public Safety intelligence officer, and the other officers were APD. There were other lawmen, like the two DPS patrolmen Heard and Stomberger were trailing when Heard was shot and the Texas Rangers Vandiver accompanied who had the same or a similar intention, but those nine turned out to be the ones who put an end to the madness.

All of the men were equally brave, and any one of them might have come out of the day the hero, the trigger puller, or as another one of the dead lined up on the floor at Brackenridge. As things turned out, two would get most of the credit.

Those two were Ramiro "Ray" Martinez and Houston McCoy. Both were from small Texas towns, Martinez from Rotan and McCoy from

Austin Police Officer Ramiro Martinez, 1966

Menard. Martinez was a devout Catholic; McCoy was an independent.

Martinez had been with the APD for five years; McCoy three. Martinez had attended U.T. for one year; McCoy attended Lamar University for a semester. Both joined the army and were sent to Germany, and in 1966 both were married, Martinez with twin daughters and McCoy with two sons. Martinez was 29 and McCoy was 26. Both men were good-looking and both acted courageously, but it took over 40 years for the correct facts of what each did and accomplished to be nailed down and understood.

McCoy reported for duty at 6:45 a.m., and after morning traffic settled down and he had some coffee, he ran into Billy Speed near the French Legation, a historic building in Austin that housed the ambassador from France during the Republic of Texas days. They talked for a while and Billy mentioned his plans to return to college, then they parted and McCoy went to the I-35 bridge over Town Lake. There he was approached by a city worker who said he'd found a social security card stuck in the branches of a young tree near the lake and a pair of shoes and pants nearby. McCoy retrieved the card and clothes—on August 3rd the body of a suicide was found in the lake—and noticed three young Latinos swimming there, which violated a city ordinance. He got close enough to be seen, hoping they would take the hint and leave, but they did not and he had to run them off. As he was returning to his vehicle the radio dispatcher called his unit number and he answered.

It was 11:52 and the first calls about what was happening on campus were being broadcast, but a combination of bad recep-tion and an overly excited dispatcher made the message indecipherable. He did not know he was the first officer called for a job that would pull in most of the entire force. After moving his car and exchanging calls, he finally heard "University Tower," and headed that way. Before he arrived the message became clearer—a shooting was in progress.

Houston McCoy and his bride, Ruth Anne Marie Gebhart, shortly after her arrival to Texas from Germany in 1963.

As he approached he could hear the shots and see puffs of either smoke or limestone dust on top of the Tower, and being one of the first officers on the scene, it is likely he actually saw gunsmoke. Modern smokeless powder lives up to its name but not completely, and McCoy knew what to look for. He drove to the north side of the Tower and parked within ten feet of its base, but there was no entrance on that side and he was concerned that a radical group of self-styled revolutionaries might be in multiple positions above, so he drove away.

He assisted two students who had their own rifles, driving one to his apartment to retrieve his, and even going to Everett Hardware and buying three boxes of 30.06 ammunition with his own money for them. He even fired a few shots at the Tower with one of their rifles, but he'd been trained on open sights and was unaccustomed to using a scope, so he gave the rifle back. He took the second student to the third floor of a building south of the Tower and while helping him get in position he saw Billy Speed get shot in the shoulder, but didn't believe the wound was serious. Telling the student to "keep shooting and keep the snipers penned down," and to "move from window to window at random so the snipers cannot pinpoint your position," he started to leave when the student asked, "What should I do if I get a bead on one of them?" McCoy replied, "Shoot the shit out of him."

He assisted a rookie officer who was arguing with a city bus driver determined to drive his regular route down the Drag, and convinced him

Austin police officer George Shepard, one of the officers who went up the U.T. Tower on August 1, 1966 to bring an end to the killing spree, being decorated for his service that day by Major K.R. Herbert, head of APD's Criminal Investigations Division.

to turn around and stay clear of the University. It was then close to 12:30 and the APD dispatcher radioed for volunteers to report to the University Police headquarters located just off of San Jacinto Street.

McCoy was the first APD officer to arrive. U.T. Police Sergeant A. Y. Barr was putting the team together. Soon Phillip Conner, Harold Moe, Milton Shoquist, and George Shepard drove up in the same APD vehicle. They brought no rifles. They had tried to find better weapons, but the only one in the Police armory, other than a tear gas gun, was what Shoquist called a Machine Gun Kelly gun—a Thompson with a round magazine—but there was no ammunition for it and none of them had fired it before. They left it but brought the tear gas gun, which fired a 3 mm. gas grenade with fins, similar to a mortar.

They agreed that the best weapon to employ for their purposes was a shotgun, but only McCoy had one, and he had only four shells for it. They were double ought buck, a load large enough to tear a man apart, but he had no way of knowing how many shots he might need. He asked the other officers for shells and searched the car they'd come in, but found none.

Barr said he would escort them to the cooling towers for the University, where he had a man named William Wilcox waiting to take them down to the tunnels. The group of six men began walking across the campus toward the Tower.

Officer Jerry Day of the APD was on patrol when he heard reports about what was happening so he drove to the campus and parked in the west alley of Guadalupe and 23rd Streets. He saw a woman who had been shot in the chest, probably Karen Griffith or Sandra Wilson, being attended to by three men. He ran across the Drag, went around one building and

William Wilcox, "the tunnel man," who led the Austin police officers through the underground tunnels from the cooling towers to the Tower.

through another until he reached the Tower, then entered through the south door.

There he ran into Allen Crum, the supervisor from the University Co-op who had come alone, unarmed, soon after the shooting started. Initially Day declined Crum's offer to help, but upon learning Crum was retired from the military and after Crum suggested he might need somebody "to watch his back," Day reconsidered.[3] Initially they discussed running onto the South Mall to assist the wounded who were lying there, but decided there was too much risk of being shot. They then discussed how Day might be able to shoot the sniper from the back of the administration building, where he tried one unsuccessful shot. They then ascended the elevator, and were approached by W.A. "Dub" Cowan. He was wearing civilian clothes and had come on his own, carrying a rifle.

Day said later that somehow he knew Cowan was law enforcement when he saw him, which was fortunate considering that a civilian carrying a rifle inside the Tower could easily have been mistaken for the shooter. He introduced himself and Day asked if he had a sidearm. When Cowan answered in the affirmative, Day suggested he give the rifle to Crum, which he did. It was an "an elderly Remington autoloading rifle, the kind made between 1906 and 1950 and much favored by law officers. This one was in caliber .30 Remington, with a magazine holding five rounds."[4] The three men took the elevator to the 26th floor, rather than the 27th, in order to have some extra room in case there was more than one shooter. There they were joined by Officer Ramiro Martinez.

Martinez was not on duty that morning, and was at home fixing his lunch when he heard what was happening on the news. After calling the station to confirm that officers were needed, he drove his personal car and parked a block off the Drag near 21st Street. From there he ran from building to building and worked his way across the campus until he reached the Tower. Along the way he saw six bodies lying on the mall, and entered through the south door.

Martinez stated in 1999 that "[w]hen I got to the Tower entrance there was a young man with a clipboard and he asked me my name and wrote it down on the clipboard and I don't know what the hell for. But anyway, at least he was doing something." He then said he got on the elevator and rode to the top floor. The identity of the young man with the clipboard has been lost. He was probably an elevator attendant. Officer Jerry

Day ran into an attendant who initially told him he could not go up, and whom Day obeyed for a few moments. If the mystery man was an attendant, neither Day nor Martinez made mention of his taking them up.

Martinez encountered a University security officer, probably L. W. Gebert or Jack O. Rodman, and borrowed his hand-held radio to call the police station to ask them to send an armored car to pick up the bodies, but he was unable to get through. He rode up the elevator to the 26th floor, where he found Day, Cowan, and Crum. Cowan was trying to call out on a telephone to request more assistance.

At the cooling towers, about 1:15, Sgt. Barr turned the five APD officers over to William Wilcox without making introductions, and for years after the officers remembered him only as "the tunnel man." They walked through the tunnels, which were both hot and a challenge to navigate. Side passages branched off, servicing numerous buildings, and without Wilcox they might have wandered about lost. When they arrived at a service elevator, Wilcox told them it would take them to the 5th floor of the Tower. They crowded in and ascended.

On the 26th floor, Martinez, Crum and Day tried office doors and found one locked. Martinez knocked. It was the room in which the two nuns and about ten other people had barricaded themselves. He identified himself as a police officer and heard them moving furniture. When they came out he directed them to go to the elevator and descend.

Just then M.J. Gabour approached, still carrying his wife's bloody white shoes. "A guy's out there," he said, obviously distraught. "I need your gun. I want to go out there and kill him. He's killed my whole family."

Jerry Day joined Martinez and told Gabour that he should go to the elevator and then to the ground floor, and that the police would tend to his family. That wasn't what Gabour wanted to hear. He became physical and tried to wrestle their weapons away. Day grabbed him and escorted him to the elevator, planning to put him inside and send him down.

Martinez was pumped. Adrenaline was coursing through his system and he was wound so tight that Jerry Day thought at one point he might need to bop him on the head with the butt of his revolver to get him calmed down. He was experiencing visual and audio "exclusion," which is a term peace officers use to describe the tunnel-vision focus that settles on a law man who is preparing to go into a high-risk, potentially deadly confrontation.[5]

When Day took Gabour down to the elevator, Martinez moved toward the stairs to the 27th floor. Crum came up behind him and asked "are you going up?" When Martinez said he was, Crum said "well you're not going up by yourself. Let's do it service style," by which he meant they should leap frog up, with one providing cover as the other moved. Being a veteran, Martinez knew what he meant and said "Fine." The two men started up.

Above, Mike and Mary Gabour heard someone approaching from below. "Play dead," Mike whispered, thinking it might be someone coming to help the shooter. Both lay still. Mike shut his eyes, waited, then peeked. He saw the two men. One was wearing a police officer's uniform. The sight was very welcome. He lifted a hand and waved for them to come on.

Frank Holder, an inspector and engineer for the Otis Elevator Company, he was in the Tower to inspect the elevators when Whitman began shooting, and he served as elevator operator for the police officers who went up the Tower after Whitman.

What Martinez and Crum saw on the landing at the top of the stairs was anything but welcome. It was ugly in the extreme. Fifteen-year-old Mark Gabour was dead, eyes open, tongue swollen and protruding. He seemed to be staring at Martinez. Mary Gabour was lying in a large pool of blood, and Mike Gabour, seriously wounded but alive, was lying beside or partially on top of her. Beyond them another woman, Marguerite Lamport, was obviously dead.

Martinez approached Mike, who managed to speak. "Come on," he said, "he's outside, he's outside on the walk." Martinez and Crum started to move past the shattered family but Mike had a request. "Can you move my mother?" he asked. "Bullets may ricochet and I don't want her to get hit." Martinez and Crum moved Mary Gabour and then Mike, but left him so that he was still lying partially on his wounded mother.

They looked up the last flight of stairs. There was the desk, blocking the way, with its legs at the edge of the top stair. Next to it was the white metal trash can, blocking the gap between the desk and the wall as though it could somehow stop anyone from getting by. Crum and Martinez gave each other a quizzical look, and Crum recalled later that the sight of the trash can "struck me as funny in a grim way."[6]

Martinez started to climb but Crum, realizing that Martinez did not seem inclined to wait for backup, had a question. "Are we playing for keeps?" he asked. "You're damned right we're playing for keeps," Martinez replied. "Then you better deputize me," Crum said. Until that instant Martinez had assumed Crum was another peace officer wearing civilian clothes, like Dub Cowan. He was startled, but did not slow down. "Consider yourself deputized," said Martinez.

Martinez started up. Rather than try to squeeze around the desk, as Mike Gabour had attempted, Martinez and Crum pushed the desk ahead of them, using it as a shield in case the shooter suddenly appeared. He did not, and soon they were in the reception area. They saw the trail of blood on the floor that Cheryl Botts thought was varnish, followed it to the couch and found Edna Townsley. Miraculously, she was still alive.

There were two windows, east side and west side, looking out onto the walkway but they did not see the shooter, only "a lot of debris, empty cartridges, and food and stuff scattered around."

Meanwhile, the five APD officers—McCoy, Shoquist, Conner, Moe, and Shepard—encountered Frank Holder, an inspector and engineer for the Otis Elevator Company, on the 5th floor. He had been in the Tower to inspect the elevators when Whitman began shooting, and he offered to serve as their elevator operator. All but one of the elevators were supposed to have attendants to manipulate the handle that would later be replaced by individual floor buttons, although there had not always been an attendant present for recent elevator rides that day. Now, Holder took them to the 26th floor.

McCoy, not knowing what might greet them, switched his shotgun off safety and pointed it toward the door as it opened. Jerry Day, standing near the elevator with M. J. Gabour and not expecting anyone from below, cocked his .38 caliber service revolver and pointed it toward the same opening door. The two officers were suddenly gun muzzle to gun muzzle, but neither was wound so tightly that he pulled a trigger. Instead they both grinned and lowered their weapons.

Day introduced Cowan, and poined out M.J. Gabour, whom McCoy described as "a peculiar acting gray-haired man in the room" who was "the father, husband, and brother of several people laying wounded and dead on the stairway leading up." Shoquist recalled him as being "glassy-eyed and obviously in shock."[7]

McCoy consulted the others. Should they go after the sniper first or try to get the wounded to safety? He asked Frank Holder if there was any way to get to the clock area above the observation deck in order to be above the shooter. Holder said there was. All McCoy had to do was

The base of the stairs to the 28th floor reception room at which the bodies of the dead and wounded of the Gabour family came to rest. APD Officer Milton Shoquist described the scene as having so much blood that it came over the tops of the officers' shoes, and made the floor so slick it was like "trying to walk on an ice skating rink."

climb up through a small door in the ceiling of the elevator to get on top of it, then Holder would take it higher, which would allow McCoy to climb outside and be above the clocks and the observation deck. McCoy thought that sounded like a plan, with the proviso that "[w]e both hoped that there was no sniper already there but he believed there was not."

They decided to remove the wounded next, bring the elevator back up, and for McCoy to try to get above the observation deck and the shooter. Phillip Conner, a former army medic, was in charge of removing the wounded while Day and McCoy provided cover. There were only two wounded, so tending to them was not perceived as creating unnecessary delay in going after the shooter. What they didn't realize was that Martinez had already eliminated the luxury they had in planning and methodically following through.

The five officers took the stairs to the 27th floor. Milton Shoquist never forgot the sight of the four bodies they encountered, and his voice caught when he described it nearly fifty years later. There was so much blood, he said, that it came over the tops of their

The shotgun used by Houston McCoy on August 1, 1966, in a display case at the Austin Police Department

WINCHESTER MODEL 1200 12 GUAGE SHOTGUN
SERIAL NUMBER 137093   APD NUMBER 19

This shotgun was used to end the life of Charles Whitman, the University of Texas tower sniper, on August 1, 1966.

It was carried to the top of the UT tower by then APD Officer Houston McCoy. It was McCoy who fired the fatal shots that ended the tower tragedy.

The tag that accompanies the shotgun used by Houston McCoy on August 1, 1966, in its display case at the Austin Police Department

shoes, and made the floor so slick it was like "trying to walk on an ice skating rink." As a result of walking through the carnage and carrying the two wounded down to the elevator on the 26th floor, he and the others became smeared with blood, so that for days afterward he would find it caked—in the eyelets for his shoe strings, in the loops for bullets on his belt, and elsewhere.[8]

Day and McCoy waded through the blood and bodies. As they were doing so, Mrs. Gabour asked McCoy if "we could get whoever was laying on top of her off of her." McCoy and Day moved Mike so that he was no longer resting on his mother, and told them the police were going to get everyone to the hospital as soon as possible. Mike Gabour then spoke up. He had lifted his head enough to see McCoy's shotgun and even though he was wounded so badly he'd not been able to stand, he decided he needed to go kill the man who'd shot him and his family. "Give me that gun," Mike said. "Let me get the son of a bitch!"

Mary Gabour winced. There was simply no excuse for such foul language.

"Don't worry," McCoy replied. "I'll get the son of a bitch for you. Just how many are up there?' Mrs. Gabour winced again. Men could be so rude. "Just one," Mike answered.

McCoy still did not know about Crum and Martinez, who were then approaching the door on the southeast side of the reception room, facing south and leading out onto the deck. It was made of wood, containing eight glass panels in two columns of four, each panel about 14 inches tall and 10 inches wide. Martinez and Crum peered out onto the south side. They saw no shooter, but could clearly see a dolly wedged securely against the door on the outside. The door pushed open rather than pulled, so Martinez pushed. The door held. He pushed again and the dolly rocked back and then forward, thudding against the door and making a loud noise, but keeping the men inside.

McCoy heard the racket, pointed his shotgun up the stairs and switched it off safety. He looked like he was about to fire. Jerry Day quickly told him about Martinez and Crum, and McCoy said later that it was a good thing they, especially "the civilian," had not come down the stairs before then, as he would have shot him.

The plan to get on top of the elevator no longer seemed appropriate. The two above McCoy and Day were apparently preparing to go after him alone. Telling Day to tell Conner and the others about the civilian so that they wouldn't shoot him, McCoy climbed the last few steps and entered the reception area. He saw Martinez in the corner at the door and Crum standing behind him. McCoy wrote that Martinez saw him, that not a word was said, but that Martinez "started banging on the glass door near the southeast corner." Martinez wrote later that he did not see McCoy until after he was outside on the walkway.

Day came up behind McCoy, who told him to cover the window on the west side of the reception room until McCoy was in position and then to cover the east window. Martinez gave a mighty shove against the door and finally knocked the dolly over. It hit the concrete floor outside with a huge clang. The door swung open and Martinez walked out. Crum turned to McCoy and said, "your fellow officer is outside and may need your help," then followed Martinez. McCoy had no choice but to do the same.

Martinez pointed his revolver west, then east. The door was at the southeast corner of the Tower, so he needed only lean around to be able to see the entirety of the east side. He did so. No shooter. Crum moved outside behind him.

Whitman spent most of his time that day shooting from the south and west sides of the Tower, and the least time shooting from the north, but he was then on that side, probably because he knew police officers were coming and the northwest corner was the most defensible. The door was on the south side and there were windows on the east and west sides, but there was no way he could be seen in the northwest corner until someone came around either the northeast or southwest corner. He didn't know which direction they would come from, maybe both, and probably heard the noise of the dolly hitting the floor. His radio was on, and he may even have heard that officers were closing in.

In the corner, he was not easy to see. The spotlights used for lighting up the Tower at night and after successful sports endeavors lined the inner wall of the deck, 13 lights to a side, each more than a foot in diameter and spaced about 18 inches apart. The looked like nothing so much as glass-topped stools, and by sitting down in the corner, only his head, shoulders, and legs were visible from the northeast corner and he had a straight shot at the southwest corner.

For all his careful planning, meticulous overpacking, and eye to detail, one may think that Whitman could have done a better job of

The north side of the observation deck of the Tower in 1966, taken from the northeast corner, the site from which Martinez and McCoy shot and killed Whitman as he was sitting in the northwest corner, where the APD officer is standing. The tower lights served to obscure the officers' view of the sniper.

barricading the door. The width of the walkway varied because the walls of the Tower contained recesses and extensions, but it was not so wide at the door that he could not have wedged the footlocker or a combination of items he'd brought into the space to keep the door shut. On the other hand, the eight glass panels in the door could be broken or shot out without much difficulty so that officers could either crawl through or reach out and remove the items barricading the door. Whitman's thinking may have been that the noise of someone forcing a way through the door would be the best defense he could muster.

Martinez and Crum waited to see if the sniper would come to check on what caused the clatter when the dolly fell, but "there was a lot of noise, because there was a lot of people shooting up at the tower and every time somebody fired a pistol or rifle or whatever it was ricocheting amongst the buildings and it sounded like thunder, so there was a lot of noise."

Martinez told Crum, "if he comes around that corner (the southwest) shoot him. I'm going to go search for him." Crum pointed his rifle west at the stretch of walkway visible from in front of the door. Martinez went east, around the corner and along the east side of the Tower, dropped to all fours and began moving slowly, almost crawling, along the walkway. McCoy came out the door, turned the corner and followed. Inside the reception area, Phillip Conner came in and took Jerry Day's position at the east window. Day joined Crum and both covered the south walkway leading to the west side.

Bullets fired from below were smacking into the side of the Tower, making what Martinez said were "soft thuds," and leaving chunks and particles of limestone on the walkway. McCoy watched Martinez moving ahead of him, "and three million splats against the wall reminded" him that they still had ground fire. Martinez turned around, saw McCoy for what he later said was the first time, and motioned for him to stay low.

McCoy did not have any intention to get down and crawl the way Martinez was doing, but was glad Martinez was doing it, because it gave him a better chance to shoot over him. Instead he bent his knees and leaned his back against the wall, sliding his feet sideways, with his shotgun aimed above Martinez's head and looking up and to both sides, not knowing where the sniper might appear and worrying that he or a second shooter was above them all the while. His thoughts were of his family and of "contact lens don't fail me now."

As Martinez crawled past a drain spout a bullet from below came through it, striking the wall between him and McCoy. McCoy made certain to move past each drain spout quickly. Martinez made it to the northeast corner of the Tower and prepared to peer around it.

Charles Whitman had only seconds to live.

Throughout history there are instances, mere collections of seconds dealing with death that are studied, debated and analyzed far beyond the expectation any increment of time might have for itself. The seconds when JFK was assassinated, as well as those in which his brother Robert and MLK were killed, are examples, as are those in which Billy the Kid, Jesse James, and John Dillinger died. Such were the seconds that made up 1:24 p.m. on August 1, 1966.

Martinez put his head around the corner, "and I looked, I saw the sniper at the northwest corner, he was sitting down pointing an M-1 carbine trying to bring it down on me."

Ten shots followed from three different weapons on the observation deck, none of them Whitman's. One of the shots was not from Martinez or McCoy, and its exact timing cannot be nailed down with certainty. It might have made a critical difference, or it may just be a footnote.

That shot was fired by Allen Crum. After Martinez left him at the door, he spotted a pump action rifle and a light green towel lying on the south walkway and, telling Day to cover him, retrieved the rifle, saw it had been hit by gunfire, and put it back down. It was Whitman's Remington pump-action rifle that Officer Burt Gerding had picked off as it was lying on top of the wall. Crum returned to the door, looked around the southeast corner, and saw McCoy and Martinez still moving north. A few seconds later he thought he heard the sniper running along the west side. There was a lot of other noise, principally gunfire from below, and Crum also thought he heard yelling. "I heard the subject running on the

The north side of the observation deck of the Tower in 2015, taken from the same position as the photo from 1966.

walkway, I fired one round in an attempt to stop him. I heard him run the other direction."[9]

Others said Crum's shot was an "accidental discharge." That is what Officer Shoquist understood and what Officer Day believed, saying later that the bullet flew right past his head. Yet its being an accident doesn't seem likely. Crum was retired military, having spent 21 years in the Air Force and, and as his son recalled in 2015, "he was very much an expert with weapons and knew how to use them and how to take them apart. If you will remember, and as I was told by my father, he did not mishandle the rife nor did he fire a round off by accident."[10] Later, Crum neither sought attention for what he did nor felt comfortable being treated as a hero. Had he fired the shot accidentally, he would have said so, and no one would have thought less of him for it. Ray Martinez referred to him later as being "like the Rock of Gibraltar."[11]

Crum believed that Whitman really was running along the west side and the shot into the west wall caused him to turn around and run the other direction. However, Officer Phil Conner was, by then, inside the reception area of the 28th floor and covering the west window. As Officer Milton Shoquist said later, "he would have seen someone running on that side. He might not have seen him going, but he would have seen him coming back."[12] He saw neither.

Even the idea that Crum fired accidentally has promoters. If Whitman was, as is almost certain, sitting in the northwest corner and waiting, the shot would have diverted his attention from the north walkway on his left, to the west walkway on his right for an instant, thereby providing Martinez and McCoy with something akin to divine intervention. Officer Martinez recalled later that when he first saw Whitman, he was pointing his M-1 carbine in the direction of the southwest corner, the direction from which Crum would have come.

Another theory, probably correct, is that Crum heard Martinez running immediately after he and McCoy fired. When interviewed on television the day after the shooting, Crum stated that "they (the officers) made contact first." Whitman was wearing soft-soled tennis shoes and would not have made much, if any, noise, whereas the APD officers were wearing boots or hard-soled shoes. The chips of limestone knocked to the floor by gunshots added extra crunch when they walked or ran. If Crum fired his shot in response to someone running, it was probably because he heard Martinez and thought it was the sniper, so he fired, after which

Martinez discharged the shotgun into Whitman's body. Thus Crum's shot came nanoseconds after Whitman had been killed, and made no real difference in the outcome. That is particularly likely if Crum fired because he heard someone yelling, which also would have been Martinez.

Crum's rifle failed to feed a second round into the chamber, and he had to thumb the cartridge into place. He then began to "creep along the south wall toward the southwest corner, when I heard rapid fire along the north corner, then nothing. Martinez and McCoy had got him."[13] If that is so, it was not Martinez whom Crum heard running or shouting, but if the "rapid fire... then nothing" was actually the last shotgun blast Martinez fired, everything fits.

Whenever it was that Crum fired, McCoy thought about it to his dying day, and concluded that it came at about the same time as the first eight shots, and all of them came almost simultaneously. McCoy's daughter, Monika, listened to her father's recollections, and came to the conclusion that Crum heard Martinez running, and then fired. In any event, the time span for all ten shots covered mere seconds.

After Martinez peered around the corner, McCoy saw him jump "out the inner wall on the north side and doing a near split with his right leg straight forward and his left leg nearly straight back, but with the left knee touching the floor," he began firing his double-action .38 service revolver one-handed. McCoy's instant thought was "that position's not a good firing one." Then he jumped around the corner to the right of Martinez and brought his shotgun up.

Harold Moe, one of the Austin Police officers who ascended the U.T. Tower on August 1, 1966 to bring an end to Whitman's reign of terror. Moe was the only officer equipped with a radio, and he was the first to report that Whitman had been killed by Ramiro Martinez.

The officers were not close to Whitman. They were at one end of the north walkway and Whitman was sitting in the corner at the other end of that walkway, some 60 feet away. Martinez said he was afraid the sniper was "drawing a bead" on him and fired as rapidly as he could, saying "I hit him and (he) sprung up like a wounded cat and turned around with his M-1 carbine trying to bring it down on me. I kept shooting and just as I emptied my gun, McCoy came around the corner and I hollered at McCoy to shoot."

McCoy said he "aimed and fired the shotgun at the white head band around the sniper's head. I had the thought that Martinez with his rapid firing was out of ammunition and I think I heard him yelling to shoot with the shotgun." Whitman's head jerked violently when the double ought slugs from McCoy's shotgun hit him in the face and neck. McCoy racked another shell into the chamber and fired again. One pellet hit Whitman between his eyes, two hit his nose, two more hit his left eye and three hit the "left temporal region." Four pellets hit in the left side of his neck, two more hit the right side, and one in the space between the sternum and heart.

McCoy pumped another shell into the chamber and looked up, thinking there might be another sniper above. Martinez threw his empty revolver to the floor and screamed what McCoy said was a war cry, and grabbed McCoy's shotgun. McCoy did not immediately let Martinez take the gun, but then thought that Martinez might have just seen a second shooter, was out of ammunition, and needed it, so he let it go and drew his revolver. Martinez ran toward Whitman "still war crying," stopped beside Whitman's prone body and fired the shotgun into it from what McCoy said was "a very few inches." The pellets hit Whitman's body in the left shoulder, left arm, under the arm, and in the "left auxiliary region," "whereupon" McCoy recalled, "the upper torso of the body rose and cleared the floor several inches."

Charles Whitman was dead.

McCoy said Martinez threw the shotgun, which still had one round in it, to the floor, whereas Martinez recalled that he immediately started waving the shotgun instead of throwing it, shouting "cease fire," but that nobody could hear. He then threw the shotgun down and "got the heck out of there."[14] McCoy wrote that Martinez started jumping up and down and shouting "I got him! I got him!" while waving both arms in the air. McCoy told him to go find Jerry Day and radio that it was all over and that everyone should stop shooting. Martinez listened, then "ran down the west walk way and resumed yelling 'I got him' over and over."

He dashed by the officers who had accompanied McCoy up the Tower, all of whom had heard the shots but without witnessing the shooting. Harold Moe had the only hand-held radio, and he stepped out onto the observation deck where there was reception and called down. "We got him," he said. "Martinez got him."[15] Moe did not know otherwise, of course, and reported exactly what needed to be conveyed, but in so doing he set the wheels in motion for a series of unfortunate events that would take years to finally resolve.

Once Martinez dashed by, Crum grabbed either the green towel or a handkerchief and waved in the air on the south side to signal those below to stop firing. Similarly, Jerry Day waved a towel on the north side for the same purpose, but the firing continued.[16]

At the home of Allen Crum, his 13-year-old son, David, was watching the event with his sisters on the family's black and white television. They

The body of Charles Whitman lying where he was killed, autographed by Ramiro Martinez and Houston McCoy

"did not have a clue as to who was up in the U.T. tower, but only that someone was shooting out from it. When it was over, someone up on the tower observation deck was waving a towel of some kind, and we all thought that the person was giving up to the police. It was only later that evening that we discovered that our father was that person in the tower waving the towel."[17]

McCoy retrieved his shotgun, put it on safety and leaned it against the wall, went back and picked up Martinez's .38, rejected the six empty shell casings, and put it in this belt. Then he went back to Whitman's body, squatted down, and "talked to it." The sniper's blood was spreading toward a floor drain near his feet and he told the body he would throw him over the tower if his blood got on his boots, to which McCoy said, "the sniper spasmodically stuck his tongue out at me" causing the officer to say, "well you sonuvabitch you."[18]

Jerry Day approached and McCoy asked his opinion. "Should we throw the son of a bitch over?" Day said "no." Day asked McCoy if he knew whether any police officers had been hurt and McCoy told him about seeing Billy Speed get shot high in the right shoulder, and started to add that he thought Speed would be all right. Just as he said the word "all," the voice of KTBC radio newsman Neal Spelce came in over Whitman's transistor radio, which was still playing. He announced that Officer Billy Speed had been D.O.A. at Brackenridge Hospital.[19]

McCoy looked at Day and asked again, "Are you sure we should not throw the sunuvabith over?" Day asked, "Who is he?" Saying, "I don't know," McCoy bent down, ripped Whitman's coveralls open and began looking for identification. Phillip Conner looked around the southeast corner of the observation deck and saw McCoy rummaging through Whitman's clothing, tearing the coveralls in the process. He later told McCoy that he was handling the body so roughly that Conner thought he really was planning to throw it over the edge.

McCoy found Whitman's Luger, stuck it in his belt, and then located Whitman's wallet and driver's license. He handed it to Day, who read it.[20] The shooting from the ground continued. Officer Milton Shoquist recalled that the shots didn't stop for at least five minutes.[21]

Others began to arrive, and McCoy asked Day one more time. "Are you sure we shouldn't throw the son of a bitch over the edge?"

Jerry Day said "no."

1. H. Crews, *Classic Crews*, 442 (New York; Simon & Schuster, 1995)

2. Ibid at 443.

3. Shoquist interview, *supra*.

4. Text for article for *American Rifleman* article about Allen Crum, Series IV, Subseries I, AHC.

5. Interview of Monika McCoy and Christopher McCoy, May 31, 2015.

6. *Ibid.*

7. Shoquist interview, *supra*

8. *Ibid.*

9. Statement of Allen Crum, Aug. 2, 1966, AHC.

10. Email from David Allen Crum to Monte Akers, April 18, 2015.

11. *Deranged Killers: Charles Whitman*, darkdocumentaries, *supra*.

12. *Ibid.*

13. Text for article for *American Rifleman, supra*.

14. Robert Nieman, "Interview with Ramiro 'Ray' Martinez, Texas Ranger Retired," conducted at the home of Ray Martinez, New Branufels, Texas, September 19, 1999, *Texas Ranger E-Book* (Waco: Texas Ranger Hall of Fame and Museum 2006).

15. Shoquist, *supra*

16. Although two or three men mentioned the green towel, it was gone, perhaps having become somebody's souvenir, when the items Whitman carried to the top of the Tower were inventoried. Crum said the next day he waved a handkerchief. The green towel may simply not been considered important enough to list. In photos of Whitman's paraphernalia a cloth item can be seen that looks like a pillowcase matching the sheets on Margaret Whitman's death bed, but which is not identified in the inventory of items.

17. Email from David Allen Crum to Monte Akers, April 18, 2015.

18. Houston McCoy's annotations of the APD radio and telephone exchanges of Aug. 1, 1966, prepared by McCoy in November, 2011, and furnished to the authors by Monika McCoy.

19. McCoy's last television interview, https://drive.google.com/file/d/0B2sFGqklP1lnT-nBDUU9FWWZNLUE/view?pli=1

20. McCoy annotations, *supra*.

21. Shoquist interview, *supra*.

CHAPTER NINE
The Immediate Aftermath

"I got him on the phone and I said, "Don are you okay?" and I will never ever forget these words. He said 'Yes Mother, but I'm lucky to be alive.'"
-Sylvia Walden, June 3, 2015

"His features and the flat top or burr haircut suggested the all-American boy."
-Dr. M.D. Heatly, Psychiatrist, August 2, 1966, during press conference to explain his analysis of Whitman on March 29, 1966

The news that the shooter was either dead or captured spread quickly and people came streaming from the buildings and other shelters where they had been hiding. All headed for the Tower. There were still bodies on the ground, and the principal background sound was what one witness called "surely every siren on every ambulance in Austin."[1]

Don Vandiver had spent most of the reverse siege with the two Texas Rangers on top of the Academic Center, from which they had fired dozens of shots at Whitman. As they did so, the portable radio left behind by a sunbather continued to play rock and roll music at a loud volume, and Don vividly remembered that at one point the disc jockey played "My Baby Does the Hanky Panky" then broke into the middle of the song and said something like, "We hear that someone is shooting at people at the Tower at the University of Texas, but we don't know any more to tell you," before returning to the whimsical song. Don was baking under the Texas sun, crouching behind a wall on the roof of a building from which he could see dead bodies

Severely wounded Mary Gabour is removed from the Tower as students and members of the public look on.

203

and people hiding all over campus, and he thought how incongruous that song was.[2]

The Rangers had their own radios, for communication, and after they had been on the roof for over half an hour one of them took a call, listened, and then said, "Okay, let's go." The shooter was down.[3]

At the top of the Tower, more police officers arrived, including Lt. Merle Wells, Sgt. Bill Landis, Sgt. T. J. Allen, Patrolman William Ligon, and others.[4] Everyone wanted to see the body of the man who had caused such havoc. Dr. Robert Stokes, a general practitioner for the Student Health Center had been attending to the wounded and was led through the underground tunnels to the Tower, where police directed him to the top at about 1:27. There he saw the "results of the slaughter that had been going on," first the Gabour family and then Edna Townsley. Police officers led him to Whitman but directed him to "walk in a bent position as people on the ground with rifles did not know the sniper was dead."

Dr. Stokes described the shooter's body as dressed in green coveralls with a military web belt filled with brass cartridges. Police emptied his wallet and Stokes used his stethoscope to determine he was dead before returning to the first floor.[5] As the officers worked, Whitman's transistor radio continued to play, providing a surreal soundtrack to the grim aftermath.

Near the Academic Center a knot of fraternity boys took up a chant of "lynch the son of a bitch!" but they were alone, both in their mob mentality and their verbosity. Forrest Preece remembered that "[t]he whole crowd was silent. No shouts, no cries for revenge—just a mass of humanity moving as one."[6] John Pipkin said, "[t]he Tower was like a magnet, everyone started walking toward it." Brenda Bell recalled that "[w]e all gathered at the Tower, as if by common agreement. We wanted to take a look at the guy who did this; we wanted to see him led out in handcuffs, or dead. That was why we were there."[7]

Instead of the shooter, the first to appear were those who shot him. "A weird tableau of three men walking west, against the grain, parted us like the Red Sea, slowing me for a few seconds," Forrest Preece remembered. "I instantly knew who they were and what they had done—that they had killed, or somehow stopped, the shooter. In the middle was a Hispanic police officer who seemed to be in a state of shock... His uniform was soaked through, as if someone had hosed him down. His eyes were locked into the thousand-yard stare. Two men were holding him up. The man on his left was whispering soothing words to him as they walked past: 'You did okay, buddy. Ease up. You did okay. It's all right.'"8

The crowd grew to a thousand people or more, standing shoulder to shoulder. They were still silent, the only sound being the continued wail of sirens far and near. It was sunny and hot with no breeze. Clif Drummond looked about him and saw that "[t]here were lots of rifles—all on safety, barrels pointed up, butts resting on waistbands. You could see the barrels sticking up out of the crowd."9

Don Vandiver and the two Rangers arrived just as a stretcher was wheeled out carrying a young man lying on his back. Don noticed that he had no shoes but wore yellow socks. He looked dead, and a murmur ran through the crowd, "he's dead, look, he's dead."

Mike Gabour rose up on one elbow and gave everyone the finger.

Mike Gabour is wheeled to an ambulance from the Tower seconds after "waving" (giving the finger) to members of the gathering crowd who made comments about his being dead.

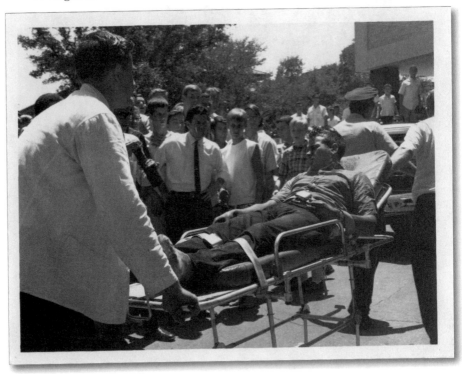

Later reports, including one written by Don Vandiver and published in the *Statesman* the next day, stated that Gabour "waved" to the crowd. He didn't, Vandiver revealed nearly a half century later. "Everyone thought he was dead and they were oohing and aaahing about him being dead and he raised up and flipped them off."[10] His mother would not have been proud, but at least he didn't use any bad words.

A deputy sheriff came out of the Tower carrying a blood-spattered shotgun. "Martinez killed the sniper. He's dead," he told the Rangers. "Everybody's dead up there. The sniper was a student named Charles

The body of Marguerite Lamport being removed from the Tower.

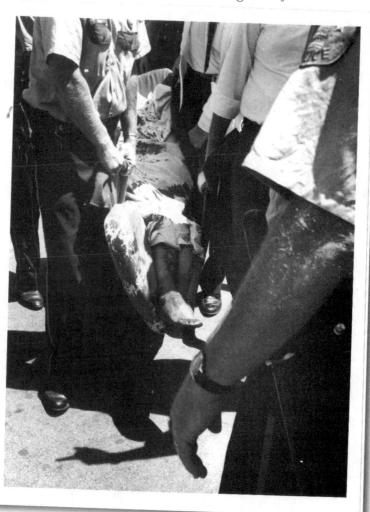

The body of Edna Townsley, the receptionist killed by Whitman in the observation tower reception area being carried from the Tower.

Whitman." This was the kind of news Vandiver had been waiting for, and it was something he needed to report as quickly as he could. He left the Tower and headed for his car to drive to the newspaper office, certain he could not find a phone to call it in and not knowing that another reporter named Al Williams would manage to get to a telephone and report the information before Vandiver could get there.

A procession of bodies followed Mike Gabour—Mary Gabour, Edna Townsley, Mark Gabour, and Marguerite Lamport. Edna Townsley was still alive when Phillip Conner found her behind the couch and felt for a pulse. People remembered her as "a scrapper," and she certainly demonstrated her toughness that day, although she would not survive much longer.

Conner, Shoquist and two others took a green army blanket from Whitman's stockpile and used it to take Ms. Townsley down. The elevators were too small to accommodate gurneys or stretchers, and anyone in either could ride down only if held vertically.

Bill Helmer was near the door at the bottom. "The cops brought out the dead and wounded," he said. "That was really grim: blood everywhere,

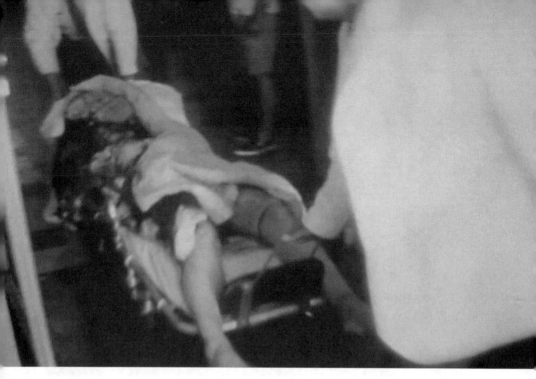

Severely wounded Mary Gabour being wheeled out of the Tower after the reign of terror ended.

heads blown apart, hands dragging on the pavement. It took fifteen or twenty minutes."

Brenda Bell and the others who wanted to see the shooter were initially disappointed. Afraid the crowd might become unmanageable, police officers put Whitman's body on a wheeled stretcher, covered him with a sheet and trundled him out a side door. Their attempt at stealth was not successful, however. Someone shouted, "That's the shooter. They got him," and the crowd broke its silence and began cheering. The sheet covering Whitman's face and upper torso was pulled back and Bill Helmer saw what was beneath. "He was all shot to hell. He looked like bloody steak tartar."[11]

Having seen what they had come to see, the crowd began to disperse but many walked about to view the damage. Store windows were shot out, bullet holes pocked curbs and sides of buildings, and Brenda Bell remembered that "there was blood everywhere. It was hot, so it had turned dark. It was on the mall, all over the sidewalk, up and down the Drag, on the carpet of Sheftall's jewelers." University Regent Frank Erwin saw the damage and directed that it be cleaned up immediately. Workers began spreading sand on the pools of blood to soak it up.[12]

Alfred McAlister did not go to the Tower. He stayed in the Student Union where "there was a bunch of shell-shocked people."

> There were some acquaintances there and we made small talk. I don't even remember what, but when I was going out to my motorcycle there was this kid that was younger than me from Westlake Hills and he came by and he saw me and came running up and said 'Did you hear that they got Paul Sonntag?' and I said 'Paul Sonntag?' and he said 'Yeah, they shot him on the Drag,' and I was like 'Oh yeah, the surfer shirt, the blond hair, that was Paul,' and that really really hit me hard, and I cried all the way home on my bike, and I'm going to start crying now. That really hurt.[13]

National news media were on the scene. A photographer for *Life* magazine named Shel Hershorn arrived too late to take any shots during the siege, so he began asking about and looking for scenes that might capture the soul of the event. Someone told him about the "foot-wide swath of blood across the carpet at Sheftall's," so, alert to the publicity maxim "if it bleeds it leads," he went to the jewelry store. The bloody swath was there, but a better image was available through the front store window. Two bullet holes lined up naturally and nicely with the Tower, and Hershorn knew it could be iconic. He snapped photos from inside the store; a close-up of the two bullet holes in the glass with the top of the Tower between them in the background.

As he was doing so, monopolizing the best space for the shots, he noticed one of his competitors pacing up and down on the sidewalk outside, impatiently waiting his turn for the same image. As soon as he was finished, Hershorn promptly kicked the window to pieces to deny anyone else the scene. When the store owner objected, Hershorn told him that *Life* would pay the damage.[14] The photo Hershorn took was on the cover of *Life's* next issue.

The world did not yet know the extent of Whitman's crimes. The bodies of Margaret and Kathy Whitman still lay undiscovered in their beds. Without knowing it, however, Don Vandiver was quickly approaching the discovery of one of them.

When Vandiver got back to the newspaper officer he immediately told the City Editor, Bill Woods, the name of the sniper. If Woods had already heard that from Al Williams, he did not reveal it. Instead he picked up a copy of the U.T. student directory, tossed it to Vandiver, and said, "find out where he lives and get out there and find out anything you can get on him."

Don looked Whitman up in the directory, wrote down his address and, realizing he might need help finding the location, enlisted the services of Mike Cox, a 17-year-old copy boy who worked for the *Statesman* and who had grown up in Austin. Together they hustled to Vandiver's car, a 1954 Jaguar, and sped off in pursuit of a potentially big story.

At the time that Don Vandiver and the Texas Rangers had been crouched on the rooftop of the Academic Center and the song "My Baby Does the Hanky Panky" by the Shondells was playing on the abandoned transistor radio, Mike Cox was at home listening to the same station and the same song, and he heard the same DJ break in to say that someone was shooting at people from the U.T. Tower. Cox was technically just a part-time copy boy, but he was allowed to write a high school news column called "Hi-Notes" that was published in the *Statesman* three times a week, which he was working on when he heard the radio report. His father was a reporter and that was Mike's plan as well, so when he heard the short report he "jumped up from my typewriter, went to my closet and grabbed a tie so I would look like a real reporter, and forsook lunch to rush to the campus to see first-hand what was going on."[15] Taking along a portable radio to keep up with the news, he headed toward the campus, heard the shooting, and saw puffs of limestone dust kicked up by shots aimed at the sniper. As soon as

In a photo dated July 1966, Don Vandiver stands beside his 1954 "fire engine-red" Jaguar in which he and Mike Cox sped from the American Statesman *office to the Whitman residence on Jewel Street*

the shooting stopped, Cox drove to the *Statesman* office, where he ran into Vandiver and "raced" in his "fire engine-red Jaguar to interview Whitman's neighbors."[16]

When they arrived at the address, on Shelley Avenue, they discovered it was no longer current for the Whitmans. They had moved. Cox remembered that he coaxed the correct address out of a phone operator, whereas Vandiver recalled that the people in the apartment next door to Whitman's previous address, Mr. and Mrs. John Morino, were renting the Whitmans the house on Jewell Street, and helpfully told Vandiver and Cox the address, adding that the Whitmans owned a little dog named Schocie, but which Don wrote down as "Scotty."[17]

Vandiver and Cox hopped back in the Jaguar and sped to Jewell Street, only a few blocks away. They knocked on the door but got no answer. Don looked in the mailbox, hoping to find mail addressed to Whitman, but the postman, Chester Arrington, had given Whitman his mail in person several hours earlier, as the latter was reconfiguring his new shotgun. Not certain what to do, Vandiver and Cox walked to the rear of the house and tried the back door, which was also locked. They circled the residence, peering in windows, but could see nothing amiss.

They crossed the street and found a neighbor, John Whitaker, at home, but other than being able to tell the pair that he saw Whitman come and go, often wearing green army fatigues, he could not tell them more. Other neighbors told them "he was quiet and kept to himself."[18]

Vandiver was in a quandary. His boss had told him to "get something; find out anything" and they were coming up empty-handed. Telling Cox to check with another neighbor, Don returned to his car, went to the tool box he carried in the trunk, and removed a large screwdriver. He had decided to break in through the back door.

Cox returned with a little news. The neighbor he had talked to had seen Whitman leave that morning after loading a big "foot locker-type chest" into his car. He had been wearing something that might have been coveralls.

Don considered further. What were the odds they would find anything in the house? What were the odds they would be arrested for breaking and entering? What were the odds that the Austin Police would not be thrilled to find them inside? What was the penalty for tampering with a crime scene, tampering with evidence, and criminal trespass? Were they even certain this was Whitman's house? The risks outweighed the possible advantages. Reluctantly, he returned to the Jaguar and replaced the screwdriver in the tool kit. When they left a few moments later, no one else, police, other reporters, or anyone had arrived. They drove away and left a BIG story, maybe THE big story behind.[19]

Ironically, there was a very good and fortunate reason for leaving, one that neither of them could possibly know. Mike Cox had taken biology at Lanier High School the previous year, and his teacher was Mrs. Kathy Whitman. Neither of the young men knew that the same Mrs. Whitman was now lying dead, naked, stiff, and bloody inside the house, mere feet from where they had stood and tried to see through a window. Had they gone inside, had they found her body, who could know the effect it may have had on the high school student?[20]

When the pair arrived back at the newspaper office, they were met by a shout from Editor Woods. "What are you doing here? They just found Whitman's wife dead in their house."[21]

Other people were zeroing in on the fate of Kathy and Margaret from different directions for different reasons. In Needville, Kathy's father, Raymond Leissner, heard his son-in-law's name on a television report at about 2 p.m. and, stunned, first tried to call Kathy at home. When there was no answer he called Southwestern Bell. When told what he most feared, that she had not come to work that day, he called the Austin Police Department to report his relationship and to urge them to go immediately to the Whitman home to make certain Kathy was okay. Detective Donald Kidd responded and had another officer, Bolton Gregory, drive him to house.

About the same time, a friend of Kathy's at Lanier High School, Mayda Tupper, heard Whitman's name and called the police to ask if Kathy was there, volunteering to come to the police station or Kathy's home to be with her. She was told the police were attempting to locate Mrs. Whitman. Similarly, the manager of Wyatt's Cafeteria heard the news and called the police to report that Margaret had not come to work that day, and that Whitman had been the one to call and say she was ill. On Jewell Street, a neighbor named Mrs. D.W. Nowotney heard Whitman's name on the news and decided she should check in on Kathy. She found the door locked and looked through the small window in the door. She saw nothing amiss, and said later that "everything was neat as a pin, like it always was."[22] Hoping everything else was normal, she returned to her house. At the Penthouse Apartments, manager Margaret Ellers heard Whitman's name, knew it was familiar and checked her files. She found the name of the occupant of no. 505, and saw who was listed as her next-of-kin. She went to the 5th floor, found the note posted on the door to Margaret's apartment, and immediately called the police.

Blood and broken glass mark the scene outside of Sheftall's Jewelry Store the afternoon of August 1, 1966. Here some of the day's greatest drama played out. Peace Corps volunteers David Mattson and Roland Ehlke were wounded on the sidewalk in front of the store, employee Homer Kelley was wounded inside, seven wounded victims took cover inside, and ambulance driver Morris Hohmann was wounded in the street while trying to pick up those wounded.

Officers Kidd and Gregory arrived at the Whitman home within minutes after Vandiver and Cox departed, a little after 2 p.m. They also knocked on the door and looked in windows until, as Gregory reported, they "were finally able to see a person lying on the bed in the southeast bedroom."[23] They cut the screen, yanked off the frame, and hoisted themselves through the open window. Kidd pulled back the covers until they pooled above Kathy's waist, revealing her bare breasts and multiple wounds. Her left hand was extended to Charlie's side of the bed, as though she had reached out to make certain of his reassuring presence. A large dark stain extended from beneath the covers and beneath her torso and arm. Her expression was peaceful. Rigor mortis had set in.[24]

Gregory saw the partially typed, partially handwritten two-pages that began, "I don't quite understand what it is that compels me to type this letter." They called the police department and reported what they'd found. Gregory went next door and interviewed the wife of John Whitaker, who reported that she'd seen Whitman take some guns into the side entrance of his garage at 9 or 9:30 that morning, but that she had not seen him bring them out. Gregory tried to enter the garage, found it locked and returned to the Whitaker house to borrow a hammer, which he used to knock the lock off of the west side garage door. Inside he found the gun butt from Whitman's shotgun, but no other firearms.[25]

When Kidd called police headquarters, he reported that the letter included a sentence that said, "similar reasons provoked me to take my mother's life." By then the calls from Wyatt's and the Penthouse had set the wheels in motion to locate Margaret. An officer named Frank Monk was assigned to go to the apartment complex and he arrived at 2:55. The owner of the Penthouse, Reuben Johnson, was waiting with the note from Room 505 in hand. They proceeded upstairs and when nobody answered the door, Johnson unlocked it. Like Kathy, Margaret appeared asleep with the covers pulled up to her chin. Like Kathy, she was not.

At the Tower, McCoy and the officers who had gone up with him, as well as others, were busy cleaning up for well over an hour after Whitman's death. Martinez did not stay behind. He had taken the elevator down, realized his revolver was missing, went back up, asked for it and was told McCoy had it. Houston gave it to him and suggested that he turn it over to Sgt. Gerald Sponholtz, the officer in charge of firearms, to be checked for damage.[26] He then returned to the ground level but he felt shaky, and supported by two other officers, Lt. Merle Wells and Lt. Lowell Morgan, he was taken to a car and driven to the police station. He was still in rough shape when he arrived, and Officer Sweeney saw him dry-heaving into a waste basket.

There then occurred the next in the long, unintentional but unfortunate chain of events, initiated by Harold Moe's radio call from atop the Tower. Police Chief Miles called a press conference for 3 p.m. It was well-attended by the media, and included diagrams of the top of the Tower and what had occurred. However, all of his information about what had happened came from Martinez, and Martinez reported only what he had done and seen. As a result, the official news reported to the world, and the first news that the officers still working at the top of the Tower heard, was that Martinez and Crum were the two involved in Whitman's killing.

Martinez did not intentionally leave the others out, but the only one he had noticed on the Tower was McCoy, so he would not have known the other officers' names if he had wanted to report them. Martinez, by his own admission, was seriously shaken up by what occurred. Off-duty officers had crowded around him when he returned to the station, shaking his hand and patting him on the back. He called his wife, VerNell, and was careful to downplay his involvement, both because he did not want her to be alarmed at how close he'd come to death and because he did not want her to detect "the emotional state I was in at the time."[27]

After getting off the phone he sat with Chief Miles and an Austin City Council Member, Hub Bechtol, and "told the story as best I could," excusing himself when the dry heaves returned. Chief Miles gave him a Valium and Martinez took it without asking what it was, and began to recover. Chief Miles suggested he not spend the night at home, as reporters were certain to descend on him. He was given a clean shirt by Sgt. Sponholtz and he began dictating his incident report to a secretary, as APD officers were supposed to do at the end of each shift.[28]

Meanwhile a procession of ambulances was proceeding to Brackenridge and to Cook Funeral Home. Even though Whitman had been identified at the top of the Tower based on the content of his wallet and other items in his pockets, it was still necessary to find someone who could identify his body. Finding such a person took awhile, and it turned out to be Professor Leonardt Kreisle, who was Whitman's academic advisor. Assistant Chief of Police Allen Hamilton and Sgt. T. J. Allen took Kreisle to the funeral home and the identification was made. [29]

At the funeral home and at Brackenridge police photographers snapped pictures. Whitman had been photographed from five different angles where he was killed. Now he was photographed on a gurney fully clothed from three angles, then without clothing with pieces of paper covering his genitals. His victims were also photographed, Margaret and Kathy in place as they were found, then at the morgue with each of the others. All shots were from the chest up, and all might be photos of people asleep except Thomas Ashton, whose left eye was half open, and Professor Boyer, whose tie was pulled down and askew, and whose eyes were both open.

The numerous possessions Whitman had carried to the top of the Tower were gathered, catalogued, and photographed. Whitman's black 1966 Chevrolet Impala was driven from where he'd parked it to the APD impoundment lot at 3:30. Milton Shoquist drove Billy Speed's unit back to the station. Police officers were dispatched to follow every lead, and before the day was over, interviews were conducted with salespersons, neighbors, classmates, friends, scouting associates, and anyone who admitted any knowledge of Whitman. The Whitman medicine cabinet was emptied and its contents inventoried. There were 26 items, including 13 bottles of prescription medicines, nine of which were Charles's, various creams and ointments, a toothbrush, and one "Voice Developer."[30] The investigators even tracked down a copy of a book entitled *Open Square*, by Ford Clark, about a young man who shot at citizens and police from atop a tower, and which someone believed Whitman had read.[31] They also checked with the National Rifle Association to find out if Whitman was a member. He was not.[32]

A phone call was made to C.A. Whitman in Florida at 3:30 by Austin Police Captain J.C. Fann. When told his son, wife, and daughter-in-law were dead, Whitman's first thought was of material possessions, and he asked that his son's house and Margaret's apartment be secured. A half hour later he called back to give directions about what to do with the bodies of his son and wife, saying he would fly to Austin to claim them, and repeated that the two residences needed to be locked up. Two hours later, he called to report that he'd made arrangements to have the two bodies sent to Lake Worth, that he would not come to Austin until after the funerals there, and that the house and apartment needed to be locked tight. There was valuable property inside the apartment, he said, and also an automobile parked nearby. As an afterthought he said he could not think why Charlie had done what he'd done, the boy being a former Eagle Scout, a Marine for five years, and an honor student at the University.[33]

Charles Whitman's record at the University involved many things, but not honor.

That night the parents of Paul Sonntag, Beverly and Jim Sonntag, sent their two younger sons, George and Barney, to stay with Jim's parents. They needed to be alone with their grief, but shortly after 8 p.m. their phone rang. Jim answered. A familiar voice was on the other end.

"We're thinking of you. Our hearts are heavy and we just wish there was something we could do." The voice was well-known to the world. It was President Johnson, calling to express deep regret on behalf of himself and "Bird," the First Lady. Jim acknowledged there was nothing that could be done and asked if the president wished to talk to Beverly, then put her on the phone when LBJ said he did. They spoke for a moment and Johnson repeated how he wished there was something he could do and that "our hearts go out to you." The tape of the conversation, preserved for all time, is remarkable because it clearly picks up Johnson's heartbeat, steady, strong, and unhurried, as the underlying score of the nation's tragedy.[34]

About an hour after that call ended, their phone rang again. It was Roger Friedman.

Sylvia Walden, the mother of Don Walden, was finally able to get a call through to her son that night. By then she was in Augusta, Arkansas, at the home of her cousin, Dorothy, after having driven all day from Illinois.

The horrible feeling that something bad was going to happen, which awakened her in the middle of the night, had persisted all day. Having presentiments or ESP-like feelings were not anything that had happened to her before, although the previous March she had had a vivid dream about people up high, in an elevated position, shooting guns down at people on the ground, and the memory of it had persisted.

About 5 o'clock Sylvia turned on the radio, while driving, and heard about the shootings in Austin. She threw one hand to her face and said, "Oh my God!" The horrible feeling now made sense and she became desperate to telephone her son to make certain he was okay.

One of the reasons they were stopping in Augusta was because a minister who was also a builder was constructing a house for Sylvia's mother and she wanted to see what progress had been made. Sylvia told the minister, as well as her mother and cousin, about her fears and asked each of them to pray for Don's safety, and then began trying to put a call through to her son. The lines were tied up. People all over the country were trying to do the same thing, and it wasn't until well after dark that she finally reached Don. "Don are you okay?" she asked as soon as he came on the line. Recalling it in June, 2015, she said, "and I will never ever forget these words. He said 'Yes Mother, but I'm lucky to be alive.'"[35]

As will be discussed by Dr. Roger Friedman in Chapter 13, the effects of trauma are significant and are not limited to persons who are injured or physically involved in violence. By the evening of August 1, such effects commenced. For some they would wear off quickly, but for others they would last for years or a lifetime for others. In the cases of Don Walden and Bob Higley, the first manifestation of those effects surfaced immediately, but were then forgotten by the men until June, 2015, when loved ones recalled them.

In the case of Don Walden, his mother said that "he told me about how he woke up, or how he set his alarm in his room to wake him up every hour or two, I don't remember whether it was one hour or two, because as he said 'I didn't want to wake up screaming.'"[36] For Bob Higley, his sister Susie recalled that she and their mother were at home when Bob returned at 3 or 3:30 p.m. the afternoon of the event. He was as white as anyone she had ever seen before or since, his white shirt and Levi's were stained with blood, and he went straight to bed. Susie shared a bedroom with their youngest sister, Betsy, next to Bob's room, and she recalled that that night and later she heard him screaming in the night, and that one of their parents would wake him, as no one else felt comfortable going near his room.[37]

The next morning, August 2, a press conference was called by the University and held in the main newsroom of the University newspaper, the *Daily Texan*. Reporters turned out in force, but none of them expected to hear more than updates on the story. Nobody was fully prepared for what the school authorities intended to present.

A long written statement was handed out. It said Whitman visited the University Health Center on March 29 and consulted with the staff psychiatrist, Dr. M.D. Heatly. It said the University was turning the records over to law enforcement authorities; that Whitman had been told to make another appointment but he failed to do so; that students were free but not required to make use of the Center; that unless a student's behavior indicated a necessity for doing so the Center would not try to commit anyone for involuntary treatment; and that Whitman gave no indication he posed a danger to himself or anyone else. "Dr. Heatly's conclusion on March 29, 1966 (was)... consistent with the impressions of the teachers, his employer, and his associates," the written statement continued, "none of whom observed anything during the intervening 4 months which reflected unusual behavior." A paragraph summarized Whitman's class load the previous semester—19 hours completed with a B average—and his satisfactory performance as a lab assistant, then it returned to discussion of Dr. Heatly.

"Dr. Heatly explained that if a student chooses to visit the Health Center for psychiatric consultation, the alternatives are: first, to determine if his is not a psychiatric case; second to schedule serial visits for further observation but the visits must be voluntary on the part of the student; and third, to determine that the patient is psychotic and/or dangerous to himself or others, in which case it is necessary to separate him involuntarily from society."

The report concluded there had been no basis for doing the latter, and "during the subsequent four months no University physician had had the opportunity to evaluate Whitman's condition."[38] Reporters may have wondered if the statement represented the dropping of a shoe to the floor, and whether the University was dangling a second one by a shoestring.

Dr. Heatly took the stage. Six television cameras were trained on him, all with harsh indoor lights. Nine microphones were arranged to catch his every word. Heatly held the report he had dictated to his secretary at the end of March and read the first two paragraphs aloud. When he got to the statement that Whitman had said that his tactics were similar to his father's, in that he had assaulted his wife physically on two occasions, Heatly paused to explain that the previous sentence meant that Whitman had admitted to beating his wife. Then he continued reading. The next two paragraphs were about Whitman's Marine service, his anxiety over his parents' separation, his feelings of hostility, and that Heatly's attempts to get him to analyze his "exact experiences" failed, except for a "vivid reference" to his "thinking about going up on the tower with a deer rifle and start shooting people."

The reporters had been scribbling notes or listening idly. Now their heads jerked up.

"Could you please repeat that entire sentence?" one of them asked.

One of the media representatives in the audience was John Economidy, editor of the *Daily Texan*. "Heatly was the brother of a very powerful state legislator," he recalled, "and that caused some embarrassment politically." Nevertheless, the University was given credit for immediately disclosing the information to the world as soon as it learned it, rather than attempting a cover-up, although, as Economidy said, the statement about going to the top of the tower with a deer rifle "was a jaw-dropper" for everyone who heard it. He also recalled that "Heatly defended himself by saying that if he committed every kid who threatened to jump off the Tower or do harm to others, there would be a lot of people in the psychiatric ward."[39]

Another press conference was held that day at which Martinez and McCoy were present, but McCoy said very little and Martinez did most of the talking. As McCoy told his daughter later, "Martinez started talking and I said 'okay' and didn't jump in. You don't want to take credit for killing a man, whether the guy is good or bad, you don't jump up and down and say 'I killed him I killed him,' you just do your job.... and when you hear somebody else talking you don't just say 'wait, that isn't what happened' in front of everyone, you know, you just let it go, so I didn't say a word." It reflected a difference in personalities that led to Martinez receiving more credit than he deserved and McCoy being rewarded with the short end of the stick.

Don Vandiver's article, published in the *Statesman* on August 2, was modified from how he wrote it. He had written about encountering James Damon, the student who fired at Whitman from the roof of the Academic Center on his own and prior to encountering the Texas Rangers, but the article was changed to say that Damon did his shooting while he was with Vandiver and the Texas Rangers. At first Don thought that the change was just an error by the typesetter or the proof reader, but then he realized there were probably political reasons for the change. The paper's editors did not want the world to know students were shooting back on their own. They wanted to convey that the shooting was done under police supervision. It was not a huge change, but it bothered Don that an eyewitness account would be changed or slanted for a political purpose. As he said, "I always went with the MacDougall Interpretive Reporting theory that reporters should report what happened, not editorialize in their descriptions of what happened."[40]

Don and other *Statesman* employees were kept busy all that day and into the week, finalizing stories, talking to witnesses, and answering phone

The cover of the August 12, 1966 issue of Life magazine, autographed by Houston McCoy. The photo was taken by photographer Shel Hershorn through the window of Sheftall's Jewelry Store on the Drag, near which several victims were shot and in which several of the wounded sheltered. After taking the photo, Hershorn kicked out the glass to prevent another photographer from obtaining a similarly iconic image.

calls. Ultimately the newspaper rewarded their hard work by giving the team a bonus of $100 each... except for Don, who received only $25. Again, it was not a huge slight, but he'd been the only reporter on the scene from beginning to end of the reverse siege and beyond, and it left a bad taste in his mouth.[41]

Copycat killings began almost immediately. On August 2, in nearby Taylor, a man named Sammy Brown "went berserk" after hearing about the shootings, broke into a home and attacked four people, after which he stabbed a police officer named Joe John Debec. Once subdued, Brown repeatedly mumbled, "they should have put me on television, they should have put me on television."[42] On November 18, 1966, in Mesa, Arizona, an 18-year-old named Robert Benjamin Smith entered a beauty college and killed five young ladies, one only three years old, with a .22 caliber pistol. Like Whitman, he was a handsome boy. Like Whitman, he planned out his spree and arrived at the college with a container of supplies—a brown paper bag containing 200 ft. of nylon cord, a package of big plastic sandwich bags, and two hunting knives. After being captured—he offered no resistance and freely admitted his crime—he revealed that he'd modeled his actions on Richard Speck, the killer of eight student nurses in Chicago the previous July, and Charles Whitman, and saying, "I wanted to get known, to make myself a name."[43]

On August 3, Sgt. Dwight Moody was assigned the task of returning the dolly Whitman had rented to Austin Rental Service. He turned it over to R. L. Parks at the store, who signed a property card for it.[44] One wonders if the dolly was simply returned to service or whether it was set aside, and is in someone's artifact collection today.

By August 4, the other officers who went to the top of the Tower, and to a lesser degree Houston McCoy, had told their versions of what occurred, and some in the APD felt like McCoy was not getting the credit he deserved. Accordingly, McCoy's sergeant approached him and said the department was prepared to call the media together, "so that they can do an interview with you and you can straighten the story out."[45] Characteristically, McCoy declined. He was a humble man who had just been doing his job. It didn't bother him that Martinez was getting most of the credit. He knew the truth and didn't see any particular advantage in appearing to be at odds with Martinez. Besides, holding a press conference just so he could stand up and appear to claim credit flew in the face of his beliefs that a man should not seek credit for killing another man. He had no idea what lay a few years down the road, and not long before he died he would tell his daughter, Monika, "Maybe I should have given that interview."[46]

Investigators for the FBI, the Austin Police Department, the Texas Department of Public Safety, the Federal Drug Administration, and even the Texas Department of Transportation contacted people who knew Whitman in Florida, the Marines, and Austin. All were interviewed, and few stones were left unturned. Additionally, some people with nothing to add to the investigations felt obligated to write letters to the APD anyway, and some sounded less mentally stable than Whitman. A man named John Gray addressed a letter to Chief of Police Miles to express his wish that the police had used a tranquilizer, "like Big Game hunters" to bring Whitman down, and asked "[h]ow do you know it was not the personnel of the Hogg Foundation who shot and killed and stabbed those people?" The Hogg Foundation for Mental Health was established in Austin in 1940 by the children of Governor James Hogg for the promotion of mental health in the state. "The shadow of doubt is real long," the writer continued. "The dead duck don't confess." One suspects the Foundation had once attempted to aid Mr. Gray.

A woman wrote on August 4 after seeing the photo of Whitman napping with his dog at his feet to declare that the picture made it "very clear" to her what the motive for the killings had been—"he had formed a hatred for people and... had come to the conclusion that a dog is man's best friend."

Other contacts and inquiries were from stable, but eccentric, individuals. A San Antonian named Bill McGuire wrote to request a bullet from each gun used by Whitman to add to his collection, offering to pay five dollars for them all. A lady who had had ten guns stolen from her home in Columbus, Ohio, saw a photo of firearms used by Whitman and went to the Sheriff's office in Pima County, Arizona to report that the .caliber Remington pump rifle was "like hers in every respect." In fact, the Remington pump, as well as the 6.35 automatic pistol, belonged to C.A. Whitman. A lady in Richardson, Texas who identified herself as the "Corresponding Secretary of the Texas Chapter of the International Grapho Analysis Society" wrote to request two photostaticcopies of each specimen of Whitman's handwriting in order to add "more samples of the unusual personality writings in order to develop accuracy in our evaluations."

Still other reports were well-meaning but not relevant. A lady named Sally O'Brien called from Washington, D.C. to report that three years earlier, during the first week of August in 1963, she and her date were walking across the mall when they heard four shots fired, followed by the sound of "the rifle being recocked," followed by the sound of someone walking and keys jangling, which she and her date took to be a night watchman. She admitted she wasn't sure her information would help, but felt like the APD needed to know.[47]

A slightly more relevant statement was received by the FBI office in San Antonio from a lady whose name was redacted from the report. She had seen Whitman's photo, and believed he might be the man she and her husband observed outside the LBJ Ranch, near Johnson City, on July 31, 1966. He had blond hair, was 26 or 27 years old, and made the remark, "Look yonder, there sits the Secret Service man with a telescopic gun across his knees. That's where our tax money goes." She added helpfully that the man had a companion who was wearing a hat. Her call was communicated to the Secret Service as a "Threat against the President."[48]

The APD was not the only recipient of reports or letters inspired by what happened on August 1, 1966. C. A. Whitman received several, including one on August 6 in which he was told, "Watch your every move. You're next."[49] At least two of the letters he received were significant enough to be recorded by the FBI. The first arrived on or about August 6. It "was derogatory of Mr. Whitman's treatment of his family and his manner of doing business, and ended 'Hope you get yours. Beware.'" It was signed "The neighbors," and was postmarked in Lantana, Florida, which is located adjacent to Lake Worth.[50]

The second arrived on December 7, 1966, but its inspiration was not confined to the Austin shootings. C. A. had done something else to startle people. On November 12, 1966, just three months after the shootings, he re-married. He was 47, and the bride was a 23-year-old—a divorcee named Ellen Ward who had a three year old son and was pregnant. Reportedly the marriage was proposed by Ms. Ward's parents and one wonders what they, and she, and C.A. were thinking. Predictably the story made the local papers, and the news led to the second letter. It was typed, postmarked in Orlando on December 6, and read as follows:

December, 1966

Dear Mr. Whitman:

You are the real killer of Charlie and the other people that died. I read about your marriage to that young girl. But you won't get a chance to kill her, too. I promise you, God strike me dead—I will kill you dead on Christmas day at exactly 3:00 A.M. 1966 with a .357 magnum. I knew Charlie. You might have known me as Tommy. Remember the night you threw Charlie in the pool? Remember? I was there but you didn't see me. Now I see you everywhere I go. When you go to the shop, I am there. When you go to the store, I am there. And on Christmas day, I will be there, too. As I said before—I promise to God—and as a God fearing catholic, you will be killed DEAD on Christmas day. Requiescat in Pace.

Be (expletive deleted)

Charles Adolphus Whitman, the father of the sniper, whom many people blamed for what happened, during his visit to Austin a week after his son's shooting spree and death.

Whitman immediately took the letter to the FBI, which notified its Washington, San Antonio, and Tampa offices, but told Whitman they could not provide him protection and turned the matter over to the Lake Worth Police Department. Nevertheless the FBI began investigating, interviewing the few people C.A. could think of who might have known about the swimming pool incident, as well as any friends of Charlie who lived in Orlando. C.A. told the FBI that he threw Charles in the pool when he was in the 10th grade, which a friend of Charles corroborated.

The FBI examined the letter and its envelope for fingerprints, investigated the type of paper, and studied the letter symbols to determine the make of the typewriter.[51] Soon they had determined that the brand of the typewriter was an Everest, and agents combed the area for stores that sold that brand and people who owned one. They interviewed both Patrick and Johnnie Mike Whitman, made the rounds of high schools to determine what brands of typewriters were used, talked to the distributor of Everest products in Florida, and even tried to determine which friends of Charlie had studied Latin.

They also interrogated Mr. Whitman further, and learned more about what kind of experiences he'd had since his son's killing spree. Whitman told them that since August 1 he had received numerous letters and telephone calls related to what Charlie had done, including letters proposing marriage and "willingness on the part of females to have an intimate relationship." Many of the communications were "nasty," but none were as threatening as the letter from December. Other letters had contained business proposals. Additionally he had been involved in a traffic accident, and a woman he had dated had filed a suit claiming fraud after he married the young Ms. Ward. In another interview with the FBI, he said that five days after he was married to Ms. Ward, a person whose name was redacted from the report filed criminal charges against him for embezzlement, although he may have been referring to the same suit claiming fraud. The local newspapers would report "every little incident" he was involved in, referring to him as the father of the "Texas University Killer." To add to the drama, Patrick Whitman was demanding to be given a share of the family business, and had forged two checks on the firm's bank account. He told FBI agent John R. Barron "with apparent tenseness and emotion that he cannot take much more and would 'blow his brains out.'"[52]

Six latent fingerprints were found on the letter that were not Whitman's, and ultimately they were matched to a man named Richard Postrozny, who was arrested and charged with extortion. The details of how he was identified as the writer of the letter and Postrozny's motives for doing so are not known, but on July 1, 1968, he entered a plea of guilty in the United States District Court in Miami, and was placed on probation for five years.

In Memphis, Tennessee a few weeks after the shootings, Volkswagen dealer William C. Dewey noticed writing in ink on a five dollar bill in his wallet. He read and discovered it said, "I Charles Whitman, have killed my wife and mother. Aug. 1, 1966, Austin, Texas," on the front, and on the reverse, at the top of the Lincoln Memorial building was printed the word "me." The bill also contained a machine date stamp of "Aug. 1, 1966." Although almost certainly a prank, the Criminal Investigation Division of the Austin P.D. wrote a letter to the Chief of Police of Memphis requesting a copy of the writing so that it could be compared to Whitman's.[53]

The five dollar bill in Memphis was not the only such item to show up. On February 9, 1967, Sgt. Joe Hawkins of the Austin Police Department was given a one dollar bill that had been received at a service station in San Marcos by a young man named Johnny Vargas, who worked there. There was nothing written or drawn on the front of the bill, but typed on the reverse side along the top, bottom and one side margin was the message, "In one more day, I will attempt the biggest mass killing in Texas. I don't know what's the matter with me. I feel sick with hatred. Charles Whitman."[54]

Despite everyone's knowledge and certainty that Whitman had been a murderer and that his shooting by McCoy and Martinez was necessary, the law required that a Grand Jury be convened to confirm the latter. On August 5, 1966, Houston McCoy appeared as its only witness at the Travis County Courthouse, after which the Grand Jury ruled that Whitman's killing was justifiable homicide. The fact that McCoy was present instead of Martinez was significant. The tradition then and now was that when a fatal police shooting occurs, the police officer who took the life is the one who appears and testifies. If more than one officer put bullets into the shooting victim, then all such officers are expected to appear and testify. An officer cannot be compelled to testify, but neither Martinez nor McCoy had any reason to decline. By sending only McCoy, Chief Miles and others in the department were suggesting they now believed that McCoy had fired the only fatal shots, and had played a larger role than Martinez.

However, the choice of McCoy instead of Martinez did not sit well with everyone. A local activist for Hispanic affairs, Rudy Cisneros, saw that only McCoy had been summoned and demanded an explanation from Chief Miles. McCoy heard Chief Miles say, "I brought the right man." Cisneros then approached McCoy, did not shake his hand or express any appreciation for what he had done, and told him to go back to the station and to tell Martinez that everyone knew what a good job he had done and how proud everyone was of him.[55]

In Florida, the funerals of Whitman and Margaret were held at the Sacred Heart Catholic Church in Lake Worth on August 5, officiated over by Father Tom Anglin. Reporters were on hand to take photos, and the double ceremony was attended by some 300 people. Charles's casket was gray; Margaret's was green and white.[56] Being a Marine, his casket was draped with the United States flag. He and his mother were then buried side by side in the Hillcrest Memorial Park cemetery. Their grave markers contain no clue about the circumstances of their lives or passing other than a common death date.

In Needville, Texas, Kathy Whitman was buried in the cemetery of the Davis-Greenlawn Funeral Chapel on August 5, by the family who adored her, far away from the man who demonstrated his love by murdering her.

On August 6, C.A. Whitman called the Austin Police Department again, and directed once more that the Jewell Street house and Penthouse apartment be locked, then asked if he could meet with the APD the following Monday. Early that day, the 8th, he called to inform the APD when he and his father-in-law would arrive—under the names of A. Smith and R. Smith—and to request access to Margaret's apartment.[57] Once at the police department, C. A. met with Ramiro Martinez, whom he understood to be the officer who killed his son. Both men were gracious and C.A. cried, saying he did not understand what had happened or why Charlie had gone on the killing spree. To a reporter for the *Austin American Statesman*, Whitman said he had come to Texas to express his sympathies and regrets and to cooperate fully with the police, adding that he had met and embraced the man who killed his son, had no animosity, and felt like doing so would "help this boy (Martinez) in years to come."[58]

C.A. met Kathy's family at the Jewell Street house, and both families gathered a few items that had belonged to their children. One possession that neither family could claim was the little dog Schocie. She was missing. A neighbor had called the police on August 2, asking to remain anonymous but reporting that the back gate to the yard at 906 Jewel was open and the dog had "gotten out of the yard and run off."[59] The animal's fate was never determined. One wonders if it sensed that neither of its owners would ever return.

On August 8, 17-year-old Karen Griffith died. Some newspapers, such as *The Washington Evening Star*, reported that she was Whitman's 17th "victim,"[60] ignoring the wounded who were still alive. Other papers reported he killed 13 or 14.[61] However, including Claire Wilson's baby, Karen was the 16th who died. There would be a 17th, but not for many years.

On the 9th, Whitman located and claimed Margaret's car, a 1966 Mercury Park Lane, which she had apparently driven to Texas from Florida the previous May, and on the 10th he wrote notes to many of the victims or their families. They were short, saying principally that the Whitman family expressed its sincere regrets.

However gracious C. A. Whitman may have acted while visiting Austin, his personality received close, critical scrutiny that was reported up the line to the very top. By letter dated August 22, 1966, to Marvin Watson, Special Assistant to the President at the White House, the FBI reported that a doctor from M. D. Anderson Hospital, the Texas Commissioner of Mental Health, the Chairman of the Department of Psychiatry at Southwestern Medical School in Dallas, and a psychiatrist who worked for the Texas Mental Health Commission had each interviewed the elder Whitman. Each "separately... diagnosed him as being dangerous, possessing homicidal tendencies, and a psychopathic personality." The M.D. Anderson doctor, R. Leo Clark, reported that he and his associates "feel that any release of information that might be damaging to the father's ego or to what he considers his rights 'could be trigger of violent response by him'" and that "Whitman's father is capable of the same type of incident perpetrated by his son." The report to the White House went on to say that Texas Governor Connally should contact Florida officials about keeping C.A. Whitman under surveillance or otherwise "containing the situation" by some means in order to prevent any possible recurrence of the holocaust perpetrated by his son," even though such surveillance would be difficult because of Whitman's "paranoid condition."[62]

Investigators who talked to neighbors of C.A. Whitman were told not only that he was a brutal man who was responsible for the killings in Austin, but more than one of them declined to be interviewed while sitting with his or her back to a window, out of fear that C.A. Whitman might shoot them. Others asked that nothing they said be made public because they were afraid that "Charles Adolphus Whitman might kill them if he knew they had discussed the matter." [63]

Had he been alive and learned that such reports were made about his father to President Johnson, Charles Whitman might have considered his mission to have been fully accomplished.

Back in Austin, various kind gestures occurred around the City. At Scholz's Beer Garten, students collected money to turn over to the ambulance drivers who risked their lives on the 1st. Someone anonymously took the newspapers that Alex Hernandez was intending to deliver when he was shot from his bicycle, sold them for twice the normal price, and had the money delivered to him at Brackenridge. A call for blood on the day of the shootings was answered by more than a thousand donors within two hours of the request. The State of Texas made a larger effort. The Secretary of State, John Hill, created a fund for the victims and their families, and placed a young attorney named Randall "Buck" Wood in charge of the collections and distributions to victims and others who applied. The fund was not huge, but over one hundred thousand dollars in distributions were made, with medical expenses for the wounded as top priority, although several of the victims never applied for any of the funds.[64]

The University's marking of the event consisted of suspending classes for one day, Tuesday the 2nd, and flying the flags at half-mast for a week, although they had already been at half-mast in honor of Professor Richard Pelton, who died on July 29, 1966 at the age of 56.[65]

At the first football game of the season in September, money was collected to assist those wounded on August 1. The game was against USC and John Wayne was in the audience to cheer on his alma mater. The rumor spread that the Duke donated generously, but the total amount given was "pitifully small."[66]

1. 96 Minutes at 196-97.

2. Interview of Don Vandiver, January 30, 2015.

3. *Ibid.*; Mike Cox, Foreword to *They Call Me Ranger Ray* by Ramiro Martinez, p. xii (New Braunfels: Rio Bravo Publishing 2005).

4. Supplementary Offense Report dated August 8, 1966 by Sgt. T. J. Allen, AHC.

5. Statement of Dr. Robert C. Stokes, M.D., August 5, 1966, AHC.

6. 96 Minutes at 197.

7. *Ibid.*

8. *Ibid.*

9. *Ibid.*

10. Vandiver interview, *supra.*

11. 96 Minutes at 197.

12. *Ibid.*

13. Interview of Alfred McAlister, Austin Texas, January 20, 2015.

14. *Ibid.*

15. Mike Cox, Foreword to *They Call Me Ranger Ray* by Ramiro Martinez, p. xi (New Braunfels: Rio Bravo Publishing 2005).

16. *Ibid.* at xii.

17. Forty-eight years later, when told the correct name of the dog, Vandiver immediately stated that it meant "little bit" in Japanese.

18. Vandiver interview, *supra.*

19. *Ibid.*

20. *Ibid.*

21. Cox, *supra*

22. Lavergne at 225.

23. Report of Sgt. B. Gregory, Austin P.D., August 2, 1966, AHC.

24. *Ibid.*

25. *Ibid.*

26. *Ibid.*; Ray Martinez, They Call Me Ranger Ray, p. 77 (New Braunfels: Rio Bravo Publishing, 2005).

27. Ramirez, *supra*, at 75.

28. Shoquist, *supra.*

29. Supplementary Offense Report dated August 8, 1966 by Sgt. T.J. Allen, APD, AHC; Lavergne at 225.

30. Supplementary Offense Report dated August 25, 1966 by Sgt. Ed Tramp, APD, AHC.

31. Report of Sgt. D. Moody, Austin P.D., August 4, 1966, AHC.

32. Report of Lt. George Phifer, Austin P.D., August 5, 1966, AHC.

33. Report of J.C. Fann, Aug. 1, 1966, AHC.

34. MP3 recording of LBJ telephone conversation with Jim and Beverly Sonntag, August 1, 1966, designated lbj_wh6608_01_10509AUG166.mp3, provided to Dr. Roger Friedman by Dr. Rosa Eberly and to the authors by email dated March 28, 2015.

35. Interview of Silvia Walden, June 3, 2015.

36. *Ibid.*

37. E-mail from Bob Higley dated June 10, 2015.

38. Lavergne at 230-31

39. 96 Minutes at 198; It would not have been comforting to the litigation-sensitive University of Texas to learn that the next day, when the FBI reported about Dr. Heatly's report, that someone—probably Deputy Director Carta DeLoach, to whom the report was addressed—underlined the portion of the report regarding the Tower and deer rifle statement and added "certainly gross mishandling by University psychiatrist" in the margin. FBI report dated August 3, 1966, from J. H. Gale to Mr. DeLoach; AHC.

40. Vandiver interview, *supra*.

41. *Ibid.* For the next two or three years, Vandiver had an aversion to firearms, and for the rest of his life he felt uneasy in large crowds, fearing another terrorist-type event. Later his thinking changed about guns. He came to the conclusion that the return fire from the ground by civilians had saved lives, and he became an advocate for not only private ownership of firearms but for concealed carry as well.

42. Connie Sherley, "U.T. Shootings Send Taylor Man Berserk," *Austin American Statesman*, August 2, 1966.

43. "Robert Benjamin Smith," *Murdepdia*, http://murderpedia.org/male.S/s/smith-robert-benjamin.htm.

44. Supplementary Offense Report dated August 5, 1966, by Sgt. Moody, APD, AHC.

45. Shoquist, *supra*.

46. Interview of Monika McCoy, March 12, 2015.

47. Report of Sgt. D. Kidd, Aug. 2, 1966, AHC.

48. Memo dated August 3, 1966 to the Director of the Secret Service from the Director of the FBI entitled "Charles Joseph Whitman, Threat Against the President." AHC.

49. Letter dated August 6, 1966 from FBI agent J. Myers Cole to Col. Homer Garrison, Director of the Tex. Department of Public Safety: AHC.

50. Airtel memo dated August 9, 1966 to Director, FBI, from SAC, Miami, AHC.

51. Reports of Agent John R. Barron, Federal Bureau of Investigation, dated December 9, December 15, and December 27, 1966; AHC; Letter from FBI agent Cole to Homer Garrison, *supra*.

52. *Ibid.*

53. Letter dated September 21, 1966 from Maj. K.R. Herbert, APD CID, to Chief James C. MacDonald, Memphis P.D., AHC.

54. Report of J.C. Fann, 6:30 p.m., February 9, 1967, AHC.

55. Interview of Monika McCoy, Kyle, Texas, March 12, 2015.

56. "The Madman in the Tower," *Time,* p. 18, Aug. 12, 1966.

57. Letter dated August 6, 1966 from FBI agent J. Myers Cole to Col. Homer Garrison, Director of the Texas Dept. of Public Safety; AHC; Lavergne at 241.

58. *Austin American Statesman*, August 9, 1966.

59. Report filed by Lt. L. Morgan at 3:30 p.m., August 3, 1966, AHC. Another minor Whitman dog mystery is what became of "Lady," the dog owned by C. A. and Margaret Whitman and commonly called "Charlie's dog." A neighbor told the FBI that she accompanied Margaret and Charles to Texas when Margaret left C. A. in March, 1966, but if so, there is no record of her having been at either Margaret's or Charles's homes thereafter.

60. "17th Sniper Victim Dies; Another Still 'Critical'," *The Washington Evening Star*, August 8, 1966.

61. E.g. "Sniper and Mother Buried in Florida," *The Washington Post and Times Herald*, August 6, 1966.

62. Letter dated August 22, 1966, to Marvin Watson, Special Assistant to the President at the White House, AHC.

63. Memo dated August 22, 1966 from the Director, U.S. Secret Service, to the Director, FBI, entitled "Charles Adolphus Whitman Information Concerning," AHC.

64. Interview of Randall "Buck" Wood, May 4, 2015.

65. Lavergne at 238.

66. 96 Minutes at 198.

When I entered the preparation room at Cook's, Whitman's body was on the table on the left and his mother was on the table on the right.

-David Orton, Mortician, Cook Funeral Home

One of the oft-repeated incidents associated with the assassination of President Kennedy involves the determination of Dallas County Medical Examiner Earl Rose that an autopsy be performed in Dallas before the president's body was removed from the city. His near-violent squabble with Secret Service agents intent on returning the body to Washington was ugly, but Rose was correct in making the demand. Texas law provided that homicides required autopsies, and even though Rose was unable to enforce it, he tried his best.

The same rule was not applied to the victims of Charles Whitman. None of his victims were autopsied. Certainly it was well-known that Whitman was the killer and that all but two of his victims had been shot, so there was no particular need. The failure to autopsy Margaret meant the exact method by which he delivered the wound to the back of her head will never be known, but otherwise no important information was lost. When asked why he believed there were no autopsies performed, David Orton said he believed it was because, in comparison to Dallas, Austin was just a small town in 1966.[1]

> *Dr. Coleman De Chenar was a neuropathologist employed by the Austin State Hospital who performed the autopsy of Whitman early the morning of August 2, 1966. He removed a small tumor from the sniper's brain but regarded it only as "an interesting find."*

Whitman was autopsied, of course, and therein lie both a tale and some minor mysteries.

After his body was removed from the Tower, it was taken first to Brackenridg

A mortician at Cook Funeral Home on August 1, 1966, David Orton drove the ambulance that carried Billy Speed, and later Claudia Rutt, to Brackenridge Hospital. He subsequently was present at the autopsy of Whitman and assisted in the embalmment of Whitman's body

Hospital, and then to Cook Funeral Home. Photographs were taken at both places, and at some point in the evening or night of August 1, his body was embalmed.

The autopsy had not been performed yet. Embalming before an autopsy is not merely unusual, but startling and potentially problematic. In fact, he was autopsied twice, and in a sense he was embalmed twice, although the second efforts at both were significantly reduced in scope. There is no record of why the embalming occurred first, but one of the morticians at Cook that day said that it was normal practice to embalm as quickly as possible after a body was received because there was no refrigeration in 1966.[2]

Embalming occurs in five steps— first, removal of clothing and disinfecting of the body; second, feature setting, particularly to close the eyes and mouth before embalming fluid is introduced; third, arterial embalming—draining the blood and injecting embalming fluid; fourth, cavity embalming to remove urine, other body fluids, feces, semi-solids, and gases; and finally post-embalming cleanup, particularly bathing, hair washing, and application of makeup. The fourth stage is sometimes accomplished with the use of a "trochar," which is a long metal tube about the size of one's pinkie finger, with a sharp blade at the tip capable of easily puncturing organs. Behind the tube and handle, it may be attached to either an aspirator or to running water, depending on the purpose of use, and in most procedures it is utilized for the purpose of aspirating fluids and semi-solid materials.

In Whitman's case, his clothes were removed, laid aside and later burned, except for his tennis shoes which were taken home by the mortician who probably embalmed him, Frank Lindner.[3] A second candidate for the embalming was David Orton, who drove an ambulance that day. Orton did, in fact, recall doing the procedure, but after studying photos of Whitman's body in April, 2015, he concluded that that was not the case, and instead he played a major role in the second, partial embalming of the body.

The doctor who performed the autopsy, early the morning of August 2, 1966, was Coleman de Chenar, M.D., a neuropathologist employed by the Austin State Hospital. The preparation room at Cook was crowded. In addition to de Chenar and the two morticians, Lindner and Orton, Justice of the Peace for Precinct 3, Place 2, Jerry Dellana, acting as coroner, was present, as were several Austin police officers.[4] Orton, who worked with Dr. de Chenar numerous times over the years, remembered him as a short, bald, bespectacled, and very cheerful man with a heavy accent which he believed to be French, but which was probably eastern European. Because he was a neuropathologist and because it was his passion, he always examined the brain first during an autopsy, and Whitman was no exception.

After removing the organ from the skull cavity and disconnecting the stem, de Chenar held it in both hands, partially rotated it to the left and right, and placed it on a cork-covered stand on the examining table, about a foot high and designed for examining organs. The brain was in rough shape, having been hit by shotgun pellets and pieces of bone. The Connally Commission report would say that Dr. de Chenar "stated that, when he removed the brain the two hemispheres tended to fall apart because of the lacerations," but Orton, who was watching, said this didn't happen.[5] The Commission report also said that "destruction of the brain by gunshot wounds was so extensive that anatomic relationships could not be completely evaluated and the examination of all the major nerve tracts and nuclei of the brain was impossible."[6]

De Chenar then began slicing the brain into pieces and, because it was already lacerated by bullets and bone fragments, he did so using a "modified Virchow technique."[7] Rudolf Virchow was a German doctor who lived from 1821 to 1902 and who is known as "the father of modern Pathology," as well as "the pope of medicine." There are several types of autopsy dissection methods, Virchow, Letulle, En Masse, En bloc, Rokitansky, and Hohn, each of which is used under different circumstances. The Virchow method involves removal of an organ and immediate dissecting. It saves time from more detailed, in situ examination, but makes forensic analysis more difficult, particularly because relationships between different organs or within the same organ are subsequently difficult to analyze.[8] As suggested in the foregoing quotation from the Connally Commission, this proved to be an issue with regard to Whitman.

Shortly after beginning his dissection, de Chenar told Justice of the Peace Dellana and others within hearing distance that he had located what he believed was a tumor "in a pool of blood and lacerated brain."[9] People in the room moved forward to get a look, and Orton saw what he described as a round object about the size of his thumbnail. De Chenar was not particularly intrigued by it, and reported "there was no correlation with this tumor to psychosis or permanent pains."[10] Later he described it merely as "an interesting find." However, it would prove to be one of the most controversial aspects of the entire Charles Whitman affair.

In Dr. de Chenar's words, "[i]n the middle part of the brain, above the red nucleus, in the white matter below the gray center thalamus, is a fairly well out-lined tumor about 2 x 1.5 x 1 cm in dimensions, grayish-yellow, with peripheral areas of red as blood."[11] De Chenar was the only physician to see the tumor in its original location and in one piece, and although various reports would later make quite an issue about the tumor's location and potential effect on Whitman's behavior, de Chenar simply reported its presence. Nowhere in his report did he mention its proximity to the amygdala or suggest that it would have affected Whitman in any manner.

After finishing his work on the brain, Dr. de Chenar continued by opening the chest and thoracic cavities, examining the organs, and noting the various places where Whitman had been shot, as follows:

Head: Between the eyes, across the nose, are three entry holes of pellets, two more around the left eye and three in the left temporal region.

Neck and chest: on the left side of the neck, around the collarbone, are four penetrations; two on the right side at the same level; one in the left fourth intercostal space close to the sternum bone (at the center of the heart); and four in the left axillary region. One under the arm is of larger diameter, close to one CM.

Left shoulder and arm: Around the shoulder, about a dozen of grazing are penetrating injuries. The left arm bone (Humerus) is severely destroyed by several large caliber penetrations.

The effect of some of the slugs was described by de Chenar—one penetrated the right ventricle of the heart, others the brain and at least one the left lung, but none of the slugs were preserved. Instead, they were left in the body or carried away as souvenirs, with Orton taking two or three and Lindner a couple more, all of which have since been lost. De Chenar concluded that Whitman's "fatal injuries (were) to the head and to the heart."

A "double ought buckshot" 12 gauge shotgun shell like that fired by McCoy and Martinez contains nine lead or steel balls.[12] Whitman was shot with three shells, two from a distance of about 55 feet, and one from inches away. Doctor de Chenar could not be precise enough about the number of penetrations to draw absolute conclusions about how many times Whitman was hit. He was very specific when counting the wounds on his head—eight—but for those on his neck and chest it isn't clear whether his count was 12 or only nine, and when he got to the left shoulder and arm he was even less absolute—"about a dozen" and "several large caliber penetrations." This may sound more like guess-work than the precise declarations of a pathologist, but the reason is that the close-up shot by Martinez chewed and shredded more than it merely penetrated. David Orton stated that Whitman's left arm was nearly separated from his body. Looking at a photograph of Whitman's body with the clothes removed, he pointed to the wound on his upper left arm and said that it went all the way around, that the bone was protruding, and the arm was attached only by skin and a piece of tissue.[13]

The question of how many pellets hit Whitman is only important for one reason—it could reveal who killed him—McCoy only or Martinez and McCoy—which will be discussed at greater length in Chapter Twelve.

Tests were also performed to determine if Whitman had drugs in his system, and the absence of bodily fluids due to the embalming inhibited the ability to do so, as well as the accuracy of the tests. There was still blood in the lungs and stomach, and no traces of drugs were identified, although a bottle of Dexedrine had been found on his body earlier.

Dr. Robert Pape, an emergency room surgeon at Brackenridge, went to the State Hospital about 9 a.m. to witness the autopsy, but it was already finished and the body was still at the funeral home. Pape thought de Chenar was Hungarian, and "did not have all his credentials and so forth" because he had received his training behind the Iron Curtain. He asked de Chenar what he'd found, and the pathologist said "a brain tumor." Pape asked where it was and de Chenar handed him "a pickle jar that had two or three pieces of brain tissue in it, each the size of a domino, and he took the lid off and said 'see that little spot on that one, that's a brain tumor,' and I questioned that. It looked like a little smudge of... of peanut butter, kind of tan peanut butter, about the size of your thumbnail."[14]

Following the autopsy, Whitman's brain and organs were treated with "Safe Powder," which is dry formaldehyde, wrapped in plastic, and placed in the thoracic cavity, which was the customary practice. David Orton and Frank Lindner then closed and sutured Whitman and dressed him, probably in clothes found at his house, and prepared the body for shipment by rail to Florida. That meant that the body was first placed in a shipping crate of heavy cardboard enforced with plywood and then placed in a large wooden box with six handles, two on each side and one on each end. However, the morning of August 3, Cook received a phone call—Dr. de Chenar needed to perform the equivalent of a second autopsy. Dutifully, Orton and Lindner opened the box, opened the crate, removed the body, and removed the clothes.

What de Chenar did when he arrived was technically a second autopsy because it was a post-mortem examination of the body, but Orton recalled that what de Chenar actually did was to open the body, remove the package of organs, and examine them.[15] He almost certainly removed more samples of the organs and took them with him, but Orton did not witness it.

When he was finished, Orton and Lindner re-sutured the body, dressed it again and returned it to its packaging for shipment. Margaret Whitman's embalmed body was placed in a similar container and was shipped on the same train.

No sooner had the two bodies been laid to rest in Florida, on the 5th, than Charles's was dug up again. The Connally Commission decided it needed more samples of his brain. Its members were debating whether there had actually been a tumor and if so, what kind it was and what effect it may have had on Whitman's behavior. A message was sent to the mortician in Lake Worth, who had the body exhumed, the casket opened, the body taken to the funeral home, the thoracic cavity opened and the package of organs placed there at Cook Funeral Home removed and sent to Austin, after which Whitman, or most of him, was returned to his grave.

This led to a classic "oh shit!" incident for the FBI.

At 6:35 p.m. on August 8, 1966, Special Agent in Charge Cole, of the San Antonio office, made a telephone report to his superiors in Washington D.C. about Whitman's brain, stating not only that the brain was damaged "extensively" when he was shot, and was dissected, but that "Whitman's brain is in numerous sections, possibly as many as four hundred."[16] The report included a statement that the brain was buried with Whitman, which was technically correct, so long as the word "permanently" was not included.

Shortly after the call was made, a teletype from the FBI office in Houston was sent to Washington with a copy to the San Antonio office, and it mentioned that research was being conducted on Whitman's brain at the University of Texas Research and Tumor Institute. This inconsistency with his earlier phone call caught Cole's attention, naturally, and he directed an agent named W.V. Cleveland to prepare a memorandum, "[s]ubmitted as a matter of information," to provide "some clarification" to J. Edgar Hoover et al. The memo explained that "the presence of Whitman's brain at the University is highly confidential," that the brain "was obtained after the casket enclosing Whitman's body was sealed and that no further explanation has been given him as to its current location at the University of Texas."[17]

The San Antonio FBI agents were in a quandary. They had a very good reason for not having acknowledged the presence of Whitman's brain at U.T., but not reporting such essential facts in a case to Hoover was probably high on the list of no-no's. Cole prepared another memo, this time in code. It arrived in Washington at 9:14 p.m., and explained that not only Whitman's brain, but all of his vital organs had been removed, obviously when the body was exhumed in Florida, but that the Whitman family had not been so informed. As far as C.A., Pat, and Johnnie Mike knew, those particular bits of Charlie were still in the casket, and Major K. R. Herbert of the Austin Police Department had requested that this information not be disseminated to anyone because he and the police were, quite logically, "afraid of legal implications."[18]

Exactly what ultimately became of Whitman's organs, other than the brain, is not known, and the fate of the brain is only slightly more certain. In all likelihood, the FBI's fears about legal implications and a corresponding paucity of records have something, perhaps everything, do to with that.

Coleman de Chenar was not merely fascinated human brains; he collected them. From the 1950s to the 1980s he amassed more than 200, all or most from mental patients who died in the Austin State Hospital, formerly known as the Texas State Lunatic Asylum, where he worked. Any time a patient with an unusual or notable ailment died, or at least when he had permission or no one protested, de Chenar preserved his prize in a jar of formalin to which was affixed a label containing a reference number, the condition from which the patient suffered, and the date of death. The labels were often in Latin, and included *Apoplexia cerebri*, where a burst blood vessel or stroke would have caused a sudden malfunction of the patient's brain; *Hemorrhagic subarachnoid idle frontotemporal*, which is bleeding between the brain and the skull in the frontal temporal area, and the more familiar Down's Syndrome.[19]

After de Chenar died in 1985, the State Hospital discovered that the brains created a previously unanticipated problem—they violated federal environmental laws regarding disposal of the formaldyhyde in which they were stored, which is both flammable and toxic. The fluid needed to be changed once a year, and the equipment required to dispose of the old fluid in compliance with the law was too expensive for the hospital, so the decision was made to transfer them to another facility. They were advertised as available and the response was significant. Six major institutions, including Harvard and the University of Texas, offered to take the entire collection, and others, particularly science teachers, asked for a single brain for class work. Ultimately it was decided to turn them over to U.T., which was just down the road, and they were packed in cardboard boxes and taken to the University's Animal Resource Center for temporary storage until a permanent site could be selected.[20]

It isn't absolutely certain that Whitman's brain, or what was left of it, was part of the collection. Those who knew Whitman had been a patient of de Chenar assumed that Whitman's brain was also included.

In 2011, a photographer named Adam Voorhes requested permission to photograph the brains for a magazine cover, and a U.T. professor named Tim Schallert escorted him to the storage closet where they were then being kept in a U.T. laboratory. Voorhes got his photos, but the sight

242

of the dozens of brains made a distinct impression on him. Some jars held two or three brains; some held only parts; others were misshapen, nearly smooth, deflated, or discolored. After taking his photographs, the experience stuck with Voorhes, and he decided to write a book about them, which he did. It was called *Malformed: Forgotten Brains of the Texas State Mental Hospital*, and it was released in December, 2014.

Perhaps it was merely a coincidence, but just before the book came out a shocking story exploded across the media. A hundred brains, including Whitman's, were missing! De Chenar had collected over 200 brains, but only about 100 were in the storage closet in the U.T. lab! It was a delightful story, just in time for Christmas. The notion that Texans had misplaced their brains was too titillating to ignore, the story was picked up across the nation. Remarkably, some of the reports even mentioned Voorhes' freshly released book.[21]

Initially there was speculation that they had been stolen, possibly as a Halloween prank, and University officials made appropriate comments. "The university... will investigate the circumstances surrounding this collection since it came here nearly 30 years ago" and is... "committed to treating the brain specimens with respect... As researchers and teachers, we understand the potential scientific value of all of our holdings and take our roles as stewards of them very seriously... We are committed to treating the brain specimens with respect and are disheartened to learn that some of them may be unaccounted for."[22] A "broader investigative committee" was appointed to examine how the decision was made to dispose of the brains, and the 100 remaining brains were moved to a different, more secure location.

Then came a less embarrassing explanation—there were not 100 brains missing, but only 40 to 60, and they were intentionally disposed of in an environmentally responsible manner in approximately 2002 because their poor condition rendered them unsuitable for research or teaching. Furthermore, U.T. said in a prepared statement, it had found no evidence that any of the brain specimens came from Tower shooter Charles Whitman, "though we will continue to investigate those reports."[23]

But that still wasn't the entire story. Whether or not any of de Chenar's collection had been destroyed, the solution to the mystery was completely different, and when solved, the explanation was accompanied by a smaller mystery.

Twelve days after the story of the missing brains first broke, another came out saying, "[a]fter the media commotion over the new book and the lost brains began to build, a faculty member at UT's other campus, the University of Texas in San Antonio (UTSA) saw an article on the brains. *That's curious,* he thought, *the brains are sitting right here at our facility."* The UTSA professor called Professor Schallert with the good news. UTSA had borrowed the missing brains in order to study the progression of Alzheimer's and other neurological diseases.[24] Schallert was relieved, and reported the good news to various newspapers.

The smaller mystery is that the loss of the brains was first reported on November 21, and their being located at UTSA was reported on December 3, but that same day the first report seemed to break again, or be re-discovered, without its solution. CBS News, the *Austin American Statesman,* and other media reported the missing brains, speculation about theft or vandalism, seemingly for the first time, on December 3, 2014.[25] It isn't recorded how Mr. Voorhes felt about so much public attention being paid to his just-published book.

Neither the reports of the solving of the mystery nor of their theft were accompanied by confirmation that Whitman's brain was recovered, destroyed, or never a part of the collection. Dr. de Chenar had no particular reason to preserve it. It was not, in his opinion, abnormal or deserving of special attention, tumor or no tumor, and it was particularly useless if, as the FBI reported, it was reduced to approximately 400 pieces.

It is not the fate of Whitman's brain, however, that continues to attract attention to the story of what he did on August 1, 1966. The mystery is what was going on in that brain that day, and the time has come to solve it.

---

1. Interview of David Orton, April 21, 2015.

2. *Ibid.*

3. *Ibid.* Mr. Orton said that it was a mystery to him and to others at Cook Funeral Home why Lindner wanted Whitman's tennis shoes, but of course they would now be a prized, if macabre, relic in someone's collection or possibly a museum.

4. *Ibid.*

5. Connally Commission Report, p. 7, interview of David Orton, *supra.*

6. "Information on the Report of Pathologic Studies Requested by Governor Connally in Conjunction with the Charles Whitman Case," (The Connally Commission Report), AHC.

7. Connally Commission, *Ibid.*

8. *An Introduction to Autopsy Technique*, p. 1, College of American Pathologists, 2005; "What is the best autopsy method of Dissection and why?" http://www.researchgate.net/post/What_is_the_best_autopsy_method_of_Dissection_and_why_The_goal_of_the_question_is_to_gain_a_better_understanding_of_the_logic_for_methods_used; Rudolf Virchow, Wikipedia, http://en.wikipedia.org/wiki/Rudolf_Virchow.

9. Orton interview, *supra*; Connally Commission Report at 7.

10. Letter dated August 4, 1966 to Marvin Watson, Special Assistant to the President, from "JMR" of the FBI, AHC.

11. Going into more detail in the "histological findings" of the autopsy report, de Chenar wrote that: "The tumor of the brain is composed of elements of the connective tissue of the brain (glia) and of blood vessels of enlarged calibers. Some of these blood vessels have thick walls, others have thin ones, with defective construction of the layers and microscopically small bleedings into the surrounding intercellular spaces, however, only a dozen or less red blood cells enter those spaces around. The cells are rather small, round or elongated, with a small amount of cytoplasm and mostly well staining nucleus. The chromatin substance of the nucleus is well organized, round or somewhat elongated or, in some places, vesicular. Cell divisions occur only very exceptionally, indicating a minimal level of activity, just on the borderline to malignant formations. There are areas of cell death (necrosis), surrounded by a fence-like arrangement (palisade formation) of elongated cells". Autopsy Protocol of Whitman, Charles Joseph, dated August 2, 1966, performed at Cook Funeral Home, AHC.

12. *Ibid.* However, different online sites contain different information, including that there are 12 double ought pellets in a shell as opposed to nine, or that there are eight pellets in a double-ought shell as opposed to nine. E.g., http://en.wikipedia.org/wiki/Shotgun_shell.

13. Orton interview, *supra*.

14. Dr. Robert Pape in *Sniper 66*, Part 4.

15. Orton interview, *supra*.

16. Teletype memo dated August 8, 1966 to Director and San Antonio, from Houston office of the FBI, AHC.

17. Memorandum dated August 8, 1966 to "Mr. Gale" from W.V. Cleveland, AHC.

18. Decoded copy of teletype to "Director" from San Antonio, dated Aug. 8, 1966, 7:05 p.m.,(Central Time) marked "Urgent" and received at 9:14 pm (Eastern Time).

19. Alex Hanford, "The Mysterious Vanishing Brains," The Atlantic, Dec. 2, 2014.

20. Ken Herman, "A Matter of Grey Matter: Texas Has the B

21. Matt Largey, *supra*.

22. E.g. "100 Brains Missing from the University of Texas," CBS News, Dec. 3, 2014, http://www.cbsnews.com/news/100-brains-missing-from-university-of-texas/; Emine Saner "The Baffling Case of the 100 Missing Brains," *The Guardian*, Dec. 3, 2015; http://www.theguardian.com/science/shortcuts/2014/dec/03/the-baffling-case-of-the-100-missing-brains; "UT says environmental workers disposed of brains" *Austin American Statesman*, December.3, 2014.rains," Associated Press, August 3, 1986.

21. Matt Largey, "The Mystery Brains of the Texas State Lunatic Asylum (Update)" Nov.

21, 2014, http://kut.org/post/mystery-brains-texas-state-lunatic-asylum-update. This article includes a slide show of many of the brains.

22. "UT says environmental workers disposed of brains, "*Austin American Statesman*, December.3, 2014.

23. *Ibid.*

24. Matt Largey, *supra.*

25. E.g. "100 Brains Missing from the University of Texas," CBS News, Dec. 3, 2014, http://www.cbsnews.com/news/100-brains-missing-from-university-of-texas/; Emine Saner "The Baffling Case of the 100 Missing Brains," *The Guardian*, Dec. 3, 2015; http://www.theguardian.com/science/shortcuts/2014/dec/03 /the-baffling-case-of-the-100-missing-brains; "UT says environmental workers disposed of brains" *Austin American Statesman*, December.3, 2014.

CHAPTER ELEVEN
The Reasons Why

Whitman's actions speak for themselves. Any cause-effect theory, whether organic (brain tumor), chemical (amphetamine psychosis), or psychological (military training or child abuse), embracing the idea that Charles Whitman's judgment or free will was impaired, is not consistent with what he DID.

-Gary Lavergne, "Charles Whitman: Why did he do it?"
Austin American Statesman, August 1, 2006

Why did the "rumor about a tumor" (in the words of a Kinky Friedman song) persist? Perhaps because everyone wanted to believe it, from state officials seeking cover from lawsuits... to a shocked public that needed simple answers to a horrifying episode. As former chairman of the Board of Regents, Frank Erwin said, "There had to be something that made him do it."

-Brenda Bell, "An Anniversary Without Answers,"
Austin American Statesman, August 1, 2006

Part One
Non-Reasons and Partial Reasons

Contrary to what newspapers declared in 1966, contrary to what the Connally Commission suggested, contrary to what the public wanted to believe, and contrary to lengthy discussions today on the Internet,[1] the tumor in Whitman's brain did not cause him to commit mass murder. It did not persuade him to climb the Tower, did not influence his behavior, was not the cause of his feelings of unease that dated back to at least 1964, and

Texas Governor John Connally speaking on the occasion of the release of the report by the commission he appointed to investigate the Whitman shootings.

249

did not unleash homicidal violence in a previously peaceful individual. It didn't even cause his headaches.

Dr. de Chenar was the first to declare it had no effect. He described the tumor as being an "astrocytoma," which is a brain tumor capable of being or becoming malignant, but which is often slow-growing, benign, and associated with long-term survival. Dr. de Chenar was made a part of the Connally Commission, but there is nothing to suggest that the work of those 32 doctors and experts persuaded him to change his mind.

Stories of the tumor hit the newspapers on August 2, right after the autopsy, and the Connally Commission Report of September 8, 1966 confirmed what the reporters had trumpeted, one of whom relied on it to write that the tumor would have killed Whitman within a year.[2] It was what a nervous public wanted to believe. Nobody wanted to think that other young men, whether good-looking, all-American ex-Marines or otherwise, might commit similar murders while in possession of their senses. The tumor fit perfectly into Whitman's own words about head-aches, uncontrollable thoughts and his hope for an autopsy.

Yet even the Connally Commission report contained statements that fell short of being an indictment of the tumor. On the one hand, the report declared without hesitation that the tumor was malignant and fast-growing, but it also stated that "[t]he data obtained provide no evidence that this man had a clinical neurological abnormality, and there is no evidence from the pathological reports that the tumor inter-rupted pathways leading to detectable neurological signs." The Commission also stated that "the application of existing knowledge or organic brain function does not enable us to explain the actions of Whitman on August first."[3]

After so saying, the version of the report released to the public contained 12 conclusions regarding Whitman's actions and behavior followed by 10 recommendations for future action. The first of the 12 conclusions stated that Whitman was "an intelligent, intense, and driven young man" and the next nine listed conditions and personality traits the Commission believed were contributing factors to the end result. The 11th stated, "It is the opinion of the task force that the relationship between the brain tumor and Charles J. Whitman's actions on the last day of his life cannot be established with clarity. However, the highly malignant brain tumor *conceivably* could have contributed to his inability to control his emotions and actions" (emphasis added). The 12th conclusion stated that the Commission found it impossible to make a formal psychiatric diagnosis of Whitman because no recent psychiatric evaluation of him existed.

If the 11th conclusion sounds suspiciously like a compromise worked out between members of the Commission with competing opinions, that is because that is exactly what it was. When Dr. Stuart Brown, a member of the Commission, was asked on April 22, 2015 if it was a compromise, he laughed and said, "that is putting it mildly." Beyond that, he declined to go into detail, saying that all of the members of the Commission had sworn at the time of their work not to reveal more than what was released to the public. This was due, he said, largely to concerns of the University of Texas that it was going to be sued, and might be found liable for some or all of the injuries and death Whitman had inflicted.[4] Another member of the Connally Commission, Pathologist Tate Minckler, M.D., was contacted a few days later about the work of the Commission and the tumor, and he responded, "Charlie's father was a nut. I think Charlie was a nut. I'm not a psychologist or psychiatrist so my Dx is worthless, but I don't think the tumor had anything to do with CWs actions or behavior that day or that week."[5]

Additionally, a 2009 research article about the evolution of the Medical Examiner system in Texas, for which at least one member of the Commission was interviewed, reported that "… some members of the (Connally) task force indicated certain doubts that the tumor, if it existed at all, was the cause of the violent outburst, and leaned toward a psychiatric diagnosis."[6]

The document issued to the public on September 8 was not, however, the complete Connally Commission report. There was additional material, stamped "Confidential" and addressed to Governor Connally. The contents of the confidential part of the report did not conflict with the report issued to the public, but it contained more detail, more medical terminology, and more explanation, as well as details considered sensationalistic or indelicate, such as the manner of handling Whitman's organs and the fact that, shortly after his body was buried, it was disinterred in order for the mortician to retrieve additional pieces of his brain.

Essentially, the discussion within the Commission was whether the tumor was, as de Chenar concluded, a non-malignant, slow-growing astrocytoma the size of a cherry pit, unlikely to have affected mental functions, or a malignant, fast-growing glioblastoma multiformae or "GBM" tumor. A GBM tumor is the most common malignant brain tumor in humans. Symptoms include seizures, nausea, vomiting, headaches, memory loss, and hemiparesis (weakness or paralysis of one side—left or right—of the body). They are more common in males than females and most common in males over 50. They are characterized by the presence of small areas of necrotizing tissue surrounded by anaplastic cells. An astrocytoma is more common among younger people, sometimes causes seizures, and can evolve into a GBM tumor.

The confidential portion of the Commission report even suggests there may not have been a tumor. It emphasized that the brain had been dissected before the Commission began its work, that not all of the pieces of the brain were recovered, and that in addition to destruction by gunshot wounds, "many parts of the brain were damaged by penetrating fragments of bone which had been created by the gunshot wounds." Scattered throughout the confidential portion of the report are what can only be considered "weasel words" that refer to the tumor in hesitant manners—it was "*reportedly* removed" by Dr. de Chenar; it "was *described*" as having certain characteristics; and "examiners *attempted* to examine parts of the brain and devoted special attention to *any* evidence of residual tumor near the *reported* location of the main mass."

At the very end of the confidential part of the report was a "List of wrapped specimens, specimen bottles, blocked tissue, and slides received" that referenced 30 different pieces of Whitman's body separated into the categories of "specimens wrapped in gauze," "specimens in glass jars," and "tumor blocked in paraffin." There were four of the latter category, two stained and two unstained, but among the specimens in glass jars were three tumor-related items, a "tumor border," "basal ganglia," and "tumor or artifact—3 pieces." For some inexplicable reason, those three items, and only those three, were followed by a question mark within the list, as though nobody was certain they were really what they were identified as being.

Offsetting these speculative descriptions were definitive statements about the tumor, such as its not having a capsule and that it was torn into two parts by a fragment of bone. This latter tidbit was not included in de Chenar's autopsy protocol and nobody who saw the tumor on August 2, 1966, mentioned it, whereas the Commission had, at most, only slide and paraffin block samples of it. Nevertheless, the fact that the Commission was furnished with those paraffin block samples, and said there was a tumor, makes it counter-intuitive to argue it did not exist.

When Dr. Robert Pape spoke to de Chenar shortly after the autopsy, he asked what part of the brain the peanut butter smudge of a tumor came from, and de Chenar told him, "the pons," which Pape described as being on the brain stem and part of the "switchboard, where you live." Pape was dubious, saying later that Whitman had had no neurological symptoms such as paralysis or any other typical indicator of a tumor, that a tumor that size located where de Chenar said it was would have been fatal, and that the part of the brain that controlled stability and instability was in the frontal cortex, not down in the brain stem. He said he left de Chenar "rather befuddled," and "not so sure this is it, but the press picked it up."[7]

Brenda Bell became a newspaper reporter and devoted years of study and writing to the Whitman case, and what she picked up was different from the 1966 reports. She interviewed not only Dr. de Chenar but members of the Commission, and said "his brain was subjected to the most sophisticated analysis available. The brain tissue was a mess, but the finding was clear: no evidence of glioblastoma multiformae or a tumor of any kind."[8] Further doubt about the tumor was delivered to Gary Lavergne after publication of his book, *A Sniper in the Tower*, in 1997. He had not attempted therein to deny the existence of the tumor, but "[a]t least two physicians closely connected to the case told me they didn't think Whitman had a tumor at all."[9]

There is no point in arguing that the tumor did not exist. Doing so is an attempt to prove a negative. There must have been one. Had Dr. de Chenar advocated that the tumor explained Whitman's behavior while the Commission drew a contrary conclusion, one might suspect that de Chenar padded the facts, but the opposite is the case. De Chenar said the tumor existed but had no effect on Whitman while the Commission said an effect was conceivable.

Instead, the relevant question is, "what would analysis of the available information about the tumor reveal today if performed by a qualified neurologist?"

Dr. Mitchel Berger is a graduate of Harvard and the University of Miami Medical School. He has been a brain surgeon for 30 years, is the chair of the Neurosurgery Department at the University of California at San Francisco Medical Center, is a recent past president of the American

Association of Neurological Surgeons, and was the co-inventor of a system for mapping the brain to safely remove brain tumors. As described by the chief executive of the UCSF Medical Center in a 2011 newspaper article titled "Mitchel Berger, UCSF Brain Surgeon, Tops in Nation," "He's the neurosurgeon that other neurosurgeons send their patients to."[10]

The foregoing description, obvious foreshadowing for the opinion Dr. Berger provided for this book, does not mean Dr. Berger conducted a long, in-depth study of the question posed above, or was part of a modern-day panel that mirrored the Connally Commission in its numbers, credentials, and work, assembled for the purposes of this book. That is not the case.

Instead, when the authors contacted the American Association of Neurology, the American Academy of Neurology, and the American Association of Neurological Surgeons to inquire whether a qualified neurologist might be willing to render an answer to the question posed above, only the American Association of Neurological Surgeons responded positively. Its Executive Director, Thomas Marshall, had been 10 years old and visiting his grandparents in Harlingen, Texas on August 1, 1966. He "vividly" remembered his father and grandfather discussing the incident, and he not only suggested we contact Dr. Berger but graciously forwarded our request to him. Dr. Berger then made time between scheduled surgeries to respond by email and by telephone, then reviewed Whitman's autopsy protocol and the Connally Commission report and promptly delivered a short, straightforward, confident opinion:

> This (the protocol and report) was helpful. He had a small incidentally found tumor that would not have caused headaches due to the small size of the tumor. In my nearly 30 years of seeing several thousands of patients with tumors very similar in size, location and histology it is my opinion that this tumor could NOT have been responsible for the behavior resulting in the shootings.[11] (emphasis by Dr. Berger)

Scientific or medical purists may take issue. As Keith Maitland, the documentary film maker of *The Tower* stated, different experts on neurology arrive at different conclusions,[12] and certainly it can be argued that insufficient time and study was devoted to the question during this project to simply dismiss 50 years of belief by thousands of people based on three sentences and one emphasized word from a single man. However, for the purposes of this book, Dr. Berger's opinion is dispositive of the question posed above. Those who disagree are invited to offer the opinion of a brain surgeon with equal or superior credentials.

If not the tumor, then what?

A simple answer is that Whitman committed suicide. There have been 10 suicides from the Tower since it was constructed. All but Whitman's were by jumping.

Decisions to commit suicide occur on a daily basis. Almost all are irrational, based on wrong-headed reasoning; the result of mental or emotional imbalances. Whitman's was particularly irrational. He was a young, good-looking, upwardly mobile, happily married man with family and friends who loved him, who impressed almost everyone who met him, who was poised to graduate from one of the nation's top universities. The problems he had were in his head, and consisted of extreme frustration over his performance at school, inability to control his temper, disgust, dismay and outrage over his parents' separation, deep resentment of his father, skewed views about money, a terror that he was going to be a failure in life instead of the superhero he had always expected to become, and acute self-loathing.

His version of the act is called suicide by proxy; sometimes suicide by cop. He decided to kill himself, but not by his own hand. His religious upbringing may have instilled in him an unshakeable belief that suicide is a sin, but it wasn't technically suicide if not by one's own hand. He left a suicide note, as many suicides do, but not a hurried, disjointed, emotion-packed scribble just before the end. Whitman's suicide note was deliberate, half-typed and half-handwritten, constructed over a nine or ten hour period some eleven hours before he died. In it he clearly announced his decision: "At this time, though, the prominent reason in my mind is that I truly do not consider this world worth living in, and am prepared to die" and "[a]fter my death I wish that an autopsy would be performed on me to see if there is any visible physical disorder."

Once he decided to die, his next step was obvious. He had been nursing a fantasy about climbing the Tower with a rifle and holding off the rest of the world for at least five years. He had told others about it on at least four occasions and perhaps more. Now he could finally do it, and in so doing he could show the world that he was, in fact, good at something. If nothing else, Charles Whitman was an accomplished marksman, and he wanted the world to know, so he killed two birds with one stone, as well as seventeen people.

He had recently visited the Alamo and might have compared what he planned to having his own private version of that battle. He was a military man and may have seen himself engaging in a "devotio," which was an ancient Roman practice in which a military leader vowed to sacrifice his life in battle, along with the enemy, in exchange for victory. It was more than just a military practice; it was a religious ritual, a consecration to the gods, a human sacrifice, a ceremony whereby a person consigns himself to destruction in order to carry out a greater good for mankind. Although no rational person would look at what Whitman did and consider it a noble sacrifice against an enemy, that is how Whitman may have viewed it.

But that still doesn't answer the "why" question, and it particularly does not solve the greater mystery of why he believed he needed to take his mother and wife with him.

A somewhat novel explanation was provided by a former member of the Connally Commission. Stuart L. Brown, M.D., was an Assistant Professor of Psychiatry at Baylor University College of Medicine in 1966. In later years he founded an organization called "Institute for Play." As stated in an article on the 40th anniversary of the U.T. Tower shootings:

> Under intense pressure from his father to succeed, Charlie made Eagle Scout at age 12, but was denied a normal childhood. He received his last beating at 18. He was never allowed to play sports; the nuns at his parochial school recalled that he didn't seem to know how to play, period.
>
> To Brown,... that explains a lot. The Whitman case led him to other studies of violent behavior; and eventually to research on the importance of play in normal brain development. Compared with thousands of individuals Brown studied, Charles Whitman offers 'the most systematic suppression of free play than anyone I've come in contact with...")[13]

This information seems at odds with the record of Whitman as a pitcher for his high school baseball team and manager of the football team, as well as his playful nature in school and at home with his brothers and pets. One of the neighbors interviewed by the FBI said that there were not many boys for the Whitman brothers to play with in the neighborhood, and that the three played together, often at a nearby school yard, but Brown and his colleagues interviewed dozens of people who knew Whitman as a child, and he concluded that Whitman was so nervous about his father's disapproval, which certainly followed almost any behavior that was playful, that he simply could not play like a normal boy. However accurate such conclusions are, however, they do not seem like a problem that leads to mass murder.[14]

A method used by the Connally Commission to seek to determine why Whitman did what he did is surprising. At least one of its members had his handwriting analyzed.

Handwriting analysis, or graphology, is a method of analyzing personalities through study of their handwriting, particularly cursive, but printing as well. Just as everyone's personality is different, so is everyone's handwriting. Although cursive handwriting is quickly becoming an educational artifact, not even taught in some modern schools, for most adults it was an elementary school subject based on an almost universal set of pictorial representations of the letters of the alphabet. Everyone who learned to write in cursive was expected to mimic the manner in which each letter was depicted in the classroom, perhaps on small flip-charts suspended above a classroom blackboard, perhaps contained in a textbook, and often demonstrated by a grade school teacher who was trained to make each letter "just so." To whatever extent each student's writing may have mirrored those stylized letters in the beginning of his or her handwriting career, within a few years it no longer did so.

Fifty years ago, and still more recently, graphology was regarded in the same category as astrology and palm-reading, such that books about the subject were catalogued with "the occult." However, by 1989 its value and the extent to which it had scientific underpinnings was officially recognized when the topic was recatalogued by the Library Bureau of Congress and moved to "Individual Psychology," with three subdivisions: 155.282 - Diagnostic Graphology, 262.2565 – Documentary Evidence, and 658.3112 - Selection of Personnel by Management.

In a memo from the San Antonio FBI office dated August 10, 1966, to Director Hoover and the Savannah office, it was reported that Dr. Tate Minckler, a pathologist on the Connally Commission, had requested an FBI document examiner "capable of analyzing handwriting of subject (Whitman) to suggest motivation or personality changes over the years."[15] Hoover apparently did not place stock in graphology, because a return message on August 11, 1966 from him to the San Antonio office stated that "[f]or your information it is felt that the Bureau should not become involved in the matter of analyzing subject's handwriting with the view of suggesting motivation or personality changes over the years... You should tactfully advise Dr. Tate Minckler that an FBI document examiner cannot be made available for such purpose."[16]

That did not dissuade Dr. Minkler. He found not one, but two graphologists and had both perform a "blind" analysis of Whitman's handwriting, utilizing samples of handwriting dating back to when he was 14, but done without the analysts knowing the identity of the writer. Although those analyses have not been released to the public and are not part of the collection of material at the Austin History Center, Dr. Stuart Brown, a member of the Commission, stated in 2015 that they "formed a large part of the basis for the Commission's conclusions" about Whitman's personality and motives.[17] However, when Dr. Tate Minkler was asked about the analysis, he did not recall it, accurately pointing out that nearly 50 years had transpired.

Not having copies of the graphological analyses used by the Commission in 1966, but being less skeptical than J. Edgar Hoover, the authors consulted a professional graphologist for the purpose of this book. Quite a bit of Whitman's writing is available, including the "autobiography" he wrote at age 14, the diary he kept while in the Marine Corps, notes he wrote to himself and, of course, the letters he wrote immediately after he killed his mother and his wife.

The graphologist selected, Eileen Page of Massachusetts, agreed to perform the initial analysis blind as well, in that she would not know anything about the subject, particularly his name, other than what his writing revealed. Having and analyzing a subject's signature is an important aspect of handwriting analysis, but she agreed to perform her analysis of the writing first in order to avoid being influenced by any knowledge of the subject or his notoriety.

Other than the fact that Ms. Page was a certified grapho-analyst, the authors had no particular reason to believe she had specific credentials for the analysis of the handwriting of a murderer. That did not come about until after she had completed her analysis and the identity of the subject was revealed to her, at which point she provided the following information:

> I am a self-proclaimed amateur expert in the field of violent personalities. After spending almost 30 years studying hand-writing analysis and the psychology behind why we do what we do, I decided to take on the challenge of understanding the mind of the murderer. I bought 125 original handwriting samples and drawings from serial killers auctioned on the internet and began my research. This past summer, after 2 years of study, I wrote a book on the subject of violence in the personality, *The Cruelty Continuum*. Framingham State University also approved a 3-credit graduate course that I developed and now teach to other educators entitled, Understanding and Preventing Violence in the Schools.

Thus, by something not much more scientific than serendipity, the analysis of Whitman's handwriting was performed by a person particularly well-qualified to do so.

The degree to which Ms. Page described Whitman accurately, in comparison to other accounts of his personality and traits, is startling. Granted, although she was not told the subject's name or that he was a murderer, the content of his last letters revealed he had killed his wife and mother, so that Ms. Page had reason to anticipate a violent personality, and she referred to those two killings as "a tragic ending" in her analysis, not knowing at the time that even greater tragedies followed.

The complete analysis, contained in the endnotes,[18] states that the subject was personified by violent behavior, learned from an early age, when he was an "extreme perfectionist (who) probably never felt that he measured up to his or others' expectations." His perfectionism—never feeling good enough, was over-compensation for feelings of inferiority. At age 14 he was a "good little boy who was on the straight and narrow path to great accomplishments" but "[b]ecause he lacked the ability to control his home life, he learned how to contain his emotions thus helping him to feel in control of some part of his life." She saw evidence of child abuse, a programmed behavior in response, and "because the abuse was a frequent occurrence and continued for so long," it "contributed to making him a walking time bomb."

By age 22 his journey toward violence had accelerated, "his emotions appear to be consuming him as he speaks of the attributes of his wife and extreme love he has for his 'Most Precious Possession.'" By July 31, 1966, "[h]e wanted to sound rational" but '[h]is thoughts were obviously clouded and distorted... Could he have experienced a blow to the head at some point in his life that caused some kind of brain damage, and because it went undetected it grew worse?" His final letter, after Kathy was dead, "occurred right after he killed his 'most precious possession' and he shifted his outlook on life and just didn't give a damn about anything anymore." Ms. Page concluded by saying that from Whitman's handwriting "it is evident that he had been traumatized from being a victim all his life, early on by others and then later held hostage by his own volition."

Following Ms. Page's completion of her analysis, she was provided with examples of Whitman's signatures, written in 1956, 1961, 1964, 1965, and 1966. However, after examining them, she concluded that "there really isn't anything significantly different that showed up from what I have already addressed. The signatures just confirm the original findings."[19]

Ms. Page's analysis corresponds with descriptions of Whitman's personality made by some of his acquaintances, by Dr. Heatly, by the Connally Commission, and by many other post-event analysts. The fact that she knew to suggest both abuse as a child and ask about possible brain damage, which could be attributable to his being involved in the Jeep accident, being attacked by other Marines and kicked in the head, or the tumor, but without knowing about either Whitman's life or autopsy, is almost unsettling.

However, the larger answer to "why he did it," as well as the implications of that answer, are best addressed through the science of psychology by a professional fully qualified to render an opinion.

Part Two
Why He Did It

by Dr. Roger Friedman, Ph.D.

The U.T. Tower shootings terrorized a community and destroyed the fabric of life for hundreds of individuals and families. It also left everyone, even the vaunted members of the Connally Commission, shaking their heads and asking, "What could his motives have been? How can someone who so many saw as a charming, all-American guy do something so horrible ?" On August 1, 2006, the lead article in the *Austin American Statesman* acknowledging the 40th Anniversary of the shootings, was headlined "Anniversary Without Answers."[20] Even today when I tell mental health colleagues or inquiring friends that I'm working on this book, their first response is always, "Why did he do it?"

I have arrived at an answer to that question after much research and thought given to the topic in the course of my teaching and clinical work as a psychologist. Stated succinctly, (1) Whitman's behavior just before and during the sniper attack shows he was a psychopath; (2) his psychopathic behavior correlates to the diagnosis of Anti-Social Personality Disorder with Narcissistic and Borderline Features; (3) against this backdrop of psychopathy and Anti-Social Personality Disorder, stressful life events began building up in Whitman's life from 1965-1966 that fueled his anger and resentment. He perceived all failures or negative consequences for his behavior as 'insults and injustices' that would justify someday activating his long simmering plan for a 'mission-oriented' sniper attack from the U.T. Tower. Though he knew he would die in the end, the goal of this military-like operation was to discharge growing rage, demonstrate his ability to gain control, and get the attention he felt he deserved if only for a day. The pre-planning and executing of the mass shooting was, for him, not sad, compulsive, or primarily suicidal, but rather, as with all psychopaths, a narcissistic and gratifying mission to gain the omnipotence he believed was his due.[21]

More discussion is needed to not only explain my answer to the question, but to put to rest the question itself. In doing so, I am fully aware that not everyone is interested in either the question or the answer. Survivors, first responders, and witnesses to the actual shootings in 1966 are generally disgusted by the continuing focus on the sniper. They feel that it leads nowhere but to more romanticizing of the "mystery killer" and contributes to the likelihood of copycat-type attacks. It's not unusual to find that even the mention of the sniper's actual name is avoided in conversations with survivors and witnesses. It's easy to understand, if one is exposed to the terror and has carried the legacy for decades, how enraging and even re-traumatizing it is to encounter popular culture's preoccupation with the sniper's life story, particularly when combined with the University's and media's almost total lack of concern for the lasting traumatic impact of the event. These very real human concerns make my diagnostic criminal and clinical inquiry into the sniper's decisions and behavior an even more somber and serious task.

An almost prurient fascination about Charles Whitman's behavior and motivation has continued to preoccupy the media and public dialogue over the past five decades, especially around the anniversary of the shooting each year. This happens in part because Whitman's school rampage was the first of its kind in America and is remembered, at least in vague detail, by everyone who was old enough to be aware of the news in the mid-1960s.

The story still sells papers and magazines, at least in Texas. Cultural preoccupation with Whitman's criminal assault is also fueled by the continuing occurrence of school rampages since 1966, and a seemingly endless stream of single factor theories of causation, from simplistic and reductive psychologizing to polemics based on the proponent's anti-military/anti-gun politics, amphetamine abuse accusations, religious views, and even surrealistic astrological readings.[22]

The challenge of explaining complex human behavior, especially that which is threatening, deadly, random and inexplicable, immediately puts us on the horns of a dilemma: Do we respond to our own and society's anxious and impatient need to explain this danger away as an accident, something that will never occur again? Or do we face the uncomfortable possibility that Whitman, only the first of a series of school shooters, exhibited a new form of public massacre, from which our society seems unable to protect itself?

So why then did Whitman do it? We can safely assume that the answer will not be hidden in another reductive, single factor theory, be it from a psychological, biological or sociological frame of reference. Let's recall the old H. L. Mencken axiom that a clinical professor of mine from Baltimore early in my training always reminded us of as we began a new client assessment, "For every problem there is a solution which is simple, neat and wrong." We do not want to err too far on the other side, however. If the answer we develop is too broad, equivocal and inclusive of every possible variable that may have affected Whitman's behavior, the resulting clinical formulation will be bewildering and of no help.

In pursuit of a satisfying explanation, I began by poring over my notes from articles and interviews from the past several months to see if I could find a new entry point or an approach to understanding Whitman's behavior that wouldn't leave me, in important ways, missing either the forest or the trees. What came to mind were my conversations in May, 2015 with Monika McCoy, an Austin Police Officer and daughter of Houston McCoy, the Officer who shot and killed Whitman on the Tower's observation deck. She had encouraged me to talk with a senior FBI Profiler in Washington, D.C., Mary Ellen O'Toole, and obtain her view of the sniper attack.

It turns out that Dr. O'Toole, former Supervisory Special Agent at the Critical Incident Response Group (CIRG) in Quantico, VA., and now Director of the Forensic Science Department at George Mason University, prepared the first monograph on school shooters. This comparative analysis of various shooters' behavior was based on a thorough review of 18 school shooting cases and the discussions held during a Conference, organized in 1999 shortly after the Columbine School tragedy, at the National Center for the Analysis of Violent Crime (NCAVC). That monograph, titled, "The School Shooter: A Threat Assessment Perspective," along with O'Toole's 2013 article, "Jeffrey Weise and the Shooting at Red Lake Minnesota High School: A Behavioral Perspective," were enough to convince me that the recent approach taken by the National FBI Behavioral Analysis Unit (BAU) and the CIRG, a perspective not available at the time of the Connally Commission Report, and not referenced in recent articles about Whitman's attack, might be an excellent starting point in our current search for answers.[23]

This behavioral approach to criminal investigations and comparative analysis of school shooters, built up over the past 25 years, doesn't start with the offender's family of origin, current relationship dynamics, or even the shooter's personality traits. The experts advocate starting with two important goals: to distinguish objective knowledge from opinion, and to differentiate an offender's motives from rational justifications for his behavior. Such an approach assumes that the most accessible, objective and therefore critical clues to the shooters' motivation are the behaviors they engage in just prior to and during the violent public event. When we describe behavior as predatory, as the CIRG suggests, within the time context of a crime it is because the offender's violence is purposeful, focused and cold-blooded. The CIRG approach assumes there can never be an explanation of the behavior that will justify to the average person what the offender did to his random victims. We will never find a "reasonable enough" explanation that would allow the public to say, "Okay, now I understand why he did that horrible crime." Nevertheless, by detailed analysis, and comparison to the behavior of other shooters, this approach provides a precise description of the offenders' behavior, from which we can fairly accurately decipher their personal motives. We may find their motives unacceptable, repulsive or plain crazy, but that has nothing to do with their validity for the offender.

In the remaining part of this chapter, I will apply, in a summary manner, the CIRG's behavioral analysis approach to Whitman's actions on August 1, 1966—and then translate that behavioral profile into the clinical language of APA's *Diagnostic and Statistical Manual of Mental Disorders* 5th Edition (DSM 5). This translation will allow us to derive a clear diagnostic statement about Whitman and to find some answers for why he did what he did. In other chapters of this book you may follow and analyze a detailed narrative of the sniper's behavior on August 1, 1966, so here I will only refer to the most pertinent behavioral elements of that day.

The CIRG's behavioral approach to understanding the motivation of mass shooters focuses on determining if the shooter's behavior fits the typical psychopathic profile in terms of pre-incident behaviors ('leakage' or disclosure of plans to carry out the mass shooting, murder of family member(s), and careful preplanning prior to the major violence) and *predatory behavior during the public massacre*. Whitman's pre-incident behavior fits the predatory profile perfectly.[24] He directly and specifically disclosed or 'leaked' his thought of conducting a mass shooting as early as 1960 to a Marine roommate in Guantanamo Bay, at least three times to a friend in 1961-62, again to a fellow student in class in 1964, and again just six months before the shootings to the psychiatrist he had an appointment with at the University Counseling Center.

The night before the incident, Whitman murdered his wife, Kathy, and mother, Margaret. Because neither Whitman, nor the other school shooters for that matter, had criminal histories or had ever murdered before, Dr. O'Toole believes the pre-incident murders served as an 'insurance' policy, committing them to going forward with their larger plans and unable to turn back.[25] Whitman explained his motivation in the notes he wrote just before and following the murders of his wife and mother. These read, in part: "I don't know if its selfishness, or if I don't want her to have to face the embarrassment my actions would surely cause her. At this time though, the prominent reason in my mind is that I truly do not consider this world worth living in, and am prepared to die, and I do not want to leave (them) to suffer alone in it. I intend to kill (them) as painlessly as possible." In these few words we can see his grandiosity and omnipotence reflected in his assumption that he knows best when his wife and mother should die. Though he says he wants to kill them "as painlessly as possible," he really doesn't have any empathy for what pain is for another person, considering he stabbed Kathy five times as she slept in their bed, clubbed his mother on the head and stabbed her with a knife in the heart.

There is also ample evidence of Whitman's predatory preplanning; he probably assessed the murder scene days prior to the event, practiced shooting, and marked the angle corrections needed for shooting at a sharp downward trajectory on a piece of tape attached to the butt of his rifle. He brought three rifles, a converted shotgun, three pistols, a machete, a hatchet, four knives, 700 rounds of ammunition, and all of the other supplies listed in the endnotes of Chapter Four, then transported it all in or with a footlocker, using a rented dolly, to the observation deck, where he blocked shut the only door that provided access to where he planned to shoot.

The sniper's predatory behavior continued throughout the event. He remained "hypo-emotional" and cool throughout. For example, when he found the elevator he planned to take to the Tower's observation deck was not working, an attendant came out of her office, unlocked it for him, and he smiled and calmly said, "Thank you, Ma'am." Other pieces of evidence for calculated and predatory behavior included his having been able to make strategic decisions when surrounded by chaos and danger: he shifted from shooting over the railing of the deck, where he was exposed, to aiming through the narrow turrets in the base of the observation deck to avoid getting hit when counter-fire from riflemen below began about twenty minutes into his shooting spree. He waited until he was on the deck to put on a white head-band, probably to keep sweat from his forehead from getting into his eyes when he began shooting, the temperature being 98 degrees that August day. He maximized his lethality by remaining in one place on the deck for periods of time and waiting for people to expose themselves, shooting efficiently at open targets and aiming mainly at moving targets, a special skill for which he had been recognized as a Marine marksman several years earlier. When he was killed officers found the transistor radio next him, tuned in to the local news station where reports of victims dead and wounded and police movements were being regularly announced throughout the day. Finally, like all the other school shooters, Whitman did not wear a mask or in any way attempt to hide his identity and, in fact, he'd brought his wallet with his student ID with him. Whitman was killed while sitting in a corner of the observation deck shooting onto the mall below, by shotgun blasts from 50 feet away from a police officer, who with his partner, had kicked their way through the door to the deck. When Dr. O'Toole, Supervisory FBI Profiler at the time, had visited Austin in 2006 to determine if Whitman's rampage was an 'outlier' or would fit into the FBI's growing model of psychopathic school shooters,she interviewed the officers who had been on the Tower and had subdued Whitman that day. She said they didn't believe a tumor caused Whitman's behavior, because they were at the crime scene and saw how prepared, organized and in control he had been throughout the whole shooting spree.[26]

This account of behavior provides a frightening picture of Whitman's psychopathic or cold-blooded actions prior to and during the mass shooting and fits the CIRG profile to a tee. This criminal and behavioral profile, in turn, straightforwardly corresponds to the clinical criteria in the DSM 5 that define Cluster B Personality Disorders.[27] A "personality disorder" is an enduring pattern of inner experience and behavior that deviates markedly from the expectations of the individual's culture, is pervasive and inflexible, has an onset in adolescence or early adulthood, is stable over time and leads to distress or impairment." Cluster B Personality Disorders include Anti-Social Personality Disorder (ASPD), Borderline Personality Disorder (BPD), and Narcissistic Personality Disorder (NPD). Whitman suffered from a primary Anti-Social Disorder with Borderline and Narcissistic features. Key attributes of

ASPD are "a pervasive pattern of lack of empathy for others, arrogant self-appraisal, display of superficial charm, thrive on high risk behaviors, may receive dishonorable discharges from the armed services, fail to be self-supporting financially, breaking the law or engaging in behavior that is illegal even if not arrested, and are more likely than people in the general population to die prematurely by violent means (e.g., suicide, accidents, and homicides.)"[28]

The cognitive abilities of individuals with ASPD are usually not impaired; in fact, they may have average or above average IQ's, though their lack of empathy and manipulative interpersonal traits usually limit their educational, military or work achievements. Individuals with ASPD may also experience depressed mood and other associated difficulties, including gambling disorders and problems of impulse control—especially with anger. All of these characterized Whitman's functioning dating back to late adolescence. Individuals with ASPD often have personality features that meet the criteria for Borderline or Narcissistic Personality Disorder, or both—as Whitman seems to have had. Co-occurring features with Borderline Disorder include a pattern of turmoil and drama in family/personal relationships and extreme dysregulation of self-image, mood and impulses. Whitman's Narcissistic features include a pattern of grandiosity, preoccupation with fantasies of power or greatness, sense of his own omnipotence, and intense desire for excessive admiration.

Increasingly stressful life events escalated Whitman's rage and sense of injustice in life. In fall, 1965 he was convicted of usury money lending, gambling and fights at Camp Lejeune Marine Base, and in addition to being demoted to a Private, was given 30 days confinement and 90 days hard labor. His father helped him get a speeded up honorable discharge but when he returned to Austin in January 1966, he failed repeatedly getting school work done or holding onto a series of jobs including bill collector, bank teller, working as a real estate agent and insurance salesman. His wife, Kathy, had finished her college degree and was teaching in a public high school—she was the only bread winner in the family and this would have been another source of humiliation and injustice to Whitman.

Particularly challenging and enraging for him was his parent's separation that took place in the spring of 1966, and his mother's, whom Whitman said he loved very much, moving from Florida to Austin. The move put Whitman in the role of helping his mother adjust to a new city and having to cope daily with angry phone calls and emails from his father in Florida who was furious about her leaving and suffered himself from an untreated Bipolar Disorder. It was at the end of this time that Whitman's father announced that he was going to stop all financial support he'd been sending regularly to his son and to his wife. Whitman's writings reveal a seething hatred toward his father that went back to early childhood, and described his father's domineering, extremely judgmental and abusive behavior toward his mother and himself.

By mid-summer, 1966, Whitman's increasing sense of rage about injustices in his life primed him for activating what was a long standing plan to climb the Tower and conduct a shooting spree that would end in his death as well. When to actually begin the preparation and execute the plan was a decision that Whitman made, like the other psychopathic school shooters, in part strategically (e.g., do it on a Monday so he had the weekend to buy supplies and kill his wife and mother on Sunday night, start shooting when classes let out) and in part by his narcissistic sense that it was just the right time for him to get it done. The well-publicized and brutal stabbing deaths of 8 nurses in their apartment in Chicago by Richard Speck occurred on July 13, 1966 and Whitman was likely to have been aware of this. Since there can be a copycat effect involved in these mass shootings, the news of Speck's crimes may have influenced Whitman's decision to actually get started on his own murderous plan.[29] But Whitman's decision of when to execute his 'mission-oriented' shooting spree was not made impulsively.

The literature refers to plans for mass shootings that end in the death of the shooter as "suicide by cop," and though Whitman certainly realized he wasn't coming down from the Tower alive, it's important to remember that the main goal for him was not suicide, but rather carrying out his mission of omnipotence with maximum lethality, skill and notoriety. The 90 minutes he was shooting from the Tower was an excruciatingly long period of time, especially compared to the briefer time frame of most recent school shootings. What can be hard to grasp about psychopathic mass killers is that every step of preparation and execution of this horror is not frightening nor depressing, but gratifying to them. The deaths, wounds and lasting trauma Whitman created during his predatory mission would not have concerned him—that would have required the capacity to feel empathy toward other human beings—the type of emotional experience of which neither he nor other psychopathic school shooters would be capable.

By starting with the behaviorally-oriented approach to criminal analysis provided by the CIRG, and using its precepts to track Whitman's psychopathic/predatory behavior during the shootings, we have come to a clear and chilling diagnosis: Whitman suffered from a long-standing Anti-Social Personality Disorder with Borderline and Narcissistic features going back to adolescence. We are then able to see the depth of Whitman's disgust and rage about the world around him, and how he was capable of carrying out this long dreamed of carnage.

Factors other than Whitman's psychopathy and growing rage did contribute to the tragedy. The fact that no one actively tried to stop him or sensed just how dangerous he was becoming fueled his plans to carry out the shootings. Remember this was in "pre-Tarasoff" America, before the clinician's "Duty to Warn" the potential victim when direct threats of violence are made by a patient was established in 1974 in the case of *Tarasoff v. Regents of the University of California* in 1974.[30] The Tarasoff family sued the University of California following the murder of their daughter because the campus therapist, who had heard his patient's direct disclosure of wanting to kill the young woman, did not warn the woman or her family about the danger. The family won in the California Supreme Court and the University settled for a large undisclosed sum of money.[31] Had "Duty to Warn" been in place when Whitman disclosed his plans to Dr. Heatly and others, perhaps the tragedy would have never happened, and if it had, the University of Texas would have likely faced lawsuits from survivors and victim families. Certainly Whitman's easy access to high-powered weaponry and large amounts of ammunition, his training and skill as a Marine marksman, his cognitive ability to carefully pre-plan the attack, and his long-held fantasy of the Tower as a perfect location to fight off the world, all added to the likelihood of the tragedy occurring. Looked at from this perspective, it seems like a perfect and deadly storm, which it turned out to be for so many.

The explanation of Whitman's motivation is complex because the ultimate causes of psychopathy and Anti-social Personality Disorder are not well understood even though it is clear that genetics, early childhood experience and socialization of entitlement, random use of deadly weapons and lack of empathy are key factors. The answer is also chilling, because psychopathic killers are difficult to identify and despite the cultural trope of being loners and lunatics, can look just like you and me. Whitman's psychopathy was hidden behind an 'all-American' handsome appearance, ability to charm, general intelligence, and a history of noteworthy achievement in his youth. Understanding this profile provides direction for schools and universities.[32] Society can be better protected from this new species of trouble, but only if we find the political and cultural will to take action on what is already known.

1. E.g. Rhawn Joseph, Ph.D., "Charles Whitman: The Amygdala & Mass Murder" http://brainmind.com/Case5.html. Gross exaggerations about the effect of the tumor are common. One recent article stated that the tumor was five centimeters in length, which is nearly three times its actual size. Alex Hannaford, "The Mysterious Vanishing Brains," The Atlantic, Dec. 2, 2014, http://www.theatlantic.com/health/archive/2014/12/the-mysterious-vanishing-brains/382869/. In others accounts, such as that by Dr. Joseph, Whitman is portrayed as the poster child for how brain tumors can put pressure on the amygdale and trigger violent, homicidal rage.

2. Derro Evans, "Whitman Had a Year to Live," *Austin American Statesman*, September 9, 1966.

3. Connally Report, Press Release, p. 8.

4. Telephone interview of Dr. Stuart Brown, April 22, 2015. When told that after 50 years it seemed unlikely he was still legally bound to keep the work of the Commission secret, he laughed and said he realized that, but that he had given his word and was a Midwestern boy with old-fashioned beliefs who did not want to either go to Hell or have his mother come down from Heaven and get after him. He added that some of his colleagues have encouraged him to either write a book or at least write down what he knows, and while he probably should, he doubts he will.

5. Email from Dr. Tate Minckler, April 30, 2015.

6. L. Maximillian Buja, M.D. "Historical Vignette Texas Tragedies and the Evolution of the Medical Examiner System in Texas," Texas Society of Pathologists, April 13, 2009, http://www.texpath.org/assets/docs/history/tsphistoricalvignette4-1-09.pdf

7. Dr. Robert Pape in *Sniper 66*, Part 4.

8. Brenda Bell, "An Anniversary Without Answers," *Austin American Statesman*, August 1, 2006.

9. Email from Gary Lavergne, February 8, 2015.

10. Erin Allday, "Mitchel Berger, UCSF Brain Surgeon, Tops in Nation," *SFGate*, August 21, 2011.

11. Email from Dr. Mitchel Berger, February 7, 2015.

12. Conversation between Keith Maitland, Nathan Akers and Monte Akers, La Grange, Texas, March 2, 2015.

13. *Ibid.*

14. Apparently the interviews conducted by Dr. Brown and his associates remain confidential. Interview of Dr. Stuart Brown, *supra*; report of agent John R. Barron dated August 11, 1966; *see also*, letter dated Aug. 17, 1966 from FBI agent J. Myers Cole to Col. Homer Garrison, Director, Tex. Dept. of Public Safety; AHC; Lavergne at 7.

15. Teletype dated August 10, 1966 from FBI San Antonio Officer to "Director and Savannah," AHC.

16. Teletype dated August 11, 1966 from "Director" to San Antonio; see also Memo dated August 15, 1966 to Director, FBI from SAC WfO, AHC, see also, teletype dated August 16, 1966 to Director and San Antonio from Charlotte (FBI office), in which Whitman's handwriting was examined for comparison with different samples to verify that Whitman was the author, but not for the purpose of analyzing motive or personality.

17. Telephone interview of Dr. Stuart Brown, April 22, 2015.

18. Anonymous Handwriting Analysis - for Monte Akers

Introduction:

Violence is a learned behavior. Violence begets more violence. The degree of violence is a cumulative process that often starts in early childhood and increases due mostly to one's chronic negative and abusive experiences. The analysis of this individual, based on the content of the letters as well as the various personality traits seen in both his printed and cursive handwriting, supports those positions. His own personal accounts along with the personality traits revealed in his handwriting affirm the longstanding, unresolved anger and resentment that he harbored during his lifetime. The time line below illustrates a lifelong continuum of what ultimately lead to such a tragic ending.

3/1/1956 – age 14

The cursive writing is contrived, controlled and image oriented…a conditioned copybook style. This means that he had rules to follow and did what was expected of him to the best of his ability. However, because his writing also shows he was an extreme perfectionist, he probably never felt that he measured up to his or others' expectations. Perfectionism, based on the concept of never feeling good enough, is considered an over-compensation for feelings of inferiority. The content of the letter is informational and safe because it is statistically focused. He fit the observable profile of being the good little boy who was on the straight and narrow path to great accomplishments. Perhaps at times, he was able to convince himself of that also. What he accomplished was that he became a good actor in order to cover up the ever present and abusive chaos of his home environment. Because he lacked the ability to control his home life, he learned how to contain his emotions thus helping him to feel in control of some part of his life. Children from abusive homes share a motto of survival, "Don't talk, don't trust, don't feel." This programmed condition of behavior, especially because the abuse was a frequent occurrence and continued for so long, contributed to making him a walking time bomb. Unfortunately, this teen's journey towards violence was well underway at this young age.

1962 – age 20

The printed writing exemplifies his insecurities from both a handwriting and a content perspective. The short, light, low and bowed t-bars represent an inability to follow through with goals that he set for himself. He had a fear of failure. The writing has a rigid and somewhat compressed appearance as he lists specific mandates. It is as if he is in a vice, desperately trying to do the right thing while internally doubting it will happen. The list of do's and don'ts continues into the typed segment below the writing…almost as if he would forget what to do if he didn't keep reminding himself. "BE GENTLE" is the last item listed but is by no means the least important. Its significance is enhanced by the use of capitals and the underlining. That point could be the one that challenged him the most.

Feb, 1964 – age 22

His journey towards violence accelerated as the tension and repression in both his printed and cursive writing increased. The spaces between words are wide representing feelings of isolation. His individual letters are very small, some looking cramped, others having a flattened appearance. The overall style is tight and rigid. It is as if he was being sucked into his analytical mind, getting lost in his thoughts. Since the slant is forward leaning, especially in the cursive letter, his emotions appear to be consuming him as he speaks of the attributes of his wife and extreme love he has for his "Most Precious Possession." Interestingly, while he was stating all these accolades, his writing tells a different story since the letters contain many weapon symbols in the form of ligatures, daggers, hooks and blunt force. It was as if he was trying to fight off his demons by saying all the right things, things he had practiced and reminded himself of using the lists that he had made. However, it really wasn't working because while the pressure from his stress was escalating, his ability to cope was diminishing. He was now fully entrenched in a dangerous and destructive path.

July 31, 1966 – age 25

6:45 pm – Part I

It makes sense that he typed this letter at first. Typing is a more controlled and detached way to communicate. Consciously or unconsciously, he was probably still in his logical, thinking/strategizing stage, sharing information about his mental and emotional struggles and his own eventual demise. He wanted to sound rational because he mentions, "It was after much thought that I decided to kill my wife." His thoughts were obviously clouded and distorted perhaps due, in part, to the extreme headaches he was experiencing. Could he have experienced a blow to the head at some point in his life that caused some kind of brain damage, and because it went undetected it grew worse? Did he take anything else to help with the pain besides the huge doses of Excedrin that he mentioned?

Time? - Part II

The hand written part at the bottom of the typed page demonstrates a loss of control. The deed was probably done. He begins writing as if to continue the train of thought in the typed letter but then goes right into talking about how he will be viewed for the brutal killing of his loved ones. There's a definite disconnect in subject matter. It is as if his mind shifted gears on its own. His writing is loose looking and spread out. The letters are malformed and large with an irregular rhythm, erratic slant and spacing. Pressure appears lighter and many weapon symbols continue to be evident. This is just conjecture on my part, but I think that there was a time lapse between the typing and the handwriting part of the letter. Because of the extreme changes in his writing style, I believe that the handwriting occurred right after he killed his "most precious possession" and he shifted his outlook on life and just didn't give a damn about anything anymore. On the second page there is another disconnect in subject matter as he started jotting things down haphazardly almost as an afterthought about his last will and testament.

August 1, 1966 – age 24

12:30 am – Part I

His plan to kill both women had been carried out. His adrenaline was subsiding slightly. I say slightly because even though the printed writing shows that he had regained some of his composure, the letter formations still contain many weapon symbols…daggers, blunt force, hooks and ligatures…all representing his surging anger and volatile nature at that time. This composure in the writing is demonstrated by a little more consistency in letter formations, rhythm, spacing and the overall organization to its appearance. Some of the changes could be due to the fact that he had already killed his wife and that might have been harder for him to do, or because he did not have the same emotional attachment to his mother and/or that he honestly believed he was relieving his mother of her pain.

Time? – Part II

The printed writing above the typed statement, "THOUGHTS TO START THE DAY" is larger and more spread out…it is as if he has succumbed to his plight in life and is done trying to fight the inevitable…his demise. His message says it all. "I never could quite make it. These thoughts are too much for me."

Conclusion:

Just as soldiers go off to war and are traumatized by the chronic violence they witness and personally experience, so also are there many individuals fighting their own personal internal war. As they try survive and make sense of what is happening and why they are feeling the way that they do, they become tortured by those thoughts and feelings. By his own words and from studying this person's handwriting, it is evident that he had been traumatized from being a victim all his life, early on by others and then later held hostage by his own volition. He mentions his extreme hatred for his father, but perhaps the hatred he felt for himself was a more influential factor in why he ultimately did what he did.

19. Email from E. Page dated January 16, 2015.

20. Brenda Bell, "Anniversary Without Answers," *Austin American Statesman*, August 1, 2006.

21. Interview of Dr. Mary Ellen O'Toole, George Mason University, Fairfax, VA, by Roger Friedman, June 17, 2015; Antonio Petri, M.D, "School Shooting as a Culturally Enforced Way of Expressing Suicidal Hostile Intentions," *Journal of American Academy of Psychiatry Law"* (December, 2008).

22. Hicks, *supra*; Anyone compelled to apply astrology to the Whitman story need only go to http://www.astrotheme.com/astrology/Charles_Whitman for a 69 page (!) horoscope and astrological examination.

23. Mary Ellen O'Toole, "The School Shooter: A Threat Assessment Perspective," Critical Incident Response Group -National Center for The Analysis of Violent Crime- FBI Academy - Quantico, VA, 1999, http//www.fbi.gov.stats-services/publications/school-shooter.

24. Mary Ellen O'Toole, "Psychopathy as a Behavioral Classification System for Violent and Serial Crime," Ch. 8 in H. Herve & J.C. Yuille (ed.), *The Psychopath: Theory, research and practice*, (Mahwah, NJ: Lawrence Erlbaum Associates, 2007).

25. *Ibid.*

26. *Ibid.*

27. Peter Langman, *School Shooters: Understanding High School, College and Adult Perpetrators* (New York: Rowman & Littlefield Publishing, 2015); M. Schroeder, K. Schroeder, R.D. Hare, "Generalizability of a Checklist for Assessment for Psychopathy," 511-16, *Journal of Consulting and Clinical Psychology*, Vol 51, No. 4, 1983; T. Bowers, E. Holmes, and A. Rhom, "The Nature of Mass Murder and Autogenic Massacre," 59-60, *Journal of Police and Criminal Psychology*, Vol 25, 2010; Theodore Millon, *Disorders of Personality*, (New Jersey: John Wiley & Sons, 2011).

28. American Psychiatric Association, (ed.), *Diagnostic and Statistical Manual of Mental Disorders* 5th Edition, (Arlington, Va.: American Psychiatric Association Publication, 2013).

29. Interview of Mary Ellen O'Toole, *supra*.

30. *Tarasoff v. Regents of the University of California*, 551 P.2d 334 (Cal. 1976).

31. Charles P. Ewing, JD, PhD, "Tarasoff Reconsidered," American Psychological Association, Judicial Notebook, Posted August, 2005 http://www.apa.org/monitor/julaug05/jn.aspx.

32. See, for example, the FBI's research and recommendations in "School Shooter: A Threat Assessment Perspective."

CHAPTER TWELVE

Lingering Effects

HARTMAN: Do any of you people know who Charles Whitman was? None of you dumbasses knows? Private Cowboy?

COWBOY: Sir, he was that guy who shot all those people from that tower in Austin, Texas, sir!

HARTMAN: That's affirmative. Charles Whitman killed twelve people from a twenty-eight-story observation tower at the University of Texas from distances up to four hundred yards. Anybody know who Lee Harvey Oswald was? Private Snowball?

SNOWBALL: Sir, he shot Kennedy, sir!

HARTMAN: That's right,.... Do any of you people know where these individuals learned to shoot? Private Joker?

JOKER: Sir, in the Marines, sir!

HARTMAN: In the Marines! Outstanding! Those individuals showed what one motivated marine and his rifle can do! And before you ladies leave my island, you will be able to do the same thing!

-Full Metal Jacket, *movie screenplay by Stanley Kubrick, Michael Herr and Gustav Hasford*

Just as the western-attired Austin businessman in Sholz's Beer Garten feared on the day of the shootings, Whitman's actions gave a boost to efforts in Congress to enact sweeping gun control legislation.

Honoring the Tower heroes. The Austin Jaycees award plaques to some of the prominent players in the Tower drama. Left to right: Allen Crum (USAF retired), Officer Ramiro Martinez, Texas Secretary of State John L. Hill

The debate and proposals about the extent to which Americans should be allowed to have firearms and exactly what the Second Amendment protects certainly were not new. They date back nearly to the beginning of American and Texas history. The Battles of Lexington and Concord in 1775 were sparked by a British attempt to take away a colonist cannon, as was the Battle of Gonzalez when Mexican military attempted to do the same to Texians in 1835. Kentucky banned the carrying of concealed weapons in 1813, and the final catalyst for the Gunfight at the OK Corral in 1881 was because members of a faction known as "the Cowboys" wore sidearms in town in violation of a Tombstone city ordinance.

The debate become more vocal after the assassination of President Kennedy. President Johnson demanded gun control legislation from Congress in a special message in March, 1965, a year and a half before Whitman climbed the Tower, and a gun control bill was under consideration in the Senate on August 1, 1966. Whitman's actions, even though involving hunting rifles and a non-felon, became a new issue around which gun control advocates rallied.

Ultimately the Whitman killings did help lead to gun control legislation, but it was two years later and the killings of Martin Luther King, Jr., Robert Kennedy, and Malcolm X played a much larger role. The Gun Control Act of 1968 placed new restrictions on the interstate sales of firearms, prohibiting the sale of certain categories of weapons except between licensed manufacturers, dealers, and importers, and banning the sale of guns to "prohibited persons."[1]

The list of prohibited persons was long, well thought-out, and comprehensive. It would not have netted Charles J. Whitman.

The University did more than just call a press conference. It appointed a committee comprised of students and faculty to determine "what the University isn't doing that it needs to do."[2] Out of that committee came a student counseling program, proposed and implemented under the leadership of Sociology professor Ira Iscoe, that was one of the best in the nation.[3] Similarly, Margaret Berry, the Dean of Women, realized there was no crisis counseling service offered to students, and within six weeks of the event she saw to it that a 24-hour hotline was established, with notices posted in all dorms and other places informing students that help was available at any time if they needed guidance or someone to advise them on how to deal with an unexpected difficulty.[4]

The Tower observation deck was temporarily closed to visitors, and in 1967, the University spent $5,000 to repair bullet holes. Doing so was not popular with everyone. A student named Harper Scott Clark remembered that "[a] bullet of Whitman's had ripped a big chunk out of one of the balustrades on the South Mall, and for the rest of the time I was at UT, whenever my friends and I would stroll by there, we would run our fingers inside it and look up at the Tower and think contemplatively. I went back years later and saw that someone had filled it in with plaster. It was gone, and I remember thinking that was a big mistake."[5]

Even with the bullet holes erased, the collective memory of what caused them floated close to the surface. A student named Patty Lankford recalled walking on the campus near the Tower, in 1972, when a large piece of plywood fell from construction scaffolding nearby. It hit concrete below with a loud smack, and students all around immediately crouched or dropped to the ground, gazing skyward.[6]

The Tower reopened in 1968, but during the next six years there were four suicides by jumping, and it was closed again in 1974.

Various magazines, including *Time* and *Life* made the Tower tragedy their cover stories in the issues following August 1, with *Time's* featuring a photo of Whitman and an article titled "The Psychotic & Society." In 1968, a poet named John Berryman made Whitman the focus of a poem called *Dream Song 135*, and in 1972, Harry Chapin recorded an album called *Sniper and Other Love Songs*, with the title song, "Sniper," being about Whitman. The following year, Texas singer and U.T. graduate Kinky Friedman recorded "The Ballad of Charles Whitman," on an album titled *Sold American*. Friedman graduated in 1966, a few months prior to the shooting. Another Whitman song called "Sniper in the Sky" was included in an album called *Sinister Slaughter* by the group *Macabre* in 1993.

The Medal of Valor awarded to Houston McCoy by the Austin Police Department. A similar medal was awarded to Ramiro Martinez, Marion Lee, and Jerry Day.

During the months and years following the incident, Ramiro Martinez received numerous awards and recognitions for his actions. Letters poured in from admirers. A young man who received a speeding ticket from him was thrilled to have a copy of the hero's autograph. United States Senator John Tower sent him a congratulatory letter. A San Antonio radio station presented him with a plaque on behalf of the Hispanic People of South Texas. A song was written and recorded in Spanish about him called "El Policia De Austin: Accion Heroica de Ramiro Martinez" (The Police Officer of Austin: Heroic Action of Ramiro Martinez). The Hispanic Society of New York City summoned him to the Big Apple for a banquet and a bronze plaque. He was parade marshal for a large parade in El Paso. Texas Attorney General Wagonner Carr presented him, as well as Houston McCoy, Jerry Day and Allen Crum, a "Bravery Award Plaque." The APD presented him with a Medal of Valor, along with Houston McCoy, Jerry Day, and Lt. Marion Lee. The Sons of the American Revolution of New York voted to give him its first "Gold Medal for Bravery Award in Law Enforcement" in Madison Square Garden.[7]

Presentation of "Bravery Award Plaques" to heroes of August 1, 1966. Left to right: Texas Attorney General Waggoner Carr, Jerry Day, Ramiro Martinez, Houston McCoy, Allen Crum, Major Burch Biggerstaff. Biggerstaff was a career officer with the APD.

Although McCoy was not totally ignored, he was recognized principally as only a supporting actor in the drama. Ramiro was the real star, and although Martinez did not dispute that McCoy played a role, he did nothing to deflect credit from himself.

Newspaper and magazine stories about the U.T. Tower shootings were cranked out in a wide variety of flavors of fact and fiction. In some, Whitman opened fire on Martinez before being gunned down. In others, Crum, Martinez, and McCoy crawled up on Whitman. In some their names were mutilated, and in others Martinez's first shot hit the carbine in Whitman's hands. In several Martinez fired McCoy's shotgun as he was running instead of point blank, and in some the airplane circling above was a helicopter.[8]

Beginning within weeks of August 1 and building over the next 40 years, there developed a very unfortunate aspect of the aftermath of the killings—unfair treatment of Houston McCoy. What makes that treatment particularly unfortunate is the fact that McCoy was a modest, or humble, man, which are characteristics that show up again and again in the recollections of those who knew him well. He not only did not consider himself a hero for what he did at the top of the Tower, he strongly disliked being called one, so much so that he once directed that upon his death, his obituary and newspaper stories not refer to the incident, and particularly not include his name in the same story with Whitman's name, as in, "hero who killed Charles Whitman." The request was forwarded to the *Austin American Statesman*, which chose to ignore it.[9] His attitude was that he was only doing his job as a policeman, no one should want or enjoy credit for killing a man, that the effort was by the entire APD, and so long as his family knew the truth about him, that was all that was necessary. With that admirable attitude in place, after risking his life and being what anyone would consider a hero whether he wanted to be one or not, McCoy became the poster child for the old saying that "no good deed goes unpunished."

Concern that the matter was not being reported fairly began in the APD. Nobody faulted Martinez for what he did, but some officers felt like he acted unprofessionally. He had gone up the Tower alone, without requesting assistance from other officers even though he knew Jerry Day and Dub Cowan were available and the five officers who came through the tunnels arrived soon thereafter. As those officers worked out a plan, he went ahead without them, accepting assistance from civilian Allen Crum who, while quite heroic himself, was there in contravention of standard police policy. There was no real reason for Martinez to accept Crum's assistance when several other police officers were on hand and ready to provide backup.

Instead, upon realizing that Martinez was proceeding alone, the other officers had no choice but to abandon their plan and follow him. The fact that he was accompanied by an armed civilian could have resulted in tragedy had Crum been mistaken for the sniper, but fortunately Jerry Day alerted McCoy to Crum's presence.

Once on the deck, Martinez continued on his own, opened fire with a weapon ill-suited for the occasion without calling to Whitman to surrender, threw that weapon down, snatched the shotgun out of McCoy's hands, shot Whitman from point-blank range, threw the shotgun to the floor, began yelling "I got him, I got him," ran down the Tower without his revolver, was so badly shaken that he needed assistance from other officers, left the scene without staying to assist, was physically ill at the police station, and then reported the incident without mentioning most of the other officers or giving credit to anyone but himself and Crum.

His frame of mind and the effect of the incident on him are completely, utterly understandable, and the foregoing should not be interpreted as criticism. Martinez was the first officer through the door and onto the observation deck, nearly alone, which took incredible courage. However, in conjunction with what happened later, and when compared to McCoy's calm adherence to standard procedure, some of his actions irritated some members of the APD.

In the days that followed, McCoy remained modest and unaffected, but others began to resent the way the event and its players were treated and that Martinez was receiving the credit instead of the Austin Police Department as a whole. One of those was Police Chief R.A. Miles. He presented Martinez with the APD Medal of Valor, but he grew weary of all the attention Martinez was getting. Some of McCoy's fellow officers were complaining, and Miles informed Martinez that all of his public appearances and fame, which were aimed at Martinez rather than the APD, were becoming disruptive, and that Martinez was prohibited from engaging in any such affairs on city time. Miles gave only one public interview about the incident, in 1979, three years before his death. In it he said, "Martinez was given all the credit, which was unfortunate, but by the time it was discovered what had actually killed him (Whitman), the reports were already out. McCoy never raised the issue, but who the heck wants credit for actually killing someone? It's not something that makes you feel good, even if the guy deserved it."[10]

Some published stories did conclude that McCoy was the officer who actually stopped Whitman, despite the credit given Martinez,[11] and the controversy probably would have died away with no further damage or consequences, had Hollywood not intervened.

The first film inspired by the U.T. killings was a 1968 movie directed by Peter Bogdanovich entitled *Targets,* about a man who murdered his mother and wife and then went on a sniping spree, first on a freeway and then at a drive-in movie theatre. Not being an attempt to tell the true story, it did no damage. However, in 1975, a genuine effort to tell the Whitman story occurred with the release of a made-for-television movie called *The Deadly Tower,* starring Kurt Russell as Whitman. As a movie it was a disappointment. As the cause of problems for some of those most closely involved with the events of August 1, 1966, particularly Houston McCoy, it was a disaster.

Both McCoy and Martinez were contacted by MGM, which was making the movie for broadcast on NBC, and each was asked for permission to use his name and character in the film. Neither were offered any compensation, and Martinez agreed and signed a release. McCoy, however, asked to read the script, and upon doing so informed MGM that he would be happy to allow the use of his name and would even serve as an advisor for the film, but only if the screenplay was revised to depict the events accurately. MGM declined, insisting that it could not be confined in the use of its artistic liberties.[12]

Artistic liberty is a marvelous thing, but in the case of *The Deadly Tower* it converted a gripping tale into a soap opera. The APD was depicted as a hotbed of racial tension. The need for gun control was an underlying theme of the motion picture. Martinez's wife was portrayed as a pregnant shrew and his twin daughters were morphed into a single individual. It also depicted a character that anyone who was familiar with the facts would conclude was Houston McCoy as ineffectual and almost a coward.

Ultimately both Martinez and McCoy sued MGM and NBC, and Martinez settled out of court for an undisclosed amount that was rumored to be substantial. Anyone who watches the movie today is greeted at its beginning with a statement on screen that the character and personality of Martinez's wife as well as incidents of his family life were fictionalized for dramatic effect.[13] McCoy, retaining his naturally modest and self-effacing approach to such things, waited and did not file suit for several years and until urged to do so by others, by which time he had waited too long. The statute of limitations had run.

Worse, Martinez's role began to take on a racial overtone. The rumors that Martinez had not actually killed Whitman were, at least by 1976, accompanied by suggestions that he received the credit or, conversely, that the only reason there was controversy about what he did was because he was Mexican-American. Martinez wrote that this allegation "really got my blood pressure up." It also meant that some people interested only in preserving the real facts became fearful that saying McCoy deserved credit might be characterized as being racially motivated.

By then McCoy and Martinez had both left the APD, Martinez to become a Texas Ranger, and McCoy first to become a flight instructor for the Air Force, and subsequently a Boy Scout Ranger, which is the equivalent of a Park Ranger for permanent scout camps. He lived on a camp near Menard, which gave his children the chance to be raised in the country, and he loved the life he was living. He still flew and worked on airplanes and gliders, gave dozens of people free flying lessons, and was a craftsman able to build anything from buildings to toys for his children. The family didn't have a television and the movie was out for over a year before he saw it, in advance of which various folks in Menard warned him that he would not like what he saw. Finally he watched it at the home of a friend, Tommy McSherry, and saw what his neighbors had warned him about. Even though not named as Houston McCoy, a character obviously meant to be him was merely Martinez's backup who froze at the last moment and never fired a shot. Not long after that, McCoy attended a reunion of his high school class at the Menard Country Club for the Menard Senior Class of 1958. He had been the star of that class, an athlete, an honor student, named Best All-Around Boy and voted Class Favorite, and he was still beloved in his home town. During the reunion he overheard two old classmates talking. One asked the other if he had seen the movie and whether Houston had been in it. The other replied, scornfully, "yeah, but he didn't do anything."[14]

It was only two guys talking, but it was bothersome, and the movie sparked new interest in the incident, so that each year as August approached, reporters would call. McCoy drank, and sometimes went on drinking binges. His family began noticing that they seemed more frequent in the summer as August 1 approached. His daughter, Monika, was born in 1971. By the time she was old enough to understand the Charles Whitman incident and her father's role, she noticed that he seemed to talk about it only after he had been drinking.[15] In 1994, McCoy and his wife, Ruth Anne Marie Gebhart, divorced after more than 30 years of marriage, although they remained such close friends and did so much together that many people believed they were still man and wife.[16] However, always looking for a gripping new way to tell the story, reporters began adding new spins, one

The corner of the observation deck where Whitman was killed. Although difficult to see without magnification, visible on the wall are marks made by bullets fired at Whitman by APD Officer Ramiro Martinez.

of which was to depict the relationship between Martinez and McCoy as having degenerated into hostility, and by characterizing McCoy as a broken man.

A 1994 article in the *Los Angeles Times* asked who deserved the credit. Was it a member of the "fabled Texas Rangers" who was "lionized in a made-for-TV movie," or a "lanky, slow-moving drifter who eventually left police work and took a twisted trail that has left him drunk, broke, and divorced?" That same article quoted McCoy as saying, "if Ramiro Martinez was sitting right here and saying he shot Charles Whitman, I'd call him a liar right to his face," and Martinez as saying, "all I can say is I feel sorry for him," about McCoy. Explaining the reason that he jerked the shotgun out of McCoy's hands, Martinez supposedly said it was because Houston "is a slow person, and he was slow in reacting."[17]

If there was animosity between the two men, it certainly was not apparent in the various television interviews each gave over the years. Time and again, Martinez and McCoy described the actions of the other for the cameras and their interviewers in a gracious, respectful manner, with no suggestion that the other did not behave admirably on August 1, 1966. To the extent that hard feelings did develop between the two, it is particularly unfortunate when one considers that if McCoy had not been there, Whitman probably would have shot and killed Martinez.

Yet once the media realized that McCoy was overlooked and treated unfairly, it became fashionable to depict him as a tragic figure. As the writer of a letter to the *Austin American Statesman* noted in 2006, "there were many victims of the tragic events of Aug. 1, 1966... [a]mong the victims must be included Austin police officer Houston McCoy."[18] There is truth to that, but McCoy was neither unhappy nor broken. Life certainly got harder for him in the 90s, but the reasons were principally health-related. He had smoked all his life, and developed COPD, which would ultimately kill him, and he was admittedly an alcoholic, although a binge drinker rather than a daily drinker. With regard to the U.T. Tower shootings, it was not so much the credit given Martinez or denied him that was unfair, but that he was sometimes singled out for derision as a result of his own, admirable modesty.

Any discomfit he did feel becomes even more ironic when one considers the probability that none of Martinez's bullets hit Whitman.

In his police report, dictated within two hours of the killing of Whitman, Martinez stated :

> Then this officer got to the north east corner and looked around, saw a subject sitting with a rifle in his hands looking south. This officer opened fire to protect MR. CRUMP (sic), who would be facing him when he would come around the south west corner. After this officer fired, the first shot hitting the subject, this subject turned and began to point the rifle toward this officer. This officer fired the remaining rounds and Officer (McCoy) fired his shotgun twice.[19]

It is possible his first bullet hit Whitman, but it would have been an incredibly lucky shot. When Martinez leaped around the corner, saw Whitman and began shooting, he could not see much of his target because of the row of spotlights along the walkway. He was also firing one-handed, using the revolver in its double-action mode. A double-action revolver is one that can be fired either by cocking the hammer and pulling the trigger or by merely pulling the trigger, whereas a single-action revolver can only be fired by first cocking the hammer. Cocking and firing is more accurate, but the distance between Martinez and Whitman, nearly 60 feet, was simply too great for accurate pistol fire in either single or double action mode.

A photograph taken shortly afterward of the northeast corner of the observation deck, where Whitman was sitting, reveals pockmarks that appear to have been made by all six of Martinez's bullets. There are a total of seven marks, three clearly from bullets, three probably being the same, and one being only a blemish. The clearest, at the top of the photo, knocked out a triangular-shaped piece of limestone. The other two distinct ones are near the bottom of the photo, at six o'clock and four o'clock. Of the other four marks on the wall, one is a little above and to the right of the one at four o'clock, but appears to be only a smudge on the wall. The other three, at nine o'clock, below and to the left of the missing chunk of limestone, and directly to the left of the one at six o'clock, appear to be the same type of pockmarks as the three distinct ones, but they are fainter, and it cannot be said with absolute certainty that they were caused by Martinez's bullets. It is unlikely any were made by shotgun pellets because they are widely spaced and dissimilar to the type of pattern made by a shotgun.

When Whitman was autopsied and embalmed, "several" slugs were removed, according to David Orton, who was present. When asked if he believed they were from a .38 caliber revolver or from a double-ought shotgun shell he declined to guess, saying he did not know enough about bullets to say. The fact that he did not notice any difference certainly suggests they were all of a similar size and were all shotgun pellets. However, the difference in size between a .38 caliber slug and a double ought shotgun slug is not dramatic, the former having a diameter of .379 inches and the latter having a diameter of .330 inches, but other differences are noticeable, even to an untrained eye. In addition to the sizes, the .38 round would be conical in front unless flattened by impact with bone, and would be flat or concave in the back and would bear the markings from both its being seated in a brass hull and from the lands and grooves of the rifled barrel. The shotgun pellets would be round, probably not distorted, and would not be marked by either a hull or by rifling.[20]

Another consideration is a remark attributed to a Cook Funeral Home mortician at a funeral that occurred several months after the Tower shootings. An Austin Police officer named Clarence Woods served as part of an honor guard at the funeral of an APD officer who was prepared for burial at Cook Funeral Home. The mortician, or student mortician, whom Woods described as young, told Woods he was present for the autopsy, and "the only things he saw from the body were shotgun pellets; no bullets that would have been from a pistol."[21] This sounds like Orton, who was five days shy of his 23rd birthday on August 1, 1966, but if so he did not recall saying it. Regardless of how many or what kind of slugs were removed, neither the pathologist, coroner, mortician, nor police made any effort to preserve them.

The single, best argument that one of Martinez's shots hit Whitman is that Dr. de Chenar recorded there being a wound under his left arm that was about a centimeter in width and larger than other wounds. Being under his arm, it had to be an exit wound, and photos of Whitman's body in the morgue, taken after his clothes were removed, reveal a wound just above his left elbow that was probably the point of entry.

Yet the angle for such a shot being from Martinez does not fit with the position Whitman was in, as described by Martinez, when he opened fire, and would correspond with being a pellet from McCoy's shotgun if Whitman was raising his left arm and pivoting to aim at the two officers, as Martinez also described. Furthermore, de Chenar did not characterize the entry wound as being larger, and an exiting slug causes a larger hole than where it entered. In fact, the larger, underarm wound was the only injury to Whitman's body noted by de Chenar that was an exit wound, all others being points of entry.

However, the lingering issue surrounding the question of who killed Whitman is not and should not be whether either man deserves to be

McCoy and his daughter, Monika (pronounced moe-nick-a). Ms. McCoy followed in her father's footsteps and now serves as an Austin police officer.

honored for his action. They both most certainly do. It was their bravery and devotion to duty that motivated them and the other officers to go to the top of the Tower and confront Whitman. The important issue is that the correct facts be recorded and credit given where it was due. Mercifully, that was accomplished well before the writing of this book, particularly at and soon after the 40th anniversary of the shootings.

Before then, more homage, if that is what it was, was paid the event in both movies and on television. In the 1987 movie, *Full Metal Jacket,* a Marine Corps drill instructor tells his recruits about two phenomenal marksmen whose accuracy was a result of their training in the Corps—Lee Harvey Oswald and Charles Whitman. Short sequences or references to Whitman were included in the movie *Parenthood* in 1989, the movie *Slacker* (filmed in Austin) in 1991, the movie *True Romance* in 1993, the movie *Natural Born Killers* in 1994, and the movie *The Delicate Art of the Rifle* in 1996. In a 1994 *Simpsons* episode called "Homer Loves Flanders," Ned Flanders climbed up a clock tower in a dream sequence and began shooting random bystanders with a sniper rifle. In 1996 Whitman was featured in an episode of *American Justice* called "Mass Murderer: An American Tragedy," and in 1997, the television program *Murder One* explored the differences between a serial killer and a mass murderer, with Whitman being a prime example of the latter. Gary Laverne's book *A Sniper in the Tower: The Charles Whitman Murders* was published by the University of North Texas Press that same year. It was subsequently re-published in 1999 by Bantam, Doubleday and Dell Books.

In 2001, *Dateline NBC* aired a special on the Tower shootings called "Catastrophe." In July, 2002, the rock & roll band Tomahawk, while playing with a band called Tool in Austin, implored the crowd to chant Whitman's name instead of booing during the show. In 2004, an episode of the animated television show called *Drawn Together* on Comedy Central, had a scene in which a character who was left out of a trip to the zoo announced, "If anybody needs me, I'll be in the clock tower," then cocked a rifle and headed toward a tower. In another animated show the same year, *King of the Hill*, one of the characters ascended a tower to spray insecticide, was mistaken for a sniper and was surrounded by police. In 2012 an episode of the miniseries *Mad Men* referenced the Tower shootings.[22]

Esquire and *Texas Monthly* magazines included occasional stories about the shootings or something related to them over the years, and numerous local newspapers included columns and reports about citizens who played a role in the tragedy. Principal characters, such as Ray Martinez, Houston McCoy, Claire James, Cheryl Botts, and Mike Gabour became accustomed and sometimes burdened by requests for interviews, particularly when a quinquennial anniversary of the event rolled around. In 2015, Mr. Lavergne wrote the authors of this book and remarked that hardly a day goes by that someone does not contact him about the book, even after eighteen years.[23]

The University of Texas considered the event the most shameful of its long and illustrious tenure. No losing football season record, player arrest, fraternity hazing event, official's ethical accusation, or faculty scandal could compare. Besides, there was always the lingering fear of lawsuits. The first person to make it publicly known, by August 23, 1966, that he intended to sue the University was not one of the wounded victims or the family of one of those killed, but C.A. Whitman.[24] He never did.

Although informal memorial services were sometimes organized by students and individuals over the years, particularly on five year anniversaries, the University essentially refused to acknowledge the event for several years, and to this day discourages anything that would "glorify" it.[25] Unfortunately, the University's understandable attempts to not glorify it have also been interpreted as cold-hearted disinterest, failure to pay homage to the innocents who were killed or injured by it, and failure to honor those who acted courageously.

That image improved in October, 1998, when University President Larry Faulkner took over. He had been at the University the morning of August 1, 1966, but Whitman started shooting a few moments after he left. As he said, "[s]ince that time, the University's stance had always seemed to be to try to erase what had happened, but with absolutely no success. It was like an injury that would never heal. And I instinctively felt that the way to get past that was to open the observation deck to the public again."[26]

He announced plans to do so and asked for the support of the University Regents in making the Tower a positive symbol of Texas pride once again. The Regents approved his plan, and on September 15, 1999, the deck was reopened. There were changes, however—a metal detector and security guards were installed on the ground floor and a high stainless steel lattice surrounding the observation deck was erected

Houston McCoy describing and reenacting the shooting of Charles Whitman.

in order to prevent suicides, falls, and maybe even copycat snipers. As Faulkner said, "we had to have a physical barrier to prevent suicides and accidents, and we had to have a credible way of screening for weapons."

Also in 1999, the University dedicated a "Memorial Garden" to the memory of the victims killed on August 1, 1966, and in January 2003, the University committed $200,000 and sought another $800,000 to redesign the garden to recognize the deaths of August 1, 1966. The one million dollar goal was not met, and what became of the $200,000 is not known, but in January, 2007, a bronze plaque that measures eight inches by eleven inches was affixed to a rock adjacent to an accurately-named but inauspicious landmark known as "the Turtle Pond." It reads: "The University of Texas at Austin remembers with profound sorrow the tragedy of August 1, 1966. This space is dedicated as the Tower Garden, a memorial to those who died, to those who were wounded, and to the countless other victims who were immeasurably affected by the tragedy." There was no mention of victims or heroes, and the site has not become a gathering place for trauma victims.

The U.T. Memorial Park and aptly named Turtle Pond in 2015.

After his stint as a Texas Ranger, Martinez became a Justice of the Peace in New Braunfels, Texas. In 2003, he published his memoirs entitled, *They Call Me Ranger Ray: From the UT Tower Sniper to Corruption in South Texas*. Houston McCoy, Jerry Day and Allen Crum are mentioned. George Shepard, Milton Shoquist, Harold Moe, and Phillip Conner are not.

On November 12, 2001, David Gunby died of long-term kidney complications from the wound he received on the South Mall. When he was shot, it was discovered at Brackenridge that he had been born with only one functioning kidney, which was nearly destroyed by Whitman's shot. After years of treatment, including a transplant that nearly killed him and dialysis three times a week, the prospect of losing his eyesight caused him to decline further treatment and he died shortly thereafter. The Tarrant County Coroner's report listed the cause of death as homicide, making him Whitman's 17th victim.[27]

The observation deck was closed again in 2001 after 9/11, and stayed closed until 2004 when it was reopened with added security.

In 2006, as the 40th anniversary of the incident approached, various people began taking steps and exerting efforts to not only memorialize the event, but to see that the record was set straight. Police Chief Miles had set the stage in 1979, having been quoted not only as saying that he believed it was McCoy's shotgun pellets that killed Whitman, but that after Martinez left the APD, he "bummed around and... would not have become a Texas Ranger except for the University of Texas Tower incident."[28] Now, particularly under the leadership of Monika McCoy, that precedent was acted on.

Ms. McCoy was destined to become an Austin police officer, but doing so was nearly seven years in her future. In 2006, while her father was still living, she reached out to the men who accompanied him up the Tower—Jerry Day, Milton Shoquist, Harold Moe, Phillip Conner, and Ray Martinez. George Shepard and Alan Crum were deceased by then, and Martinez declined the invitation, but the others reunited, essentially for the first time since August, 1966.

A television broadcaster named Ron Oliveira received a phone call. He worked for KEYE-TV in Austin, and was told that the story of the U.T. Tower shooting had not been reported accurately. There was going to be a reunion of the officers who went up the Tower that day 40 years ago, he was told, and they wanted to "set the record straight." They had approval of the University of Texas to film the reunion and reenactment of what happened, and they wanted just one media representative to record their recollections.

Oliveira was thrilled to participate, and he acted as narrator for a news story that followed the five aging men through the tunnels (William Wilcox was also deceased), up the elevators, up the stairs past the place where the Gabours and Lamport families were gunned down, and out onto the observation deck. Houston McCoy provided his recollections in a straight forward manner, describing how Ray Martinez came around the corner with his police revolver in one hand, essentially doing the splits as he emptied the firearm at Whitman, whose head was barely visible in the northwest corner, and how McCoy came around on the right, crouching, firing one shotgun blast that hit Whitman in the head, not liking that shot and standing up straight to fire a second time, seeing Whitman's head rock back and his body slide down to a prone position.[29]

Following the broadcast, Oliveira received numerous calls expressing appreciation that someone had finally told the story correctly. Never in the broadcast was there a critical word spoken about Martinez, but Oliveira was nevertheless concerned that someone would complain, and particularly that someone would accuse him of bias against a Hispanic hero. He was relieved that there were no such calls.

Another person who met with the officers at the top of the Tower was Dr. Mary Ellen O'Toole, an FBI Profiler who was preparing a monograph on the characteristics of school shootings. She talked to the police officers, got details of the crime scene, and was told, particularly by Houston McCoy and Jerry Day, that they strongly felt the idea that a tumor caused his behavior did not make any sense because of how prepared, organized and methodical he was on the Tower and in his shooting.[30]

After a different event that year, at which Monika McCoy spoke, she was approached separately by two widows of Austin police officers. Both thanked her and said the same thing—their husbands went to their graves angry about how the affair was handled and how one man, not necessarily the right man, got so much credit while the APD received so little.

Credit continued going to Martinez. The City of Austin declared August 1, 2006, as "Ramiro Martinez Day," and a state office building was named in his honor. There has been no Houston McCoy Day in Austin, but the headquarters of the Austin Police Association is named the Speed/Martinez/McCoy Building, and is typically referred to merely by McCoy's name. In August, 2008, a black and silver metal historical plague was unveiled at the Travis County Precinct 3 headquarters building in Oak Hill, several miles from the Tower, listing the names of law officers and civilians who were involved.[31] The plaque also honors "all law enforcement officials, medical workers, students and civilians who risked their lives by returning fire, assisting victims, and directing traffic... who were heroes on August 1, 1966. Many of their names will never be known."

Following the 40th anniversary, a friend of McCoy's gave his daughter a USB drive on which was recorded all of the radio dispatch calls and "chatter" from August 1, 1966. The sounds of that day not only refreshed and re-vitalized the memories of the officers who lived it, but gave McCoy a new lease on life. He listened to the recordings over and over and constructed a detailed, accurate, and final version of the incident before he passed away on December 27, 2012. A year and a half earlier he'd been given only six months to live, but the radio chatter project, which he transcribed and annotated, plus the writing of his final account, yielded three times as many months of life. His final account of the incident is available today online at a website associated with west Texas boy scouting history.[32]

Since 2006, principally as a result of Ms. McCoy's efforts, the credit due her father has been forthcoming. The old, inaccurate images of him as a tragic, broken man, or of him and Martinez feuding, still pop up from time to time, but at least two television documentaries and interviews have been broadcast in which McCoy is recognized as the one who genuinely brought an end to Whitman's killing spree, even concluding that all of Martinez's shots missed.[33]

In April, 2008, Austin Police officer Jason Huskins began the Austin Police Officer Memorial project, which involved the placing of granite memorials at every location in Austin where an Austin Police Officer was killed in the line of duty, there having been 24 since 1875.[34] Most of the memorials are 5 feet 4 inches tall, 20 inches wide and 6 inches thick, constructed of gray granite, donated to the project by Rockdale Memorials. However, some are more suitable due to their location as plaques, 20 inches wide by 24 inches high and mounted on a wall, in a sidewalk, or in a street at or near the site of the officer's sacrifice.[35] When the University was approached in 2009 about placing one of the latter at the site of Officer Billy Speed's death it declined to allow it, even though the site—along the wall at the base of the Jefferson Davis statue—seems ideal.[36] If a memorial for Billy Speed was going to be placed, it would need to be on city or state property two blocks or more from the place where he was killed.

However, the reply that Officer Huskins received from the University was not official, and apparently came from a low level public relations representative who repeated what he'd been told to say on other occasions. Based on a recent interview with a U.T. representative who is helping finalize the University's plans for the 50th anniversary of the event, there is reason to believe that the school will now officially reconsider, and hopefully grant, Officer Huskins' request.[37]

Other odd, serendipitous, "small world" events occurred.

Immediately following the shootings, so many people visited the observation deck whenever they pleased that it was decided to change the locks on the door leading out of the reception area to prevent either damage from souvenir hunters, a possible suicide, or other unwelcome events. The U.T. employee who did so kept the old lock cylinder and key. He did not do so as a souvenir hunter, but because he felt like the artifact should have a home. When he retired 20 years later, in 1996, he turned to lock system over to his successor and told him it should be given to the right person whenever he or she, whoever it might be, appeared.

Toby Hamilton was the 12-year-old boy scout whose scout master was Charles Whitman, who was cared for during the summer of 1966 by Claire Wilson and Tom Eckman, Whitman's first two victims, and who watched the shootings from his home with a telescope. The incident had haunted him and had a devastating effect on Boy Scout Troop 5. As he recalled:

> It was a very hard experience for me, finding out that Mr. Whitman did that. He was a Marine, he'd been the youngest Eagle Scout. This was a guy young boys looked up to. And he's a cold-blooded ass. We all left the Scouts after that. We hardly spoke to each other about it. In those days, children were to be seen and not heard so no one interviewed any of us.[38]

He not only quit the scouts after it occurred but his grades began to suffer. He had only boys his age to talk to about it, no counselors and no school psychologists. His father discussed it with him some, but the fact that Whitman would do such a thing caused him to lose respect for all authority. He considered the event the "defining point" in his life, but not in a good way. In 2006 he wrote a short article for the *Austin American Statesman* about his memories of the incident, saying that doing so "released demons from me that have been there for 40 years."[39]

Publication of the story led to his meeting Houston McCoy, and their bond was almost instantaneous. Monika McCoy said they were "two peas in a pod." They became as close as brothers, and began planning to write a book together. McCoy's health was declining, and Hamilton became his best and most constant friend.

Hamilton worked for Dell Computers, but downsizing caused him to lose his job, so that he became the manager of a 7-11 convenience store in the summer of 2008. One day he told one of the employees at the store about his experiences of August 1, 1966, and she carried the story to her boyfriend, who worked at the University. The fellow employee was Hamilton's age, and her boyfriend, Jeff, was a few years older. Sometime later the same employee asked Hamilton when his birthday was and learned it was December 10. On Tuesday, December 9, Toby received a phone call from Jeff, who told him he knew that his birthday was the next day and that he had a present for him that he had been holding onto for 12 years. A bit baffled, Hamilton arranged to meet Jeff, who presented him with a box containing the lock cylinder and key. Jeff was the maintenance man who had succeeded the man who removed the lock in 1966.

Toby joyously emailed Monika and Houston McCoy, relating the story and describing the lock as "one of my most prized possessions." He also talked to Jerry Day about it, who responded that "he had been visualizing doors opening for a couple of days before I got it. He spoke of the door of truth opening. If you are not a believer, please send me an explanation that makes sense. I see no way this happens without faith."[40]

But as Christmas approached in 2011, tragedy struck. McCoy's wife of 31 years, Ruth Anne, passed away. Although they had divorced in 1994, she and he remained the best of friends and she took care of him faithfully after he became ill, literally until the day she died.[41] Whereas McCoy was already in a rest home in Menard, suffering from the COPD that would take his life in another year, Mrs. McCoy had not been ill and her death was not expected. Monika McCoy and one of her brothers were with their father at the home and did not want to leave him alone as they made arrangements for their mother's funeral, so on Sunday, December 18, Hamilton and his wife, Ede, agreed to drive down to stay with him.

While driving near Llano, Toby suddenly lost consciousness. Ede grabbed the wheel, turned off the ignition and guided the car off the road, where it came to a stop against a highway sign.[42] He was dead, only 52 years of age, having passed away enroute to see Houston McCoy, one final link in the chain that inexplicably bound his life to the events of August 1, 1966.

Rita Jones, who bravely came to Claire Wilson's aid on the South Mall, subsequently divorced Jeff Jones and, rather than return to her maiden name of Murphey, decided to change it to something distinctive and in keeping with her passion for art. After making lists, discussing the matter with her friends and rejecting playful monikers like "Rebecca Woodpecca," she settled on Rita Starpattern. She became very active in the Austin arts community, focusing on the work of women, and opened a gallery called "Women & Their Work," which is still in operation at 1710 Lavaca and which has brought dozens of well-known dancers, poets, and artists to the city. She died of cancer in 1996.[43]

Neither of Whitman's brothers had a happy ending. Patrick was deeply affected by what his older sibling did, and made it a point to go to Mass each August 1 after the incident, but he found no peace. He told the *Austin American Statesman* on the 20th anniversary of the shootings, "I don't think I know what happiness is."[44] Pat was gay, but he never "came out," and not quite three years later, on June 30, 1989, he died of AIDS in Los Angeles.[45]

Johnnie Mike, once described as the wildest of the three boys, married the year after the shootings, at age 18, to Gayle Clifford, who was then 16. In 1971 he went to work for his father, and seemed to settle down. The couple had a daughter, Kathleen, and in 1973 he signed up to take the exam to become a licensed plumber. The date of the exam was July 5, and the night before he took his wife out for an Independence Day drink at a lounge in Lake Worth called Big Daddy's. The bar was having a special—25 cent drinks—and it was crowded with nearly 300 people. An argument started inside, someone announced an intent to get a gun, and about 100 of the patrons moved to the parking lot. In the ensuing fight six shots were fired from two .22 caliber pistols. One bullet hit a 23-year-old named James Girot, and another hit Johnnie Mike in the stomach. He died in a hospital-bound ambulance. A 21-year-old named Cootis Burgis was charged with murder and a 30-year-old named Clint Jones was charged with conspiracy to commit a felony. At 24, Johnnie Mike was a year younger than Charles had been. His wife remarried, but became addicted to heroin and committed suicide in 1992.

C.A. Whitman's marriage to Ellen Ward lasted five months. She initiated the divorce proceedings. He married again to Betty Clifford, the mother-in-law of Johnnie Mike and together they raised little Kathleen. That marriage ended in 1993. A neighbor had one clear memory of C.A. during that time—seeing him chasing Betty across their yard and driveway, trying to whip her with a belt. Whitman was diagnosed with Parkinson's disease in 1989 and with Alzheimer's in 1995. He died in a Florida nursing home in 2001.

Visitors to the Tower today must purchase a ticket and accompany a guided tour group with a specific time table in order to ascend the Tower. Along the way and at the top the guides provide interesting detail—when the Tower was built, its height in comparison to the Texas Capitol building, and the purpose of the girders that serve as its skeleton. Not once will a guide mention August 1, 1966 or Whitman's name. No attention will be drawn to the drain spouts through which he fired his rifles. No explanation will be provided for the numerous patched holes in its walls. If asked a specific question about the event that a guide can answer, he or she will do so, but typically one on one with the person asking, out of hearing of the others.[46]

Ironically, the University's attitude has accomplished the exact opposite of what was intended: the glorification of Charles J. Whitman. To some degree such glorification was inevitable. Americans are fascinated by bad boys and killers. Depending on the nature of the crime, the fascination may be admiration, repugnance, or something in between, but it is still fascination. Indeed, numerous readers of these words are reading them out of such fascination, and granted, the Whitman story is a multi-layered tale, complete with mystery and room for wild speculation, but it is and will always be a story of brutal, heartless assassination of innocents, coupled with noble sacrifice. As follows, described in Chapter 13 by Dr. Friedman, a result of the University's silence is that when people learn about what happened on August 1, 1966, it is unofficial, and what they hear, practically all they hear, is about Charles Joseph Whitman.

One of the overlooked victims, killed but often not even counted as such, was the baby boy Claire Wilson was carrying on August 1, 1966. At eight months the baby was viable and moving, but that movement stopped almost immediately after Ms. Wilson was shot. Lying in the hot sun, she felt the stillness and knew what it meant before the infant was removed by Caesarian at Brackenridge Hospital later that afternoon,

It was buried in an unmarked grave, but in 2014, as the 48th anniversary of the shootings approached, author Gary Lavergne, who wrote the single most comprehensive book about the event, obtained permission from Ms. Wilson, now Claire Wilson James, to place a headstone on the grave at his expense. He had researched and found the grave in a plot that had been leased to Ms. James's stepfather, even though Mrs. James did not know of its exact location. The permission was granted and the gravestone, in Austin Memorial Park Cemetery, reads "Baby Boy Wilson, August 1, 1966." "To know that the child was buried is very precious to me," James said in an interview. "It means a lot more now than it would have back then." "Graveyards are not for the dead," Lavergne said. "They are for the living. Maybe the argument would be that, after a while, people will forget you and no one will visit your grave. And maybe that's true, but there's something about a grave that makes you immortal."[47]

No one associated with the tragic killings in Austin, Texas on August 1, 1966, will achieve true immortality. After 50 years the event, its victims, its heroes and its villains, are still bright in the minds of hundreds, but the memories and concern will fade. Dedication of a more fitting memorial on the campus at U.T. would go a long way toward the type of immortality that the dead, injured, and heroic deserve, and there are strong indications now, in 2015, that such a memorial, or monument, will be erected and dedicated. Until then, and in addition, the writing of the tale, such as this, must serve as a mobile memorial for all concerned.

1. Defined as: anyone who: (1) is under indictment for, or has been convicted in any court of, a crime punishable by imprisonment for a term exceeding one year; (2) is a fugitive from justice; (3) is an unlawful user of or addicted to any controlled substance . . .; (4) has been adjudicated as a mental defective or has been committed to any mental institution; (5) who, being an alien— (A) is illegally or unlawfully in the United States; or (B)... has been admitted to the United States under a nonimmigrant visa... ; (6) who has been discharged from the Armed Forces under dishonorable conditions; (7) who, having been a citizen of the United States, has renounced his citizenship; (8) is subject to a court order that restrains such person from harassing, stalking, or threatening an intimate partner of such person or child of such intimate partner or person, or engaging in other conduct that would place an intimate partner in reasonable fear of bodily injury to the partner or child, except that this paragraph shall only apply to a court order that— (A) was issued after a hearing of which such person received actual notice, and at which such person had the opportunity to participate; and (B) (i) includes a finding that such person represents a credible threat to the physical safety of such intimate partner or child; or (ii) by its terms explicitly prohibits the use, attempted use, or threatened use of physical force against such intimate partner or child that would reasonably be expected to cause bodily injury; or (9) has been convicted in any court of a misdemeanor crime of domestic violence. 18 U.C. 922 (d):

2. Interview of Clif Drummond, May 8, 2015.

3. *Ibid.*

4. Keith Maitland, presentation to the Fayette County University of Texas Exes Association, March 2, 2015.

5. 96 minutes at 199. Considering that two bullet holes are now visible, it is likely that the University's repair was undone over the years.

6. Recollection of Patty Lankford Akers, wife and mother of the authors.

7. Ramiro Martinez, *They Call me Ranger Ray,* at 80-86.

8. E.g., "Sniper: Reign of Terror at U.T.," *Austin American Statesman*, August 2, 1966; "The Chief," *San Antonio Evening News*, August 2, 1966; "Policeman Makes 1st Shot of Career Important One," *Fort Worth Star Telegram*, August 2, 1966; "Officer Left His Steak to Kill Sniper," *San Angelo Standard-Times*, August 2, 1966; "Officer Recalls Facing Sniper, *Fort Worth Star Telegram*, August 3, 1966; "Compulsion—The Evil Forces That Left a Town Drenched in Blood," *Confidential Detective Yearbook*, No. 13, 1967.

9. Email from Monika McCoy, June 29, 2015.

10. Mona Ross Trotter, "Miles Broke Silence Shortly Before Death," *Austin American Statesman*, August 3, 1979.

11. E.g Jack Keever,"Sniper Horror Recalled," AP, August, 1970; "Former Austin Officer Says Show is 'Bull,'" *San Angelo Standard*, October 22, 1975.

12. Interview of Monika McCoy, March 12, 2015; Martinez, *supra*, at 88-89.

13. https://www.youtube.com/watch?v=BiHRY2njJvM

14. Monika McCoy interview, *supra*

15. *Ibid.*

16. Interview of Monika McCoy and Christopher McCoy, May 31, 2015.

17. Richard Serrano, "Massacre and Myth in Texas: One Man Ended Charles Whitman's Coldblooded Austin Slaughter. Was it the Hero of Legend, or a Second Officer in the Tower, Who Says He Fired the Crucial Shots?" *Los Angeles Times*, July 29, 1994.

18. Jim Echols, letter entitled "A hero who became a victim," *Austin American Statesman*, August 8, 2006.

19. The statement about protecting Mr. "Crump" was not included in later recollections, and one wonders if Martinez added it to his first report out of concern that he had been hasty in opening fire without calling to Whitman to put his rifle down or to surrender. He also did not mention Whitman jumping to his feet, as he recorded in later accounts.

20. Email from Milton Shoquist, April 28, 2015.

21. Email from Clarence Wood to Milton Shoquist dated April 29, 2015.

22. "The Awe-Inspiring JoelleDrees," kingwood underground.com/topic.jsp?topicid=11169404.

23. Letter dated January 6, 2015 from Gary M. Lavergne to Monte Akers.

24. Letter dated August 23, 1966 from the FBI to Marvin Watson, Special Assistant to the President, AHC.

25. *Austin American Statesman*, December, 2014.

26. 96 Minutes at 199.

27. Dennis McLellan, "David H. Gunby, 58; Hurt in '66 Texas Shooting Rampage," Obituaries, *Fort Worth Star-Telegram*, November 16, 2001.

28. Martinez, *supra* at 87.

29. Phone conversation with Ron Oliveira, March 23. 2015; "U.T. Tower News Special, KEYE," August 6, 2006, https://www.youtube.com/watch?v=-A8hgoACMpM.

30. Interview of Dr. Mary Ellen O'Toole by Dr. Roger Friedman, June 17, 2015.

31. Cowan was a DPS agent but not a peace officer.

32. "Houston McCoy's Own Story, West Texas Scouting History," http://www.westtexasscoutinghistory.net/McCoy-story.html

33. *A Crime to Remember the 28th Floor*, Full Episode, https://www.youtube.com/watch?v=Z54c-CAnUpbo; Interview of Houston McCoy by Noel Newton, https://drive.google.com/file/d/0B2sFGqklP1lnTnBDUU9FWWZNLUE/view

34. "Officers Killed in the Line of Duty," http://www.austintexas.gov/page/officers-killed-line-duty.

35. "The Austin Police Officer Memorial Project" http://austintexas.gov/news/austin-police-officer-memorial-project-6

36. Telephone interview of Officer Huskins, *supra*; Interview of Milton Shoquist, March 12, 2015. The statue of Davis has since been removed by the University.

37. Division of Diversity and Community Engagement, The University of Texas at Austin, June 29, 2015.

38. Toby Hamilton, "Memories of a Smaller Town and a Tragedy That Became Personal," *Austin American Statesman*, August 6, 2006

39. *Ibid.*

40. Email dated December 9, 2008, from Toby Hamilton to Monika McCoy, provided the authors by Monika McCoy.

41. Email from Monika McCoy, April 28, 2015.

42. Brenda Bell, "Man Entwined with Shooting at UT Tower in Life, Death," *Austin American Statesman,* Dec. 21, 2011.

43. Forrest Preece, "*Westside Stories,*" June 9, 2011.

44. *Austin American Statesman,* August 1, 1986.

45. Telephone interview of Dr.Stuart Brown, April 22, 2015.

46. When the authors of this book visited the Tower in 2015, one of the guides seemed tempted to expand on an answer to a question so posed, then turned away and said, soto voce, "I don't want to lose my job."

47. Reeve Hamilton, "After 48 Years, Whitman's Unborn Victim Gets a Headstone," *Texas Tribune*, August 1, 2014, http://www.texastribune.org/2014/08/01/after-48-years-whitmans-unborn-victim-gets-headsto/.

CHAPTER THIRTEEN

Reflections on a Traumatic Legacy

By Dr. Roger Friedman, Ph.D.

It is 1:30 a.m. in the morning on April 16, 2015, in Blacksburg, Virginia. I'm walking up a winding black-topped path that crosses a concave meadow that everyone here at Virginia Tech calls the Drill Field. The dome-shaped street lamps that border this public commons look like old-fashioned gas lights, each lamp haloed by a misty glow in the cold drizzly night air. Behind the street lamps is a semi-circle of large box-like dormitories, in some of which are dorm room windows lit by desk lamps; students up late studying. Finals are coming in about three weeks.

I'm not alone on the dark path. There are four college girls, each wearing almost identical outfits of dark North Face winter vests, torn blue jeans and Hokie ski caps, walking somberly, arm in arm, ahead of me. Nearby, three late night runners, cheeks red from exertion, jog across the meadow heading west, silently sprinting up an incline. There's a boy and girl strolling down from the dorms in matching school hoodies, walking slowly close together, each holding a string of Rosary beads. We are all heading in the same direction, to the same location, to visit the same quiet hallowed space, set aside for solace and remembering; we're just a few minutes into the 8th Annual Observance Day of the shooting of 32 students and faculty on campus on April 16th, 2007—the largest school rampage shooting since that on August 1, 1966 in Austin, Texas.

Thousands of Virginia Tech students, faculty, and staff join families of survivors and victims on April 16, 2015 for the 8th Annual Candle Light Memorial Service on campus to Remember and Honor the 32 members of their community killed on April 16, 2007. The tragedy at Virginia Tech was the first campus shooting to surpass the lethality of the UT Tower sniper on August 1, 1966.

The Memorial is on the far edge of the meadow, in front of Burruss Hall, a chiseled rock administration building built in 1936. The Memorial itself is simple; an elegant semi-circle of 32 granite stones, each illuminated at night and engraved with the name of someone killed during the campus rampage. In the hours following the tragedy on April 16, 2007, a group of students spontaneously gathered and placed the 32 granite Hokie Stones on the Drill Field. That poignant impromptu monument quickly became a container for grief, the place on campus to gather, mourn, and reflect about the horror that had occurred. Such a simple, heartfelt commemorative place, with the addition of walking paths, plants, and the night lighting, is the official University Memorial. It was formally dedicated in August, 2007, five months after the tragedy.

Earlier this evening several thousand people stood on the Drill Field holding candles as they listened to the reading of the names of those who lost their lives. In the morning the ceremonies will involve the placing of wreaths, a statewide moment of silence, and the sounding of "Taps." Thirty-two members of the Virginia Tech Corps of Cadets will stand guard, symbolically protecting the families of victims and the many first responders and hundreds of students and faculty who will silently gather in the soft, chilly, Appalachian rain to remember and honor those who are gone.

But tonight it's all very quiet, hushed, and hallowed. I have the same sacred, sad feeling as when I visit the Vietnam War Memorial on the Mall in Washington, but these weren't soldiers, they were students and teachers. The memorial feels like a very grown-up space on a college campus full of kids, all of whom were in middle school when the tragedy occurred. The freshness of youth and adventure has been woven into a campus tapestry of loss and memory caused by the shootings. Hopefulness is tempered by terrible knowledge about life. Community on this campus now means more than cheering at a football game; it means helping each other survive a tragedy in everyone's own backyard. "We'll help you carry all of this and find meaning in it," the Memorial seems to be saying to the young people who gather here tonight. I think they are listening.

The 2007 rampage at Virginia Tech and the 1966 sniper shootings at the University of Texas had emotional consequences for local communities similar to the upheaval faced by most of the nation on and after September 11, 2001. The tragedy in Texas, the first campus mass shooting of its kind in America, occurred nearly fifty years before that in Virginia, but had many similarities in regard to the culture of the two Universities, both being large historical state Universities with lots of school pride and gridiron spirit that experienced a random mass killing of students and faculty on campus.[1] However, the public response of the University of Texas was the inverse of what I saw on the Drill Field at Virginia Tech.

Trauma is a social and individual experience. In contrast to Virginia Tech, during the immediate aftermath of the Texas shootings individuals who'd personally experienced the shootings became painfully isolated from each other and from the larger community. The President of the University cancelled summer school classes for the following day, flags on campus were flown at half-mast for a week, and the Observation Deck of the Texas tower was closed while officials tried to decide what to do next. The President of the University expressed deep regrets and Governor Connally convened a Commission to study the tragedy and come up with recommendations. Some of those recommendations and other developments were novel at the time and have become common place today, including the establishment of SWAT Teams, Emergency Medical Services, and 24-Hour Mental Health Hotlines on campus. While these were important administrative steps in enhancing the capacity for crisis response on a college campus, neither the University nor the City of Austin provided leadership to create a publically supportive environment for the individuals, families, and a campus community that had been fractured by shock and violence. For forty years, these institutions made little effort to bring the wounded city together, publically memorialize the dead, honor the survivors, celebrate the bravery of the police officers who shot the sniper, or acknowledge the many student volunteers who risked their own lives to help fellow students during the rampage.

This chapter identifies and explores how some of the people devastated by the shootings in Austin on August 1, 1966, were affected by the lingering traces of trauma over the past five decades. A personal dimension will be present because my best childhood friend, Paul Sonntag, was killed on that day in the 18th summer of our lives. It will also touch on how the University of Texas and the City of Austin failed to provide the leadership needed to promote a healthy, healing process or create an accurate public narrative of that terrible event until challenged to take action by an informally organized, compassionate, media-aware group of trauma survivors, witnesses, concerned citizens, and retired police officers. Conversely, it will describe how those local community efforts, truly from the bottom up, served as catalysts for a cultural intervention that is now changing, in hopeful and healing ways, the frame of reference toward trauma itself for the Austin community and generations of UT students and faculty to come.

Since the Texas Tower tragedy in 1966, more than 70 mass shootings have taken place in America, resulting in hundreds of deaths, many more wounded and traumatization of countless survivors, witnesses and first responders. The frequency of such terrible events has increased since 1996, with 29 multi-victim shootings occurring in the past 15 years alone.[2] The five most lethal school shootings to have occurred in the United States over the past half-century were the Texas Tower shooting on August 1, 1966; the Columbine School Shooting, April 20, 1999, The Red Lake Minnesota High School shooting on March 21, 2005; the Virginia Tech University Shooting on April 16, 2007; and the Sandy Hook Elementary School Shooting in Newton on December 14, 2012. Though rare, the frequency of school shootings is increasing, and when they occur are life-changing and destructive events for many individuals, families and communities involved.[3] Mass killings of all kinds, including the March 24, 2015 intentional crashing of the Germanwings passenger plane and the June 17, 2015 killing of nine members of the Emanual African Methodist Episcopal Church in Charleston, South Carolina, are becoming prevalent enough that from an anthropological perspective it's possible to view them as new idioms of distress in modern society.[4] What's clear is that a person does not have to be a combat veteran to be exposed to trauma in America. Hardly. In the past 50 years since the shootings at the University of Texas, we have learned that trauma happens to each of us, as well as our kids, friends, and neighbors.

To fully comprehend this "new species of trouble," we must first come to grips with the contemporary understanding that exposure to trauma inevitably influences who we are for generations.[5] We now know that trauma is not just an event that takes place sometime in the past; it is also the imprint left by that experience on our mind, brain, body, and relationships. Humans are a hardy, resilient species, but trauma leaves its traces in our lives, families, communities and culture. Our culture is becoming increasingly trauma-informed. The arrival of this broader understanding came to mental health circles in 1980, when a group of Vietnam veterans and their allies in psychiatry persuaded the American Psychiatric Association to create a new diagnosis: Post-traumatic Stress Disorder (PTSD), which appeared in the third edition of the *Diagnostic and Statistical Manual of Mental Disorders* (DSM-III). PTSD described a set of symptoms that was common to war veterans, and finally gave a name to the suffering of people who were overwhelmed by horror, help-lessness, and terrible knowledge about life.[6] This new language led to an explosion of research and attempts to find effective treatment.

The clinical definition of trauma has evolved since that time, and the recently published DSM 5 describes trauma as the "exposure to actual or threatened death, serious injury or sexual violence... the following ways: direct experience as a victim, witnessing the event in person, learning of the trauma occurring to a close relative or friend, or repeatedly being exposed to aversive details of the trauma in your line of work."[7]

As valuable as hard data and clinical definitions are for intellectual clarity and background, in order to truly grasp the meaning and human impact of the sniper shootings we need to engage in a particular and personal conversation about trauma.

Claire Wilson James was a freshman at UT in 1966, and now teaches elementary and junior high school in Texarkana. The first person to be shot and seriously wounded, whose unborn baby was killed by a sniper bullet, she recalled her return to classes six months later. "I was in intensive care for seven weeks, and I wasn't released from the hospital until November. I had to learn how to walk again. When I went back to school in January, no one said anything to me or talked about it around me. I almost felt like I had imagined the whole thing. Not one person ever called together the students who'd been injured that day and said, 'How are you?' or 'We're so sorry.' I guess that's just the way it was—it was a measure of the times. We didn't have the vocabulary at that point to deal with what happened. If it was mentioned at all, it was always called 'the accident.'"[8]

Barton Riley, a faculty member in architecture at the time, now deceased, remembered that "the fall semester started right after the shooting and life went on, just like nothing had ever happened. I never heard it mentioned. Isn't that amazing? I was rather stunned."[9] Forrest Preece, then a junior at UT, recalled "sitting with the rest of the Longhorn Band in Memorial Stadium at the first football game that September when the announcer, Wally Pryor, asked us to remember those who had been injured. He suggested giving to the designated people who would be standing with donation cans at the exits.... But a story in the next issue of the *Daily Texan* said that the total take was pitifully small. A friend who was part of the collection effort said he was amazed at how quickly everyone seemed to forget."[10]

The first exploration into the meaning and public response of the Tower shootings in Austin began 29 years later, in 1995, when Dr. Rosa Eberly, an Assistant Professor of Rhetoric and Composition at U.T., proposed to teach a course entitled, "The U.T. Tower and Public Memory." Her Department approved the course and it rapidly filled up each of the semesters it was offered between 1996 to 2001. Eberly had noticed for several years that the University seemed to have gone out of its way to erase the Tower shootings from memory, and yet there was constant talk about the tragedy on the radio around August 1st each year. On the 29th Anniversary of the shooting, in 1995, she was listening to a three-hour talk/call-in show on KTBC radio in Austin, and heard Neal Spelce, a UT alumnus who had been news director of the station in 1966, comment:

> I was out at the University of Texas commencement in May. Wonderful evening. Pageantry like you wouldn't believe; not like when we graduated out there. It was festive; there was music; there were colors. It was an unbelievable evening. And then the Tower lit up orange. And, for a moment there, even though I was wrapped up in the events of the commencement, for a moment there, all of a sudden, it just comes back.

"Even more remarkable than the lack of an official history of the event is the active repression evident on the University's website," Dr. Eberly said. In April, 1996, for instance, the University launched "Scenes from the Top," a series of still photos and video clips of the view from the top of the Tower in eight directions. Professor Eberly was amazed and the students in her course that fall were incredulous to find that the texts for "Scenes from the Top," the University's official chronology of the Tower, began in 1974 rather than 1937, when the Tower was constructed, and made no mention of what occurred in 1966.

She and her students were further struck by how the memory vacuum created by the University drove the remembering of the tragedy "underground," leaving individual survivors to cope with their sorrows on their own, while at the same time allowing pop culture to usurp the narrative and turn the public memory of the sniper into a cool antihero. Charles Whitman was the subject of films, at least one novel, and even a Website created by an alum that was called "The Charles Whitman Fan Club." One of her students conducted an email survey of 1,500 randomly selected U.T. students, in the spring of 1996, to find out how they first heard about the Tower shootings and what they knew. The survey revealed that such information was mainly spread by rumor and word of mouth, and was focused on Charles Whitman, the shooter, not on the victims and the terrible trauma suffered by so many. Moreover, the information about Whitman came mainly from cultural texts such as the movie, *Deadly Tower*, and singer song-writer Kinky Friedman's *Ballad of Charles Whitman,*[11] which, according to Eberly, contributed most to disseminating the "cruel" coolness of Whitman as an anti-hero.[12]

Gary Lavergne's seminal history of the tragedy, *The Sniper In The Tower: The Charles Whitman Murders,* published in 1997, was the first piece of serious historical writing about the shooting. Lavergne contributed a valuable archival resource to nourish public memory. Of necessity he focused particularly on Whitman's life and the chronology of the event, but he also documented that there was a painful legacy of trauma that extended far beyond the immediate atmosphere of terror and was still palpable 31 years later for everyone who was there that day.

We now know that traumatic events are recorded in the brain's hippocampus in very different ways than the ordinary humdrum of everyday life. The total mind/body experience and all the atmospherics are encoded in multi-sensory high definition color. This intensified archiving of experience leads to rapid and passionate recall when activated by similar stimuli. It's the job of the limbic system, and more specifically the amygdala, to scan the environment, 24/7, for threatening stimuli, and it knows what's threatening because of instantaneous check backs with the archives in the hippocampus. When there is a near match between a current stimulus and a traumatic memory, the amygdala automatically signals the body and the neo-cortex to engage in fight, flight, or freeze response. Sometimes this alarm system is accurate, but often it can be sloppy and provides a false alarm that creates highly anxious responses to stimuli that aren't nearly as threat-ening as the brain perceives them to be. The recorded information is archived in the present tense, our recall is immediate, totally present and in high definition; it feels as if our body and mind are actually re-experiencing the trauma.

This is simply how exposure to trauma impacts the memory and retrieval system of the human brain, primarily the hippocampus and the related limbic system and amygdala. This alarm mechanism provided protection from predators for our evolving species 20,000 years ago. Today, however, when this neural alarm gets activated from trauma and remains aroused for long periods of time following the event, our nervous system and biology become seriously impaired and we develop a set of behaviors and internal experiences that we now describe as post-traumatic stress disorder.

In an interview for the August, 2006 issue of *Texas Monthly*, Bob Higley, a U.T. junior in 1966, recalled what the scene looked and felt like when he and Clif Drummond, a senior and the student body president, stepped outside into the eerie heat and silence of that August day. They did not merely experience what is described in Chapter Six, but became forever linked to the young victim who is at the heart of this story for me and, accordingly, to my life.

It was shocking to see the name "Paul Sonntag" suddenly appear in Bob's story. The objectivity I needed for my research was suddenly swept away and I again fell into the dark vortex that Paul's violent death holds for me, and for days I could not continue writing. My own traumatic memories were activated by the images of Paul's slumped body, Bob pulling him close, Paul's head falling over, the blue fingers, the heaviness of my dear childhood friend's body. It occurred to me that Bob and Clif were the first to reach out to Paul at the end of his life. I thought how I'd love to meet them in person, introduce them to Paul's parents and his brothers, and let them know how much we all appre-ciated their courage that moment fifty years ago.

Knowing they put themselves in harm's way to help Paul was a gift for me, and I know it would have been to Paul's family—to have known that he was not alone, that loving strangers tried to save what was left of him and get him to the hospital as quickly as they could. Believe me, to have known that would have provided some solace almost 50 years ago when

I visited with Jim and Beverly Sonntag; sitting back in Paul's room on the night of August 1, 1966, when we wept together about his terrible death and the empty tragedy of life that it revealed so starkly to each of us.

Now managing director of an investment firm in Houston, Higley responded in writing to questions I prepared for him in May, 2015. He told me he is still friends with Clif Drummond, a high-tech executive in Austin, "but the first and only time in our lives, Clif and I relived the hours we spent together on August 1, 1966 was in 2006, when Pam Colloff, a *Texas Monthly* writer, called and set up a telephone interview with us. The call acted as a catharsis for me. I got it all out and in front of me. Clif recalled things I had forgotten, I things he didn't recall, and... we accepted that our gaps in memory were there for a reason. From then on I have been more comfortable in dealing with others on the events... In retrospect, I let the U.T. response to the event become my response: the Heisman stiff arm and the age old whistle past the graveyard. Pretend it never happened and it will go away. I should have reached out for help immediately and coughed up the emotions, met with others, moved on with a greater sense of confidence and helped others back then. UT fumbled the ball on their end and I bit my tongue."

Alfred McAlister was 18 years old when he witnessed the sniper attack and rushed to help victims, particularly his and my dear friend, Paul. Now a Professor of Behavioral Sciences at the U.T. School of Public Health, he wrote in 2014, "I never realized I had PTSD until there was a name for it, and only one symptom has distinctly endured. I am hypervigilant and almost nothing around me escapes my observation. Any movement or unusual feature draws my eye instantly."

Alfred also reminisced about his admiration for Tom Eckman and Claire Wilson James who had been leaders in the anti-war movement on campus before the sniper attack, and how "proud" Claire seemed to be about being pregnant. In an informal email response, Claire said that she was grateful both for Alfred's recollections of her being "proudly pregnant" that morning fifty years ago, and for his comment about Tom and what a special couple they were. Alfred and his wife have become very close friends with Claire just within the past year. It is a paradox that the shared experience of trauma can bring us together in incredible intimacy, and can also cut us off from each other and the communities whose support we so desperately need.

If no one intervenes to create a safe interpersonal space and validating conversation about a trauma, we come to believe that only those who were "there" can really understand us, and that it's too painful to talk about it with them as well. So we carry the trauma alone. This is the position of those who suffer from Post-Traumatic Stress Disorder. The failure after the shooting in August of 1966 to create a place and process for communal grieving reinforced the isolation and the stifling ambivalence that the trauma victims felt about bearing their souls; especially when the community seemed to prefer to forget what happened. The campus shootings of 1966 created lasting human wounds and fractures of distrust and disassociation within the larger University community for half a century. The lack of empathic public response and mobilization on the part of the University at the time seems startling to us today.

It is certainly true that in 1966 we did not have the knowledge or the language in our culture to describe such traumatic experience, nor did we understand how exposure to violent trauma, other than during combat, inevitably affects the human brain, body, nervous system, and the social environment in which the trauma occurs. The sniper attack was the first public human disaster of its kind in the country, and no one had any kind of a road map for how to respond to the emotional intensity and grim human loss caused by such a massive public rampage. It's also good to remember that the cultural mores of Texas, today and certainly in the 1960s, have always championed emotional stoicism, a solitary "do it alone" cowboy spirit, and dictated that no "real man" would show any public signs of hurt or helplessness. This aspect of Texas culture is a mixed blessing; at times it does help to just soldier through a tough situation like an unconquerable John Wayne, but in the aftermath of a major trauma like the rampage on campus in 1966, this stoic façade needs to be set aside so that traumatized individuals and communities can have an opportunity to heal.

Nevertheless, the University's stance seems oddly determined to erase what happened. Perhaps their position came out of a desire to manage public image, to protect themselves from liability, and to promote a sense of safety on campus by describing the trauma as an "accident" that will never happen again. Maybe no one could figure out how to honor the dead without also enshrining the sniper and contributing to copycat shooters. More likely the Board of Regents and University Administration wanted to protect the iconic symbol of the University Tower from a tragic association with the sniper, not to mention legal liability. For perhaps understandable but mistaken reasons, both of commission and omission, the University long ago decided to sustain its effort to minimize the emotional impact of this tragedy, and to remove the event as much as possible from the formal history and public memory of the Austin campus. They have not been successful, but they have been persistent.

Remarkably, no memorial plaque or marker was put in place until over forty years after the shootings. Like so much of the legacy of the shootings, the story behind the plaque is a multi-layered, intensely interpersonal and revealing lesson about the corrosive impact of trauma. It shows the ways in which the lack of public memory and erroneous historical narratives influence how the tragedy is experienced by survivors. It also reveals how a tender relationship between a father who was intimately involved in the campus shooting, and his daughter who wasn't even born at the time, can shape its traumatic legacy for a whole community many years later.

In the year 2000, Monika McCoy, then a 29-year-old military veteran of two overseas tours in the Army in Germany, returned home to Austin. Her father, Houston McCoy, 39 years earlier in August of 1966, had rushed to the Tower's Observation Deck along with other officers and civilians, and from 55 feet away fired two loads of buckshot in short order from his 12 gauge shotgun, killing Charles Whitman and stopping the sniper attack after 90 minutes of terror. Houston was tall, lanky, and 62 years old when Monika got home from the Army. Her father's ethic of hard work, honesty, and always being willing to help others out, alongside his west Texas cowboy humor, had been an important influence on her as she grew up. Monika was born five years after the sniper shooting, and she told me that she and her older brothers had always known about it, but she didn't really understand how important it was to her father, the Police Department, or the City of Austin until she was an adult.

I spent an evening at Monika McCoy's kitchen table in May, 2015, talking with her about her father and the effect of the sniper's attack on her family, the Police Force, and the City of Austin. She is a dynamic, athletic forty-four-year-old, with longish blond hair, and was dressed casually in a white sleeveless blouse, jeans, and flip-flops on her day-off from the Austin Police Department. In March, 2013, she entered the

Austin Police Academy at 42, by eighteen years the oldest member of her class, graduated eight months later and started as a Patrol Officer on the street in December, 2013. She's currently assigned to patrol Baker Sector, a part of which had been her father's beat almost fifty years ago. It still includes all of the U.T. west campus. Monika is a multi-tasker. Even as I settled down at the table to begin the interview, she got up to slide a tray of chicken tenders into the electric oven and set the timer for an hour or so, getting her meals prepared for the week ahead. She loves to tell stories though. She speaks quickly with much emotion and rich detail, usually looking me straight in the eye; sometimes she stood up and gestured with her hands and taut muscular arms to make her point more powerfully.

Monika began matter-of-factly, "I went on a five-year humanitarian project, starting in 2006." She knew that her father was troubled by the false depiction of the shooting of Whitman in the 1975 TV movie, *Deadly Tower*. In the confusion surrounding the shooting of the sniper, Officer Ramiro Martinez, the first officer to push his way through the barricaded door and step onto the Observation Deck, was credited with killing the tower gunman and this misinformation persisted for years. The public narrative that seemed to be accepted by the media in 1966 and reinforced by the movie *Deadly Tower*, was that Martinez first shot Whitman in the shoulder with his pistol and then, after he'd emptied the bullets from that gun, grabbed the shotgun from McCoy's hands and made the fatal shot that killed Whitman. In the movie, McCoy's character was portrayed as passive, if not cowardly, instead of as the officer who actually shot Whitman first, and with two shotgun blasts killed him, all of which McCoy recounted in his written report of the event. As discussed in the previous chapter, information now indicates that McCoy's two shotgun blasts to Whitman's head were the fatal shots, whereas Martinez's final shotgun shell at close range went into Whitman's upper left arm. It was obvious from Houston's original written report and his final writings in the fall of 2012, before his death, that maintaining the integrity of the sequence of events on the observation deck was of great importance to him.

It is remarkable to remember that on August 1, 1966, the officers who went up the Tower were operating without bullet-proof vests, police radios, or any communication or plan among themselves. They weren't even sure at the time if there was more than one sniper. The only facts of which they were certain were that they were outgunned, that whoever was up there had no concern for life, that the sniper(s) possessed expert and lethal shooting skills, and that they might never come back down alive.[13]

Monika said that it seemed like "Papa could never ever get away from the history being wrong. He was constantly reliving it year after year." In the months before Houston McCoy entered hospice care and died from Chronic Obstructive Pulmonary disease on December 27, 2012, he again wrote down his full account of the sniper attack and the shooting of Whitman. He included the blow-by-blow narrative of that day on the Tower's observation deck; a narrative different from the one described in the movie and in the press years earlier, and finally validated with the release of reports and autopsy records that had been sealed for a decade. In his writings toward the end of his life, Houston also shared that "In 1998, I was diagnosed with Post Traumatic Stress Disorder for mental anguish and depression related to the tower incident, the movie and untruths presented by different media."

Around the kitchen table on May 18th, 2015, Monika told me that, "My first step in 2006 was to bring all the officers together who were on the Tower that day to sit and talk with each other…I had a vision of getting justice and closure for my father and the other officers, but I knew it would take some time. They had never talked about what happened among themselves, in all these almost 40 years—for the most part they didn't know what each other had been doing until they all got off the elevator on the top of the Tower. It was amazing to watch them talk together…they so enjoyed it."

The group met at Monika's home, and one of the officers who was there, Phillip Connor, told me on the phone in early June, 2015, "I found (meeting with the other officers) very therapeutic personally—finding out minute details of where everyone was that day… what our time lines were like back then. That's the sort of thing we talked about. We each talked one by one. You know Billy Speed and Houston were the only officers officially on duty that day, the rest of us had come in to help out when we heard what was going on." Phillip said that their wives came to the meetings as well. He said, "Of course our wives all knew each other back then. I remember they were sitting and talking in a different room, but would come over sometimes to hear what we were talking about. None of us had ever talked to our wives about that day. Getting together like this gave us a chance to get things off our chest and tell them about what happened as well. It was a good thing for me. You know I was a combat medic in Korea and had lots of exposure to trauma and death over there, but this thing affected me because it was so unique."

Houston's report from the incident said that he actually saw Billy Speed get shot in the shoulder from where he had been standing earlier in the day, on the roof of the Education Building, but it hadn't looked serious at a distance. Houston and Billy were both in their mid-twenties and were patrol partners and friends. Later, after Houston and then Martinez shot the sniper, Houston walked slowly to the shooter's limp, bloody body in the northwest corner of the observation deck, and as he searched for an ID, he heard an announcer's muffled voice from Whitman's little transistor radio on the cement floor next to the dead body, that "Officer Billy Paul Speed, twenty-three year old Patrolman, has just been brought in an ambulance to the Hospital, dead on arrival." That was how McCoy learned of his friend's death. Monika said, "Papa felt a lot of survivor's guilt about what happened to Billy. He always felt that if he could've gotten up there quicker and gotten to Whitman sooner, he could have saved Billy."

By 1969, three years after the sniper shooting, all of the officers on the Tower that day except one had left police work for better paying jobs. "They were mostly in their mid-twenties, making $2.55 an hour on the force at that time. Papa and Mom had their third baby and they needed more money to get by." Houston had always told Monika that he didn't leave the force because of the trauma, but because of the low pay and how frustrating it was becoming, with all the politics and continuing media coverage.

"I don't think it was until 10 years later when the movie came out, that he really got depressed. The Whitman incident was important in Papa's life, but it was just a part of his life. He was an experienced pilot and loved flying, having been in the Army in Germany and flown glider planes in the late fifties. He quickly got a better paying job as a civilian flight instructor for the United States Air Force in Del Rio in 1968. In January, 1975, we all moved again, and this time it was out to the country where Papa had been offered the position of Camp Ranger at Boy Scout Camp Sol Mayer near Ft. McKavett. That's where he and mom stayed until 1987 and raised me and my three older brothers."[14]

It wasn't easy for Monika to get in contact with all the officers that had been on the Tower. The Police Department helped informally and she was finally able to reach Officer Phillip Conner, Officer Jerry Day, Officer Ramiro Martinez, Officer Harold Moe, Officer George Shepard, Officer Milton Shoquist, and of course, Officer McCoy. The men who came together that summer at Monika's home included Conner, Day, Moe, Shoquist, and Houston McCoy.

This group of retired officers and their wives coming together with Monika's coordination was just the beginning of a remarkable series of interpersonal events, revelations, new connections and re-connections of old acquaintances among survivors, police, and witnesses who over the past forty years had either never met, or if they had, had never spoken with each other about that terrible day. The shared conversation that started in the summer of 2006 was immediately recognized by all involved as an essential element that had been missing in their decades-long individual struggles to cope with the effects of the sniper's attack. Monika and those five retired police officers provided the beginning leadership for what has become a continuing public healing process that the University of Texas and City of Austin had failed to lead or even to recognize the importance of for over forty years.

"All kinds of amazing things started happening after that group of officers got together that summer," Monica said with delight. In October of 2006, with help from the Austin Police Department, the retired officers piqued the interest of TV Reporter Ron Oliveira at KEYE NEWS in Austin. Oliveira met the five men on campus, and asked them to lead him through their story of what happened to them that day on the Mall, going up into the Tower and finally shooting Whitman on the Deck. The most moving narrative was told by McCoy. It was the first time since 1966 that all the officers had gotten together again on the Observation Deck. He took the reporter through the shooting of Whitman, step by step. Monika was there during all the video-taping. At one point McCoy was standing at the spot where he'd aimed his shotgun and shot Whitman twice in the head 40 years earlier, and gesturing slowly with his right hand to show how the body "just kinda slithered down" onto the floor from a sitting position after his second shot hit him in the left side of the head. McCoy said he then "jacked in that third shell" and Officer Martinez grabbed the shotgun. Pointing toward the corner where Whitman's body was lying that brutally hot August afternoon in 1966, McCoy said, "Martinez ran…all the way down to that body down there," and shot him again. Monika turned to me and softly said, "We all got the chills up and down our spines when Papa pointed and said "that body down there," because we knew he was actually reliving it, he was really back there right then."

The *Secrets of the Tower Tragedy* aired on KEYE TV in Austin in November, 2006, forty years after the tragedy.[15] It was the first public broadcast of what happened that day told by the police officers who were actually there. Monika showed me a clip of it, and I was struck at how the retired officers reminded me of grey-haired, no nonsense, laconic cowboys, showing the city boy newsman around the fields on their West Texas spread. They seemed like Larry McMurtry's *Lonesome Dove* characters Gus McCrae and Woodrow Call, wise, matter of fact, and country smart. They spoke with little emotion, very matter-of-factly even about the most terrifying moments during the event. As Houston McCoy would later say, "We weren't the heroes…we were just doing our jobs. The heroes were the people who ran out on the Mall and risked their lives to help the fallen victims just because they thought it was the right thing to do."

There's nothing in the video that tells you these retired police officers had, in the previous few months, re-united and talked for the first time about how they'd been affected all these years by that day, or that they risked their own lives repeatedly and faced down a mass murderer on a narrow observation deck nearly 300 feet in the air above the campus. It was just their job as police officers, to do what had to be done to protect lives in Austin that day.

In the video, Phillip Connor publically shared the somber sentiment that police in Austin had been privately feeling for years, "It's our blood spilled on that campus…they should have something recognizing the victims on the campus as well." When I spoke with Connor on the phone while researching this chapter, he remembered clearly his feelings back then, "The University did the ostrich thing and pretended like it never happened. I was shocked." Just a month after the *Secrets of the Tower* was aired, in December, 2006, the University placed a small bronze marker on a granite stone near the base of the Tower in the middle of a sliver of green space universally known as the Turtle Pond. The marker reads in part, "remembering with profound sorrow the tragedy of August 1, 1966."

Administrators christened the small space the "Tower Memorial Garden." Monika well remembers when the plaque first went up, "The fact that after all this time the University recognized the need for this and placed it in a peaceful spot by the Tower, meant a lot to all of us then." Ironically, a University press release at the time of the plaque's unveiling concluded, "A detailed plan for a more extensively landscaped Tower Garden, including memorial elements, has been developed but private fund-raising efforts have been unsuccessful to date."

On August 1, 2007, at the 41st Anniversary of the Tower shooting, the first memorial service to occur on campus for the sniper shooting took place at the Memorial Garden. It was organized by Monika and Forrest Preece, and attended by retired Officers McCoy, Shoquist, Moe, Connor, and Day, their families, Claire Wilson, Gary Lavergne, and a small group of friends of victims and survivors.

Four of the U.T. Tower Officers at the base of the Tower on April 21, 2010. Monika McCoy, who was present, stated that the photo was taken an instant after one of them mentioned the death of fellow Officer Billy Speed, which caused all to become silent and reflective. L. to R.: Phillip Conner, Houston McCoy, Milton Shoquist, Jerry Day

"We all chipped in and bought roses and laid them around the marker—black ones for victims, red for survivors, and yellow for heroes. I think it was retired Officer Jerry Day who said that it took forty years to get to the Promised Land in the Bible, and it's taken us forty years in the desert to get here. I remember seeing Claire Wilson and Papa standing together, and she reached up and gave him a big long hug around the neck. She was crying and thanking him for saving her life that day," Monika said.

Houston McCoy relished his relationships with surviving victims of the attack, their family members and others affected by Whitman's rampage. McCoy met Toby Hamilton at the 2007 memorial service and developed the close brotherly relationship that continued until Toby's untimely death in 2012 from a heart attack while on his way to be with McCoy.

McCoy also corresponded for many years with Becky Davis, who was 18 months old when her father, Billy Speed, was fatally shot by the sniper. Monika remembers that Becky graduated from the University of Texas. Becky recently told Monika that whenever "I walked past the place on the Mall where my father had been shot, his memory inspired me to not be fearful and to embrace life with the hope that he would be proud of me."

If the City of Austin failed in the beginning to take ownership of August 1, 1966, it has now done so. In addition to various recognitions and events over the years, the City responded in 2007, when Monika reached out to staff in the Mayor's Office about honoring the officers on the Tower for the contributions each made that day. The City organized a ceremony in which the Mayor recognized 11 former officers and three civilians who worked together on the Tower to subdue the sniper. On August 8, 2007, Mayor Will Wynn, presented 14 Distinguished Service Awards and described briefly how each of the men "performed bravely and without consideration for their own safety to protect the residents of Austin, the University of Texas and citizens of Texas by ending the UT Tower shooting spree." The following received the awards: APD Officer Billy Paul Speed (Deceased), APD Officer Phillip Conner, APD Officer Jerry Day, APD Lt. Marion Lee (Deceased), APD Officer Ramiro Martinez, APD Officer Houston McCoy, APD Officer Harold Moe, APD Officer George Shepard (Deceased), APDOfficer Milton Shoquist, DPS Agent W.A. 'Dub' Cowan, Civilian Jim Boutwell, Civilian Allen Crum (Deceased), Civilian Frank Holder (Deceased), Civilian William Wilcox (Deceased).[16]

A year later, in August of 2008, Forest Preece worked with Travis County officials to name the new Precinct 3 Building in Austin "The Tower Heroes Building." A large metal plaque was placed outside the front door of the building, with all the names listed and the building being dedicated to their honor. As part of the Austin Police Association's 60th Anniversary Celebration in 2009, McCoy, Conner, Day, Moe, Martinez and Shoquist reunited and each received a plaque, pin and honorary APA membership. On August 1, 2009, the APA dedicated "Speed, Martinez, and McCoy Hall," the new police union building in East Austin.

It was 9:00 p.m. before I walked out of Monika McCoy's home in Kyle, Texas and my mind was swirling with all the emotions and complicated information that she had shared. I felt like I'd been with a remarkable person. It took forever to find IH-35 and then get to US-183 North that would take me to Monte and Patty Akers' rambling ranch house in Cedar Park where Monte and Nathan were up waiting to talk. Driving slowly through a dark, wet Texas night, I tried to get some perspective about what Monika McCoy had humbly called her "humanitarian project." Her simple effort to assemble the retired police officers had become a catalyst that is still unfolding, fostering a rich gold mine of multi-layered relationships, revealing traumatic memories, and uncovering historical facts.

Such a flood of meaning is probably spawned by every mass shooting and may continue to build in strength and twist through the lives of those involved in the trauma forever. However, it seemed clear; when these traumatic experiences were finally and vulnerably brought into public space, people were more than ready to participate, listen to the truth and begin the process of communal mourning, memorializing and honoring that was so long overdue. The dark intensity that the tragedy generated and which separated people for so long began to transform into a more positive force, bringing people together, so that the first objective and public narrative of what really happened that day on the Tower emerged. From this finally open narrative a public memory can be built that will be textured enough to capture the complexity of the traumatic event itself, and last for generations. I was finally finding my way in this intricate web of relationships organized around the sniper attack so many years ago.

Along with all of these public efforts that occurred from 2006 to 2009, Keith Maitland began working on a powerful HBO documentary called

"The Tower" in 2011. The video project documents the reflections of many of the survivors, officers, and witnesses that are quoted here. He video-taped the 48th Memorial Gathering at the Memorial Garden in August, 2014, that was organized by a group of radio-TV-film students. He followed the speakers as they conducted a 'living memorial,' walking to the various locations on the Mall where each victim was shot, and reading a brief biography of that person. Alfred McAlister spoke about plans for a future memorial design. Claire Wilson James, Forrest Preece and Jim Bryce were there, as well as a clutch of new students who quietly stood near the plaque listening and learning.

Maitland is bringing people together who were exposed to the sniper shooting for taped discussions for the first time. Maitland's work, like that of those before him such as Monika McCoy, Forrest Preece, Claire Wilson James, Alfred McCallister, Jim Bryce, Gary Lavergne, Pamela Colloff and Rosa Eberly, did for the survivors, their families, the police force and the campus community what the University has yet to be willing to do, and what the City did belatedly. It brought traumatized people together to support each other, to honor the dead, celebrate the heroes, and create an accurate historical narrative that will shape public memory for all time. Many of those in the documentary are staying in touch with each other and meeting regularly in the Austin area. They are building new friendships and rekindling old ones, and lobbying the University to design in the Tower Memorial Garden a memorial that is commensurate with the impact that this public human disaster had on the community and so many individual lives.

We know now that when people are exposed to serious trauma, they desperately need a communal, safe, and personally validating process to grieve their losses and celebrate those who risked their lives to help them. No matter how mature, professional, or stoic each may feel or be, exposure to severe trauma penetrates skin and implants itself internally. Doing so is a natural part of the brain's response to life-threatening stimuli. As we saw beginning to develop in the summer of 2006 and still building dynamism in Austin today, the social and public aspect of mourning the dead and celebrating the living is a central part of coping with communal trauma. Those exposed to a mass shooting need to reach out to one another, stay in touch and remain organized over the years to help each other avoid drifting into silent, morose isolation. Over time, they need the opportunity to re-visit a memorial space or location on anniversaries of the tragedy, to have available a safe and personal peer-support setting where they know that even their darkest thoughts and feelings will be validated by others who understand what they are going through.

Given the increasing frequency of mass shootings accompanied by the shooter's suicide around the country and the world today, a key responsibility of the public health sector is to disseminate information about how trauma impacts the brain, and to normalize and teach strategies for coping with disturbing symptoms of traumatic stress like flashbacks, hypervigilance, and sensitive startle responses. The field of behavioral health is helping us understand that trauma requires the survivor to be much more intentional and mindful about calming their own highly activated nervous systems through regular aerobic activity. It has also pointed to the importance of close attachments and human touch, healthy high protein/low sugar nutrition, consistent sleep patterns, mindfulness or stress-relaxation strategies and active combating of the tendency to isolate ourselves after the serious crisis has passed. Public education in classrooms, religious institutions, social media, radio and TV needs to focus on de-stigmatizing the use of mental health services and psychotropic medication when the burden of acute or post-traumatic stress seriously impairs going to work, attending school, being an effective parent, or maintaining secure attachments.

For many adults who've been exposed to major trauma, it is valuable to have the opportunity to be proactive and get involved in establishing memorials to honor victims, or lobbying for new policies or programs that may prevent the reoccurrence of such public tragedies. Testifying for gun control laws, advocating for more accessible mental health services for students, and training parents, teachers and police to be more trauma-informed are just some of the meaningful activities that help us constructively work on our own recovery by making the world a safer place for others. Of all the many lessons that the traumatic legacy in Austin teaches us, perhaps the most important is that, without an ongoing public conversation and continuing dependable social support systems, trauma victims have little option but to withdraw into isolation from each other and their community, and the acute stress they naturally experience in the aftermath of the tragedy may well consolidate into a post-traumatic stress disorder.

In the process of completing this chapter, I have also found some solace that had been missing in my own life. Unaware for many years, it's clearer to me that I had become just as isolated as all the other survivors of this tragedy. I am now much more conscious of the importance of grieving my loss of Paul Sonntag with others, and in so doing face with others the terrible knowledge of how vulnerable, frail and unsafe all of us are in the world. By returning to the people, memories and places of fifty years ago, I have learned that I'm not the only one whose internal life has been shadowed by the edgy legacy of that traumatic day. It seems such a "common sense enlightenment," but if I can stay connected to those who shared that experience with me, I don't have to pass this way alone.[17] What an unexpected gift to discover as we approach the 50th Anniversary of the sniper shootings in Austin; to be reminded of the profound and intricate web of inter-connections, in ways visible and not, that crosses time and space and binds all humans together.

1. Peter N. Stearns, "Texas and Virginia: A Bloodied Window into Changes in American Public Life," *Journal of Social History*, (Winter, 2008).

2. Michael Rocque, "Exploring School Rampage Shootings: Research, Theory and Policy," 304-313, The *Social Science Journal*, (2012); available online at www.elsevier.com/locate/soscij.

3. Mary Ellen O'Toole, "Psychopathy as a Behavioral Classification System for Violent and Serial Crime," Chapter 8 in H. Herve & J.C. Yuille (ed.). *The Psychopath: Theory, Research and Practice* (Mahwah, NJ: Lawrence Erlbaum Associates, 2007).

4. Mark Nichter, "Idioms of Distress Revisited" *Culture, Medicine, and Psychiatry*,Vol.34, No. 2, (2010).

5. Kai Erikson, *A New Species of Trouble: Explorations in Disaster, Trauma and Community* (New York: W.W. Norton, 1977); Bessel van der Kolk, *The Body Keeps the Score: Brain, Mind, and Body in the Healing of Trauma* (New York: Viking Penguin. 2014).

6. Van Der Kolk, *Ibid.*

7. American Psychiatric Association, *Diagnostic and Statistical Manual of Mental Disorders*, 5th Edition (Arlington, VA: American Psychiatric Association Publications, 2013).

8. 96 Minutes at 198-199.

9. *Ibid.* at 198.

10. *Ibid.*

11. Full disclosure: Kinky Friedman is my brother, and when the *Ballad of Charles Whitman'* was released on his first album in 1973 by Vanguard Records, I was his Personal Manager. We both lived in Nashville at the time.

12. Rosa A. Eberly, "Everywhere You Go, It's There: Forgetting and Remembering the University of Texas Tower Shootings" Chapter 3, in *Framing Public Memory*, Kendall R. Phillips, (ed.), (Tuskaloosa: University of Alabama Press, 2004).

13. Mary Ellen O'Toole, in Foreword to "Houston McCoy's Own Story," West Texas Scouting History http://www.westtexasscoutinghistory.net/McCoy-story.html

14. Interview of Monika McCoy by Roger Friedman, May 18, 2015.

15. UT Tower Documentary News Special from 2006 - KEYE TV News, https://youtube/-A8hgoACMpM.

16. Honoring Police Officers 8/9/2007 by Mayor of Austin, Part 1: https://youtu.be/DER-rib_lswo; Honoring Police Officers 8/9/2007 by Mayor of Austin, Part 2: https://youtu.be/65dPgYN-kg4.

17 Erik Erikson & Richard Evans, Dialogue with Erik Erikson. (Lanham, MD: Rowman and Littlefield Publishers, 1969).

CHAPTER FOURTEEN

Taking Back the Tower

It is a very important anniversary, and important that we be proactive.

-Erica Saenz, Associate Vice President for Community and
External Relations, Division of Diversity and Community
Engagement, The University of Texas at Austin

One of the officers who went to the top of the Tower to subdue Whitman, Milton Shoquist, remarked to another Austin police officer, in regard to how the University of Texas seemed to want to divorce itself and the Tower from what occurred there on August 1, 1966, that "if that is their attitude, they should just tear the Tower down."[1]

It will happen someday. Apparently the fire escape systems inside the Tower are so inadequate that most of the floors are now used only for storage. Perhaps it will not only be the cost of bringing the 80-year-old fire escapes up to code, but all maintenance efforts for the Tower that will finally become so expensive that demolition and replacement are the most cost-beneficial steps the University can take. When it happens, loss of the Tower will not be popular with thousands of Texas alumni and will be particularly painful to those who view the Tower as a symbol of more than just Longhorn pride. There are some who view the Tower in a manner similar to how others view the Twin Towers or Pearl Harbor—as a symbol of human sacrifice and bravery, a place

The University of Texas Tower immediately before the shootings began. Dated August 1, 1966, this photo depicts the Tower and a flag flying at half-mast, not for the shooting victims but in honor of Lt. Col. Richard B. Pelton, a university professor who died on July 29, 1966 at the age of 56. Although difficult to be certain, the time on the clock appears to say 11:30, which would be 18 minutes before the shootings began, and by which time Whitman was already inside the Tower and on his way to the top.

where Americans died at the hands of an aggressor, and where others nobly stepped forward to aid their fellow men and women in a time of great crisis, and where memorializing the events does nothing to glorify the aggressors.

Understandable, and over decades that attitude has caused a few of the people personally affected by the events of August 1, 1966 to decide that the school let them down. Some of the proudest, most loyal Texas alumni in the world nevertheless feel as though their beloved alma mater decided to "cut and run." Now that the 50th anniversary of the event is approaching, there is hope that something will happen to eradicate that feeling.

Happily, there are strong indications that that is what will occur. During the course of writing this book its authors attempted to find the right people at the University to speak to about what might be planned, and finally, on June 29, 2015, the connection was made.

The University, which is operating under new leadership, has been working with a committee comprised of victims and participants of the shootings—the Texas Tower Memorial Group—to establish a more fitting memorial that will identify those who were killed. The design has been selected and plans to construct it from Texas granite and limestone are nearing finalization. The University's arborist is assisting in plans to plant a tree, probably a Montezuma Cypress, to commemorate the event. Each year the University conducts a "U.T. Remembers" ceremony to honor alumni and other persons associated with the University who passed away during the previous year, and a special edition of U.T. Remembers to honor those lost on August 1, 1966 is proposed. Several student leaders and groups are supportive and are actively making plans for the commemorative events and fund-raising efforts. At least $25,000 has been appropriated and more may be forthcoming, in addition to donations from the public.

As a spokesperson for the University stated on June 29, 2015, "I think it's important that the University be proactive and positive... Something we hear a lot from the Texas Tower Memorial group is that they don't want to glorify the shooter. They don't want to make this about him and the violence of that day. They want it to be about perseverance and love for the university, sending a positive message, and we want to honor that as well."[2]

Although it is too early as of the writing of this book to know what will ultimately occur, there is a year-long timeline being finalized for the numerous steps that will be needed to make it all come to fruition by August 1, 2016. The existing plaque on the boulder near the Turtle Pond will be replaced, and in all likelihood the plans will be publicized and established well before this book is published.

Whatever occurs, the same University spokeperson certainly said the kind of words that many of those interviewed for this book would want to hear.

> *I feel really confident and positive that it will end up being, not just positive, but an honorable event. I think it will meet the needs of the Tower Memorial group... and should be a positive thing for the University as well... The most important message that I would want to relay to you is that we want to honor the group and the survivor's perspective, not glorify the shooter or the violence of that day. We want to focus on the perseverance of the students and that "survivor's spirit," not just of the group that lived to tell the story of that day but also what it signifies for all students and all community members around Austin who are familiar with the events. The positive spirit extends beyond such a tragic occurrence. If you want that to be the focus of your book, that would be our (the University's) focus as well.* [3]

What occurred on August 1, 1966 is not the story of an angry, unbalanced, misguided, youth living out a large personal delusion. It is the story of crisis in a near-sacred place, lives lost, people hurt, and the reactions of those who did right. It is the story of Rita Jones, John Fox, James Love, Alfred McAlister, Claire Wilson James, Roland Ehlke, Clif Drummond, Bob Higley, Brehan Ellison, Chip Jansen, Morris Hohmann, David Orton, Milton Shoquist, Phil Conner, George Shepard, Allen Crum, Harold Moe, Dub Cowan, Mary Gabour, M. J. Gabour, Mike Gabour, Sandra Wilson, Nancy Harvey, Carla Sue Wheeler, Paul Bolton, Don Vandiver, Joe Roddy, Dr. Albert Lalonde, Camille Clay, Dr. Robert Pape, Ramiro Martinez, Houston McCoy, and dozens of others, many of whom are still alive, and particularly the 17 people whose lives ended on or because of that day.

It is the story of people who did not look or walk away when they saw strangers in need. It is a story of humans at their finest.

1. Telephone interview of Austin Police Officer Jason Huskins, May 21, 2015.

2. Interview of Erica Saenz, Associate Vice President for Community and External Relations, Division of Diversity and Community Engagement, The University of Texas at Austin, June 29, 2015.

3. *Ibid.*

BIBLIOGRAPHY

Primary Sources

Austin History Center

The Austin History Center's collection is the single largest depository of primary materials related to the Whitman mass murders in existence, with its guide and table of contents alone numbering 79 pages. The preferred method of citation to the collection is Police Department Records of the Charles Whitman Mass Murder Case, AR.2000.002. Austin History Center, Austin Public Library, Texas. While the entire collection was consulted in the preparation of this book, the following specific documents are specifically cited:

Decoded teletype 13 page memo to the Director of the FBI and Assistant to the Director de Loach dated August 15, 1966

Interview of Brock Huffman by Fishel of DPS

Interview of Dr. Clyde Lee, by Officer Boyd, DPS

Interview of female Fla. Neighbor, name redacted, by FBI,, p. 13 in report filed as MM 62-5533

Interview of Lt. John C. Drolla, 25th Transportation Co., U.S. Army, interviewed August 4, 1966

Interview of Dr. Ada Simond by T. Galyen, 1986

Interview of Neil Spelce (tape recording), year not identified

Department of Public Safety memo to O.N. Humphreys, Agent in Charge, from Donald R. Fishel, Intelligence Section

Recollections of Houston McCoy provided by request to Bill Helmer, *Playboy* magazine, 1985

Report for Offense No. 968193, Assault with Intent to Commit Murder, dated August 1, 1966 by Sgt. D. Kidd, Austin P.D

Statement of Anton Jacobson to Lt.George Phifer, Austin P.D., August 4, 1966

Statement of John and Fran Morgan to agent O.M. Humphreys, Jr., Texas Department of Public Safety, August 2, 1966

Text for article for *American Rifleman* article about Allen Crum, Series IV, Subseries I

Assault with Intent to Murder Report filed by Sgt. D. Kidd, APD, regarding Roland Ehlke, August 2, 1966

Reports of Agent John R. Barron, Federal Bureau of Investigation, dated December 9, December 15, and December 27, 1966

Report to the Governor, Medical Aspects, Charles J. Whitman Catastrophe, Austin, Texas September 8, 1966 (Connally Commission Report released to the public by Press Release)

Decoded copy of teletype to "Director" from San Antonio, dated Aug. 8, 1966, 7:05 p.m.,(Central Time) marked "Urgent" and received at 9:14 pm (Eastern Time)

HOR by E. Tramp, August 1, 1966

Report of Officer R. Jones, August 1, 1966

Report of Officer Ligon, August 1, 1966

Statement of Cheryl Botts to the APD, August 1, 1966

Statement of Oscar Royvela to the APD, August 1, 1966

Report of J.C. Fann, Aug. 1, 1966

Affidavit of Allen Crum dated August 2, 1966

Autopsy Protocol of Whitman, Charles Joseph, dated August 2, 1966, performed at Cook Funeral Home

Department of Public Safety memo dated August 2, 1966, to O.N. Humphreys, Jr., Officer in Charge, from Howard W. Smith, Intelligence Section

Report of Sgt. B. Gregory, Austin P.D., August 2, 1966

Report of Sgt. D.L.Moody, Aug. 2, 1966

Report of Sgt. A.E.Rugledge, Aug. 2, 1966

Report of Officer Morehead, August 2, 1966

Report of Sgt. B. Gregory, Aug. 2, 1966

Statement of Allen Crum, Aug. 2, 1966

Statement of Brock Huffman to DPS, August 2, 1966

FBI Teletype Report dated August 2, 1966, 1:37 a.m., to Assistant to the Director DeLoach

FBI report dated August 3, 1966, from J. H. Gale to Mr. DeLoach

Report of R. Wisian, Austin Police Dept., August 3, 1966;

Texas Dept. of Public Safety report dated August 3, 1966 from Maurice Beckham to O. N. Humphreys

Memo dated August 3, 1966 to the Director of the Secret Service from the Director of the FBI entitled "Charles Joseph Whitman, Threat Against the President."

Report filed by Lt. L. Morgan at 3:30 p.m., August 3, 1966

Affidavit of Don W. Walden, dated August 4, 1966

Letter dated August 4, 1966 from FBI agent J. Myers Cole

Report of Sgt. D. Moody, Austin P.D., August 4, 1966

Report of Sgt. Moody, 4:05, August 4, 1966

Statement of Dr. Robert C. Stokes, M.D., August 5, 1966

Report of Lt. George Phifer, Austin P.D., August 5, 1966

Supplementary Offense Report dated August 5, 1966, by Sgt. Moody, APD

Letter dated August 6, 1966 from FBI agent J. Myers Cole to Col. Homer Garrison, Director of the Tex. Department of Public Safety

Letter dated August 6, 1966 from FBI agent J. Myers Cole to Col. Homer Garrison, Director of the Texas Dept. of Public Safety

Supplementary Offense Report dated August 7, 1966, by Sgt. R. Kelton

Interview of Larry Fuess, August 8, 1966

Supplementary Offense Report dated August 8, 1966 by Sgt. T. J. Allen

Supplementary Offense Report dated August 8, 1966 by Sgt. T.J. Allen, APD

Teletype memo dated August 8, 1966 to Director and San Antonio, from Houston office of the FBI

Memorandum dated August 8, 1966 to "Mr. Gale" from W.V. Cleveland

MM 62-5533, August 9, 1966, FBI Miami

Airtel memo dated August 9, 1966 to Director, FBI, from SAC, Miami

Teletype dated August 10, 1966 from FBI San Antonio Officer to "Director and Savannah,"

Teletype dated August 11, 1966 from "Director" to San Antonio

Report of agent John R. Barron dated August 11, 1966

Memo dated August 15, 1966 to Director, FBI from SAC WfO

Teletype dated August 16, 1966 to Director and San Antonio from Charlotte (FBI office)

Letter dated Aug. 17, 1966 from FBI agent J. Myers Cole to Col. Homer Garrison, Director, Tex. Dept. of Public Safety

Letter dated August 22, 1966, to Marvin Watson, Special Assistant to the President at the White House

Memo dated August 22, 1966 from the Director, U.S. Secret Service, to the Director, FBI, entitled "Charles Adolphus Whitman, Information Concerning,"

Supplementary Offense Report dated August 25, 1966 by Sgt. Ed Tramp, APD

Letter dated September 21, 1966 from Maj. K.R. Herbert, APD CID, to Chief James C. MacDonald, Memphis P.D.

Report of J.C. Fann, 6:30 p.m., February 9, 1967

Interview of Morris Hohmann by Sara Rider, May 31, 1983, Original Tape No. 0513

Interview of Dr. Albert Lalonde by Sara Rider, June 2, 1983, Original Tape No. 0511A.

Interview of Judge Jerry Dellana by Sara Rider, June 2, 1983, Original Tape No. 0511B

FBI report to Director and San Antonio Office dated August 15, 1966 from the Anchorage, Alaska FBI office

Interviews: in person, by telephone, and by electronic mail

(by or to Monte Akers and/or Nathan Akers, unless noted otherwise)

Emails from and telephone conversations with F.J. Schuck, various dates, February-May, 2015

Conversation between Keith Maitland, Nathan Akers and Monte Akers, La Grange, Texas, March 2, 2015

Telephone conversation between Dr. Roger Friedman and Claire Wilson James, May 18, 2015

Telephone interview of Austin Police Officer Jason Huskins, May 21, 2015

Interview of and calculations performed by Kyle Wineman, firearms consultant, May 15-27, 2015

Email from Monika McCoy, June 29, 2015

Emails from Otis Shearer, December 29, 30, 2014, & January 2, 2015

Emails from Rachael Penman, Exhibits Manager, Crime Museum, 575 7th Street, NW, Washington, DC 20004, May 18 & 19, and June 23, 2015

Interview of Patricia Lankford Akers, November 3, 2014

Email from Paul Stoker, of Dallas, Texas, November 15, 2014

Telephone conversation with Bob Higley, December, 2014

Email from E. Page January 16, 2015

Interview of Alfred McAllister, Austin, Texas, January 20, 2015

Telephone conversation with Dr. Roger Friedman, January 30, 2015

Telephone interview of Don Vandiver, Lubbock, Texas, January 30, 2015

Interview of Erica Saenz, Associate Vice President for Community and External Relations, Division of Diversity and Community Engagement, The University of Texas at Austin, June 29, 2015

Email from Gary Lavergne, February 8, 2015

Interview of Dr. Robert Smalley, La Grange, Texas, March 2, 2015

Interview of Milton Shoquist, March 12, 2015

Interview of Monika McCoy, March 12, 2015

Email from Dr. Don Walden, San Antonio, March 17, 2015

Interview of George Cofer, Austin, Texas, March 19, 2015

Telephone conversation with Ron Oliveira, March 23. 2015

Interview of George Russell, Mayor of Marble Falls, April 7, 2015

Email from David Allen Crum, April 18, 2015

Interview of David Orton, April 22, 2015

Telephone interview of Dr. Stuart Brown, April 22, 2015

Emails from John Fox, April 25, 2015

Interview of John Fox, April 25, 2015

Interview of Dr. Mary Ellen O'Toole, George Mason University, Fairfax, Va., by Roger Friedman, June 17, 2015

Email from Milton Shoquist, April 28, 2015

Email from Dr. Tate Minckler, April 30, 2015

Interview of Kyle Wineman, experienced firearms consultant, May 15, 2015

Interview of Randall "Buck" Wood, May 4, 2015

Email from Clif Drummond dated May 15, 2015

Telephone interview of Orville, "Chip" Jansen, May 15, 2015

Interview of Monika McCoy by Roger Friedman, May 18, 2015

Email from Harold Moe, May 24, 2015

Telephone interview of Brock Huffman, May 27, 2015, and email dated June 15, 2015.

Telephone interview of Keith Hamilton, May 29, 2015

Interview of Monika McCoy and Christopher McCoy, May 31, 2015

Interview and hand-written account of Sylvia Walden, June 3, 2015

Interview of Dr. Don Walden, June 3, 2015.

Email from Bob Higley dated June 10, 2015

Email from Dr. Mitchel Berger to Monte Akers dated February 7, 2015

Miscellaneous

Page, Eileen, Graphological Analysis of the Handwriting of Charles J. Whitman, dated March 20, 2015

Information on the Report of Pathologic Studies Requested by Governor Connally in Conjunction with the Charles Whitman Case," (Confidential portion of The Connally Commission Report)

Recordings of all radio dispatches related to the Whitman mass murders on 8/1/66, with ; Houston McCoy's annotated transcript of same, provided by Monika McCoy, March 15, 2015

McAlister, Alfred, Testimony regarding Senate Bill 11, before the Texas Senate State Affairs Committee, Austin, Texas, February 12, 2015

James, Claire Wilson, Testimony regarding Senate Bill 11, before the Texas Senate State Affairs Committee, Austin, Texas, February 12, 2015

Bryce, James, Testimony regarding Senate Bill 11, before the Texas Senate State Affairs Committee, Austin, Texas, February 12, 2015

Tarasoff v. Regents of the University of California, 551 P.2d 334 (Cal. 1976)

The Gun Control Act of 1968, 18 U.C. 922

MP3 recording of LBJ telephone conversation with Jim and Beverly Sonntag, August 1, 1966, designated lbj_wh6608_01_10509AUG166.mp3, provided to Dr. Roger Friedman by Rosa Eberly and to the authors by email dated March 28, 2015

Email dated December 9, 2008, from Toby Hamilton to Monika McCoy, provided the authors by Monika McCoy

DVD prepared by David Orton for his family on March 9, 2012

Letter dated January 6, 2015 from Gary M. Lavergne to Monte Akers

Secondary Sources

Books

American Psychiatric Association, *Diagnostic and Statistical Manual of Mental Disorders,* 5th Edition (Arlington, VA: American Psychiatric Association Publications, 2013)

Bockler, N. et al. (ed.)*School Shootings: International Research, Case Studies and Concepts for Prevention,* Chapter 8, (New York: Spring Science Media, 2013)

Brown, Stuart, M.D., and Vaughn, Christopher Vaughn, *Play: How it Shapes the Brain, Opens the Imagination, and Invigorates the Soul* (New York: Penguin Group, 2009).

Chesterson, G. K., *The Defendant* (London: R. Brimley Johnson, 1901)

Crews, Harry, *Classic Crews* (New York; Simon & Schuster, 1995)

Erikson, Kai, *A New Species of Trouble: Explorations in Disaster, Trauma and Community* (New York: W.W. Norton, 1977)

Erik Erikson, Eri & Evans, Richard, *Dialogue with Erik Erikson.* (Lanham, MD: Rowman and Littlefield Publishers, 1969)

Fahrenthold, Lisa, and Rider, Sara, *Admissions: The Extraordinary History of Brackenridge Hospital* (Austin: Brackenridge Hospital, 1984)

Lamport, Mary Gabour, *The Impossible Tree,* (Austin: Ginny's Copying Service, 1972)

Langman, Peter, *School Shooters: Understanding High School, College and Adult Perpetrators* (New York: Rowman & Littlefield Publishing, 2015)

Lavergne, Gary, *A Sniper in the Tower:* The Charles Whitman Murders (Denton: North Texas State University, 1997)

Martinez, Ramiro, with Foreword by Mike Cox, *They Call Me Ranger Ray* (New Braunfels: Rio Bravo Publishing 2005)

Nieman, Robert, "Interview with Ramiro 'Ray' Martinez, Texas Ranger Retired," conducted at the home of Ray Martinez, New Branufels, Texas, September 19, 1999, *Texas Ranger E-Book* (Waco: Texas Ranger Hall of Fame and Museum 2006)

O'Toole, Mary Ellen, "Psychopathy as a Behavioral Classification System for Violent and Serial Crime," Chapter 8 in H. Herve & J.C. Yuille (ed.). *The Psychopath: Theory, Research and Practice* (Mahwah, NJ: Lawrence Erlbaum Associates, 2007)

Phillips, Kendall R., *Framing Public Memory* (Tuscaloosa; University of Alabama Press, 2004)

True Crime: *Mass Murderers* (Alexandria, Va.: *Time-Life Books*, 1993)

van der Kolk, Bessel, *The Body Keeps the Score: Brain, Mind, and Body in the Healing of Trauma* (New York: Viking Penguin. 2014)

Williams, Shelton L., *Summer of '66* (Denton: Zone Press, 2007)

Periodicals

"17th Sniper Victim Dies; Another Still 'Critical'," *The Washington Evening Star*, August 8, 1966

"Compulsion—The Evil Forces That Left a Town Drenched in Blood," *Confidential Detective Yearbook*, No. 13, 1967

"Deranged tower sniper rained death on UT campus," *Houston Chronicle*, July 8, 2001

"Former Austin Officer Says Show is 'Bull,'" *San Angelo Standard*, October 22, 1975

"Gun Bill Up to .S Eastland," *Washington Daily News*, Aug. 3, 1966

"Gun Laws Can't Stop Killing, Connally Says," *The Washington Post*, August 4, 1966

"Officer Left His Steak to Kill Sniper," *San Angelo Standard-Times*, August 2, 1966

"Officer Recalls Facing Sniper, *Fort Worth Star Telegram*, August 3, 1966

"Policeman Makes 1st Shot of Career Important One," *Fort Worth Star Telegram*, August 2, 1966

"Sniper and Mother Buried in Florida," *The Washington Post and Times Herald*, August 6, 1966

"Sniper: Reign of Terror at U.T.," *Austin American Statesman*, August 2, 1966

"Surviving History - For 48 Years: In the UT tower with Sniper-Killer Aug. 1, 1966," *Rockdale Reporter*, May 22, 2014

"The Chief," "*San Antonio Evening News*, August 2, 1966

"The Madman in the Tower," *Time*, August 12, 1966

"The Psychotic and Society," *Newsweek*, August 15, 1966

"The Psychotic and Society," *Time*, August 12, 1966

"The Texas Sniper," *Life*, August 12, 1966

"UT says environmental workers disposed of brains," *Austin American Statesman*, December.3, 2014

Allday, Erin, "Mitchel Berger, UCSF Brain Surgeon, Tops in Nation," *SFGate*, August 21, 2011

Austin American Statesman, numerous articles, 1966, 1986, 2006, 2014, "Show-World" section, July 31, 1966

Bell, Brenda, "An Anniversary Without Answers," *Austin American Statesman*, August 1, 2006

Bell, Brenda, "Man Entwined with Shooting at UT Tower in Life, Death," *Austin American Statesman*, Dec. 21, 2011

Bowers, T., Holmes, E., and Rhom, A, "The Nature of Mass Murder and Autogenic Massacre," 59-60, *Journal of Police and Criminal Psychology*, Vol 25, 2010;

Colloff, Pamela, "96 Minutes," *Texas Monthly*, p. 199 (August, 2006)

Criss, Nicholas C., *Los Angeles Times*, September 8, 1966

Daily Texan, August 1, 1986

Echols, Jim. letter entitled "A hero who became a victim," *Austin American Statesman*, August 8, 2006

Hamilton, Toby, "Memories of a Smaller Town and a Tragedy That Became Personal," *Austin American Statesman*, August 6, 2006

Hanford, Alex, "The Mysterious Vanishing Brains," *The Atlantic*, Dec. 2, 2014

Helmer, Bill, "The Madman in the Tower, *Texas Monthly*, August 1966

Herman, Herman "A Matter of Grey Matter: Texas Has the Brains," Associated Press, August 3, 1986

Keever, Jack, "Sniper Horror Recalled," AP, August, 1970

McLellan, Dennis, "David H. Gunby, 58; Hurt in '66 Texas Shooting Rampage," Obituaries, *Fort Worth Star-Telegram*, November 16, 2001

Millon, Theodore, *Disorders of Personality*, (New Jersey: John Wiley & Sons, 2011)

Nichter, Mark, "Idioms of Distress Revisited" *Culture, Medicine, and Psychiatry*, Vol.34, No. 2, (2010)

O'Toole, Mary Ellen, "Jeffrey Weise and the Shooting at Red Lake Minnesota High School: A Behavioral Perspective," (Bockler, Seeger, Sitzer and Heitmeyer, 2013)

O'Toole, Mary Ellen, "The School Shooter: A Threat Assessment Perspective," Critical Incident Response Group -National Center for The Analysis of Violent Crime- FBI Academy, Quantico, Va., 1999

Petri, Antonio M.D, "School Shooting as a Culturally Enforced Way of Expressing Suicidal Hostile Intentions," *Journal of American Academy of Psychiatry Law"* (December, 2008)

Pett, Saul & Loe, Jules, "Trail Through the Sniper's Mind: What Made Charley Whitman Tick?" *The San Antonio Express,* August 27, 1966

Rocque, Michael, "Exploring School Rampage Shootings: Research, Theory and Policy," The *Social Science Journal,* (2012)

Schroeder, M, Schroeder, K, & Hare, R.D., "Generalizability of a Checklist for Assessment for Psychopathy," 511-16, *Journal of Consulting and Clinical Psychology,* Vol 51, No. 4, 1983

Serreno, Richard, "Massacre and Myth in Texas: One Man Ended Charles Whitman's Coldblooded Austin Slaughter. Was it the Hero of Legend, or a Second Officer in the Tower, Who Says he Fired the Crucial Shots?" *Los Angeles Times,* July 29, 1994

Sherley, Connie, "U.T. Shootings Send Taylor Man Berserk," *Austin American Statesman,* August 2, 1966

Stearns, Peter N. "Texas and Virginia: A Bloodied Window into Changes in American Public Life," *Journal of Social History,* (Winter, 2008)

Trotter, Mona Ross, "Miles Broke Silence Shortly Before Death," *Austin American Statesman,* August 3, 1979

Unidentified witnesses, apparently from Kathy Whitman's hometown, quoted in *Newsweek,* p. 24, Aug.15, 1966

Online

"100 Brains Missing from the University of Texas," CBS News, Dec. 3, 2014, http://www.cbsnews.com/news/100-brains-missing-from-university-of-texas/

"Borderline Personality Disorder Symptoms," http://psychcentral.com/disorders/borderline-personality-disorder-symptoms/

"Camp Lejeune water contamination," http://en.wikipedia.org/wiki/Camp_Lejeune_water_contamination

"Officers Killed in the Line of Duty," http://www.austintexas.gov/page/officers-killed-line-duty

"Quoted from the Journal of Charles Whitman," Aybeesea's Blog, http://aybeesea.wordpress.com

"Robert Benjamin Smith," *Murdepdia,* http://murderpedia.org/male.S/s/smith-robert-benjamin.htm

"Rudolf Virchow," Wikipedia, http://en.wikipedia.org/wiki/Rudolf_Virchow

"Texas Society of Pathologists Historical Vignette Texas Tragedies and the Evolution of the Medical Examiner System in TexasL. Maximilian Buja, M.D. Chairman, Heritage Council April 13, 2009, p. 5; http://www.texpath.org/assets/docs/history/tsphistoricalvignette4-1-09.pdf

"The Austin Police Officer Memorial Project," http://austintexas.gov/news/austin-police-officer-memorial-project-6

"The Tower Fire," https://www.utexas.edu/tours/mainbuilding/news/index.html

"U.T. Tower News Special, KEYE, August 6, 2006, https://www.youtube.com/watch?v=-

"A Crime to Remember the 28th Floor," Full Episode, https://www.youtube.com/watch? v=Z54cCAnUpbo

"*An Introduction to Autopsy Technique*," p. 1, College of American Pathologists, 2005; "What is the best autopsy method of Dissection and why?" http://www.researchgate.net/post/What_is_the_best_autopsy_method_of_Dissection_and_why_The_goal_of_the_question_is_to_gain_a_better_understanding_of_the_logic_for_methods_used

Austin Aqua Festival, http://en.wikipedia.org/wiki/Austin_Aqua_Festival

Awe-Inspiring JoelleDrees. The, kingwood underground.com/topic.jsp?topicid=11169404

"Borderline Personality Takes Center Stage on Discovery Channel," http://www.borderlineblog.com/borderline-personality-criminals-take-center-stage-on-discovery-channel.php#sthash.Vu31aciR.dpuf, February 14, 2010

Boren, Jon, & Wright, Byron, "Controlling Rock Squirrel Damage in New Mexico," New Mexico State University, March 2003, http://aces.nmsu.edu/pubs/_circulars/CR574.pdf

Buja, L. Maximllian, M.D., "Historical Vignette Texas Tragedies and the Evolution of the Medical Examiner System in Texas," Texas Society of Pathologists, April 13, 2009, http://www.texpath.org/assets/docs/history/tsphistoricalvignette4-1-09.pdf

Burr, Beverly, "*History of Student Activism at the University of Texas at Austin* (1960-1988)," TC 660H, Spring 1988, Supervising Professor: Harry Cleaver, Economics. http://www.campusactivism.org/server-new/uploads/burrthesis.pdf

"Charles Whitman," en.citizendium.org/wiki.Charles_Whitman

Day, Jerry, interviewed in *Deranged Killers: Charles Whitman*, darkdocumentaries, Discovery Channel, (2006), https://www.youtube.com/watch?v=Jy1B5mfzC-BA

"*Encyclopedia Dramatica,*: Charlie Whitman's Tumor," https://encyclopedia-dramatica.se/index.php?title=Charles_Whitman's_Tumor&diff=next&oldid=227497

Ewing, Charles P., JD, PhD, "Tarasoff Reconsidered," American Psychological Association, Judicial Notebook, Posted August, 2005 http://www.apa.org/monitor/julaug05/jn.aspx

Feldman, Bob, "*Civil Rights:, SDS, and Student Activism in Austin, Texas,* 1954-1973," http://www.theragblog.com/bob-feldman-civil-rights-sds-and-student-activism-in-austin-texas-1954-1973/

Film footage at http://www.texasarchive.org/library/index.php/Special:GSM-SearchPage?fulltext, and https://www.youtube.com/watch?v=MAET3gFy5E8

"Flickr," photo of the Texas Tower, https://www.flickr.com/photos/atxj2007/2890749909

H.D. "Doc" Quigg, "Doc Quigg's Report on Texas Tower Shooting," UPI, 1966, http://www.downhold.org/lowry/doc.html

Hamilton, Reeve, "After 48 Years, Whitman's Unborn Victim Gets a Headstone," *Texas Tribune*, August 1, 2014, http://www.texastribune.org/2014/08/01/after-48-years-whitmans-unborn-victim-gets-headsto/

Hannaford, Alex, "The Mysterious Vanishing Brains," The Atlantic, Dec. 2, 2014, http://www.theatlantic.com/health/archive/2014/12/the-mysterious-vanishing-brains/382869/

Honoring Police Officers 8/9/2007 by Mayor of Austin, Part 1: https://youtu.be/DERrib_lswo

Honoring Police Officers 8/9/2007 by Mayor of Austin, Part 2: https://youtu.be/65dPgYN-kg4

Largey, Matt, "The Mystery Brains of the Texas State Lunatic Asylum (Update)" Nov. 21, 2014, http://kut.org/post/mystery-brains-texas-state-lunatic-asylum-update

McCoy, Houston, "Houston McCoy's Own Story," West Texas Scouting History, with Foreword by Mary Ellen, O'Toole, http://www.westtexasscoutinghistory.net/McCoy-story.html

Newton, Noel, Interview of Houston McCoy, https://drive.google.com/file/d/0B2sFGqklP1lnTnBDUU9FWWZNLUE/view

O'Toole, Mary Ellen, "The School Shooter: A Threat Assessment Perspective," Critical Incident Response Group -National Center for The Analysis of Violent Crime- FBI Academy - Quantico, VA, 1999, http//www.fbi.gov.stats-services/publications/school-shooter

Preece, Forrest, *"Westside Stories"*, http://trysomethingmore.com/westside-stories-by-forrest-preece/

Rhawn, Joseph, Ph.D., "Charles Whitman: The Amygdala and Mass Murder," http://brainmind.com/Case5html

Rocque, Michael, "Exploring School Rampage Shootings: Research, Theory and Policy," www.elsevier.com/locate/soscij

Saile, Jean W., "History of Apache Shores" http://www.apacheshorespoa.com/web124/news24_historyofapacheshoresbyjeansaile.asp

Saner, Emine, "The Baffling Case of the 100 Missing Brains," *The Guardian*, Dec. 3, 2015; http://www.theguardian.com/science/shortcuts/2014/dec/03/the-baffling-case-of-the-100-missing-brains

"Shotgun Shells," http:en Wikipedia.org/wiki.Shotgun_shell

"Sniper 66," https://www.youtube.com/watch?v=hRDHYeH82OA

Spelce, Neal, *"The Neal Spelce Collection, No. 3 - UT Tower Shooting,"* http://www.texasarchive.org/library/index.php?title=The_Neal_Spelce_Collection,_No._3_-_UT_Tower_Shooting

"Spree Killers," https://truecrimes.wordpress.com/tag/charles-whitman/, January 23, 2008

UT Tower Documentary News Special from 2006 - KEYE TV News, https://youtu.be/-A8hgoACMpM

"The Deadly Tower (aka Sniper) Kurt Russell 1975 [Full Movie]" https://www.youtube.com/watch?v=BiHRY2njJrM

PHOTO CREDITS

Monika McCoy

Austin History Center

Monte Akers

David Orton

UT Texas Student Publications, (di_02852, di_02853, di_080733, di_10392, di_10393)
The Dolph Briscoe Center for American History, The University of Texas at Austin

Frank Armstrong. UT Texas Student Publications, di_08072, The Dolph Briscoe Center for
American History, The University of Texas at Austin

Footage provided by the Texas Archive of the Moving Image, www.texasarchive.org.
Donor: Cactus and Peggy Davis Pryor, Neal Spelce, Gordon Wilkison, Texas Archive
of the Moving Image

Map prepared by Adam Allen

Brock Huffman

Bob Higley

Alfred McAlister

Don Vandiver

Virginia Tech

Neal Douglass: University of Texas Tower; Aerial View of the University of Texas Campus;
The University of Texas, Austin; UT Austin Tower, South Mall

Cover photo by: Larry D. Moore

INDEX